THE EMERGENCE OF IRANIAN NATIONALISM

THE
EMERGENCE
OF
IRANIAN
NATIONALISM

RACE AND THE POLITICS OF DISLOCATION

REZA ZIA-EBRAHIMI

COLUMBIA UNIVERSITY PRESS / NEW YORK

COLUMBIA UNIVERSITY PRESS
PUBLISHERS SINCE 1893
NEW YORK   CHICHESTER, WEST SUSSEX
cup.columbia.edu

Library of Congress Cataloging-in-Publication Data

Zia-Ebrahimi, Reza, 1977– author.
The emergence of Iranian nationalism : race and the
politics of dislocation / Reza Zia-Ebrahimi.
pages cm
Includes bibliographical references and index
ISBN 978-0-231-17576-0 (cloth : alk. paper) — ISBN 978-0-231-54111-4 (e-book)
1. Iran—Intellectual life—History.   2. Nationalism—Iran—History.   I. Title.

DS266.Z53   2016
320.540955—dc23
2015029286

Printed in the United States of America

COVER DESIGN: CHANG JAE LEE
COVER IMAGE: HELMUT R. SCHULZE © EDITION HRS

To the memory of the departed:
Michel Justrich, my dearest friend;
Fattaneh Farzaneh-Rahmanian, my beloved aunt;
and Fred Halliday, my teacher and guide

CONTENTS

ACKNOWLEDGMENTS

THE VAGARIES OF MY PERSONAL HISTORY ARE THE RAW MATERIAL for my reflection on Iranian nationalism. Yet, if not for a fateful discussion I had with the late Fred Halliday in October 2006, this reflection would have never become the subject of my research. It was also Fred who suggested that I approach Homa Katouzian at Oxford University to seek his guidance. From the winter of 2008 to the summer of 2011, Homa spared no effort in supporting my work and helping me navigate complex historical events. I am indebted to him for his generosity and mentorship.

My parents, Simin and Gholamreza, represent the spiritual backbone of this enterprise, which they encouraged from the onset. I am forever devoted to them. Behind every man is a great woman, they say. But I like to believe that I humbly stand behind my wife, Kaja Ystgaard, who made great sacrifices to allow me to finalize my book, and whose similar views on most aspects of nationalism and ethnicity are precious and always comforting.

Informal discussions with close friends provided me with arguments or for-mulations that are now integral part of this book. Where I did not incorporate their ideas, it has never been without anxiety. I would like to mention and thank Ali Tavakoli-Khoo, for our discussions of the "traumatic encounter with Europe"; Vassilis Paipais, for his encyclopedic knowledge and comparative views of Greek history; Stephan Davidshofer, for his command over arcane theoretical concepts; William Stockland, for his insights into medieval Iran and its literature; Khodadad Rezakhani, for enriching my arguments dealing with ancient history and sources; Sara Mashayekh, for her constructive criticism; Rasmus Christian Elling, for his healthy skepticism toward established ethnic myths; Leah Feldman for her familiarity with Akhundzadeh; and Daniel Matlin, for much-needed last-minute feedback.

I was very fortunate to benefit from the guidance of a number of established scholars in the field. Ali Gheissari spared no effort to throw his light on Qajar intellectual history; Maziar Behrooz, to elucidate the birth of modernism; Stefan Arvidsson, to offer his knowledge of the Aryan discourse, Nikki Keddie, to temper my take on Indo-European linguistics; Mehrdad Kia, to share his insights into Akhundzadeh and language reform; Touraj Daryaee, to revive ancient Iran before my eyes; Houchang Chehabi, to shape my own views of some early Pahlavi policies (and many other things); Dick Davis, to help me demystify the myths surrounding Ferdowsi; Michael Banton, to refine my views of race theory; Hamid Tafazoli, to summarize his painstaking work on classical German views of Iran; Monica Ringer, to provide me with a vista into war and education in the Qajar era; Cyrus Masroori, to reveal facets of Kermani's thought that I had heretofore neglected; Firoozeh Kashani-Sabet, to share invaluable archival sources with me; Ali Ansari, to mentor me in the uncertainties that follow the completion of a PhD; Faisal Devji, to read through and comment on tedious passages; and, finally, Eric Hooglund, for his steady boosting of my morale. I must thank the staff of the St. Antony's College Middle East Centre at Oxford, Michael Willis, Edmund Herzig, and especially Stephanie Cronin for comments on earlier drafts, and Mastan Ebtehaj, who rules over the library like a queen over her realm.

Very special thanks must go to John Breuilly and Afshin Marashi, to whom I am irremediably indebted for very extensive comments and invaluable support.

My alma mater, the London School of Economics, and Sheffield Hallam University, where I held my first academic post, must both be thanked for providing me with research facilities and stimulating environments to work on the final draft. Anne Routon, Kathryn Jorge, and Whitney Johnston at Columbia University Press and Patricia Bower of Diligent Editorial deserve unconditional praise for their professionalism and expertise. Last but not least, I must express my gratitude to the organization that funded my work. Without the generous support of the Swiss National Science Foundation, I might have been irrevocably diverted from scholarship. Grateful thanks must also go to the late Miss Isobel Thornley's Bequest to the University of London for a grant covering some of my publication expenses.

NOTE ON TRANSLITERATION AND SPELLING

THIS BOOK USES A SIMPLIFIED SYSTEM OF TRANSLITERATION, which privileges oral recognizability over written reversibility in a slight deviance from Marshall Hodgson's suggestions.[1] There are a few exceptions to this transliteration system. Names that have a conventional spelling in English, including many proper nouns (Nasser, Tehran, Shaykhism, Qajar, Hassan, Hossein in Persian, Hussein in Arabic, etc.) or common nouns that have made it into the English language such as "ulama," are spelled as such.

In complying with the principle of oral recognizability, this book avoids using the Library of Congress transliteration system or any other system designed for the Arabic language and wrongly applied to Persian. Because Persian speakers pronounce the same letters differently from Arabic speakers, these systems impede oral recognizability while they also frequently offer the same transliteration for different words. Such is the case, for instance, of حاکم and حَکیم in Persian that these systems would both transliterate into *hakim* (as opposed to *hākem* and *hakim*, respectively, in my system). For the reader fluent in Persian, such systems present a third challenge, that of doubling the transcription effort: often one must mentally transliterate the word into Arabic first and from there try to identify it in Persian.

All translations from Persian, French, and German are mine, unless specified in the notes.

THE EMERGENCE OF IRANIAN NATIONALISM

INTRODUCTION

ANYONE WHO HAS LIVED OR TRAVELED IN IRAN, OR WHO HAS come into contact with Iranians abroad, might have come upon some of the ideas that are analyzed in this book. One often encounters among Iranians a longing for Iran's pre-Islamic grandeur and glory. This permeates popular and elite understandings of the nation's origins and "essence" and is also prominent in artistic and literary production. It partly explains why an incalculable number of Iranian-owned restaurants and businesses across the world bear names such as "Persepolis," or "Cyrus." The most visible aspect of this longing is of course an imagery inspired by pre-Islamic forms and symbols, which is nothing short of ubiquitous. One need only see the neo-Achaemenid public buildings erected in the 1930s and neo-classical houses built by upstart Iranians today; observe the iconography of Iran Air; scrutinize some of the motifs used in jewelry, carpet, and souvenir design; or browse the Iranian cyberspace to be overwhelmed by the recurrence of a limited number of Persepolitan ornamental elements such as the immortal soldiers, the King of Kings on his throne, the lion biting the bull, the winged man-bulls of the Gate of All Nations, the Zoroastrian winged figure of Faravahar, or the eagles and bulls that decorate the columns of the Apadana Hall.

Related to this pre-Islamic frenzy is the popular belief in some sections of society that the history of Iran after the advent of Islam is a long process of degeneration, as if Iran was suddenly and irremediably demoted from its high rank among the greatest nations of the earth. The great scientific and literary achievements of the Islamic era are somewhat passed over or repackaged as cases of a reemergence of the pre-Islamic genius in Islamic garb. Equally frequently one meets Iranians who matter-of-factly blame their country's predicaments on Islam and argue that Mohammad's message does not suit the temper of Iranians as well as it does that of desert-dwelling Arabs. In this reading, the advent of Islam to Iran is ethnicized into an "Arab invasion," an event that seems to be about cultural imposition rather than territorial conquest, the expansion of a taxation base, or even the propagation of a new religion. It is not uncommon to hear that the Islamic Republic is only the last manifestation of age-old Arab animosity against Iran's distinct culture as embodied in the Persian language and an attitude to life, which is more hedonist than that of the putatively coarse and literalist Arabs. Indeed, the founders and high-ranking officials of the Islamic Republic are often called *tāzi zādeh*, or Arab-descended, for their profession of Islam, and the dense Arabic-mixed jargon they use places them outside the nationalist definition of Iranianness.

From among the same cluster of ideas, Iranians' belonging to the "Aryan race"—along with Europeans—is trumpeted with great pride. Inscribing Iranians within a notion of Aryanness allows one to hit two birds with one stone. First, it reiterates one of the pillars of Iranian identity: the deep cultural and linguistic distinction between Iranians and Arabs. Arabs, we are told, are not Aryans, they are Semites, and a gulf separates these two races. Second, it makes Iranians distant cousins of Europeans. This is no mean feat. For all the animosity against "Western imperialism," the reality is that many Iranians are profoundly flattered to perceive themselves as related to Europeans. It has been reported that even the diplomatic team of Mahmoud Ahmadinejad, arguably the most West-bashing figure in recent Iranian memory, proudly brought up the matter of the shared Aryan heritage when meeting European counterparts.[1] In a time when Arabs are perceived to bask in division, civil violence, and economic stagnation while the West is—still—on top, who wouldn't try and associate himself with the latter?

This book treats these ideas not as ahistorical, common-sense elements of the Iranian collective psyche but as historical objects begging for critical analysis. These ideas are part of a variety of nationalist ideology that I call "dislocative nationalism." It is an ideology predicated on a number of core ideas. First, Iran is a primordial nation that has been in uninterrupted existence for 2,500 years (although this figure is often inflated to 5,000 and even more). Second, Iran's essence and glory is to be found in its pre-Islamic golden age. Third, Iran's shortcomings and decadence must be blamed on Islam, which Arabs imposed upon Iranians at the point of the sword. And fourth, Iranians are part of the Aryan race, thus akin to Europeans and racially quite distinct from Arabs. I argue that dislocative nationalism is an identifiable body of thought with an elaborate ideological apparatus that includes doctrinal texts and established dogmas produced by recognizable ideologues. This ideology is, at a fundamental level, concerned with history; indeed, its adherents have produced the dominant historiography of Iran.

The core claim of this book is that dislocative nationalism is a modern ideology without any antecedent before the late nineteenth century. It emerged in the late Qajar period, sometime between the 1860s and 1890s, and later became integrated into the official ideology of the Pahlavi state (1925–1979). Thus it became part and parcel of the teaching of history in the national curriculum for several decades and shaped the understanding of history, nation, and race of generations of Iranians. It is therefore deeply embedded, and its influence in Iranians' identity and self-perception seems, for the foreseeable future, indelible. Moreover, its core doctrine enjoys remarkable stability. It is a lively ideology today, and since the 1980s it has become the most conventional form of secular opposition to the Islamic Republic. Even the officials of the Islamic Republic themselves do not seem to be immune from its appeal and quite frequently tap into its imagery to shore up their patriotic credentials. That sediments of dislocative nationalism are to be found on both ends of the political spectrum is only testimony to the dominance of this ideology in modern Iran.

The second core claim concerns the origins of dislocative nationalism's main tenets. This book suggests that the elevation of the pre-Islamic past as the embodiment of the essence of the Iranian nation, the centrality of the Iranian/Aryan versus Arab/Semite opposition, and the racialization of Iranian history can be safely traced back to nineteenth-century European scholarship on the Orient and on race, and not to local traditions or narratives. This is not to suggest that these ideas were imported wholesale or unchanged from Europe. A complex process of selection and indigenization took place, at the end of which European ideas were hybridized by Iranian thinkers to serve their ideological needs. It is the modalities of this indigenization/hybridization that have been overlooked so far and are analyzed here.

I do not claim that dislocative nationalism is the only form of nationalism in Iran. Quite the contrary, this book suggests that a multiplicity of nationalisms can be concerned with the same "nation"—that is, the same territory and the same group of people. There are indeed other forms of nationalism in Iran, and I touch upon some of them in due course, in particular the nationalist aspect of the Constitutional Revolution of 1906–11, the nationalism of Mohammad Mosaddeq (1882–1967) and the movement for the nationalization of oil, and the nationalism of the Islamic Republic (which would very much benefit from further scrutiny in history and the social sciences). One form of nationalism is not replaced by the next in a historical sequence, but they coexist alongside each other. However, my argument is that none of these forms of Iranian nationalism can claim to have the degree of ideological development of dislocative nationalism. This latter's doctrine was clearly articulated in ideological texts, and the Pahlavi state put all its strength behind the propagation of dislocative tenets. It is the dominant nationalist ideology in Iran.

Before moving on to a more theoretical discussion, I must ask the reader for some leniency. I often refer to Europe, European scholarship, European orientalism, European imperialism, and European authors in a manner that will seem essentializing and totalistic. Europe is a complex and contested geographic and historical concept, as highlighted by Norman Davies, among others.[2] My aim is to use this broad European category only to highlight the alien origins of some of the core ideas of an ideology that considers itself homegrown and deeply rooted in the national self. I discuss some "European" authors mostly hailing from Western European backgrounds and discuss ideas with some traction on this continent in the nineteenth century. However, my focus is clearly on Iranian authors and ideologies, and I hope to be forgiven for not highlighting the subtleties of European intellectual history: such is simply not my aim.

Similarly, I hope to be forgiven if I sometimes take liberties with chronology. This book is a work of history, but it aims to be thematic and topical rather than strictly chronological. The core chapters elucidate the origins, development, and uses of particular ideas that form the ideological backbone of dislocative nationalism. Concurrently, I try to keep the reader aware of the stability of dislocative nationalism—in other words, to show that it is still lively among Iranians *today* and relevant for an understanding of present-day Iranian views on a range of matters. This double preoccupation explains the temporal shifts that the reader used to traditional historiography might find unusual or unconventional. However, there is no confusion between periods, and references to events outside of the chapter's coverage are made only in passing, and the text hurriedly reverts back to the historical period under study.

DISLOCATION

Why is this nationalist ideology "dislocative"? I do not use the idea of dislocation in the sense one can find in diasporic studies, meaning geographic displacement as experienced, for instance, by migrants and refugees. Dislocation here refers to an operation that takes places in the realm of the imagination, an operation whereby the Iranian nation is dislodged from its empirical reality as a majority-Muslim society situated—broadly—in the "East." Iran is presented as an Aryan nation adrift, by accident, as it were, from the rest of its fellow Aryans (read: Europeans). When I say that this ideology dislodges Iran from its empirical reality, it is not my intention to claim that I hold the truth about such reality, or to reify a particular definition of the "essence" of Iran as Islamic. I do believe, however, that to make the idea of dislocation analytically viable, two very basic premises must be granted.

The first is that the majority of Iranians profess Islam, or at least come from a Muslim background, and that the country's history is intimately intertwined with that of this faith and the various religious, cultural, and administrative practices Islam has brought about over the centuries. This is no disavowal of the many religious minorities that are an important part of Iran's social fabric, or the religious, cultural, and administrative practices whose origins do *not* lie in Islam. It is simply recognition that Iran and Islam have something to do with each other: nothing more, nothing less. In light of this very straightforward (and fairly incontrovertible) proposition, the dislocative nationalist dissociation of Iran from Islam and its claim that the two are fundamentally incompatible will be problematized and treated as an object for historical inquiry. It is not a claim to be merely brushed aside as a fallacy but something sufficiently remarkable to deserve close examination. The Aryan race hypothesis—in particular its formulation of differentiation and opposition between the Aryan/ Indo-European and Semitic races—is the intellectual mechanism that allows dislocation to take place. In other terms, only a racial formulation of difference and opposition between Iranians and Arabs can bring about the dislocative nationalist reading of Iranian history and the dissociation between Iran and Islam that lies at its heart. Equally, only such a racial lens can allow for imagining a kinship between Iranians and Europeans, an assertion that is not quite obvious to the dispassionate observer, to say the least.

Second, it is hardly deniable that no definition of European civilization—however broad—includes Iran, apart precisely from the particularly Iranian reading of the Aryan race hypothesis (as we will see, European theorists of Aryanism mostly stopped short of considering Iranians as full-fledged members of the Aryan race). If these two basic principles are granted, then my contention that Iran is being dislodged from its empirical reality becomes an acceptable premise for analyzing the modalities of this imaginary process and the objectives it aims to serve. I argue that dislocation was one intellectual strategy to manage the trauma of the encounter with the seemingly more advanced Europeans. It is the discursive response to the challenge posed by European modernity and the need to make digestible a novel and painful sentiment of deficiency. Dislocative nationalism is thus discursive in the sense that the solution it provides to the predicament of (European) modernity is in the form of a discourse, specifically, a historicist narrative of Iran's past glories and rank among nations. In other terms, dislocative nationalism does not provide a blueprint for reforming the Iranian state; rather, it is almost exclusively concerned with the imaginary operation of dislocation, and in terms of reform it satisfies itself with calling for the return of Iran to its pre-Islamic past, its stage of racial purity. Hence the nationalist endeavor to uproot what is perceived as the influence of Arabs in Iran: mainly Islamic practices and Arabic loanwords. Uprooting such "alien" elements, it is believed, will purify Iran's Aryan ethos from Semitic contamination and automatically resuscitate Iran's lost glory. Dislocative nationalism provides a comfortable explanation for Iran's perceived deficiencies: it identifies scapegoats to be loathed and absolves Iranians themselves from any responsibility in bringing about contemporary Iran. The agency of Iranians in their own history is limited to their maintenance—time and again—of a distinct culture, language, and way of life after a series of invasions by alien races. These invasions are in turn described as mainly concerned with cultural matters, particularly the destruction of the Persian language.

I said earlier that dislocation is an imaginary process. There is a parallel here with Benedict Anderson's concept of imagined communities. At the core of any form of Iranian nationalism—dislocative or otherwise—Iran is imagined as a cohesive national unit. Anderson claims that we are here in the realm of imagination, for "the members of even the smallest nation will never know most of their fellow-members, meet them, or even hear of them, yet in the minds of each live the image of their communion."[3] However, the peculiarity of dislocative nationalism is that it adds an additional layer by imagining the Iranian nation twice: once as a cohesive nation and again as a nation that is culturally and racially out of place, unrelated to its surrounding, racially different from its neighbors, and only accidentally Islamic. Iran is *imagined* as Aryan and as foreign to its natural environment. This is what I mean by dislocation. This idea is encapsulated in Mohammad Reza Shah Pahlavi's claim (discussed in chapter 6) that Iran's situation in the Middle East is a mere "accident of geography."

Herein lies an important theoretical question: as a mental device, is dislocation specific to this form of Iranian nationalism? I would like to suggest that some cases of ethnic imagination across the world can remind one of an Iranian-type dislocation, but a closer look either puts the claim into question or reveals a somewhat weaker or less consistent case of dislocation.

Kemalist identity in Turkey is an interesting parallel. Under the impetus of Kemalism, Turkey took a decisive turn toward Europe that involved the adoption, *inter alia*, of European dress codes and alphabet.[4] Previously the Ottomans had adopted European military and administrative practices, in particular in instituting conscription and reforming the empire's tax system. Is the definition of modern Turkish identity as European a case of dislocation in the sense referred to earlier? Some authors argue that modern Turkish culture is "imitative and derivative."[5] However, large sections of Turkish society and foreign observers of Turkey alike would certainly dispute that modern Turkish identity is a case of dislocation, and they might have a point. Turkey's geographic situation bridging Europe and Asia, its very visible Roman and Byzantine legacies, the Ottomans' long rule over European territories (today's Greece and the Balkans in particular), and its intense interaction with European states through warfare and trade would warrant Turkey a claim to Europeanness. It should also be borne in mind that a very sizable portion of the top Young Turk and Kemalist cadres (officers, bureaucrats, and intellectuals) hailed from the European provinces of the empire (Mustafa Kemal was born in Salonika), as were quite a few of the viziers and pashas before them. Given that there is no consensus on where Europe starts or ends, the Kemalist declination of Turkish identity as European is neither outlandish nor an obvious case of dislocation: at the very least Turkey is adjacent to the most conventional conceptions of geographic Europe. Iran, on the other hand, is neither adjacent to Europe nor has it a common history with Europe running so deep. The greater gap between Iran and Europe makes the Iranian nationalist imagination a more unambiguous case of dislocation.

In addition to Iran, Aryanism had a successful career in India. High-caste Indians made similar uses of the Aryan race hypothesis to claim parity with their British rulers.[6] Indian intellectuals even used Vedic sources to develop their own theories of Aryan origins, such as Bâl Gangâdhar Tilak and his *Arctic Home in the Vedas*. However, their endeavor did not result in the elaboration of an ideology complete with doctrinal texts, core beliefs, and a sizable following. Crucially, this case of dislocation was not taken up by the Indian state as official ideology. Part of the reason may lie in the gradual realization by Hindu reformers that the narrative of the migration of Aryans into India made them out to be as "foreign," similarly to the Muslims to whom they directed their ire. It also established tribal peoples and low castes as India's "original" non-Aryan inhabitants. The Aryan race hypothesis in India did not serve the interests of nationalists as well as it did in Iran. We can therefore infer that there is a case of dislocative imagining in Indian identity politics; however, it did not benefit from the same consensus and legitimacy as it did in Iran.

Afrocentrism in the Americas is perhaps a closer parallel. In a diasporic context—in North America or the Caribbean, for instance—Afrocentric claims that all people of African descent share a particular destiny and that they should return to an idealized Africa that is intrinsically theirs could be construed as a case of dislocation. In the United States, for instance, it minimizes the immediate reality in which African Americans live and have lived for generations in favor of a link to the ancestral land of Africa that is tenuous at best. This point was made by a number of African American critics of Afrocentrism, for instance Ralph Ellison and Albert Murray, who fiercely opposed the pan-Africanist and separatist black nationalism of the 1960s and 1970s.[7] Both viewed black Americans as fully American, and Murray in particular derided claims of belonging to Africa.[8] Some authors have also stressed that the Africa of Afrocentrism is imaginary.[9] One could retort that, then again, American Afrocentrism is not a clear case of dislocation since African Americans' descent (or partial descent) from an African origin is incontrovertible. However, this argument should not invalidate the comparison: as we will see, Iranian Aryanists make similar claims of descent from an Aryan Urheimat or proto-fatherland.

This is not an attempt to draw a comprehensive list of cases in which some form of dislocative imagination can be discerned. It simply serves to suggest that dislocative nationalism in Iran may not represent a unique instance of imaginary dislocation, although it certainly is a particularly unambiguous, perhaps even archetypical case. In my endeavor to scrutinize dislocation, I hope that I will be able to provide students of nationalism with a useful concept that can perhaps in turn be applied to the cases I briefly touched upon here or, indeed, in cases that I have overlooked.

AKHUNDZADEH, KERMANI, AND INTELLECTUAL HISTORY

Dislocative nationalism was born in the seminal texts of Mirza Fath'ali Akhundzadeh and Mirza Aqa Khan Kermani between the 1860s and 1890s. This book is very much concerned with the lives and ideas of these two authors who lived through a period of turmoil and self-questioning among Qajar thinkers. All the traditional certainties of the Iranian elite had been shattered by a traumatic confrontation with Russian and British imperialisms earlier in the nineteenth century. Their dilemmas and predicaments were those of a whole generation who attempted, sometimes desperately, to make sense of European modernity and to decide how (and not whether) Iranians needed to emulate it. However, it will be shown that Akhundzadeh's and Kermani's responses significantly diverged from other intellectuals' recipes for offering effective resistance to and closing the gap with Europe.

Some of their ideas had been around for some time but had been marginal, to say the least. Akhundzadeh's importance lies in his systematic compilation of these disparate ideas into ideological form, allowing the development of dislocative nationalism as a body of dogmas with a degree of fixity. Were it not for Akhundzadeh's work of systematization, these ideas would probably have subsisted in their initial form, unrelated and with fluid contours. Kermani further consolidated Akhundzadeh's thought in its ideological form and developed its racial component. My focus is therefore on the modalities of the two authors' selection, combination, hybridization, and radicalization of existing but disparate dislocative ideas. I also devote significant space to determining where exactly the two authors found the ideas that they then promoted.

Intellectual history is the method of choice in this investigation. This book traces the origin of the core ideas of dislocative nationalism to the two authors' texts, analyzes the historical and ideological context in which they emerged, accounts for the complex process of hybridization that brought them about, and examines the purposes they were meant to serve. I carry out some textual comparisons with the European texts that provided the templates of this new ideology. The book also makes inroads into other non-European sources, including Parsi discourses of origins prevalent in nineteenth-century India. Following Quentin Skinner's methodological cues, I see Akhundzadeh and Kermani's texts as neither typical products of the historical context in which they were born nor as fully autonomous from such historical context.[10] First, although both authors were products of their times and very much involved with the self-questioning that the encounter with the West brought about among Qajar thinkers, they were marginal thinkers. As such, they were hardly representative Qajar intellectuals. Indeed, at first their ideas failed to have any impact. Only in the 1910s were the historical conditions for such impact gathered, and as a result, dislocative nationalism started its rise to official sanction. Second, as already mentioned, their ideas were not entirely of their making, as they both drew on European sources, and Kermani also significantly drew on Akhundzadeh. Their texts can therefore not be analyzed on their own either. My purpose in this book lies elsewhere: beyond my objective of tracing the archetypical ideas that the authors hybridized and demonstrating the modernity of their thought, I aim to show *why* some ideas were given precedence over others, and why, at some historical conjuncture, they became so appealing as to become one of the dominant ideologies of modern Iran.

It is worth clarifying what I mean by ideology, which is a notoriously difficult concept to define. For Friedrich Engels, ideology was a mental process distinguished by "false consciousness."[11] Ever since, ideology has been widely assumed to operate some distortion of reality and has been used to describe one's opponent's political stance rather than one's own. However, John Breuilly provides a definition of ideology that is relevant to this book's endeavor. Breuilly defines ideology in a nationalist context as "an intellectual attempt to solve some puzzle about society as a whole."[12] There are, however, several stages in the birth of an ideology: "Because such puzzles and related predicaments are shared generally, the answers offered at a fairly sophisticated level by intellectuals can, in a simplified form, be adopted by others as ideology. So one must begin by examining the sorts of puzzles, and the initial non-ideological responses they provoked, which could give rise to nationalist ideology."[13]

Intellectuals produce a response to a predicament, which must then be translated into symbols and ceremonies for the masses to be able to take them on. In other terms, the intellectual responses must become simplified to allow for mass adoption. Breuilly then goes on to illustrate what he means by intellectual responses to social predicaments by examining the texts of Johann Gottfried Herder on Germans, František Palacký on Czechs, and Jomo Kenyatta on the Kikuyus. I would argue that Iranian dislocative nationalism differs slightly from these examples: Akhundzadeh and Kermani's texts, as we will see, were not sophisticated, at least not in the sense understood by Breuilly. They were not complex philosophical analyses of society's puzzles by any stretch of the imagination. On the contrary, their ideas were quite straightforward and could immediately appeal to masses. The later dislocative nationalism of the masses differs little from the dislocative nationalism of these authors. Symbols (pre-Islamic generally) and ceremonies (the Ferdowsi millennium celebrations in 1934, the 2,500th anniversary of the "Persian empire" in 1971) were added, but the core ideology was already there, ready to be taken on, already in Akhundzadeh and Kermani's texts. The simplicity of their texts is not necessarily the result of inherent intellectual limitations on the part of their authors but simply of their intention to produce an ideology precisely in this sense. These texts were *meant* to be ideological treatises. In other words, they were meant to be simple and appealing ideas about Iran's past addressing some puzzle in society (namely, Iran's perceived deficiencies vis-à-vis Europe).

Skinner's signposts in his classic piece on intellectual history, *Meaning and Understanding in the History of Ideas*, can here shed light on the ideological underpinnings of Akhundzadeh and Kermani's texts. Observing linguistic models, Skinner warns against reading too much into the social context of texts, as the context says little about the text's illocutionary force or, in other words, the meanings the author aimed to bring about through the use of a particular utterance. This model emphasizes the intention of the author over the social context in which the text was produced. In this light, it is my contention that Akhundzadeh and Kermani intended their texts to bring about a new ideology, although of course they never used the term ideology but rather referred to "convincing" and "changing views."

Finally, to close this theoretical discussion, I state what the alert student of nationalism will already have gathered: this book largely adheres to the modernist approach in nationalism theory, emphasizing the modern character of nations and nationalist ideologies. Formulations of Iran as a national community based on ethnic, cultural, linguistic, or racial grounds are undoubtedly unique to the modern era. Although the term "Iran" existed in premodern times, its meaning was fluid: it could be geographic, broadly cultural, and often purely territorial or political.

I should add that although my approach is modernist, I do take issue with the eurocentrism and social determinism of some modernist authors, who attribute the birth of nationalism to specific modern social processes alone, and generally ones closely associated with European history. Ernest Gellner's argument that nationalism is a by-product of industrialization and the re-sulting need to create a large mass of skilled and interchangeable individu-als to tap into for purposes of expansion cannot be applied to the Iranian case, where nationalism appeared when industrialization was a very distant pros-pect. Similarly, Anderson argued that nationalism is a necessary outcome of the decline in appeal of universalist religion, coupled with the advent of what he calls "print-capitalism," but religious sentiments in Iran were strong and dislocative nationalism owes nothing to print-capitalism, which in late nine-teenth-century Iran was embryonic at most.[14] In this context, it is important to note that the founding texts of Iranian nationalism were only published late in the twentieth century (or early in the twenty first), and their influence was entirely due to oral circulation and the transmission of manuscripts. The emergence of modern definitions of the Iranian nation can, of course, be traced to the social process of Iranian modernity, which was initiated by what I call the traumatic encounter with Europe, but I believe that the social deter-minism of the above authors does not give sufficient weight to either local social processes or the imprint of individuals. In my view, the Iranian expe-rience of modernity in addition to individuals such as Akhundzadeh and Kermani, played an equally determining role in shaping the ideological con-tent of dislocative nationalism.

THE ACADEMIC DEBATE
ON IRANIAN NATIONALISM

For a long time, nationalism was one of the most neglected aspects of Iranian studies. Large segments of Iranian historiography generally considered nation-alism to be a natural element of the country's history, rooted in distinct racial and cultural characteristics.[15] In other words, modern Iranian historiography was largely written with the primordialist assumptions provided by either the orientalist literature produced in the West or the nationalist literature produced in Iran. It is only recently that Iranian nationalism has started to be approached critically. Richard Cottam's *Nationalism in Iran* (1964) was the first attempt to study the topic. This laudable enterprise suffers today from obsoleteness as it appeared before the development of nationalism theory. It thus lacks theoretical relevance and largely focuses on the events of 1951–53 and the nationalization of oil by Mohammad Mosaddeq.

Mostafa Vaziri's *Iran as Imagined Nation* (1993) is an appraisal of the con-struction of identity in modern Iran, which sets out to challenge the perennialist idea of a continuous Iranian entity since time immemorial. Vaziri uses Benedict Anderson's model of "imagined communities" to argue that the idea of an Iranian nation was constructed by orientalists and adopted by nationalists. The methods of Vaziri's modernist approach to nationalism prompted strong reactions from scholars of Iran. Although it is hardly deniable that *Iran as Imagined Nation* is a controversial work due to its polemical tone and some conceptual inconsistencies, it does however have the merit of attempting, for the first time, to critically reassess Iranian identity myths. Yet, by doing so, it goes too far by way of modernism and pushes the argument of the European origin of the Iranian nationalist discourse beyond what is reasonable. It dismisses as "imitation" the role of Iranian thinkers, the modalities in which they filtered European nationalist ideas and scholarship through Iranian forms of expression, and the strategies they pursued in doing so. The work remains an important landmark nevertheless.

Mohammad Tavakoli-Targhi criticized Vaziri's approach and methodology, arguing that to "challenge the nationalist historiography it is not sufficient to construe it as a fabrication of Orientalists and Aryan supremacists."[16] Tavakoli-Targhi himself set out to investigate the intellectual origins of Iranian modernity in a number of articles that were compiled in 2001 into the *Refashioning Iran* volume in English, and in 2002 in *Tajadod-e bumi va bāz andishi-ye tārikh* (Vernacular modernity and the rethinking of history) in Persian. Analyzing the narratives of Iranian nationalism is an important component of Tavakoli-Targhi's research. For instance, he conducts important semantic work shedding light on the evolution of terms such as *vatan* (homeland) from denoting one's village or town to signifying "motherland" in a national sense.[17] But most importantly, Tavakoli-Targhi offers a new theory of the origins of the nationalist discourse on pre-Islamic Iran, including in Akhundzadeh and Kermani's work. According to him, a series of seventeenth-century texts produced in Mughal India in Persian (the *dasātiri* texts) provided the model used to retrieve memories of Iran's pre-Islamic past.[18]

Where Vaziri attributes the conceptual framework and narratives of Iranian nationalism to European orientalists alone, Tavakoli-Targhi keeps them squarely within the Persianate domain, seeing the origin of many nationalist myths in local sources exclusively. Vaziri rejects the agency of Iranians themselves (beyond their mere "imitation") while Tavakoli-Targhi refutes any claim that European models could have been used to reimagine the Iranian nation. The works of these two authors are important milestones: Vaziri has influenced my systematic reappraisal of nationalist discourse in Iran, while my analysis of modernity and culture is partly indebted to Tavakoli-Targhi's. While acknowledging my debt to these authors and to the theoretical contributions of postcolonialism in general, my work aims to move beyond theoretical partisanship, and as such I can only reach different conclusions on the origins and elaboration of the tenets of nationalism. I see my book as a third alternative, endeavoring to do justice to the central role of specific individuals such as Akhundzadeh and Kermani in selecting, adopting and instrumentalizing ideas they found in European scholarship. That these ideas were first expressed by European authors rather than in any local tradition, *dasātiri* or otherwise, is in my view incontrovertible, and I offer evidence to that effect. However, it was Iranian thinkers who are to be credited with the hybridization of these ideas into the ideology of dislocative nationalism, and this intervention should not be ignored or dismissed as imitation: it was a complex process whereby particular ideas were selected at the expense of others. As already mentioned, it is the strategies pursued by these Iranian thinkers that should be the main object of study of any work on the nationalist ideologies. Not seeing this process is missing out on one of the most fundamental aspect of the history of nationalism in Iran.

With his *Nationalizing Iran* (2008), Afshin Marashi provided the field with a new milestone. The book is an analysis of the changing state–society relationship and modernizing transformations in Iran in the period 1870–1940, and of how this process affected or even shaped the modern definition of Iranian identity. Through the case studies selected, Marashi offers a comprehensive overview of the ideas of the Iranian nation that had currency during that period and ultimately influenced the state's formulation of identity—in other words, of the convergence of cultural production and state-building. Marashi's approach and mine differ to some extent. Marashi is concerned with state–society relations, and with the modalities of transformation of this relationship in the latter part of the nineteenth century and the early twentieth. I, on the other hand, am concerned with tracing the historical and intellectual circumstances in which a set of ideas emerged, and with the individuals who streamlined them into ideological form. There is, however, a great degree of convergence as well. In particular, we both see the nationalism of the early Pahlavi period within a larger process of maturation, thus cutting across conventions of periodization in Iranian historiography. In other words, we have an overarching interest in analyzing how the nationalist ideas that had currency in the Pahlavi period came about rather than simply look at their implementation.

Firoozeh Kashani-Sabet's *Frontier Fictions* (1999) is a study of the place of land and geography in the maturation of the Iranian national imagination. Kashani-Sabet's main contention is that, besides language, historiography, and religion, territory is a fundamental source of Iranian identity, something that has so far been neglected by students of Iran. Kashani-Sabet's historical coverage is similar although slightly broader than mine (1804–1946); thus we do discuss some of the same historical events (the Russo-Iranian wars, the period of modernist thought, the Constitutional Revolution, the rise of the Pahlavi state). Kashani-Sabet also actively engages with nationalism theory, arguing, for instance, that Anderson's "imagined communities" concept overlooks something very tangible in bringing about a national community: territory.

Ali M. Ansari's *The Politics of Nationalism in Modern Iran* (2012) argues that the constitutionalist origin of Iranian nationalism is essential in understanding nationalist politics in the twentieth century, and that the impact of constitutionalism extends far beyond the revolutionary period or even the Pahlavi era. There are essential differences between Ansari's analysis and mine. I focus on a particular brand of nationalism; Ansari looks at nationalist politics from a broader perspective. I consider dislocative nationalism to be highly rigid—to the point of fixity—and one of the dominant ideologies of modern Iran. Ansari's is a more fluid nationalism that evolves from its constitutionalist origins throughout the different stages of Iran's recent political history. Ansari also rejects the centrality of race to the formulation of nationalism.

Rasmus Elling's recent *Minorities in Iran: Nationalism and Ethnicity after Khomeini* (2013) is the latest attempt to approach the matter of ethnicity, minorities, and nationalism critically. It is very much the first full-length analysis of the highly sensitive subject of minorities in Iran. In some sections of his book, Elling assesses the impact of nationalist identity myths on the concrete day-to-day treatment of minorities in Iran (which essentially translates into a denial of cultural rights and administrative independence). Elling also makes an important contribution by analyzing the origins (modern and Western) of the idea of the "Persian majority." Therefore, although hailing from a different methodology than mine and covering a different period, I believe that Elling's theoretically sophisticated work is highly relevant to any historical appraisal of Iranian identity myths.

Other authors have more specifically looked into the works of Akhundzadeh and Kermani, chiefly Fereydun Adamiyat, who produced two hagiographies of these authors in the second half of the twentieth century, to which I will have the opportunity to return.[19] Other more impartial works have informed my evaluation of the two authors, in particular a number of articles by Mangol Bayat-Philipp and Cyrus Masroori on Kermani, and by Juan Cole, Mehrdad Kia, and Maryam Sanjabi on Akhundzadeh.[20] But my aim is to conduct a full-length piece of research on the two authors, show the deep spiritual affinity between them, identify their sources and reflect on Akhundzadeh's work at the service of the Russian Viceroyalty.

The analysis of Iranian nationalist discourses is therefore ongoing, but a reappraisal of the racialization of Iranian history, the definition of Iranianness against its Arab "other," and the uses and abuses of the Aryan discourse that are at the core of dislocative nationalism has been overdue. With this book, I aim to fill this gap. My priority is the examination of the texts that Akhundzadeh and Kermani produced along with the European templates they used. However, I will not leave it there, as I emphasize the startling impact of the dislocative nationalist ideology by tracing its evolution into the contemporary period. I hope that this work will shed a new light on utterances and policies that derive from dislocative nationalist tenets but had so far been analyzed in a void. For instance, the persistent endeavor since the early twentieth century to eliminate Arabic loanwords or the Pahlavi policy of forced unveiling cannot be fully elucidated without reference to the dislocative nationalist horror at cases of racial and cultural miscegenation and its insistence on uprooting Islam from Iran in order to recreate the grandeur of ancient Iran.

1

THE PALEONTOLOGY OF IRANIAN NATIONALISM

IRANIAN NATIONALISM IS A MODERN IDEOLOGY, A TRIBUTARY
of fairly recent social and cultural developments that allowed for its formulation, dissemination, and reception. But when did Iranian modernity start? I
would argue that it started during the rule of the Qajar dynasty (1796–1925),
more specifically in the context of two wars against Russia in 1804–1813 and
1826–1828, when the state elites encountered European military might for the
first time. Therefore, the backdrop of the emergence of Iranian nationalism is a
traumatic encounter with Europe, which was made possible by modern means
of communication and warfare.

Modernity is a contested concept. A now-outdated Eurocentric historiography had established a sequence of historical developments (the Reformation,
the Renaissance, the Scientific Revolution, the Enlightenment, and industrialization) as the milestones of modernization. This reading construed
modernity as a Western achievement. In this narrative, religion receded in
favor of "reason," and the West initiated the rise of global capitalism, the
nation-state, and imperialism. Non-Western societies were deemed mere observers or aspirant imitators of this European modernity. According to Mohammad Tavakoli-Targhi, "from within this hegemonic paradigm, non-European
societies were 'modernized' as a result of Western impact and influence"; in

other words, they were in transition between "tradition" and "*western* modernity."[1] This narrative conflating modernity and the West has been challenged, most notably by Stuart Hall.[2]

Obviously, if there is such a thing as specifically Iranian modernity, it did not follow this path. Therefore we need an alternative to the Euro-derivative understanding of modernity to locate its beginning; for instance, we can define modernity within the context of the globalization of certain political, social, economic, and intellectual processes and Iran's incorporation into these. These processes could be said to comprise, inter alia, the integration (even incomplete) into global networks of trade and power and the advent of a set of ideas about progress and—precisely—"modernity," on which intellectuals would reflect and argue transregionally. This definition of modernity has the advantage of being applicable globally, and it also makes it possible to consider the modern age as having started at different times in different places (it does justice to what many authors refer to as "multiple modernities"). This process was no benign transition; in fact, modernity in Iran was experienced as a violent historical rupture, and I am not necessarily referring to the classical "tradition versus modernity" binary of modernization theory. Rather, I refer to a rupture between a safe and familiar world where the Iranian elite knew who its immediate neighbors and rivals were (the Ottomans and Mughals) and a new, unsafe world that is populated by many more actors, thanks to spatial compression, and that presents a set of at first incomprehensible challenges (imperialism), impregnable enemies (European militaries and financiers), and intellectual dilemmas (what to do). Ironically, this definition of modernity seems to suggest all the same that modernity emanates from Europe. I suggest that it was triggered by an intellectual, economic, and military encounter with Europe, which is not quite the same thing as endorsing a new form of modernization theory. But the presence of Europe in this story is incontrovertible. As I argue throughout this book, Iranian nationalism is intimately and organically intertwined with the intellectuals' fear of, and infatuation with, things and ideas European, and their anxiety to bring Iran to the same level of advancement as soon as possible. There is nothing exceptional in this Iranian experience. If one looks at it from a regional perspective, there are parallels with Muhammed Ali's Egypt and the Ottoman Empire under the Tanzimat period. However, there is more to the history of this period, as I am not assessing nationalism as a wholesale import from Europe: a very complex process of selection and hybridization of European ideas took place, and the end product was something quite novel and distinctly "Iranian modern."

The traumatic discovery of the European "other" also meant a discovery of European texts, and in this chapter I also argue that modern Iranian historiography is conceptually indebted to a specific definition of Iran as instigated by orientalist scholarship in Europe. I do not claim that European orientalists "invented" Iran. Rather, I mean that a hybridization of Iranian sources with a European nationalizing mindset (rooted in European concerns) produced a national historiography of Iran that gave a clearer contour to the otherwise variable realities to which the term referred to previously. In fact, this new historiography liberated the history of Iran and Iranians from the universalism of the Islamic *umma* and the restricted deeds of kings and prophets. It transformed them into vessels of history endowed with a degree of agency.

THE TRAUMATIC DISCOVERY OF THE EUROPEAN "OTHER"

Throughout the eighteenth century, "Europe" had been a distant continent. The Silk Road, which had once connected Iran to remote societies in Europe and Asia under the Pax Mongolica, had long since disintegrated. The European fortune-seekers and missionaries that had flocked to Isfahan in the Safavid era had become rare: encounters between Iran and Europe were close to nil, and even diplomatic exchanges were unusual. Comparatively, Arab Ottoman subjects had received far more exposure to Europe through trade, war, or the settlement of European merchants from the eighteenth century onward. Iran in the meantime led an isolated life behind its formidable natural barriers and was more concerned with its immediate surroundings than with Europe. When the Qajar dynasty ascended the throne in 1796, the expansion of European empires and the intensification of intercontinental transport by modern means brought Iran into sudden contact with European military power and imperial designs.

The first episode of this encounter came in the form of the 1804–1813 (First) Russo-Iranian war. It was the result of a clash between the Iranian sovereign Fathʿali Shah Qajar's (1797–1834) keenness to preserve Iran's traditional suzerainty in the Caucasus and Tsar Alexander I's (r. 1801–1825) determination to secure his empire's southward expansion. Russian encroachments led to war in 1804, and Russia prevailed thanks to its more tactical warfare and superior technology. The shah was forced to pay ruinous war reparations to Russia, and the 1813 Treaty of Gulistan formalized the tsars' hegemony over Georgia and other parts of the Caucasus. Russia's continued infringements along with calls for intervention from Muslims persecuted by their new Russian overlords created a new momentum for intervention. Thus, the second Russo-Iranian war broke out in 1826.[3] The second defeat was even more disastrous than the first, and the 1828 Treaty of Turkmenchay added Yerevan, Nakhchivan, and other strategic provinces to Russian gains while imposing a tough diktat on Iran.

Defeat at the hands of "infidels" left a deep imprint on the popular mood. Testimony to Qajar subjects' anger was the notorious murder of Alexander Griboyedov, the Russian envoy.[4] Yet, it took the Qajars a few other setbacks to take full measure of their comparative military weakness, and this time it was Britain's turn to deliver them a blow. Mohammad Shah Qajar's (r. 1808–1848) plans to invade Herat had alerted London. Herat was of strategic importance to Britain, as military commanders believed the Russians could use the valley of the Hari River south of Herat as a passageway into India. When the shah launched his attack on Herat in 1837, British reinforcements repelled his tribal forces.

Simultaneously to these military confrontations, Iran's geostrategic position brought about political interference in its affairs. Iran became a de facto buffer state in the strategic rivalry between Britain and Russia in Central Asia, later called the "Great Game" by British diplomats. Both empires considered their presence in Iran to be vital to their imperial interests—Russia, regarding the Caucasus and Central Asia, and Britain, concerning access to the Sub-continent. However, neither could make a definite move to turn Iran into a colonial possession without incurring the risk of an all-out military confrontation. Thanks to this fragile balance, the Qajars managed to maintain some nominal sovereignty, but it came with foreign presence and interference. With time, the two European powers' intrusion into Iranian affairs became increasingly bold, and the Qajar state could not offer effective resistance. In 1907 the Great Game was settled through the Anglo-Russian agreement, which divided Iran into three zones: a British zone of influence in the southwest, a Russian zone in the north, and a neutral zone in the remaining part of the country.

The two powers also pressured the Qajar kings to gain the concession of various special privileges to their subjects. In 1872 Nasser ed-Din Shah Qajar (r. 1848–1896) granted a "comprehensive country-wide monopoly" to Baron Paul Julius de Reuter, a British subject, partly to pay for his first royal voyage to Europe and partly out of sincere belief that it could contribute to Iran's development. Lord Curzon, then viceroy of India, famously said of the Reuter concession that it was "the most complete and extraordinary surrender of the entire industrial resources of a Kingdom into foreign hands that has probably ever been dreamt of, much less accomplished, in History."[5] It was indeed a serious limitation on Iran's independence to exploit its own resources, although it is important to stress that it was a private matter between Reuter and the shah, and that it was not backed by the British government (hence, perhaps, Lord Curzon's comment). Facing tremendous pressure from the Shi'ite clergy and the Russian legation (both united in their opposition to British influence), the shah ultimately repealed the concession. The tobacco concession of 1891 prompted a countrywide boycott of the *qaliyān* (water pipe). The tobacco uprising was the country's first-ever peaceful political mass movement, and it successfully forced the sovereign to back down—an unprecedented outcome that shows the extent to which foreign interference was resented by the populace and the clergy that led it into the uprising.[6]

Some concessions were thus repealed, but the Qajars paid a high price for them. The cancellation of the Reuter concession had to be settled with the establishment of a British bank in 1889. Likewise, a Russian bank was set up after the termination of a railway concession granted to a Russian subject. The Qajars faced tremendous financial difficulties and European pressure. They were in a vicious spiral that they only deepened by offering more concessions in the financial, mining, infrastructure, and later oil sectors, despite public and clerical discontent. All of these concessions yielded handsome revenues to their British and Russian concessionaires as well as their Iranian counterparts. Nasser ed-Din Shah's successor, Mozaffar ed-Din Shah Qajar (r. 1896–1907), started his reign by contracting a colossal loan of over three million pounds sterling from the Russian Loan Bank to finance his trip to Europe.[7] In order to obtain the loan, the sovereign, among other things, pledged the revenue of the customs (with the exception of the Persian Gulf ports) as security. Thus was the state of Iran's relationship with its newly found neighbors.

But let us come back to the Russo-Iranian wars. Iran's military defeats at the hands of Russia caused consternation among the self-contented princes, courtiers, provincial overlords, intellectuals, clergymen, and Sufis who composed the Qajar elite. Several reasons may explain the magnitude of their disbelief and anguish. First there is the medieval Islamic tradition of holding all things Christian in contempt, a sentiment that survived in Iran into the early nineteenth century because the Qajars had been relatively sheltered from European traders and colonial agents. Anything stemming from Europe was considered undesirable.[8] This line of thinking stemmed from a period in which the Islamic empires were at the forefront of scientific advancement and political power while Europe seemed to vegetate in the midst of what was later called "the Dark Ages." Although this biased perception of Europe had started to recede by the eighteenth century among Ottoman elites, it remained strong in Iran until the period under study.[9] Such a punishing defeat from "infidels" was particularly unpalatable. Second, and more specifically, Russians had been objects of scorn in Iran since the Safavid period (1502–1736). According to historian Rudi Matthee, they were associated with the "Biblical and Qur'anic notion of Gog and Magog, Ya'juj and Ma'juz, the foggy lands to the north inhabited by brutish, dimwitted, and bibulous people and separated from the civilized lands of Islam by a wall supposedly built by Alexander the Great"; indeed, Russian envoys and merchants were often treated undiplomatically or contemptuously by Safavid officials, as even Sir John Chardin testified in his travelogue.[10] By Qajar times, perceptions were starting to change due to Peter the Great's and Catherine II's reforms, but Russians were still generally seen as an inferior and boorish people—albeit now they were also aggressively expansionist.[11]

Third, there was a traditional and more indigenous sense of superiority associated with Persian high culture that was strong within the Qajar elite. If the testimonies of foreign travelers are any indication, there is reason to believe that this chauvinism pervaded the traditional upper class. Indeed, early-seventeenth-century European travelogues often relayed their authors' observation that Iranian subjects displayed a natural sense of superiority over foreign travelers, and were easily offended.[12] Sir John Malcolm (1769–1833) identified Iranians as "a nation distinguished for vanity."[13] The Comte Arthur de Gobineau (1816–1882) also took notice of the self-contentment of Qajar subjects. He described them as being "universally" endowed with "a firm sentiment of superiority, which constitutes one of their shared ideas and an important component of their moral patrimony."[14] Twenty-four centuries earlier, Herodotus had already noticed that Persians thought of themselves as the most civilized nation on Earth.

Iranian sources, be they travelogues, archives, or poems, provide us with further indications of this cultural chauvinism. Iranian travelogues prior to the nineteenth century display no interest in Europe and Europeans, certainly in comparison with later accounts. Most of their authors did not consider Europe to be a relevant source of inspiration for Iran.[15] Archives confirm this aloofness: the Safavid official historians, for instance, hardly ever considered European travelers and ambassadors worthy of being mentioned in court documents, unlike their Ottoman or Mughal counterparts.[16] When they did mention

Westerners, accounts were scornfully dismissive, displaying a sense of both religious and cultural arrogance. Eulogies of Iran, on the other hand, abound in literary sources. Similarly to the premodern Chinese, premodern Iranians saw their land as the center of the universe and were reluctant to travel or learn languages other than Arabic and Turkish.[17] It has to be stated that along with Iran, premodern poets writing in Persian eulogized a number of other geographical and cultural entities and even foreign lands, but this should not invalidate my point that the Qajar elite was imbued with a sense of religious and—although in a less visible way—cultural superiority.

Thus, the encounter with Europe brought the merry-go-round of Islamic self-righteousness and the sense of cultural superiority of the Persian high culture to a juddering halt. The Qajar elite was brutally awakened and came to realize—albeit timidly at first—the extent to which European powers had advanced in the arts of warfare. The scar was deep and permanent. Sources on the elite's assessments of the Russo-Iranian wars are rare due to the official chroniclers' wariness not to offend their courtly patrons. Nevertheless, two extant testimonies relay the scope of the Qajar court's incomprehension after the defeats. First we have Crown Prince and military commander Abbas Mirza Qajar's (1789–1838) naïve and frankly bitter question to a European dignitary as early as 1805: "What is the power that gives [Europe] so great a superiority over us? What is the cause of your progress and of our constant weakness? You know the art of governing, the art of conquering, the art of putting into action all human faculties, whereas we seem condemned to vegetate in a shameful ignorance."[18]

The French diplomat and traveler who conveyed these words has no doubt deliberately exaggerated their tone for self-aggrandizement. However, a second source—Iranian this time—seems to confirm the general astonishment of the high dignitaries involved in the planning of the wars against Russia. Mirza Abolqasem Qaʻem Maqam Farahani (1779–1835), a high-ranking Qajar official and minister to Crown Prince Abbas Mirza, recorded his personal reflections on these events with a candor that contrasts with the obsequious tone of courtly reports and panegyrics.[19] In these poems, Qaʻem Maqam's many references to destiny and fortune, which he blames for Iran's defeats, show his almost desperate attempt to make sense of the painful outcome of the wars: "It is the cycle of the time that chances to exalt and to humiliate / The playful wheel [of fortune] has so many such puppets."[20] Elsewhere, Qaʻem Maqam compares Russian imperial domination to Napoleonic France and again interrogates destiny rather than providing any answers, confirming his failure to grasp the immediate realities he confronted: "Who knows what this concealed secret is / Or the purpose of this cockfight?"[21]

After the immediate shock, these events engendered a long and painful process of questioning, which gradually paved the way for the emergence of what came to be known as Iran's modernist movement (*nehzat-e tajadod*). Abbas Mirza's words are illustrative of the first phase of modernist thought, which was largely concerned with increasing Iran's military might to confront European encroachments. Abbas Mirza's reform program, the *nezām-e jadid* (new army), was exclusively designed to import military and technological expertise from Europe, and in this sense, it echoed similar Ottoman military reform programs in the same period, and was even named after them. Gobineau noted, as late as 1865, that the European books that were highest in demand in Iran "were not the kind that bring ideas" but rather were "treatises of artillery or of infantry theory; abstracts of medical practice and essays of French grammar."[22] Domestic resistance, the absence of a strong state apparatus, and Abbas Mirza's premature death in 1833 brought the ambitious program to a halt and led the way to less radical military reforms.

Early modernism's somehow simplistic belief that the casual import of military technology would solve Iran's problems stemmed from the absence of concrete understanding of the historical, political, social, and economic factors behind Europe's strength or the causes behind Iran's own deficiencies, even among the most enlightened Qajar subjects in the early nineteenth century, as Abbas Mirza's question clearly exemplifies.[23] This situation made the first Iranian assessments of Europe's strength superficial at best or outright fanciful, as nothing in Iranian forms of knowledge could help make sense of the mechanisms behind European advances. To make matters worse, Iran adopted the print fairly late. This was the result of the prohibitive price of imported paper and high rates of illiteracy.[24] Thus, circulation of information was slow and erratic, and it took some time until accounts of Europe became accessible in print, for the literati to ponder.

As part of the vague policy of catching up with European militaries, Iranian students were sent to Europe for purposes of higher education. In the process, these students acquired a tangible experience of European modernity and brought about a dramatic change in Iranian perceptions of Europe. Abbas Mirza himself opened the way by sending a group of Iranian youngsters to study in England in 1811 and 1815. Upon his return, one of these students, Mirza Saleh Shirazi, established a print shop, published one of the first newspapers in Persian, voiced his admiration for British democracy, and held unheard-of anticlerical stances.[25] This was only a foretaste of the ideas that would soon become widespread with an ever-growing number of sons of princes, dignitaries, and wealthy merchants making their way to Europe, Russia, the Ottoman Empire, and India to attend university, and this increasing famil-iarization with Europe would have tremendous bearing on modernism's evo-lution throughout the reign of the Qajars. Upon their return, these Iranian students would gather in their modernist circles to discuss representative gov-ernment, economic development, technical advancement, and social reform. The traditional contempt for things "infidel" soon turned into an unquestion-ing reverence for Europe's achievements.

The first "technological" phase of modernism brought about tangible changes, although few in numbers. First, Iranian higher education was es-tablished with the opening of the polytechnic school Dar ol-Fonun, the first modern Iranian academic institution—and ancestor of today's University of Tehran—in 1851. It was first exclusively manned with European teachers to train the progenies of the Iranian upper class in, unsurprisingly, modern skills ex-ploitable in warfare (including languages and medical science). Gobineau was very critical of the institution; he found the European teachers staffing the school, "with the exception of two or three," to be "very ignorant" and com-plained that "the public, except the students who must be paid to attend classes, take no interest in [the school] at all."[26] For him, imparting knowledge that is "immediately applicable" could never awaken the Iranians' interest in the real achievements of Europe. Edward G. Browne (1862–1926), on the other hand, attended a *majles-e sehhat* (medical council) at the Dar ol-Fonun a few decades later and was positively impressed by a discussion of the state of health and hygiene in the realm.[27] Whatever a fair assessment of the Dar ol-Fonun may be, fierce opposition to it among the ulama and other circles hostile to European influence is testimony to the institution's role as a conduit for Eu-ropean ideas.[28] In addition to the Dar ol-Fonun, a number of European and American missionary schools operated in Iran, particularly among the reli-gious minorities, contributing to the slow spread of Western ideas. Second, as already mentioned, there were attempts to modernize the armed forces. These attempts were erratic at best, and Stephanie Cronin has argued that switching away from the traditional tribal forces in reality weakened Iran's overall military power.[29]

These half-hearted efforts at reform were nowhere near the late Ottoman reformism, which brought about one of the largest standing armies in the world and transformed the lives of Ottoman subjects through taxation and

conscription. Thus, they could only lead to disappointment among modernists. A number of events in the 1850s highlighted the inadequacy of technological modernism. First, court intrigues caught a reformist-minded and extremely able chief minister of Nasser ed-Din Shah in the wings. Amir Kabir
(1807–1852), arguably the most inventive figure of the entire Qajar period, a
talented diplomat, military strategist, founder of the Dar ol-Fonun, and initiator of the first official newspaper in Iran, was executed in 1852 after a tenure of
only four years. Part of the reason for this tragic end was that he had alienated
all his potential supporters.[30] That a man with such potential to accomplish
reforms could be slain unceremoniously and in such an arbitrary fashion
seemed to indicate that Iran's ills were not limited to comparatively lower military might but could be blamed on the arbitrary nature of royal power. The
arbitrariness of Nasser ed-Din Shah's rule would be confirmed two decades
later when another able politician, Mirza Hossein Khan Moshir od-Dowleh
(1828–1881), would also fall due to court intrigues.

Second, yet more military defeats proved that decades of haphazard modernization of the armed forces had been entirely ineffective. In 1852 and 1856
Nasser ed-Din Shah followed in the footsteps of his predecessor, Mohammad
Shah, and launched two fresh attacks on Herat. They met the same fate as the
previous attempt in 1837: British reinforcements disarmed the Iranian forces
and roundly defeated them. The incursions into Herat led to harsh peace
terms for Iran, which included capitulatory privileges to be granted to Britain
and her subjects. The Qajars were lucky not to be stripped of their throne. The
military gap between Iran and the European powers in fact increased throughout the nineteenth century. Whereas during the first Russo-Iranian war Iran's
tribal forces stalemated Russia in a war of attrition for several years, Russian
armies in the early twentieth century could violate Iran's sovereignty in impu-
nity and without encountering any resistance.[31]

Modernists who served in the state apparatus and attempted to implement
reforms were increasingly frustrated as they realized that the task at hand was
impossible and systemic resistance insurmountable. Mirza Yusef Khan Mostashar od-Dowleh, a high-ranking official serving in the Ministry of Justice and
an enthusiastic modernizer, confided to his friend Mirza Fath'ali Akhundzadeh (1812–1878) in 1871 that he felt "exhausted and powerless": "we have not
been able to do a grain of service to the nation and the fatherland."[32] As a
result of this realization, modernist thinkers became aware of the necessity for
deeper and more far-reaching reform. Among these more sophisticated modernists, Mirza Malkam Khan (1833–1908; also spelled Malkum or Malkom)
clearly stands out. Invested with a far deeper knowledge of life in Europe than

his predecessors, Malkam Khan recognized that the main difference between Europe and Iran resided in the structure of political power. In Europe, power—even that of an absolute monarch—was tempered by certain laws or the rights of other groups such as landed gentries and nobilities, whereas in Iran the power of the shah went unchecked. In practice, the monarch's power was only constrained by the anarchic nature of politics, the absence of any nationwide institution, the deteriorating state of the court's finances, and the encroachments of foreign powers. Yet no legal framework made the exercise of royal power predictable.

Malkam Khan advocated that law should "condition" (*mashruteh sākhtan*) the shah's powers, and his doctrine paved the way for the demands formulated in the 1906–1911 Constitutional Revolution (thus called, following the Ottoman model, the *mashruteh* revolution in Persian.) This idea of power conditioned to law had stricken deep roots among the reformers of the time, and even Nasser ed-Din Shah admitted after his first trip to Europe that "all the order and progress that we witnessed in Europe in our recent visit is due to the existence of law."[33] Malkam's influence brought the concept of law (*qānun*) to the very core of modernist thought for the next half century. Yet modernism ultimately failed to achieve the hopes of its advocates. Their progressive projects necessitated a drastic change in the nature of the state, which was still rigidly arbitrary. Needless to say, there was tremendous resistance from the monarchs, their courts, and the ulama, although occasionally one at least of these groups advocated reform but ultimately failed to garner enough support from the others. Modernists' attempts to place checks on the monarch's ability to grant concessions were also unpopular with all those who benefited from concessions, or who thought that they contributed to Iran's development. As a result, although Nasser ed-Din Shah had a degree of sympathy for some modernist ideas, he ultimately shied away from fundamental reforms. As the British minister to Tehran observed, "The Shah fears the approach of civilization as being likely to curb his power and to check his autocratic and arbitrary tendencies."[34] The monarch's French physician echoed, "the Shah's best intentions were too often paralyzed by the people interested in the maintenance of the *status quo*."[35]

THE COMING OF HISTORICAL IRANOCENTRISM

The response to the encounter with Europe was the defining moment of Iranian modernity. It also provided the historical backdrop to the advent of the ideas that would gradually be fused into Iranian nationalism. In the next chapter, I argue that nationalism was the second trend running parallel to the pragmatic modernism of Malkam Khan and the constitutionalists. The failure of technological modernism brought about a chasm between this pragmatic and more decidedly reformist version of modernism centered on the concept of law and a historicist narrative, that of dislocative nationalism. Before getting to these distinctions, it is essential to make a detour by the evolution of the historiography of Iran in the same period, which brought about a national history of Iran centered on a new notion of Iran and its Volk as a perennial and self-conscious collective body.

In this section, national history refers to a work whose object is a nation (or so assumed) within its current borders, or variations thereof, that is then projected onto the past. The protagonists of a national history are the people—Volk—of that nation, usually assumed to have always been aware of their national belonging. Johann Gottfried Herder (1744–1803) was the initiator of the concept of Volk used here. He understood it as "people," not in the ancien régime sense of the underclass mass but rather as an all-encompassing "national" body to which both the king and the peasant equally belong.[36] This *völkisch* focus is the main element distinguishing modern national histories from prenational epics and traditions centered on kings, heroes, prophets—in one word individuals—that were common in many premodern societies.

In Europe, "national histories" appeared in the midst of the political and social upheavals that accompanied the emergence of the nation-state. These upheavals were systemic transformations caused by the French Revolution, the rise of the industrial society, the 1848 uprisings, colonial expansion, and an early form of globalization. National histories consolidated old identities, defined new ones, or aimed to protect freshly built nation-states and their individualities against the dying specter of religious universalism or the budding internationalism of the socialists. The works of Herder, Johann Gottlieb Fichte, and Leopold von Ranke on German history; those of François Guizot and Jules Michelet in France; and Macaulay among others in England established the canons of this discipline early in the nineteenth century. They turned the inhabitants of the Holy Roman Empire, Gaul peasants, and pre-Norman Saxons into incipient Germans, Frenchmen, and Englishmen. Soon the ancient inhabitants of the Iranian plateau would be assumed to have been endowed with similar national loyalty.

In this sense, John Malcolm's *History of Persia* (1815) was a decisive first step toward a national history of Iran, which—as we will see—was tributary of specifically European historiographical methods and stemmed from the expanding use of a national lens to write history. This European—as opposed to home-grown—historiography of Iran is largely responsible for the transformation of Iran and Iranians into vessels of a national history, autonomous from the broad universalism of the Islamic *umma*, or the restricted deeds of kings and prophets. Before reviewing the traditional historiography produced in Iran, two preliminary clarifications must be made.

For the purpose of showing the novelty of a "national history" of Iran, it is advisable to divide the Iranian time into three separate periods. Such division, however arbitrary, simply aims to show that traditional Iranian histories never covered these three periods in one full narrative and that an uninterrupted history of Iran is a novelty of modern historiography. First, a pre-Islamic period stretches from antiquity to the advent of Islam in the seventh century AD. A second period of about 850 years follows the Islamic conquest when Iran ceases to exist as a unified political unit and when no state consistently refers to itself as "Iran," although Iran survives as a cultural and geographical idea. A third period starts with the re-creation of an Iranian state by the Safavids around 1500 and extends into modern times. Traditional epics and histories either covered only one period (the pre-Islamic), were Islamic-universal with a broader scope than Iran itself, wove the history of Iran into a Quranic sequence of events, were dynastic in nature, or combined two or several of these features.

Second, broadly speaking but particularly in the Iranian context, the distinction between national history and epic poem must be stressed. Iran possesses an archetypal epic in Hakim Abol-Qasem Ferdowsi Tusi's *Shāhnāmeh* (Book of Kings; ca. 977–1010), and confusing the *Shāhnāmeh* with a national history would obscure the argument that is being articulated here. Many societies have preserved epic traditions in oral or written form. In nineteenth-century Europe, the nationalizing mindset of the time produced a trend that Joep Leerssen calls "literary historicism" based on the belief that "old texts could inspire the nation in the present."[37] Literary historicism involved a rediscovery of these traditions, sometimes their retrieval from oblivion, or their outright rewriting: the *Niebelungenlied* was retrieved and published in 1807, oral Finnish traditions were compiled into the *Kalevala* and published in 1835, and *La Chanson de Roland* was discovered in the Bodleian Library and printed for the first time in 1836.[38] These premodern traditions were reinterpreted as *national* epics, a radically new genre, and have been used to substantiate the modern claims of the national community to go back to time immemorial. Since then, a national epic has become an essential element in the paraphernalia of nation-states, and this explains their recrudescence.

Literary historicism has of course had a similar career outside of Europe too. It is interesting to note that in other parts of the world, several epic poems have not necessitated a revival, as long-lived written or oral traditions have kept them readily available for the task at hand.[39] Arguably, the most famous of them is the *Ramayana*, originally written in Sanskrit at an uncertain date. Its status as India's national epic is undisputed, although, interestingly, the *Ramayana* has been extensively indigenized outside of India from Burma to Bali. In some of these places, the local version of the *Ramayana* plays an identical role as a national epic, one case in point being Thailand and its *Ramakien*. Similarly, the Iranian nation can tap into the *Shāhnāmeh* to base its claim to primordial existence. It is deemed by some authors to be "the main evidence of our nation" (*sanad-e mellat-e mā*).[40] It recounts the stories of kings and heroes of the past in no less than 50,000 couplets. In a similar fashion to the *Ramayana*, the *Shāhnāmeh* needed no revival as it had been conserved in its present state for about one thousand years through copying and a sustained oral tradition called *Shāhnāmeh* reading (*Shāhnāmeh khāni*), to which I will come back.

There are essential differences between the works of the *Shāhnāmeh* tradition and modern national histories, which must be kept in mind. First, the *Shāhnāmeh* tradition is limited in coverage to the pre-Islamic period. Second, it focuses almost exclusively on the deeds of kings and heroes, to the detriment of the Volk. Third and most importantly, they are simply not historical but largely mythological and legendary. Ferdowsi's work accounts for the mythological dynasties of the Pishdadids and the Kayanids while ignoring all of the historically attested Achaemenids and only cursory mentioning the Parthians. Even the "historical" Sasanian section is populated with fabled heroes and witness to extraordinary events. Epics have their importance, but the object of this chapter is Iran's national history, and the underlying argument is that a modern history precedes the nationalization of an epic poem. It is in light of modern historicism that epics acquire a new *national* meaning. However that may be, the *Shāhnāmeh* is a good starting point for our analysis of traditional Iranian histories or mythistories.

Texts of the *Shāhnāmeh* tradition were known as "histories of the kings of Ajam (Iran)" (*tavārikh-e moluk-e ʿajam*) and existed before the advent of Islam in Iran. This tradition resurfaced with the emergence of Modern Persian as a language of culture in the ninth and tenth centuries AD. There are therefore older sources than Ferdowsi, on which he admittedly relied, chief among which were the Daqiqi and Abu Mansur *Shāhnāmehs*, some pre-Islamic sources, and probably also a sizable oral tradition.[41] This literature never covered the period following the Islamic conquest. The explanation lies in the mode of production of this literature, which was often the work of the *dehqān* class, to which Ferdowsi belonged. The *dehqāns* constituted the backbone of the late Sasanian empire's military and played a crucial role in the imperial economy as tax collectors. As such, although they converted to Islam in order to maintain their privileges, they remained the repository of pre-Islamic cultural practices, especially when it came to epics and legends. This concern with cultural and narrative preservation is not unusual among postconquest literate elites troubled with the disappearance of the ancient culture associated with their genealogy and its substitution by that of the conquerors. Parallels exist elsewhere: it has been referred to the similar and almost contemporaneous undertaking of Geoffrey of Monmouth with his History of the Kings of Britain (*Historia Regum Britanniae*, c. 1136) written after the Norman Conquest.[42]

In contrast to the *Shāhnāmeh* tradition, the works of many early medieval historians were principally concerned with the Islamic revelation and its development. They produced a different type of narrative in which Quranic prophetography (*tārikh ol-anbiyā*) took precedence over the kings of Ajam. The monumental *History* of Muhammad Ibn Jarir at-Tabari (839–923) is a quintessential illustration of this Islamic historiography. It starts with accounts of the Creation and the histories of prophets and patriarchs before moving onto pre-Islamic Iranian kings.[43] The Iranian past, however, merely gives a historical introduction to the single most significant event in this sort of work: the revelation of the Quran to Prophet Muhammad. For instance, in the midst of his account of the Sasanians, Tabari inserts a passage on the birth of Prophet Muhammad in order to maintain a Quranic synchronicity, whereas Ferdowsi's *Shāhnāmeh* takes no notice of the birth of the Prophet.[44] There was no anti-Islamic feeling in this omission, as Ferdowsi professes being a devout Muslim, but this simply shows that he had a different focus and different sources.

Thus, for authors like Tabari, Islam was the main affair. Others, like Abolfazl Beyhaqi (995–1077), for instance, even considered the history of pre-Islamic Iran to be altogether irrelevant.[45] These works were historical inquiries with an Islamic perspective. Iran was occasionally the backdrop but never the predominant subject. They creatively recontextualized pre-Islamic Iran into the traditional narrative of prophetography, flanking it with Abrahamic benchmarks such as the birth of Adam or Noah's flood: there were even theological attempts to reconcile the Zoroastrian first man, Kiyumars, with its Abrahamic equivalent Adam.[46] It must also be said that Islamic works were generally historical as opposed to mythological. Muslim historians were genuinely concerned about the authenticity of their sources, especially when it came to the life of the Prophet, hence a great deal of attention devoted to the reliability of the chains of transmission of historical documents.

The Mongol period was a turning point and witnessed the flourishing of a new historiography that completed the abandonment of Arabic in favor of Persian, and that drifted away from the Islam-centered character of the previous period. Some even consider this period to have witnessed the true birth of Iranian historiography;[47] others have surmised that this new recalibration proceeded from Mongol Iran's approximate territorial congruence with the former Sasanian heartland and the interest that Mongol rulers saw in promoting "a record of its achievements."[48] Indeed, an interest on the part of Mongol rulers to record their own deeds within their Iranian realms, and for the consumption of their kin, allowed for a more Iran-centered historiography to emerge, although this Iranocentrism was imperfect and opportunistic. One case in point is Ata-Malek Juvayni's (1226–1283) *Tārikh-e Jahān Goshā*, a history of the "World Conqueror"—that is, Genghis Khan—which covered Iranian lands but through the prism of its Mongol rulers. For the reasons discussed earlier, the Mongol period reinforced the official and dynastic focus of Iranian historiography.

That kings and local rulers commissioned historical works, or were their dedicatees, explains to large extents why they often—if not always—had a dynastic focus. Rather than address the deeds of the people, in a modern *völkisch* fashion, histories were in fact chronicles of the rise and fall of kings and dynasties and the incidence of these successive sequences on the affairs of the realm. Dynastic history writing was the rule down to the Qajar era. Examples abound. The sixteenth and seventeenth centuries, for example, saw the production of several partial histories of the Safavid kings. Two of these must be mentioned: first Sadr ed-Din Ebrahim Amini's *Fotuhāt-e Shāhi* (1531) and then Eskandar Beg Turkoman's *ʿĀlam Ārā-ye Abbāsi* (1629). It is in reference to dynastic histories that Tavakoli-Targhi calls the object of traditional historiography "cyclical time" (*zamān-e charkhandeh*), in which the divine grace (*farr-e izadi*) is transmitted from one king to the next, creating a chain of self-contained episodes, as opposed to the evolving "linear time" (*zamān-e bālandeh*) of modern national histories.[49] In the Mongol period, there were very few inroads into the lives of ordinary people.

Traditional Iranian histories thus complied with rules that sharply distinguished them from the modern historiography of Iran. The *Shāhnāmeh* tradition was largely mythological and covered exclusively the pre-Islamic past. Medieval Islamic histories were universal in nature; predominantly preoccupied with Islam as a political, social, and religious phenomenon; and only occasionally extended the narrative to Iranian lands and kings. Both genres obeyed to the rule of dynastic focus.[50] The three periods of Iranian history were never covered in full. Although there were examples of long continuous narratives, one could only find them in the form of urban or provincial histories, which were another established tradition: for example, the anonymous *Tārikh-e Sistān*, written in Persian ca. 1062, Fakhr ed-Din Zarkub's *Shirāz-Nāmeh* (1343) and Shams ed-Din Ali Lahiji's history of Gilan, *Tārikh-e Khāni* (1514?).

One has to wait until the seventeenth century and travel thousands of miles westward to see a history of Iran that fuses the above-mentioned periods of Iranian time into one narration. The Jewish Portuguese merchant and traveler Pedro Teixeira's (1563–1645?) *Kings of Persia* (1610) pioneered the modern time of Iranian history two full centuries before Malcolm, although this assertion needs qualification. Teixeira's *Kings of Persia* was essentially a translation of an Iranian fifteenth-century universal history written by Mirkhwand (1433–1498) and titled *Rowzat os-Safā* (the Garden of Purity). *Kings of Persia* was therefore not an original work but it had one characteristic that is of interest here: Teixeira only selected the information that the original work held on Iran and left the rest out. Talking of the *Rowzat os-Safā*, he said "Having perus'd, and finding [it] very extensive and universal as to the Affairs of *Persia*, I extracted as much as the Publick is here presented with."[51]

Without having produced an original work, and while preserving the *Rowzat os-Safā's* tone and dynastic focus, Teixeira's *Kings of Persia* is nevertheless the first-ever attempt at historical Iranocentrism. Teixeira combined all periods of Iranian history up until his time in a radical digression from any traditional history written in Iran itself. He thus pioneered the national narrative of modern Iranian historiography. While the early seventeenth century was far from an age of nationalism, the Safavid state was in place and possessed a discernible territorial contour. This reality can explain Teixeira's vision of a continuous Iranian history, or perhaps one could surmise that he had been influenced by the recently published *Luciads* of Luís de Camões (known in English as Camoens; 1524–1580), today considered the national epic of Portugal. However it may be, Teixeira singled some Iranian entity out of a universal history, and this is a remarkable proto-national undertaking that has gone un-noticed in the works of students of Iranian historiography.

Teixeira was a pioneer, but far more systematic was Malcolm's *History of Persia* (1815). An original inquiry, it is truly a national history of Iran. First, it covers the three previously mentioned periods in full. Second, its subject is a clearly defined "Persia" (within its modern borders projected onto the past). Malcolm relied on many sources, including European travelogues and partial histories (inter alia Teixeira's), but the defining feature of his work is the wealth of Iranian sources that he consulted in contrast to the sketchy orientalist litera-ture of his time (and even later), which exclusively relied on Greek, Latin, and biblical sources.[52] These local sources include the works of Bal'ami, Mirkh-wand, Mohammad Kamel bin Esmail, Mirza Mehdi, Lotf Ali Beg, and others. Malcolm even discusses Iran's own Zoroastrian founding myths, as he believes they "have an influence on the character of the people."[53]

Although Malcolm's narration is dynastic in nature, he does experiment with *völkisch* history in interesting ways. Indeed, the *History* is the result of Malcolm's diplomatic mission and sets as its objective to survey Iran's govern-ment, armed forces, and climate. Thus, a large section of the *History* in fact deals with various aspects of Iranian life. Malcolm reviews Iran's religions on the account that "religion has always exercised a supreme power over the human mind."[54] He then offers an analysis of demography, the character of the population, a description of cities and roads, and an assessment of the general stagnation of Iranian arts, crafts and sciences: "the people is neither in a state of improvement, nor has it fallen behind their forefathers."[55] Malcolm de-scribes the fondness for poetry prevalent in the Qajar lands in flattering terms that stand out from his generally paternalistic—if not disdainful—tone. He uses an entire chapter to dwell upon "Persian" "manners and usages," first those of the "exalted ranks" and then, through a progressive social descent, those of the "lower classes of the citizens," including a critical assessment of the posi-tion of women in society.[56]

That Malcolm himself was fully aware of the novelty of his endeavor is doubtful. It seems that he saw his work as simply a necessary undertaking within a strictly British context: "Persia seems hitherto to have been generally neglected [by British writers]. It must, therefore, be allowed to be highly desir-able that this blank in our Literature should be filled up."[57] Moreover, Mal-colm was an untrained historian whose work had political purposes: it was commissioned by the British administration of India, which was keen to chart the Iranian lands. Hence, Malcolm's national category of "Persia" was a geopolitical concept suited to policymakers and the maps of their imperial aspirations. It was not intended to be some radical historiographical experimentation. This furthers my point that the birth of modern Iranian historiography was initiated in response to European standards and concerns, not Iranian. Nevertheless, all historians who succeeded Malcolm adopted his signposts. The *History of Persia* became very popular in Iran later in the nineteenth century and was read to Nasser ed-Din Shah before sleep.[58] To this day it is a popular read.

While the *History of Persia* remained dynastic, it was followed by a series of works by prominent orientalists that were increasingly less so. These orientalist works displayed an increasingly *völkisch* focus—in other words, an interest in defining the Iranian nation through a study of its cultural and ethnographic specificities. Many of these first attempts were still largely prisoner of their Iranian dynastic sources. Friedrich Spiegel's *Erânische Alterthumskunde* (1871–1878) dwells a lot upon kings and is limited in its coverage to pre-Islamic Iran. However, in producing this work Spiegel also investigated ethnology—although through the today discredited lens of racial history—and took a sincere interest in Iran's ancient religions, social life, and languages. His *Iranian Art* is a study of architecture from a historical perspective. Similarly, George Rawlinson published an extensive history of pre-Islamic Iran in his series the *Great Monarchies of the Ancient Eastern World* (1871–1876), which, although slightly more dynastic in focus, attempted further investigations of the Iranian Volk in racial terms. All these works were produced within the strict national framework pioneered by Teixeira and Malcolm.

The definition of the Iranian Volk in cultural and linguistic terms took center stage when philological studies started to appear in the 1880s. These were not historical works *stricto sensu*, but they engaged with Iran's past in ways that justify their mention in the context of the volkization of Iranian history in the nineteenth century. James Darmesteter devoted his *Études Iraniennes* (1883) to the language, ancient myths, and religions of Iran. Italo Pizzi conducted important studies of Persian poetry in the 1880s and 1890s, and Browne produced the monumental *Literary History of Persia* (1902–1924). These undertakings culminated with the publication in 1895–1904 of the *Grundriss der Iranischen Philologie* (Encyclopaedia of Iranian philology), recognized as the "*summa* of 19th-century Iranian studies."[59] Thus, not only had Iran emerged from the mist of traditional histories as an independent and continuous entity, but attention also started to be paid to its cultural, religious, and social characteristics as a primordial nation. This endeavor, informed by a European nationalizing mindset, helped define Iran's people, its Volk, in the sense of modern national historiography.

In Iran itself, historiographical evolution was slower and less radical. However, in this context the work of Jalal ed-Din Mirza Qajar (1826–1870) was essential in cementing some proto-nationalist ideas. He was arguably the first Iranian author to reconstruct Iranian history within a "national" lens. One of Fath'ali Shah's numerous progenies (his fifty-fifth son) and, as such, a junior Qajar prince, Jalal ed-Din Mirza received some education at the Dar ol-Fonun where he learned French, among other things.[60] He was also a leading member of Malkam Khan's *farāmush khāneh* (house of oblivion), a semisecret society of modernists and reformers molded on the freemason model. Jalal ed-Din Mirza's contribution to the nationalization of the idea of Iran in historiography came in the shape of a mythistorical work called *Nāmeh-ye Khosrovān* (Book of Sovereigns, hereafter *Nāmeh*) written between 1868 and 1870.

The *Nāmeh* is the first Iranian text to perform a fusion of the three periods of Iranian time in the manner of Teixeira and Malcolm.[61] It is thus Jalal ed-Din Mirza who introduced the idea of Iran as a continuous historical entity to Iranian intellectual circles.[62] Not only that, the *Nāmeh* is far more Iranocentric than traditional histories, as events taking place outside of Iran's borders are deemed irrelevant and relegated to a secondary status (if ever mentioned), including Quranic—or generally Abrahamic—episodes. In complying with this nationalizing principle, Jalal ed-Din Mirza went so far as to avoid use of any foreign—in particular Arabic—loanwords. This linguistic puritanism is, to this day, a hallmark of nationalist writing. Other historical works produced in the same period usually started with the advent of Islam in Iran, including Mohammad Taqi Sepehr's *Nāsekh ot-Tavārikh* (The abrogator of histories) or Reza Qoli Khan Hedayat's *Rowzat os-Safā-ye Nāseri* (a sequel to Mirkhwand's medieval work).

Jalal ed-Din Mirza turned Iran into a national unit with an uninterrupted history that would later serve as a template for the nationalist narrative. In the first volume covering the history of pre-Islamic Iran, Jalal ed-Din Mirza labels the monarchs whose history he writes "kings of the land of Iran" and he refers to the people of the realm as Iranians and occasionally *pārsiyān*, or ancient Persians.[63] He further clarifies the contours of this new category of Iran by continuously referring to the "great men of Iran" (*bozorgān-e Irān*), the "armies of Iran" (*lashkar-e Irān*) and the "land of Iran" (*khāk-e Irān*). Pre-Islamic Iranian kings are unequivocally eulogized: not a single criticism is leveled at any of them. Jalal ed-Din Mirza reifies ethnic categories such as Arabs—whom, following the *Shāhnāmeh* tradition, he calls *tāziyān*—in addition to Turks and Mongols. In passages addressing invasions by these ethnic others, he praises Iranians' resilience in preserving their cultural distinctiveness and resisting foreign occupation. Arabs in particular are treated negatively, and as such the *Nāmeh* pioneered one of the central themes of nationalist historiography.

Some contemporaries believed that Iranian historians should adopt the standards of European history writing, and they praised Jalal ed-Din Mirza for being the first one to uphold such standards. The Parsi envoy Manekji Limji Hataria, whom I will discuss in more detail in chapter 3, was among them. In a letter to Jalal ed-Din Mirza, he first complained that the language of traditional histories was "mixed" with Arabic and Turkish, and that they generally contradicted what European historiography had to say about Iran; he then praised the *Nāmeh* for being short, written in pure Persian (*pārsi*), and being "like" the histories written in Europe.[64] Mirza Kazem Beig, a philosopher and orientalist, also praised the *Nāmeh* for "following the methods of European histories" and "being the first work complying with such methods in Iran."[65]

Claims regarding Jalal ed-Din Mirza's compliance with European canons of historiography are exaggerated. Notwithstanding the continuous national narrative of Iran and the negative treatment of Arabs, the *Nāmeh* remained heir to traditional Iranian forms, rather than attempt to replicate orientalist scholarship (such imitations will come later). For instance, its focus is entirely dynastic and even national-biographical. Indeed, dynastic histories were still the rule at the time, as works such as Sepehr's *Nāsekh ot-Tavārikh* clearly demonstrate. His sources account for this dichotomous merger of a European national and continuous category *à la* Malcolm with a purely traditional mythistorical and dynastic narrative. As far as the influence of specific European works is concerned, it is highly likely that his education at the Dar ol-Fonun had exposed him to orientalist works held at the school's library, and these included Malcolm's *History of Persia*.[66] This assumption seems to be corroborated by the *Nāmeh*'s frequent references to *farangiyān* (Europeans) and their scholarly works, although the sources are never revealed in full. Yet this exposure to European works seems to have been limited to the idea of a continuous Iranian history, as Jalal ed-Din Mirza does not seem to have been aware of crucial recent discoveries. He does not know of the Achaemenid dynasty more than Ferdowsi does, and he is entirely uninformed about Henry Rawlinson's decipherment of the Bisotun inscriptions in the 1840s and the valuable information they imparted on ancient Iran. Nor was he well versed in the writings of Herodotus. His superficial exposure to orientalist scholarship resulted in his new national category of Iran and his use of prose, but overall the form and content essentially relied on the *Shāhnāmeh* model. He was also informed about the neo-Zoroastrian *dasātiri* texts, which he mentions in his introduction and occasionally in the text.[67] In sum, it is fair to say that Jalal ed-Din Mirza's work was hybrid and, as such, a harbinger of works that appeared later with growing awareness of orientalist scholarship.

That being said, what sets the *Nāmeh* apart from its predecessors and contemporaries is its reconstruction of the Iranian past for political purposes, and this is a revolutionary and modern enterprise. Political aims were not absent from previous historical works. Clearly, the "mirrors of princes" (*āyeneh*) genre—used to instruct young princes in the art of ruling upon their accession to the throne—was eminently political in nature. Dynastic histories themselves, aiming to celebrate or defend a certain ruler, dynasty, or decision, were rarely free of political motivations. In the case of the *Nāmeh*, however, we are dealing with a private individual not involved in government (in spite of his princely status, he was more of an outcast) offering a particular reading of history that promotes a certain course for the future. Indeed, all in the *Nāmeh* praises Iran's pre-Islamic past, which is transmuted into a blueprint for the future. Alien invasions are wholly blamed for Iran's decay, and recovering the culture of pre-Islamic Iran is presented as the key to the nation's regeneration. Hence, the avoidance of any Arabic loanword, so much so that he does not even directly name "Arabs" or call the Prophet Muhammad by his name.

In order to disseminate his regeneration agenda, Jalal ed-Din Mirza intended his *Nāmeh* to be a popular reading rather than some obtuse treaty for the literate few. His Persian is clear and concise, devoid of the sometimes arcane and pompous style of traditional histories. He makes it clear in the title that he intends the *Nāmeh* to be an educational tool, so that new generations of Iranians come to share his own vision of Iranian history: the full title of the *Nāmeh* is "The Book of Sovereigns: Stories of Persian kings in the Persian language (*pārsi*—avoiding the Arabic f), beneficial to *people, especially children*" (my emphasis). In this sense, Jalal ed-Din Mirza's work is an important milestone in Iranian historiography and preludes future works in this field that will increasingly reflect the political inclinations of their authors.

It will take several more decades for Iranian authors to start moving beyond traditional mythistories and start using scientific methods developed in the West for history writing. Yet, until well into the twentieth century, their attempts remained imperfect and heavily reliant on the orientalist heritage, to which they failed to add any new discovery.[68] A crucial work was the *Tārikh-e Irān* (History of Iran; 1901) by Mirza Mohammad Hossein Forughi (known as Zoka-ol-Molk; 1839–1907). To a large extent, Forughi's book was a replica of orientalist work in the Persian language, without any innovation. The 1920s and 1930s saw the contribution of Hassan Pirniya (known as Moshir od-Dowleh; 1871–1935). Because Pirniya and his contemporaries' worked in the context of the Pahlavi state's official nationalism, they are dealt with in a later chapter covering that period.

To give a full account of historiography in the period under consideration, it should be added that the Constitutional Revolution and the momentous events that followed it gave birth to a new generation of historians who had been participants in, and desired to relate their own accounts of, the revolution. Ahmad Kasravi's *Tārikh-e Mashruteh-ye Irān* (Constitutional history of Iran; 1940), itself based on Nazem ol-Eslam Kermani's *Tārikh-e bidāri-ye Irāniyān* (The history of the awakening of the Iranians; n.d.) are prominent examples. Another influential author was Mehdi Malekzadeh, whose seven-volume *Tārikh-e Enqelāb-e Mashrutiyat-e Irān* (History of Iran's Constitutional Revolution; n.d.) is an important primary source.

In this period, dynastic historiography was gradually being abandoned in favor of Volkization. Mirza Aqa Khan Kermani lamented in the 1890s that "Fath'ali Shah's cachinnations are part of history." In his view, in addition to "biographies of sultans, accounts of wars and epopees of heroes," history should relate "a nation's character and beliefs, the qualities of each province, the laws, the nature of the rule" and should compare them with those of other peoples and nations.[69] When Kermani was writing these lines, European orientalist literature had already transformed the Iranian collective body into a genuine "national" protagonist of history whose fate was no longer a footnote to the history of Islam or the deeds of its rulers. Orientalists did not carry out this historiographical revolution out of sympathy or a desire to equip Iranians with a history of the people but instead to keep up with their own "national" habits in history writing.

Another element in this conceptual transformation of Iran was the systematized fusion of the three periods of Iranian time that Teixeira and Malcolm had pioneered. A new continuous time became the theater of Iran's national adventure. In Iran itself, the influence of this transformation was limited in scope and appeal to a handful of marginal intellectuals, among whom Jalal ed-Din Mirza led the way. Iranian authors will, however, increasingly tap into this growing orientalist corpus of research, gradually generalizing its theoretical

outlook. It was assumed in an Iranocentric reading of history that Iran had
been into uninterrupted existence as a nation-community populated by na-
tionally conscious "Iranians," since "time immemorial." Thus, Iran became a
"homeland" (*vatan*), and a range of other patriotic designations were subsequently formulated to refer to it: *keshvar-e Irān* (the country of Iran), *khāk-e
Irān* (Iran's soil), *khalq* or *mardom-e Irān* (the people of Iran), and so on.[70]

There is yet another reason why the *Nāmeh-ye Khosrovān* deserves particular attention in this context: it shows that the web of intellectual interaction
with Europe was complex. Transmutations in history writing are a clear indication that a gradual hybridization of form and content was taking place, but
European trends had little impact beyond the literate elite until assimilated
into local sources, reinterpreted in traditional aesthetics, and—needless to
say—accessible in Persian. This trend would not be perfected before the
twentieth century and the advent of mass schooling. It is interesting to
note that the first schoolbooks printed by the nationalist Pahlavi state largely
echoed the themes of the *Nāmeh-ye Khosrovān*. As we will see, some of these
themes will serve as the pillars of dislocative nationalism.

From the 1860s onward, dislocative nationalism would emerge as a radical
alternative to modernism. As we will see in the next chapters, this new thought
was an entirely discursive response to the dilemmas of modernity, as opposed
to the more pragmatic modernism of Malkam Khan. The encounter with
Europe provided the sociopolitical background to the emergence of dislocative
nationalism. An equally important evolution was taking place in historiography, giving new meaning and contours to the very concept of Iran. Indeed,
nationalist ideologues will rely on the notion of the continuous Iranian nation
as brought about by historical Iranocentrism to take the process of ethnogen-
esis to its fruition. The progressive transmutation of a fluid geographical and
cultural idea into a perennial nation-community allowed for this new idea of
Iran to become a suitable object for a nationalist thought. History is the cultural tool par excellence in the definition of a nation's past and the creation
of its desired future trajectory or, in Eric J. Hobsbawm's words, "the raw material for nationalistic, ethnic or fundamentalist ideologies, as poppies are the
raw material for heroin addiction."[71] The Iran of Teixeira and Malcolm became the raw material for the ideological nationalism of Akhundzadeh and
Kermani.

2

AKHUNDZADEH AND KERMANI

THE EMERGENCE OF DISLOCATIVE NATIONALISM

That some people simply disagree with Akhundzadeh or Kermani and dislike
them, only reveals their own intellectual deficiency.
— Fereydun Adamiyat, 1970

[Kermani's] idiotic enemies call him an extreme archaist.
— Harun Vohouman, Kermani's editor, 2007

FOR ERNEST GELLNER, NATIONS AND NATIONALISM ARE COROLLARIES
of the industrial age—in other words, the results of modern social transformations that took place primarily in Europe. Benedict Anderson, too, although in
a less explicit way, suggests that nationalism is the end product of a historical
process of modernization that originated in Western societies (which he extends
to include Spanish America) and involved the triumph of reason over religion,
the vernacularization of communication, and the advent of print-capitalism.
Both Gellner's and Anderson's theories of nationalism were groundbreaking
and contributed significantly to the academic discussion of this topic. However, two issues emerge when one attempts to apply these authors' models to a
non-Western experience of nationalism.

First, modernist readings of nationalism can produce problems similar to
those of modernization theory and other hegemonic paradigms (as touched
upon in the introduction to chapter 1). Such reading condemns the non-Western
world to either imitate well or lag behind. The application of a sequential
model whereby nationalism follows a process of rationalization, vernacularization, and industrialization does not quite help to investigate the rise of
dislocative nationalism, for instance, unless we assume that non-European
nationalisms derive from the European experience. Even if we acknowledge

the centrality of European models, ideas, and texts, as I do, we still have to explain why the rise of dislocative nationalism in Iran, for instance, was not immediately accompanied by the advent of print-capitalism (which hardly existed in Qajar times) and at a time when industrialization was a very distant prospect. How could nationalism be a product of European industrialization and yet develop in a nonindustrialized setting? How could it be grafted in a different environment? While acknowledging the transregional character of non-Western forms of nationalism, we need to take them seriously as genuinely relevant historical phenomena that are not purely imitative or derivative. We must identify the *local* processes of modernity that formed the historical context of their rise, and against that backdrop analyze the modalities of a complex intellectual exchange with Europe that involves selection, amnesia, and a great deal of invention. Partha Chatterjee, for instance, has endeavored to unearth this new layer of complexity and detail in his analysis of Indian nationalism. For him, Indian nationalism does to some extent comply with European models, but Chatterjee is more concerned with the agency of the Indian intellectuals who produced its hybrid discursive apparatus.[1] In other words, nationalism is not a ready-made package that you adopt or reject but a tool shop that offers myriad possibilities of combination. It is these combinations, and why some prevail over the others, that should be at the core of the analysis.

Second, I feel that a concern with broad social processes, which is central to Gellner's work particularly, runs the risk of glossing over crucial microprocesses, in particular the determining imprint of specific individuals. Within "national" or "prenational" public spheres, nationalist ideologues, intellectuals, historians, and political agitators dispose of a substantial margin of maneuver to shape the content of nationalism—in other words, to develop the historical interpretations and political objectives of its doctrine, sometimes even arbitrarily.[2] In the history of dislocative nationalism, a few individuals did have a determining imprint, and Jalal ed-Din Mirza was one of them. Most importantly however, one individual, Mirza Fath'ali Akhundzadeh, played a crucial role in compiling disparate ideas about Iran's past and true national essence, amalgamating them with some of his own radical stances, and organizing this new corpus into a polemical discourse of nationalism, an ideology ready to be adopted by his followers. His was a complex work of transregional selection and hybridization, which, as we will see, has been wrongly assessed as either wholly rooted in the Iranian national consciousness or a wholesale import of European ideas.

The result of this selection and hybridization is an ideology. It is my contention that Akhundzadeh intended his thought to take on ideological form. Mirza Aqa Khan Kermani, Akhundzadeh's spiritual heir, although largely building on his predecessor's work, significantly intensified the racist outlook of the nascent ideology, radicalized its tone, and perhaps ensured its transition to the next generation of ideologues, who would become the standard-bearers of a new form of identity discourse. This standard would become firmly anchored into the body of the Pahlavi state from 1925 onward.

The contingency of the formative process of dislocative nationalism is remarkable, and it directly relates to the role of individuals. The previous chapter showed that in this period, Iranian authors were very much preoccupied with making sense of European modernity and Iran's deficiencies. Numerous schools competed in explaining this dilemma, and there were as many ideas about the way forward as there were segments in the literate elites. Modernism and later constitutionalism were only the most prominent of these schools and even there, great variety existed between individual authors. Akhundzadeh used his command over Russian and his situation in Tbilisi to select isolated ideas in the orientalist literature on Iran and the "East," heretofore unknown in Iran itself, to construct his nationalist thought. This process did in no way have to happen the way it did, and its complex and accidental nature exposes the contingency of his doctrine, an important caveat that I believe broad sociological analyses of nationalism have somewhat overlooked. This ideological contingency is precisely the result of the convergence of specific sociohistorical spaces with isolated individuals who try to make sense of them. This is why this book focuses on these influential individuals. A biographical account is here inescapable.

AKHUNDZADEH, THE FOUNDING FATHER

Fathʿali Akhundzadeh (or Akhundov, in Russian and Azerbaijani parlance) was only to some extent a product of the zeitgeist described in the previous chapter. His situation in the Caucasus under Russian rule and what this meant in terms of the influences that shaped his views made him a complex and hybrid figure among Qajar intellectuals, even an outcast. He was influenced by the new historicist definitions of the Iranian nation as brought about by orientalist scholarship filtered through a Russian lens while also drawing on the kinds of Jalal ed-Din Mirza (with whom he held a correspondence). He was also deeply affected by Iran's encounter with European imperialism, even at a personal level. He was born in 1812 in the town of Nukha (today Shaki). Like most towns in what was at the time called "Arran and Shirvan" (today Azerbaijan), it was home to a religiously and linguistically heterogeneous population that included Shiʻites, Sunnis, Yazidis, Jews, and Christians, and, aside from Turkish speakers, there were also communities of speakers of Talyshi, Tati, Kurdish, Persian, Armenian, and Arabic. Russian forces annexed Nukha the year following Akhundzadeh's birth, and it is today situated in the Republic of Azerbaijan. As we will see, Akhundzadeh did not harbor any negative feeling against Russia—quite the contrary.

As a youngster, his family destined him to join the ulama. However, this plan was thwarted by the teachings of his mentor, an anticlerical mystic and poet named Mirza Shafiʻ Vazeh (next to whom he is buried in the Muslim cemetery of Tbilisi). Instead of the legalistic teachings provided at religious seminaries, Mirza Shafiʻ inculcated the young Akhundzadeh with Sufi mysticism and skepticism toward orthodox religion. Akhundzadeh claimed that the teachings of Mirza Shafiʻ shaped the aversion that he will nurture throughout his life for both the ulama and religious dogma.[3] This teaching probably did not do more than predispose Akhundzadeh: as we will see, European and Russian readings played an even more important role in informing his stance toward Islam and tradition. In 1834 he moved to another multiethnic city, Tbilisi (today capital of Georgia) and, thanks to his command of several languages, became translator in the service of the Russian viceroy. He would perform this job for the rest of his life, visiting Qajar Iran only once thereafter in 1848. In the service of the Russian state, Akhundzadeh would choose never to criticize the annexation of his homeland.

Tbilisi was a multicultural city with Armenian, Georgian, Turkish, Iranian, Jewish, Chechen, Abkhaz, and Russian communities. During Akhundzadeh's time it was also in the midst of an intellectual florescence, which provided him with a stimulating environment for the maturing of his thought. He quickly acquired Russian and extensively used it to inform himself on European ideas. He did not acquire his knowledge of the West and Western ideas through direct contact with Europe, which he never visited, but through the prism of the Russian language. A mixed environment and broad readings explain the syncretical nature of his thought, which blended, not always in a coherent manner, ideas selected from the Enlightenment and liberalism with tendencies that quite outright contradicted them, mostly borrowed from nationalism, and possibly Russian orientalism. As a result, he would acknowledge being equally influenced by the secularist stances of Voltaire and the racialist views of Ernest Renan, with whom all students of nationalism are familiar.[4]

His social circle included prominent Caucasian intellectuals, and there have been claims that he befriended Russian Decembrists, and even met the renowned Russian author Mikhail Lermontov.[5] As I argue in chapter 5, Akhundzadeh was a faithful servant of the Russian state, and as such it is unlikely that he shared the views of the Decembrists or Lermontov. Be that as it may, he also corresponded with modernist personalities in Iran, among whom were Mostashar od-Dowleh and Malkam Khan, but also radical *literati* in the vein of Jalal ed-Din Mirza and the Parsi envoy Manekji Limji Hataria. His experience of the historical upheavals of nineteenth-century Iran was therefore that of the uprooted exile rather than a genuine actor or victim, and this explains the radicalism of his ideas. The realities on the ground did not sober his anti-religious stances like they did Malkam Khan's, for instance, who admitted that he would "clothe [his] material reformation in a garb [Iranians] would understand, the garb of religion."[6] Similarly, Jamal ed-Din Asadabadi (known in the West as "al-Afghani"; 1838–1897), one of the pioneers of Islamic modernism, spoke the language of piety so that his modernizing ideals could appeal to the masses.[7] Nor was Akhundzadeh subject to the censorship and repression of the Qajar state, like many other modernists. In sum, he did not take any risk by holding his stances and was to some extent out of touch with the constraints—and even the realities—of Iranian society.

In the first period of his intellectual career, Akhundzadeh became a renowned playwright, writing in Azeri Turkish. His plays were soon translated into Russian and then several other European languages, giving him some fame as the "Tatar Molière."[8] His plays were social critiques of what he considered to be the backwardness and superstitious nature of Islamic societies, and he addressed with some passion the status of women. He advocated opening these societies to European rationalism and progress. The theme of European modernity and rationalism as opposed to "Islam" is the leitmotiv of his work, recurrent throughout his life in his literary and political writings. It has also been suggested that Akhundzadeh transformed literature in Azerbaijani Turkish and Persian by writing in a language accessible to anyone who could read, and writing about situations to which the ordinary man could relate.[9]

After this initial period of literary creativity, he devoted fifteen years of his life to reforming the alphabet used to write Persian, Turkish, and Azeri. Akhundzadeh was the pioneer of alphabet reform and saw a reformed script as a tool to forcibly modernize the lands of Islam. The presumed connection between alphabet and progress, an idea that had then currency in Russia, may today seem fanciful—as a complex script did not prevent Japan, for instance, from developing. Fanciful ideas about language also had currency in Europe, where some believed that Eastern languages including Persian "greatly darken the mind and vitiate the heart" and were not "an adequate medium for communicating a knowledge of the higher departments of literature, science, and theology."[10] Be that as it may, alphabet reform was a fundamental pillar of Akhundzadeh's thought. He traveled to Istanbul in 1863 to present his proposal for a new Turkish alphabet to the Ottoman Scientific Society. But his projects of alphabet reform would remain dead letter both in Istanbul and in Tehran. Although the Ottoman Scientific Society's decision was pragmatic, informed by the technical and logistical difficulties of changing script, Akhundzadeh believed—typically, in view of his anti-Islamic stances—that the decision was due to "fanaticism."[11] This failure made him bitter and led to the next period, one of increasingly radical anticlerical stances and the first articulation of Iranian nationalism.

Thus, it was late in his career that his nationalist thought took shape and was laid in the *Maktubāt-e Kamāl od-Dowleh beh Shāhzādeh Jamāl od-Dowleh* (Letters from Kamal od-Dowleh to Prince Jalal od-Dowleh; 1860, hereafter *Maktubāt*). Although intended as a treatise of Iranian nationalism, Akhundzadeh (unlike Kermani) does not insist on the linguistic nature of the community, and the *Maktubāt* was in fact originally written in Azeri Turkish; it is only at some later stage that Akhundzadeh translated it into Persian with the help of his friend Mostashar od-Dowleh. The community is defined in vaguer ethnic terms, and Akhundzadeh uses the term *"nezhād"* on a few occasions: although today *nezhād* has come to mean race, at the time it was associated with descent. This is not to mean that racial concepts are absent from Akhundzadeh's work. In fact, Iranians are defined negatively. We are told what they are not rather than what they are. And they are not Arabs.

The *Maktubāt* was crafted as an epistolary exchange between two fictional princes, Kamal the Indian—who expressed Akhundzadeh's own views—and Jamal the Iranian—who spoke laconically for Akhundzadeh's opponents, especially the clergy. This format is rather unusual for a nationalist treatise and was possibly inspired by Montesquieu's *Persian Letters*, but Akhundzadeh was candid about its purpose. As he put it, the "liberal, progressive and *civilisé*" objective of writing this treatise was to "sow the seeds of zeal, honor, patriotism."[12] Elsewhere he addresses Iran in these terms, "all you need is unity of thought and direction," implying the sort of unanimity of purpose and esprit de corps that a nationalist ideology precisely promotes.[13] In the *Maktubāt*, Akhundzadeh constructs a new Iranian identity based on a selective reading of history and forthrightly advocates the complete abandonment of religion to open the way for rationalism and progress. He thus squarely scorns religion as a body of superstitious beliefs responsible for the arbitrariness and backwardness of Qajar society. He also considers the *Maktubāt* to be a work of *"qertikā"* (his transliteration of *Критика* or "kritika," Russian for critique or criticism, meaning critical and rational thinking).[14] While upholding an acute sense of historicism, he elaborates an atavistic definition of Iranian ethnic identity. Yet his work is also idealistic, as he believed that one could turn an arbitrary and traditional society like Qajar Iran into "the light of all nations" by applying his prescriptions. The *Maktubāt* is the pioneering work of a long series reproducing its themes, and it can be safely considered—for reasons that will be demonstrated—as the founding treatise of dislocative nationalism. It compiled previously disparate ideas about Iran's history for the first time in a systematic fashion and laid the ground for an ideology that has many followers to this day.

As our brief review of Jalal ed-Din Mirza's work showed, for a number of authors Iran's pre-Islamic past had become a golden age embodying the past grandeur of Iran (more on this in the next chapter). In his idealization of the pre-Islamic past, however, Akhundzadeh went further than any of his predecessors. He transformed pre-Islamic Iran into a utopia that bore more resemblance to the Garden of Eden than to any real human society. The *Maktubāt* opens with the first letter of the Indian prince Kamal od-Dowleh to his Iranian friend Jalal od-Dowleh about his recent trip to Iran and the misery and backwardness he witnessed there, and it immediately moves on to offer Akhundzadeh's account of the pre-Islamic past. Contrasting the dreadful state of contemporary Iran with the utopian account of ancient Iran is here meant to stress the unfulfilled potential of the Iranian nation.

He describes the "splendor and felicity" of the times of Kiyumars, Jamshid, Goshtasb, Anushiravan, and Khosrow Parviz.[15] These names uttered in passing give an indication of the frames of thought Akhundzadeh relies on to convey this past to an Iranian audience. Only the latter two are attested Sasanian kings; the other three are legendary figures. In similar fashion to Jalal ed-Din Mirza, Akhundzadeh's style derives from the mythical tradition, and he seems quite uninformed about recent discoveries. For instance, he ignores all about the Achaemenid dynasty, probably because he had not read Herodotus and was unaware of the decipherment of Achaemenid royal inscriptions, which took place around the middle of the nineteenth century.[16] Although one could argue that Russian translations of important works may not have been available to him, it is clear that Akhundzadeh's prime concern was not to provide an accurate and factually objective account of Iranian history. Rather, he selected disparate data, often of a legendary nature, which he tied into an imaginary narrative offering a new historicist assessment of the ills of Iranian society.

Ancient Iranians, according to Akhundzadeh, lived under the "rule of benevolent kings" who were free of any moral failing.[17] People at the time did not know poverty, and there were no beggars.[18] Hospitals gave shelter and treatment to lonely souls and the needy poor. Akhundzadeh even goes on to assess the tax system that unsurprisingly he deems to have been just, so much so that the commoners would freely pay twice as much tax as they owed. The tax revenue was safely kept and wisely spent. "Sanctified" by such "divine blessings," Iranians were "free in their country, respected in foreign lands, and the prestige and grandeur of the kings of Iran were well-known in the whole world, as Greek—and not Iranian—historians have testified."[19] This equivocal reference to Greek historians, of which he gives no precise detail, is not designed to support his claims but to fill the gap left by the alleged disappearance of the books and laws of the kings of Iran. In his correspondence we later learn that he believed that the Arabs—of which there will soon be abundant talk—destroyed all written material produced by ancient Iranians.

Similarly to Jalal ed-Din Mirza, Akhundzadeh granted a quasi-divine status to ancient kings, with all the virtues this presupposes: superior wisdom, righteousness, justice, and benevolence. Reappraisal of these kings according to his self-professed commitment to *qertikā* (critical thinking) is entirely absent from the *Maktubāt*. Local governors, we are told, could not put anyone to death, even if execution was well deserved. The kings had to approve such verdicts, and they would endeavor to avoid the life sentence whenever possible. Wise companions surrounded the King and they would "always encourage him toward kind deeds," and so did his knowledgeable high Zoroastrian priest, who would assist him in taking difficult decisions. The King was a sort of Saint Louis, giving audiences to the common folk on specific days, dispensing justice on their behalf, and eating at their table.[20]

Akhundzadeh portrays a realm where a just law is implemented by a body of virtuous agents of the crown, whose only concern is the well-being of their fellow subjects: "for every matter, Persians had regulation."[21] If someone was found guilty, nobody from the King's entourage would intercede in his favor, while anyone serving the community was rewarded deservingly. One can only notice the contradiction in his assessment of pre-Islamic laws, when only two pages before he asserted that there were no traces left of ancient Iranians' "writings and laws," destroyed as they were by the Arabs.[22] Akhundzadeh goes on to reaffirm that "the Persian people were chosen among all peoples," which is a customary claim of all nationalisms. The even-handedness of the "sultans of Furs" (kings of Persia) was such that it is "proverbial in the languages of the world to this day." Akhundzadeh, like many nationalists after him, also displays pride in the sheer stretch of the territory under the rule of ancient kings: "To the north, the Jayhun river [the Oxus or Amu Darya], [and] the Aral lake . . . ; to the south, the Persian Gulf and the Oman Sea; to the east, the Sutlej river between Sind [the Indus] and Hindustan; to the west, the Bosphorus"; all the people of this sizable empire lived in "dignity and prosperity."[23]

Kamal od-Dowleh had started his letter to Jalal od-Dowleh by confiding his sorrow and grief at the state of Iran: "I wish I had not come here, had not seen the inhabitants of this land, who are my brethren in faith, and had not become informed of their condition."[24] That glorious pre-Islamic past of perfect happiness is then contrasted with the present state of Iran, which is all superstition, despotism, and misery. Such disparity between Iran's past and present of course begs for an explanation. How could the heavenly empire in which nobody ever begged or was killed have become a wretched land that disheartened Kamal od-Dowleh to such a degree? Akhundzadeh's hypothesis is strikingly simple and is the very core of his thought.

Unlike the musings of modernists, there is here little scrutiny into the technicalities of Iran's dysfunctional state system. Malkam Khan, for instance, had identified the lack of *qānun* (law) as the main hindrance to Iran's progress, rendering the exercise of royal power unpredictable and arbitrary. Mostashar od-Dowleh shared Malkam's advocacy of judicial and legal reform but held corrupt state officials and obsequious courtiers for the main culprits of Iran's backwardness. "Al-Afghani's" indictment of European imperial interference as undermining the Islamic world's progress is nowhere reflected in Akhundzadeh's thesis either. Instead, Akhundzadeh lays the blame for "1280 years of misery" by the doorstep of "naked and hungry Arabs."[25] In fact, he partly shares the analysis of great modernist thinkers but relates all the shortcomings they highlighted to the legacy of the Arabs and Islam. Arabs are wholly responsible for having destroyed Iran's power, made her inhabitants ignorant and nescient of world *"civilisation"* (always in French in the original text), deprived them from the blessing of freedom, and turned their kings into *"despotes."*[26] The advent of Islam becomes, in Akhundzadeh's thought, a teleological mo- ment making sense of all subsequent events, and all the complexities of such a long history are brushed aside.

In Akhundzadeh's view, Arabs did not do the job of causing Iran's downfall from the fullness of the pre-Islamic period to the altogether negative experi- ence that followed the advent of Islam on their own. They were the evil gar- deners who sowed the seeds of decay. These seeds grew into two distinct groups of individuals who carry out the day-to-day work of perpetuating the destruc- tion of ancient Iran on behalf of Arabs: the *despotes* and the ulama. It is the tyranny of the former and the *"fanatisme"* of the latter that perpetuates Iran's "weakness and impotence."[27] To further his point, Akhundzadeh initiates what has become a consistent tradition in nationalist writing, that of quoting an- cient authors selectively and manipulatively to further their modern political stances. He quotes from Ferdowsi's *Shāhnāmeh*:

When the Arab fortune overtook that of the Persians
Luck turned against the Sasanians'
. . .
Iranians made me sad and teary
As for Sasanians, they burned my heart
. . .
Hereafter they will be defeated by Arabs
Their star would not turn but against them
When the pulpit replaces the throne
There would remain no name other than Abu Bakr and Omar
. . .
From among Iranians, Turks and Arabs
Will emerge a people
All of them Turkish and Arab but no *dehqān* [here meant as a member
    of the Sasanian nobility]
And culture will decline
. . .
From drinking camel milk and eating lizard
The Arab's fortune has reached the point
That he wishes for the Persian crown
Spit be upon you O' wheel of fortune[28]

Then Akhundzadeh proceeds to a long and thorough critique of present-day Iran. Iranians have become ignorant and superstitious to the extent that they are not aware of the adequate use of printing, do not know how *poésie* should be written (quite a claim in view of Iran's rich poetic tradition) or how to cultivate hygiene, and they "bear expenses of 100 or 200 tomans to go to Hajj, [and] feed hungry Arabs." Anathema to Akhundzadeh is the Shiʻite religion, as he abhors to see his fellow Iranians "hit their chests and pull their hair" because "a thousand and two hundred and something years before, ten or fifteen Arabs killed ten or fifteen other Arabs in the Kufa desert [allusion to the yearly Shiʻite commemoration of the martyrdom of Imam Hussein ibn Ali, who was murdered in Karbala and not Kufa]."[29] He also draws attention to the lack of a functioning judicial system and then moves on to a meticulous roast of the Qajar ruler (Nasser ed-Din Shah) that he lambasts for his own ignorance and superstition, and his presumed belief that "planet Earth is located on a cow's back, and the cow on the back of a fish."[30] Among the many aspects of Iranians' daily practices that he condemns, he rightly points at violence against children in traditional education and the inhuman dismemberments and other mutilations that the authorities afflict upon even minor offenders.[31]

Kamal od-Dowleh's second letter is a methodical refutation of religion from a materialist perspective and an indictment of the ulama as the "charlatans" instilling superstitious beliefs among the people to preserve their status and hold over society. In equal fashion although not in order, he dissects the general monotheistic faith in the existence of God or miracles and some Islamic beliefs in addition to more specifically Shiʻite convictions, such as the occultation of the Imam of the Time. Although he does discuss articles of faith that are not particular to Islam (such as the very existence of God or Hell) and could also be attributed to pre-Islamic Mazdean and Zoroastrian faiths in Iran, he entirely imputes their contemporary prevalence in Iran to Arabs: "After the Arabs' domination in Iran, religions multiplied there."[32] He considers Arabs to be particularly skilled at propagating superstition: "The Arab tribe is unique among the tribes of the world in its capacity to weave lies and create tales, and the people of Iran are unmatched in their propensity to believe lies and tales."[33]

Occasionally and in particular contexts, he takes it out on both God as defined by Islam (or, broadly, the Abrahamic faiths) and the Prophet Muhammad. He affirms that a revengeful God that punishes his creatures in the fires of Hell is worse than any "hangman" or "butcher."[34] When relaying Muhammad's controversial marriage with Zaynab—the wife of his adopted son Zayd—which was imposed upon him by God according to tradition, Akhundzadeh proclaims that if there is a god, "undoubtedly it is not this god who has accepted the employment of a pimp called Muhammad, an Arab" and extolled him to marry his own adopted son's wife; for him, conferring such qualities to God amounts to blasphemy.[35] The only religious figure that he approves of is Hassan Ala Dhikrihi as-Salam (d. 1166), a little-known Ismaili ruler of Alamut, who announced that he was the promised imam and abrogated Islamic law before being assassinated by a more orthodox member of his community. Akhundzadeh calls his movement *protestantisme*; he holds the belief that if Iranians had supported this suspension of Islam and Islamic law, "England and the New World today would only be the candle-holders to Iran's greatness."[36]

Kamal od-Dowleh's third letter mostly reiterates the antireligious stances of the second. Here Akhundzadeh concerns himself with some distinctly Shi'ite beliefs and practices (like *ta'ziyeh*, the Shi'ite passion play) and, beyond religious orthodoxy, attacks the Shaykhi movement. The conclusion of this shorter letter summarizes Akhundzadeh's ideas about reform in Iran. He believes that once people have decidedly opted in favor of "*progrès*," science will prevail and they will realize that these miracles they believed in were irrational. From there they will step onto the path to *civilisation*, the people will "be freed from ignorance . . . and chaos, and also from the *despotes*."[37] In other words, he believed that uprooting religious beliefs was an entirely achievable goal. He says nothing of the modalities of bringing about this objective but assumes that there is no such thing as religiosity in Western countries or preIslamic Iran. And finally, once the elimination of religion is fulfilled, Iran will instantly become a paradise "devoid of all corruption . . . and rid of all internal and external enemies."[38] The third letter is followed by Jalal od-Dowleh's only response, which distinguishes itself by its much shorter length and its less thorough argumentation, which even occasionally seems to indirectly corroborate Akhundzadeh's points (for instance, that Ferdowsi was a closet Zoroastrian). More importantly, this last letter's central rebuttal is not so much leveled at Akhundzadeh's reading of Iranian history as it is at India and its presumed deference to Britain (Kamal od-Dowleh being an Indian prince). Clearly, Akhundzadeh did not intend Jamal od-Dowleh's reply to be even remotely a challenge to the dogma he worked to establish earlier in the *Maktubāt*.

The issue of an author's intentionality could be brought up here to argue that the *Maktubāt* is fictional and does not reflect Akhundzadeh's deep convictions. This brings up the issue of an author's intentionality: what did he try to achieve? Akhundzadeh, who was self-professedly a rationalist and material-ist thinker, could possibly not believe in these fanciful descriptions, the argu-ment would go, as they are only metaphoric and are intended for educational or amusement purposes. There would be some plausibility to the argument if Akhundzadeh's private correspondence were not there to confirm, if not that these were deeply held beliefs, at least that these were beliefs that he consid-ered as his mission to propagate. His correspondence with Jalal ed-Din Mirza, whom he held in high esteem and about whom he said "I found someone on the face of Iran in whom I can confide," is particularly revealing in this re-gard.[39] They both thoroughly loathed and despised Arabs and never missed an opportunity to vilify them. "You wrote that Arabs have overwhelmed your heart with sorrow. True! True! I sympathize with your feelings," wrote Akhun-dzadeh.[40] One prominent feature of their exchange was the two authors' con-cern with uprooting everything that they considered to be of Arab or Islamic origin. Akhundzadeh expressed his admiration for Jalal ed-Din Mirza's *pārsi negāri*, his habit to write in pure Persian and avoid all foreign—and particu-larly Arabic—loanwords, which is to this day a defining feature of nationalist writing. Akhundzadeh equated Jalal ed-Din Mirza's endeavor with his own attempts to "rid our nation of the Arabs' alphabet."[41]

Another prominent element of Akhundzadeh's correspondence is his con-viction that it is patently unpatriotic, almost an act of betrayal, that Iranians hold some Arabs in high regard. By this he refers to the respect and veneration in which the Prophet Muhammad, his daughter Fatimah az-Zahra, and the twelve Imams of Shi'ite Islam, among others, are held among pious Iranians even as Arabs, according to him, "destroyed [Iranians'] homeland and threw them in such abjectness." He fulminates at Iranians' "favoring" of "Arabs, who are the enemies of their lives and possessions," rather than the Zoroastrians, who are "their brothers who speak the same language, their compatriots, the living memory of their glorious forefathers, and their guardian angels."[42] This theme arises particularly in his exchanges with Manekji, the emissary of the Zoroastrian Parsis in Iran, and it shows the reification of the categories of "Arab" and "Iranian" in the articulation of their project to "purify" Iranian-ness by eliminating features that they had identified as "Arab" or "Islamic."[43]

KERMANI, THE RADICAL DISCIPLE

More than anybody else, Mirza Abolhossein (known as Mirza Aqa Khan Ker-mani; 1853–1896) was an heir to Akhundzadeh's nationalist thought. Kermani's work was the only reclamation of Akhundzadeh's legacy until World War I. In two books written at unknown dates, but probably sometime in the 1890s during his protracted exile in Istanbul, Kermani retrieved Akhundzadeh's thought and complemented it with his own additions. These books are *Seh maktub* (Three letters; in a clear homage to his spiritual master's *Maktubāt*), and *Sad khatābeh* (One hundred lectures; in fact only forty-two of them).[44] In many ways, *Seh maktub* is a sequel to Akhundzadeh's *Maktubāt*, with the same epistolary exchange between Kamal od-Dowleh and Jalal od-Dowleh extended for a few more rounds.

Kermani was born in 1853 near Kerman to a literate family with a penchant for religious heterodoxy. His grandfather was a Zoroastrian judge who converted to Islam.[45] Kermani spent his formative years in Kerman, which was at the time a breeding ground for political and religious sedition and therefore a focal point of repression and violence. It was an important center of spirituality too. The city was home to a large Zoroastrian community and had witnessed the birth of several important religious movements, in particular Shaykhism and Babism. It has been argued that this particular environment left a deep imprint on Kermani's personality and intellectual outlook, engendering his fascination for ancient Iranian history, Zoroastrianism, and mysticism; his aversion to religious dogmatism; and his hatred of despotism and corruption as well as the untamed rage and blind anger that stem from—and significantly undermine—the arguments he laid down in his treatises.[46] The city of Kerman's culture of almost customary dissent may also explain his conversion to Azali Babism: he later married one of the daughters of Sobh-e Azal, the disputed successor to the Bab. Ultimately, however, he would fall out with all religions.[47]

Kermani had a choleric nature, which is displayed in his writing, and an incisive tongue that he never managed to tame. These two attributes created much enmity toward him, and early on he was forced out of his hometown and soon the Qajar lands altogether. He spent the last decade of his life in a protracted exile in Istanbul, teaching and writing—notably in the modernist publications *Qānun* and *Akhtar*—to make a living. It has been claimed that his command over English and French allowed him to acquire modern Western ideas.[48] In fact, it is doubtful that he had any command over these languages: he aimed to transliterate the French term *"civilisation"* like Akhundzadeh, whom he emulated, but he consistently used his own corruption, *"sivinirāsiyon,"* an indication that he had in fact no workable command over French or any other European language; one can even doubt that he could read the Latin script.

There is therefore no evidence that his rather sketchy familiarity with a set of European ideas he conveys were acquired from perusing books in their original language. He probably became acquainted with them in sources in Persian (including Akhundzadeh) in addition to some Arabic and possibly Ottoman Turkish sources. Indirect transmission probably played an important role too, either orally in discussion with literate Iranians in Istanbul, or through correspondence. Indeed, he worked with some of the most eminent Iranian modernists of the time, in particular Malkam Khan—whom he never met but to whose newspaper, Qānun, and pseudo-Masonic activities he contributed a significant lot—and "al-Afghani," the pioneer of Islamic modernism.

Back in Tehran, the shah was most irritated by Kermani and his revolutionary ideas. Due to his association with "al-Afghani," his reputation as a Babi, and his alienation of anyone who could have helped him against Tehran's fury, Kermani was ultimately deported from Istanbul back to Iran. Upon arrival in Tabriz, he and his two companions, Sheikh Ahmad Ruhi and Mirza Hassan Khan Khabir ol-Molk—believed to be coconspirators in the assassination of Nasser ed-Din Shah in 1896—were savagely murdered on the orders of the Crown.

It has been claimed that it is not an easy matter to categorize Kermani within a given school of thought, as his writing is characterized by "a hopeless synthesis of the most disparate philosophical and social ideas."[49] Indeed, according to Bayat-Philipp, who extensively analyzed Kermani's written legacy, "The voluminous disorderly corpus of his works, which included newspaper articles, poems, historical and philosophical treatises, political pamphlets and theological essays, are a trial to anyone who attempts to discover in them a logical sequence of ideas. He claimed to be a Muslim, a Babi, an agnostic philosopher all at one and the same time."[50]

This is hardly surprising, as any thinker's views evolve during the span of her lifetime.[51] Authorial intentionality must be taken into account, and the historian should wonder whether there is any other explanation than Kermani's alleged instability. Perhaps some of his works—his Babi treatises, his history of pre-Islamic Iran and his monuments of dislocative nationalism— were aimed at different readerships. Perhaps some arguments were used rhetorically or in an instrumental fashion, rather than reflecting his deep convictions. This work concentrates on his contribution to dislocative nationalism, which is in reality cohesive and which he intended—just like Akhundzadeh's—to be an appealing and readily available nationalist ideology, complete with a historicist view of the origin of Iranians, "others" to serve as scapegoats, and a more precise definition of the Iranian national community as can be found in Akhundzadeh, defined in linguistic and racial terms. The impression that European orientalist and racialist ideas made on him can safely be considered as the formative experience in his espousal of Akhundzadeh's dislocative nationalism. In his early years, renowned tutors thoroughly educated Kermani in the traditional Iranian curriculum, focusing mostly on metaphysics and mystical philosophy. His later contact with modern European thought, however, transformed him into a freethinker, who came to exhibit only the most intense contempt for the methods, objectives, and established dogmas of Iranian knowledge. "Freethinker" is of course a relative word, for concurrently to his occupation as a merciless critic, sparing no aspect of Iranian culture and traditional knowledge, he displayed the most unquestioning veneration for European science, although his understanding of it was sometimes—as we will see—approximate to say the least.

The first few pages of Kermani's *Seh maktub* are but a paraphrase of Akhundzadeh's *Maktubāt*. Then Kermani imparts his own fantasies of ancient Iran's achievements, which in many ways are a step higher than even Akhundzadeh's on the scale of overstatement. For instance, he claimed that "the stretch of the country was such that the sun could not traverse it from coast to coast in one day," quite a statement for an author professing veneration for science and rationalism.[52] Again, it is said that the "kings ate at [common folks'] tables" and were cherished by all their subjects. "When cities or countries were conquered, [the people] were safe, their lives and possessions preserved from plunder and prisoners of war were treated kindly." Women enjoyed such status that they would share in all their husbands' activities and were their confidantes.[53] Kermani consciously imitated his predecessor's style and imagined pre-Islamic Iran as a sort of Garden of Eden. That he brought this project to new heights is noteworthy given that one of his other works, the *A'ineh-ye Sekandari* (Alexandrian mirror, n.d.) is a comparatively sober history of pre-Islamic Iran, which is informed by Iranian, ancient Greek, medieval Islamic, and modern European sources. It may be that his nationalist works were written at a later period when his thought had become more emotional, radical, politically driven, and less constrained by serious scientific considerations.

Be that as it may, Kermani's hypothesis about Iran's decay is identical to that of Akhundzadeh's: it is clearly imputed to Arabs and Islam. He does attempt a methodical critique of Islam, but it is not as informed as Akhundzadeh's, and the emphasis throughout is clearly on Arab-hatred, expressed in even harsher terms. *Seh maktub* is a long and fairly redundant invective against Arabs and their alleged visceral enmity against Iranians. The substance of this idea could be summarized in a few pages, but Kermani stretches it over hundreds, leaving the reader with the impression that, through his lengthy treatise, he is simply venting his personal fury and antipathy. His angry nature transpires through his continuous use of rather colorful phrases such as "I shit on" this and that, the wife of so and so is a "whore," he "licks cunt," and so forth.[54] What Kermani blames Arabs for, in essence, is nothing less than the annihilation of what he assumes to have been the previous way of life of Iranians. It should be noted in passing that the recent historiography of this period has highlighted numerous linguistic, cultural, and even religious continuities between pre-Islamic and Islamic Iran, although of course this should have no bearing over our assessment of Kermani's work, judging an ancient author by the standards of the day being the worst offense an intellectual historian could commit.[55]

He calls Arabs "bare-arse, savage, hungry, vagabonds."[56] He goes on: "I spit on them . . . naked bandits, homeless rat-eaters . . . vilest humans, most vicious beasts . . . camel-riding thieves, black and yellow scrawny lot, animal-like and even worse than animals."[57] He describes the "destruction" that Arabs inflicted upon Iran "in the last 1280 years" (the same figure used by Akhundzadeh thirty years earlier) as if it was an ongoing process: bloodbath, death, imprisonment, destruction, barbarity, the sale of the King's daughter in a slave market "like a load-carrying animal," and the decapitation of one thousand Iranians in Mazandaran seem to be daily events.[58]

In terms of his criticism of Islam, his chief argument is that this religion was revealed to "improve the Arabs, and address the persistent maladies of this uncivilized people"; it is thus not adapted to the Iranians' temper.[59] It has been argued that this idea was inspired by Montesquieu and the English deists, who suggested that religions are only suited to the very people to whom they were revealed, and thus incompatible with other populations.[60] He defends himself against preferring any religion to Islam as he considers all of them to be myths and lies (we could assume that at the time he wrote these lines he had abandoned his Azali Babi beliefs, although we could also surmise that in his endeavor to convince Iranians to abandon religion, he privileges a more radical antireligious tone). Yet, according to him, nowhere are the "roots of religion and the foundations of superstition" as unwavering as among Jews, Hindus, and Muslims who are particularly "persistent in their ignorance."[61] In comparison, Akhundzadeh's theory of Iran's decay was more sophisticated: he blamed Arabs for having brought Islam to Iran, but most importantly, Akhundzadeh insisted on the role of the *despotes* and ulama as perpetrators of the Arabs' oppression. These themes are also present in Kermani's *Seh maktub,* as it is an extensive imitation of the *Matktubāt.* He does also lament the ulama's grip over society. For instance, he blames the Safavid dynasty for having co-opted the Shi'ite ulama and cemented their authority over ordinary Iranians. He considers this legacy to be worse than that of the Mongols, who "invaded Iranians and shed much blood," because in his view the Safavids "impaired their brains" by giving free rein to the superstitious and charlatan ulama.[62] However, in spite of these few qualifications, scapegoating Arabs is clearly Kermani's chief objective.

What is remarkable in this context is Kermani's open attempt to attribute every single Iranian shortcoming to Arabs, and to absolve Iranians from any responsibility in their current state of affairs, thus entirely denying their historical agency. He makes this objective abundantly clear: "Whenever I touch a branch of the ugly dispositions of Iranians, I find its seed to be planted by Arabs."[63] According to him, "in the past 1200 years, all the kings that have invaded this country" have been ruling on behalf of "the ill-mannered *tāziyān.*"[64] Such was the magnitude of the contamination of Iranians by the Arabs that since their invasion, Iranian women had lost the "hypnotic eyes" that used to characterize them, and they are not "as tall as cypress trees" as they used to be in the pre-Islamic days.[65] He quotes almost the same verses from Ferdowsi's *Shāhnāmeh* as Akhundzadeh but inserts "those savage Arabs" in between two verses to force Ferdowsi's verses into his own views.[66]

Although his work is a slightly simplified and radicalized imitation of Akhundzadeh's, he displays far better awareness of racial theories then *en vogue* in Europe, and he can be considered the pioneer of modern European racial thought in Iran (more on this in chapters 4 and 6). He is, for instance, aware of Linnaeus's classification of the white race as "Caucasian."[67] He imparts one of the fundamental pillars of "scientific racism" when he insists that "knowledgeable people believe that civilized customs and habits modify natural temperament and essence." Kermani shows a good grasp of this now discredited science that was racial anthropology, which aimed to classify people into different racial categories according to their physical features, with irreversible mental and behavioral characteristics attached to every category in a deterministic fashion. He believes that if one were to observe "an Iranian, a Greek and an Englishman, and then an Ethiopian Sudanese, a Negro (*zangi*) and an Arab, [one] would clearly be able to judge which one is clean and civilized and which other savage."[68] The origins of his ideas about the social environment affecting the physiognomy of a group are likely to lie in the social application of Lamarckism as developed by Herbert Spencer (who famously coined the phrase "survival of the fittest").[69] For Kermani, the blood and brain of "civilized" and "savage" humans tell them apart: "the blood of a Negro (*zangi*) and the form of an Ethiopian's (*habashi*) brain [are different from] the blood of an Englishman and the shape and form of a Parisian brain."[70] This observation might indicate that some of Kermani's sources were out of date, since in the second half of the nineteenth century European racial thinkers had come to agree that there was no difference in, at least, the blood color of different races. The conviction that the blood and brain of "Negroes" were black was more of an eighteenth-century curiosity, which survived until the early nineteenth century, but no later.[71] But then again, Kermani's priority lay in the development of a nationalist ideology rather than ensuring that his scientific sources were up to date.

Kermani was also the first Iranian author to directly refer to the Aryan race (to which I will come back in chapter 6). He equated the *majus* (magi) or ancient Zoroastrian priests to the "great Iranian people" and the "noble Aryan nation."[72] Similarly, in another work he mentions the "good Aryan people of good extraction."[73] Kermani transcribed into an Iranian context the opposition between Aryan and Semite, which European racial thinkers had erected into an overarching anthropological principle. He affirms that "the philosophers of Europe write that we have never seen two nations more antagonistic and opposed to each other in character than [Aryan] Iranians and [Semitic] Arabs."[74] His dehumanization of Arabs is so excessive that he even implies that they may deserve no less than extermination. "If it was not for the ruthless ulama of Iran," he warns, and their relentless praising of the Arabs, Iranians would have taken revenge over their ancestors' blood, and they would not have spared "one single tribe of the barbarian Arabs on the face of the earth."[75]

Miscegenation also causes his hair to rise in horror, a reaction rooted in the typical tenets of nineteenth-century racial thought best expressed by Gobineau in his *Essay on the Inequality of Human Races* (1853–1855) and without any precedent in an Iranian text. Furthermore, he imparts anti-Semitism with obvious European flavor: Jews are passive, dirty, homeless, treacherous, and ugly.[76] Kermani's preoccupation with racial purity translates into his concern about the syncretism of the Persian language. He incorrectly believes that the use of the Persian language in ancient times was universal, and this somehow explains that "the Iranian nation was the father of all these civilized nations."[77] He suggests in a typically clumsy formulation that "the impairments that penetrated Iranians from the Arabic language are more numerous and harsher than all the tyranny and oppression of Arabs."[78] These impairments are due to the replacement of the Iranians' "simple language and sweet wording" by—as he sees it—the futilely turgid style of Semitic (*semetik*) languages.[79]

In compliance with his objective of aggrandizing Iran and its place among nations, and in compliance with his dubious methods and resourceful imagination, he attributes Iranian roots to a number of words in different languages. This is not an attempt to show the common root between, for instance, a Persian word and one from a European language. His claim is that any foreign word sounding like its Persian equivalent in fact originates in the Persian language, hence giving his mother tongue the ascendency over others. He particularly focuses on French and sees Persian roots in no less than five thousand French words. He mentions *mort* and *mord*, *père* and *pedar*, *dent* and *dandān*, *genou* and *zānu*, and so on. His assessment of these similarities derives from the Aryan hypothesis that attributed the linguistic similarities of Indo-European languages to racial kinship:

> One *brother* migrated to the West and like France attained that degree of progress, civilization, wealth, grandeur and humanity, while this other *brother* who is Persian, became tied down in the Orient with veteran ghoulish thieves, crooked camel-breeders, fierce lizard-eaters, evil Arabs, who stripped him of all embellishment and ornament of reason, gems of knowledge, insight, refined mores, excellence, ethical nature, *morale* [in French], and spirit of innocence and splendid beauty, and forced him to wear old and ragged clothes, coarse and ripped sacking covered in dirty Arab patches, lice, ticks and tatters. (My emphases)[80]

In his etymological analysis, the French word "*Dieu*" (God) is derived from the ancient Persian term "*div*" (meaning giant or demon in modern Persian), and the Egyptian Ottoman title "Khedive" is in fact the Persian word "*mahādiv*" (the overlord of *divs*). Another French term, "*ville*" (town, city) is assumed to derive from Persian "*il*," "*vil*," "*bil*," and "*bol*." It is because ancient Persians called the sun "*zhu*" or "*zhā*" that the Land of the Rising Sun is called Japan, ignoring that the Japanese themselves call their land *Nippon/Nihon*. By extension, the word "*zhu*" or "*zhā*," Kermani's argument goes, allows us to trace the origin of various and entirely unrelated French words such as "*jeune*" (young), "*joue*" (cheek), "*jour*" (day), "*juin*" (June), "*juste*" (just), "*genou*" (knee;

again), and even "Jupiter" to Iran.[81] Under Kermani's pen, any word anywhere in the world containing the sound "zh" is indebted to ancient Iranians. He also famously contends that the French word "*histoire*" derives from Persian "*ostovār*," which means "firm," adding that "for the firmness of a nation's foundations, we have no better device than history."[82] By engaging in comparative linguistics, Kermani was attempting to mimic the great Aryanists of the nineteenth century, authors such as Friedrich Schlegel, Max Müller, and Adolphe Pictet. But unlike their work, which can be considered to be at least pseudo-scientific, Kermani derives sweeping conclusions on Iran's grandeur from anecdotal and fortuitous semantic similarities (a habit that is still common among dislocative nationalists). Kermani's espousal of the idea of Aryan kinship is made evident in his use of the word "brother" in the earlier quotation to describe the alleged affinity between an Iranian and a Frenchman. I return to these matters in chapter 6.

Overall, *Seh maktub* is rather cavalier with any "scientific" method. On numerous occasions, Kermani exhorted Iranians to visit Europe and see with their own eyes the miracles of science and progress.[83] He assured them that science will "turn the world into a rose garden and bring about the promised paradise."[84] Yet he dismissed the need to back his arguments by evidence in these terms: "I can attribute each item to ten natural, rational and *antique* [historical] causes, which I would not be able to fit into this essay."[85] The reader is therefore requested to take all Kermani's allegations at face value and trust that there are rational explanations somewhere, although it would be a waste of time to actually discuss them.

AKHUNDZADEH AND KERMANI IN IRANIAN HISTORIOGRAPHY

Akhundzadeh and Kermani's historicist narrative of an Iranian nation pitted against its Semitic other largely complied with the standards of their time, in spite of the clumsy slips and contradictions so prominent, particularly in Kermani's writings. Our understanding of "nation" and "race" has undoubtedly evolved a lot since then. After the discovery of Nazi Germany's death camps, the success of emancipation movements in the vein of the civil rights movement in the United States, the dismantlement of European empires, and of course significant advances in sociology as well as natural sciences, the concept of race has been thoroughly discredited. The socially constructed nature of race is today part of the scientific consensus. Similarly, the appearance and

significant growth of the field of nationalism studies since the 1960s has de-
mystified nations, and there is some consensus, although not complete, on
their modernity and constructed nature. In this context, it is remarkable that
Akhundzadeh's and Kermani's vision of pre-Islamic Iran and the racial hatred
that emanates from their pages, in spite of their obvious dissonance with the
standards of the past half century or so, have so far been sheltered from any
systematic criticism, with only a handful of exceptions, all in English and
inaccessible to most Iranians. In this latter category, Bayat-Philipp's new approach to Kermani's work has been essential in highlighting its racist tendencies.[86] A few authors have questioned Akhundzadeh's construction of identity
and have qualified claims that he was a modernizer.[87] However, with the
exception of this handful of publications, Akhundzadeh and Kermani are
generally adulated by a slanted scholarship so concerned with "backwardness"
that it sees any critical evaluation of authors praising modern European ideas
as tantamount to high treason.

In compliance with the principle of preserving the sanctity of these authors,
contemporary nationalist literature does not hesitate to explicitly call names
anyone who would dare to offer a sober reassessment of Akhundzadeh and
Kermani's thought. Fereydun Adamiyat, for instance, wrote that in "the analysis of the xenophobic (*zedde ajnabi*) thought [of Kermani] as a cultural and
social phenomenon, one must consider all aspects"; that "some people simply
disagree with Akhundzadeh or Kermani and dislike them, only reveals their
own intellectual deficiency."[88] The editor of Kermani's *Sad khatābeh*, although
not an established scholar, deserves to be mentioned, as he is more candid: in
his preface, he simply calls Kermani's critics "idiots." His admiration of Kermani is of a devotional character. He states that *Sad khatābeh*'s angry prose is
"lively, strong, rich, rational and convincing," and he considers Kermani to be
"a sharp-minded genius" and no less than "the most important political figure
of the Qajar era."[89] Kermani's baseless guesswork on the alleged Iranian origin
of French and Japanese words is considered to be part of his "rationalism,
positivist scientism" and his "astonishing grasp of etymology," while his racist
utterances are rebranded as his command over "the science of race," a remarkably anachronistic term for a preface written in 2007.[90] Similarly, the editor of
Akhundzadeh's *Maktubāt* calls him the "founder of revolutionary thought in
Iran" and affirms the *Maktubāt* is "the most important philosophical and
sociological Iranian work of the nineteenth, even twentieth, century" and a
"masterpiece of critical analysis."[91] The cover bears a strap line linking the
Maktubāt to the one hundredth anniversary of the Iranian Constitutional

Revolution. Chapter 7 shows that Akhundzadeh's thought had nothing to do with Iranian constitutionalism.

Nowadays, opposition to the Islamic Republic has given new lease of life to this form of intellectual repression. Passing the slightest judgment on thinkers who have disparaged Islam has become equivalent to supporting Islamist extremism or the regime in place in Tehran. For the secular opposition, hatred of Islam—which is as dogmatic and fanatic as the regime's ideology itself—is often seen as a healthy guard against religious extremism. These nationalist opponents argue that Akhundzadeh and Kermani's warnings against the clergy were vindicated when the latter took power in 1979. Akhundzadeh's editor claims that the latter was the leader of an awakening against "Islamic despotism."[92] Mashallah Ajoudani, who is a widely read amateur historian, is one of the main present-day representatives of this trend. He oftentimes refers to Akhundzadeh and Kermani as "enlightened intellectuals (*rowshanfekr*)" and holds Akhundzadeh for the most distinguished "social thinker and critique" of his era.[93] The works of Shoja'ed-Din Shafa, to which I return in the epilogue, reflect similar views.[94] These authors conveniently ignore Kermani's propensity to instrumentalize religion to suit his purposes: on one occasion he even called on the clerics to take the lead in opposing the Qajar monarchy.[95] It should be added that the sole fact that the nationalist authors' treatises are censored by the Islamic Republic lends them some aura of respectability in the eyes of many opponents to the regime.

The scholar who more than anyone promoted an uncritical attitude toward our nationalist authors is Fereydun Adamiyat (1920–2008). To investigate the reception of Akhundzadeh and Kermani, this book focuses on Adamiyat's publications, and for good reason. First, his work enjoys almost absolute and unconditional authority in Iran.[96] Second, in 1967 and 1970 he wrote the only biographies of the two nationalist authors available in Persian (and of course outlawed by the censors of the Islamic Republic).[97] Third, almost all subsequent literature largely refers to Adamiyat's work rather than engage with it critically.[98] Part of the reason for this overbearing influence was the unavailability of Akhundzadeh and Kermani's works when Adamiyat wrote his biographies, allowing little reassessment. But perhaps the most significant reason is Adamiyat's reputation as the "father of the science of history in Iran" and the most methodologically thoroughgoing of its practitioners.[99] What follows is not a reassessment of Adamiyat's work as a historian, as this would clearly lie outside of this book's scope. Rather, I investigate his role in establishing the image of Akhundzadeh and Kermani as important modern intellectuals who are to be credited for Iran's awakening from the somnolence of tradition and march toward progress and modernity. In other words, what I am interested in is how Adamiyat's own political sympathies have distorted his appraisal of Akhundzadeh and Kermani. The fact that subsequent authors have almost exclusively relied on his two biographies is a reflection on the shortcomings of modern Iranian historiography rather than Adamiyat himself.

Adamiyat's biographies of Akhundzadeh and Kermani, although painstakingly detailed, are the works of a partisan. His use of historical sources is often selective or outright manipulative.[100] He consistently refused to acknowledge, devote necessary critical attention to, or even interpret our authors' audacious rewriting of history, their utopian and potentially violent approach to modernization (more on this in chapter 5), and their racist endeavor to identify an absentee scapegoat to be reviled. Adamiyat's nationalist bias is evident in two instances. First, he himself fervently believed in the perennial character of Iranian nationalism. As the following quotation makes plain, he took Iranian nationalism for a primordial fact rather than a historical phenomenon to be investigated by historians. Thus, he could hardly exercise the necessary intellectual detachment that would allow him to offer a serious and impartial study of Akhundzadeh or Kermani's doctrine:

> Nationalism was not a phenomenon akin to knowledge and modern technology that could have been directly imported into Iran from the West. Before even the emergence of the philosophy of nationalism in Europe itself, all the elements composing it existed in Iran and were recognized: the representation of the land of Iran, the Aryan nation, racial pride, a common language and faith. Most importantly, historical consciousness and a common intellectual outlook were not things that were exported to Iran from abroad. Our ancient history and culture have created and preserved these elements.[101]

A second element is his approach to non-Iranian nationalisms, which is tainted with a condescension that contrasts with his leniency toward the most absurd utterances of the founding fathers of dislocative nationalism. He affirms, not without some derision, that Egyptians have been ruled by foreigners since ancient times. He then imputes the Egyptian "invention" of Arab nationalism to "al-Afghani's" thought. The aim of this proposition is evident, although erroneous; Adamiyat infers that it took Arabs an Iranian thinker to come up with their own nationalism. He also scorns Namık Kemal, the Young

Ottoman intellectual, for having overstated the contribution of Turks to world civilization.[102] Kemal's claim that Turks were "the educators of the world" is a typical case of nationalist self-aggrandizement. Although this quotation pales in comparison to the wildest claims of Akhundzadeh and Kermani, Adamiyat ridicules it while refusing to apply even a fraction of this critical approach to the authors whose work he actually examines. Thanks to his status and reputation and the unavailability of Akhundzadeh and Kermani's works, he got away with this deliberate sloppiness. He has had a disproportionate impact in shaping the mainstream view of Akhundzadeh and Kermani as modernizing patriots, whose aplomb in rewriting history, escaping empirical reality, and promoting aggressive Arab-hatred are to be revered rather than examined.

In his study of Akhundzadeh's life and work, Adamiyat never assesses Akhundzadeh's noncompliance with his own norm, that of *qertikā* (critical thinking). Adamiyat in fact descends into hagiography wrapped in the language of modern history writing. He calls Akhundzadeh an "essentially good man," "that wise patriot," "the representative of the era of rationalism and liberalism," or he adorns his name with other flattering adjectives.[103] When it comes to Akhundzadeh's dehistoricization of pre-Islamic Iran, Adamiyat contents himself with praising his "historical awareness."[104] Adamiyat, the "methodological historian," entirely shuns the issues that arise from Akhundzadeh's rewriting of history.[105] Akhundzadeh's favoring of pre-Islamic over Islamic Iran is recast as "comparative political history."[106] In fact, Adamiyat himself reappropriated Akhundzadeh's Manichaean terminology to describe these periods. He sweepingly calls pre-Islamic Iran an "era of grandeur and power" and the Islamic period one of altogether "weakness and chaos."[107]

Adamiyat's method is apparent in his take on an exchange between Akhundzadeh and Jalal ed-Din Mirza. Replying to Jalal ed-Din Mirza's request to retrieve information on kings from the Ilkhanids to the Safavids for the last volume of his *Nāmeh-ye Khosrovān*, Akhundzadeh writes and insists that "in my opinion these kings do not deserve to be mentioned in your publication" because, in the history of Islamic Iran, "the rulers of this land were all *despotes* and plunderers (*harāmi bāshiyān*)."[108] In other words, entire segments of Iranian history should be overlooked because they do not comply with Akhundzadeh's ideals. Now, by any standard, such an approach to the writing of history is purposefully selective and deceitful. It openly attempts to induce amnesia. Adamiyat relates this episode, but rather than take the logical conclusions, he uses it to argue that Akhundzadeh did not attribute the destruction of pre-Islamic glory to Arabs only but also to Turks and Mongols. According to

Adamiyat, this should show the sophistication and balanced nature of Akhundzadeh's thought.[109]

This brings us to the very reasons for Adamiyat's refusal to impartially analyze the racial lens through which Akhundzadeh viewed the world. It is reasonably doubtful that a historian trained at the London School of Economics, the birthplace of nationalism studies, and writing in 1970 had not been exposed to critical literature on race and ethnicity.[110] He almost certainly did, but one can doubt that an author whose anti-Semitism and anti-Baha'ism are well known[111]—and as we will see a certain dislike of Arabs is not all absent from his writings—would have a valuable insight into the nationalist authors' racist prejudice. One can also argue that in pursuance of his strategy to portray every facet of Akhundzadeh's thought as ethical and upright, he was determined to obscure the racial component of the *Maktubāt*. Adamiyat devotes all in all three paragraphs to Akhundzadeh's hatred of Arabs, even though this aspect unremittingly arises in the latter's writings and correspondence. The objective of these three paragraphs is of course to whitewash Akhundzadeh's scorn toward the racial other, not to evaluate it impartially. According to Adamiyat, Akhundzadeh's "love for ancient Iran and aversion toward the *tāzi* (Arab)" is neither specific to him nor to other nationalist Iranian authors; rather, it is allegedly natural for any society that has experienced a "brilliant past" to "be nostalgic of it" and become wary of "aliens," especially if these are held responsible for their decline.[112] For Adamiyat, "hatred of aliens is a complex sociological phenomenon, and in its analysis one must take into account all of its historical, political and psychological components."[113] Yet Adamiyat's reader is left without even the beginning of such analysis, merely a cursory validation: hatred of aliens is beneficial because "it consolidates the foundations of nationality." There is therefore nothing to analyze, criticize, or evaluate; what matters above all is the consolidation of the nationalist doctrine, not scientific inquiry. The ideological legitimation of Akhundzadeh's thought, in all its aspects, is complete. Adamiyat concludes by a contradiction that Akhundzadeh, while "scorning the figure of the Arab, holds Iranians responsible for their historical failure"; according to him, this is proof of Akhundzadeh's "historical realism."[114] As my earlier analysis showed, Akhundzadeh blames the state of Iran on Arabs, *despotes*, and the ulama, but by no means have Iranians as national community any responsibility or agency in this state of affairs.

Adamiyat offers a candid explanation of Iranian history to his reader, in case this latter was left with any doubt on the Weltanschauung of the greatest of modern Iranian historians. This explanation startles as much by its defiance of any serious historical methodology as by its resemblance to the theories of his spiritual master Akhundzadeh. He affirms that "the ascension of the rulers of the Turkish race, drowned in ignorance and religious fanaticism, is one of the most important factors in the intellectual decadence of Iran." He then goes on to blame "the supremacy of ignorant and bloodthirsty Turks" in Anatolia for Iran being cut off from the great achievements of the West, inadvertently suggesting that progress comes exclusively from the West, not Iran, and only direct contact with the West could have kept Iran "civilized."[115] The stratagem of simplifying history to its most basic features—in this case essentializing almost one thousand years of history—and blame aliens for Iran's decline, is entirely identical to Akhundzadeh's, although here the figure of the Turk replaces that of the Arab. Assuming that Iran has always been declining since the Islamic conquest in fact flies in the face of historical facts that could have been known to both Akhundzadeh and Adamiyat, in particular the scientific and literary achievements of medieval Iran.

One aspect of Akhundzadeh's life that is wholly swept under Adamiyat's rug is his inglorious work at the service of Tsarist Russia, a despotic government and enemy of Iran. Akhundzadeh served a viceroy that headed the legation that signed the Turkmenchay Treaty, probably the most humiliating peace terms ever imposed upon Iran. Akhundzadeh also indirectly supported Russian exactions in the Caucasia wars. Adamiyat actively attempts to conceal Akhundzadeh's career and beliefs. These questions are thoroughly analyzed in chapter 5.

In Adamiyat's pages, flattering designations also rain on Kermani: "founder of the historical philosophy of Iran," "renowned national poet," "oracle of freedom and national rule," "pre-constitutional revolutionary thinker," endowed with a "broad and worldly mind," a "promoter of the humanist creed," an "authentic representative of Iran's culture."[116] Adamiyat's approach is so uncritical that when analyzing Kermani's preoccupation with language, he steers clear of quoting this latter's linguistic delirium for his readers, let alone critique it, as he tries to preserve and promote an image of Kermani as a knowledgeable revolutionary. Others before Adamiyat had taken notice—for instance, the prominent literary historian Mohammad-Taqi Bahar (known as Malek osh-Sho'arā) referred to Kermani's work as "worthless due to its baseless investigations into etymology."[117] Adamiyat's assessment of Kermani's work is equally sympathetic when it comes to Kermani's reading of pre-Islamic history, which, as we saw in the earlier quotations, is even more simplistic than Akhundzadeh's and therefore more open to criticism. Yet Adamiyat praises Kermani's "modern historiographical method, and his critical evaluation of sources," before declaring Kermani "the most prominent representative of the field of modern historiography in the nineteenth century" and asserting that Kermani's "rank in historical thinking is unsurpassed," making anyone who has read Kermani's treatment of history to jolt with stupefaction.[118] He not only approves of Kermani's vision of pre-Islamic Iran but claims it to be the result of suitable historiographical research: "to this day, his discussion on Mazdakite social philosophy and also his argument in regards to the reasons for the degeneration and decline of the Sasanians is the richest of all writings in Persian."[119]

Kermani's analysis of these issues is precisely where a criticism of his "methods" would have been warranted. Failing that, the historian would be expected to offer his interpretation of the reasons behind Kermani's outlandish claims. Both are absent from the pages of the "father of Iranian historiography." On the matter of the downfall of Sasanians, Kermani's "rich" argument—continuously recurring throughout *Seh maktub* and *Sad khatābeh*—can be summarized into one word: Arabs. Yet even the apparent simplicity of this hypothesis fails to conceal a degree of confusion very much typical of Kermani's often jumbled writing. He venerated ancient Iranian kings uncritically and constantly emphasized their justice and wisdom while at the same time admiring Mazdak, who led a plebeian revolt against those same kings. Mazdak was a religious figure and reformer who declared himself a prophet and promoted redistribution of wealth and the possibility of mixing between classes in the Sasanian Empire.[120] The sheer number of his followers is an indication of the level of disaffection with the Sasanians' rule, the hierarchical structure of Sasanian society, and the repression of the Zoroastrian clergy.[121] Ironically, when Mazdak and his followers were massacred, it was in Arabia—in particular, in Mecca—that they survived.[122] However that may be, Kermani considered Mazdak to be the precursor of "French anarchists, Russian nihilists and English socialists," who only now "after 700 years of progress and civilization" have found the "aptness for equality (*este'dād-e mosāvat*)" that Iranians experienced "2000 years ago."[123] On the one hand, he presents ancient Iran as a paradise of justice; on the other, he portrays Anushiravan—the Sasanian king who put Mazdak and thousands of his followers to death—as a *despote*, thus digressing from his otherwise consistent veneration of pre-Islamic kings. He then blames Anushiravan for having obstructed the triumph of Mazdak's "egalitarian" and "republican" thought, and hence causing Iran's downfall.[124] The reader of *Sad khatābeh* is left mystified about the actual reason for Iran's decay in Kermani's mind. Was it not the Arabs that destroyed Iran's glory? Is it Anushiravan now who is to be blamed for the fall of the Sasanian Empire? Or for the Arabs' invasion, because he obstructed Mazdak's success? Or is it Mazdak's failure to bring justice and equality to a society that was supposed to be fundamentally just and egalitarian in the first place?[125]

Inconsistency even taints his approach to Arabs and Islam. As mentioned before, he claimed that one can tell by observing "an Iranian, a Greek and an Englishman," that they were "clean and civilized." Yet, in only the next paragraph, he gives us a description of the physical features of Iranians that runs boldly counter his earlier claim. There he says that Iranians have "stern and sour faces, curved and humped statures, their necks thrust into their shoulders with crooked discolored cheekbones," and so on. Unsurprisingly, this is the result of the passage of Arabs, whose "nature is visible on [Iranians'] foreheads."[126] How can they look "clean and civilized" then, one wonders? In similarly contradictory fashion, he charges Islam to be a regressive force that caused Iran's disgrace and rarely misses an opportunity to curse the religion, its clergy, or its followers in his nationalist writings. Yet—as pointed out earlier—he did not hesitate to "identify himself as a Muslim" whenever political expediency dictated it.[127] He also collaborated with "al-Afghani" on the project of pan-Muslim political unity practically at the same time that he was writing *Seh maktub*. He occasionally even called for a Protestantism of sorts to revive that same Islam's now "truth and purity."[128] In his historical work *Āʾineh-ye sekandari*, he calls the Prophet Muhammad "that great honorable man" (*ān bozorgvār*) and displays only a fraction of the Arab-hatred that covers the pages of *Seh maktub* and *Sad khatābeh*.[129] All these positions were held during his time in Istanbul, therefore practically simultaneously.

His hatred of Arabs—intense even by the standards of nineteenth-century Europe—is the main flaw of Kermani's work. It arises in more instances and in more mutually unrelated contexts than one wishes it to, in a manner more fanatical than Akhundzadeh's. Kermani's simplistic attribution of all Iran's shortfalls to that one teleological event, the Islamic conquest, does not stand up to careful examination; neither does the solution he offers, which consists in reversing that conquest. That Adamiyat and the nationalist literature have consistently refused to discuss these matters in any detail is revealing about the serious flaws from which Iranian historiography suffers. It is not a matter of judging Kermani from today's moral standpoint. We stand on the shoulders of giants, and we cannot expect a nineteenth-century Iranian thinker to demonstrate the critical detachment that we can afford toward race discourse.

However, a serious examination of Kermani must at the very least investigate the objectives he was pursuing. Instead, Adamiyat only praises Kermani for consolidating patriotism and bringing about modernity and progress.

The close examination of these inconsistencies is all the more indispensable as Kermani professes blind submission to science. His twentieth-century biographer had both sufficient historical detachment and access to sources to evaluate at the very least the sources Kermani relied on in the development of his thought. Instead, Adamiyat himself promotes racial prejudice (including, as mentioned, anti-Semitism and anti-Baha'ism). To him, Kermani's theories that the "natural environment" influences the character of "nations" are not obsolete, but the products of "the sophisticated (*por maghz*) writings of European thinkers" that Kermani has been right to consult.[130] In fact, Adamiyat seems rather enchanted by Kermani's hypothesizing that the Arabs' natural environment (the desert) inclines them toward "obdurateness and grudge, generating their malevolence and discord," theories that he approves before adding that the Arabs' lifestyle in the desert explains their "cruelty and murderousness" and their lack of "civil development."[131] One wonders whether Kermani and Adamiyat have traveled through their own country, where desert is not a rare sight (in particular around Kerman). Adamiyat's objective is to place Akhundzadeh and Kermani within a nationalist pantheon and grant them a semi-sacred status, brushing aside any critical reassessment, however scientifically legitimate. That Adamiyat himself in time became a member of that same pantheon is testimony to the potency of ideology in Iranian historiography.

In conclusion, the appearance of Akhundzadeh's and Kermani's nationalist thought marked a decisive turning point in Iran's modern intellectual history. By that time, mainstream modernism had left its initial "technological" phase behind and had become increasingly concerned with reforming the state. This programmatic character was at display in the thought of Malkam Khan, for instance, and the reform movement represented by the Constitutional Revolution. Modernism devised a concrete reform agenda centered on the concept of law and its indispensability if Iran was to shake off the arbitrariness of its rulers and make its way into the realm of modernity.[132] It was a practical path to modernity, although the chaos that followed the revolution took the wind off its sails.

Yet, around 1860, from among a few thinkers disillusioned with reform, suddenly there emerged a radicalized offshoot, or rather an alternative path to modernism. Akhundzadeh can safely be considered the founder of this nationalist thought. Kermani reproduced Akhundzadeh's work and ensured its transmission to a later generation of nationalists, which will in time adopt Kermani's definition of Iranianness in linguistic and racial terms. This is Kermani's contribution: transmission, radicalization, and the addition of a conceptually informed version of European racial thought. This nationalist doctrine only perfunctorily attempted to provide Iran with a valid project of reform and adaptation to modernity. Instead, it took the shape of a predominantly discursive and historicist ideology whose main objective was to soothe the pain of the traumatic encounter with Europe while making sense of Iran's backwardness.

This ideological tradition is not without incoherence or ethical ambiguities, and the bizarre contradictions highlighted here should not be taken as evidence of Akhundzadeh and Kermani's ignorance or malevolence. What should really come up for historical scrutiny is the authorial intentions behind these texts. Here Kermani's work sheds a particular light on his intentions. Kermani's historical texts such as Āʾineh-ye sekandari, written in the same period (1889–1891, according to Bayat[133]), show that he could conduct—certainly for the standards of the time—works of history that, although not entirely impartial, were at least not ridden by obvious contradictions and outlandish claims. Therefore, it does not seem that Kermani has "got it wrong" or lost his mind, but rather that his vision of pre-Islamic Iran and his hostility toward Arabs and Islam pursue a particular objective. This objective is the creation of an ideology, which is appealing and digestible enough to command mass conversion. He does not aim to provide his readership with facts or a compendium of scientific discoveries. His aim is to promote dislocative nationalism, and he makes this aim abundantly clear in the concluding paragraph of Seh maktub when he announces that his wish is to awaken Iranians' patriotisme, to strip them off their Semitic nature and through a changement subit (French for "sudden change") revitalize this "buried-alive lot."[134]

Akhundzadeh himself echoed this objective three decades earlier by clarifying his aim: to "sow the seeds of zeal, honor, patriotism," and give Iranians "unity of thought and direction."[135] This ideology addresses the needs of Qajar intellectuals at the time and soothes their predicaments. Trumping up the achievements of pre-Islamic Iran and overplaying Iranians' difference with Arabs is a strategy to claim parity with those Europeans with whose achievements they were obsessed. As an ideology, dislocative nationalism had clear objectives. The next three chapters offer a thorough analysis of its three core components: archaism, Arab-hatred, and a convoluted relationship with European modernity.

3
PRE-ISLAMIC IRAN AND ARCHAISTIC FRENZY

"A Contradiction: The Iranian Soul and the Islamic Spirit"
—Title of an article by Nader Naderpour, 1984

IN 2010 THE BRITISH MUSEUM LOANED THE CYRUS CYLINDER to the National Museum in Tehran for exhibition. The Cyrus Cylinder was discovered by a British expedition in the ruins of Babylon in today's Iraq in 1879. Its surface bears inscriptions carved in clay that Cyrus the Great (d. 530 BC), the founder of the Achaemenid dynasty, commissioned after his armies conquered the Neo-Babylonian empire. In these inscriptions in Akkadian, one of the ancient languages of Mesopotamia, Cyrus presents himself as a benevolent new king who is blessed by Marduk, Babylon's very own chief deity, and he commits to be a benefactor of the newly conquered people, support them in rebuilding their temples, and help the displaced to return to their homelands.

In an eccentric outburst of anachronism that only a nationalist ideology can engender, the Cyrus Cylinder has been referred to as the "first charter of human rights" by Mohammad Reza Shah Pahlavi and dislocative nationalists (the first such reference was made at the 2,500th anniversary of the foundation of the Iranian monarchy in 1971). That a declaration dating from the sixth century BC could address "human rights," a concept developed by the Enlightenment *philosophes* in the eighteenth century AD, is quite intriguing. More sober analysts have argued that Cyrus's declaration, rather than a declaration of rights, is a classical case of Babylonian propaganda, a shrewd political ma-neuver to bring on board the Babylonian religious and economic elites; in-deed, Cyrus did not hesitate to use force when expediency required it.[1] Antiq-uity was not concerned with "human rights" and Cyrus the Great was no exception. Moreover, his successors never applied anything remotely resem-bling human rights; therefore, even if the Cyrus Cylinder *had* the characteris-tics presumed by dislocative nationalists, their legacy did not last very long. Be that as it may, the ephemeral passage of the cylinder in Tehran in 2010 had more anachronism and nationalism in store. The divisive then-president of the Islamic Republic, Mahmoud Ahmadinejad, seized the opportunity to appeal to the cult of pre-Islamic Iran still very much alive in the country, especially among those who oppose the Islamic regime and see it as yet another alien invasion in disguise (Islamic, therefore Arab). Indeed the Islamic Republic's attachment to the Islamic fate and the refusal of some of its dignitaries to ac-knowledge the preponderance of Iranian national culture and interests over that of the umma, although simple ideological devices with serious practical limitations, stand in sharp contrast to the pre-Islamic focused nationalism of the ancien régime.

With a bluntness quite unprecedented in the annals of the Islamic Repub-lic, Ahmadinejad attempted a fusion of the Iranian and Islamic components of Iranian identity that have been seen as incompatible ever since the appear-ance of dislocative nationalism. When unveiling the cylinder at a grand ceremony, the president presented Cyrus as "the King of the world" and his controversial chief of staff, Esfandiar Rahim Mashaei, later equated him with a prophet.[2] The ceremony turned outright grotesque when Ahmadinejad adorned an actor in full Cyrus-the-Great-outfit with a black-and-white keffi-yeh, which is an item that the pro-regime Basij militia wear in solidarity with Palestinians. The staging sparked a storm of protests among the advocates of both components of Iranian identity, Islamic and pre-Islamic. On the one hand, a conservative member of parliament was outraged that the president should praise Cyrus, whose "actions were not in line with the Prophet's teach-ings" because he "did not abolish idolatry." On the other extreme of the iden-tity spectrum, a fuming blogger asked, "Why is Cyrus the Great, the symbol of Iran, being decorated with the symbol of another country—Palestine?"[3] Another equally outraged blogger found the move "insulting," asking "How can one mix two very different symbols that go against each other?" before as-serting confidently that the "keffiyeh is the symbol of bloodshed, war, and terrorism in Palestine and Lebanon."[4]

This episode confirms the extent to which the pre-Islamic past and Islamic Iran are still hotly contested in Iranian identity politics, are opposed to each other as incompatible, or are the subject of attempts at incongruous reconciliation. It also shows how Arabs—even their contemporary Palestinian incarnations—still are either loathed as the implacable "others" looming from the dark of ages to finish the job of destroying Iran's separate identity or as brothers in faith within the Islamic umma. This fracture within Iranian identity, this constructed antagonism between Iran and Islam, goes back to the writings of Akhundzadeh, Kermani, and their myriad heirs.

Before the times of Akhundzadeh, there was no trace of such archaistic frenzy. A new interest in the pre-Islamic past had certainly already been "in the air" for a few decades. Indeed, the views of European scholars were making themselves known, although these occasional shows of interest for a distant past were far from the infatuation that would characterize later nationalist writing on the subject. A few Qajar authors had started to refer to Iran's pre-Islamic past as "bright" (derakhshān) and "glorious" (bā shokuh). Fath'ali Shah (1772–1834) is the first on record to make this interest manifest. This is quite remarkable as the Qajars traditionally emphasized their Turkic roots and their alleged descent from one of Genghis Khan's generals (a claim that lasted well into the nineteenth century). Fath'ali Shah commissioned rock engravings and reliefs in the style of pre-Islamic kings near the Allah-o Akbar gate in Shiraz and at Taq-e Bostan in Kermanshah.[5] There is no evidence that Fath'ali Shah's objective was to glorify the nation's pre-Islamic history; rather, it seems that these engravings were the expression of his status. Be that as it may, he also gave distinctly pre-Islamic names to his younger progenies; thus, the elder Abbas Mirza, Mohammad Ali Mirza, and Hossein Ali Mirza were followed by the younger Khosrow Mirza, Keyqobad Mirza, Keykavos Mirza, and Kiyumars Mirza.[6] Deeper into the nineteenth century, reliance on the pre-Islamic period could come from widely different schools of thought and serve diverse objectives; it was in no way an exclusive domain of incipient nationalists. For instance, E'temad os-Saltaneh (1840–1896), a monarchist ideologue, developed a theory of national identity centered around the monarchy and in so doing relied extensively on memories of pre-Islamic kingship. Even Abd ol-Baha (1844–1921) the leader and son of the founder of the Baha'i faith, invoked pre-Islamic Iran as "the heart of the world" and praised ancient Iranians' multiconfessionalism in his Maqāleh-ye shakhsi sayyāh (A traveler's narrative, 1888) to further his own calls for religious tolerance.[7] Toward the end of the nineteenth century, a number of historical works on the pre-Islamic period appeared, among them Mohammad Nasser Forsat od-Dowleh's *Āsār-e 'Ajam* (History of the Persians; 1896).[8]

The appearance of this cult of pre-Islamic Iran raises several questions that this chapter will address. Was pre-Islamic archaism a novel trend—effectively initiated by this generation of Qajar literati—or was it a traditional view with a long history in Iranian culture? If it was modern, where did it stem from, what particular sources was it the tributary of, and what strategy did it serve? Finally, was the pre-Islamic Iran that these authors described a historical reality or was it invented?

INDIGENOUS SOURCES

Rooting the nation in the distant past is nothing exceptional in the construction of modern national pedigrees. The case of Greece is illustrative as the ideologues of Greek nationalism had at their disposal two pasts that could narrate the identity of modern Greeks: the classical and the Byzantine. There are indications that the rural populations of Greece in the nineteenth century considered themselves to be primarily Orthodox Christians as noted by an American traveler in 1824: "The modern Greeks know nothing of Thucydides, Aristotle, Solon and other worthies of olden times; their traditions go no further than the Byzantine Empire."[9] This identity narrative emphasizing religion—hence, the Orthodox Byzantine tradition—was promoted by the Church as in this injunction of Kosmas Aitolos, a prominent eighteenth-century monk: "Ye are not Hellenes, ye are not impious, heretical, atheistical: ye are pious Orthodox Christians."[10] Yet it was the classical age of Euripides and Plato that became that glorious past of Greek nationalism. With a remarkable success, it should be added, that can perhaps be attributed to its broad popular appeal and uncontested character.[11] The Byzantium "model" was first relegated to an alternative narrative. At a later stage, however, the two golden ages, classical Greece and Orthodox Byzantium, were fused into a coherent nationalist reading of Greek identity and legacy.[12] In the case of Iran, on the other hand, the narratives deriving from the pre-Islamic and Islamic pasts have not yet been successfully fused into a single, continuous Iranian nation reconciled with the full length and complexity of its own history.

In the Middle East, other forms of nationalism endeavored to use a pre-Islamic past as the site of the nation's essence. In 1920s Egypt, for instance, particularly after the discovery in 1922 of the tomb of Tut-Ankh-Amon, a num-

ber of nationalist intellectuals started dismissing or downplaying the country's links to both the Islamic umma and the community of Arabic speakers, to
instead call for the revival of Pharaonic Egypt. This movement has been referred to as territorial Egyptian nationalism with Muhammad Husayn Hakyal
as its most important figure (although he would later switch to pan-Arab nationalism).[13] Pharaonism was particularly prominent in the ideology of the
Young Egypt party. From a comparative perspective, what is of interest here is
the short-lived nature of Pharaonism in Egyptian territorial nationalism as
Arab and Islamic orientations became increasingly prominent in the 1930s and
1940s and pan-Arab nationalism supplanted the Pharaonic longings of the previous generation. In that period, Arab nationalism emerged as a more efficient
instrument to oppose imperial domination, and it was believed that Egypt
could assume a role of leadership in bringing about Arab unity.[14] In Iraq, it
was in the 1950s that interest for the country's pre-Islamic Mesopotamian heritage emerged, a recalibration of local identity that was supported by Brig. Gen.
Abd al-Karim Qasim in 1958–1963 and significantly strengthened by the Ba'ath
party after 1968. While preserving a modicum of Arab nationalism to emphasize Iraq's leadership role in the Arab world, the ideologues of Mesopotamian
nationalism hoped that their brand of Iraqi identity could appeal equally to
all the constituencies of Iraq, thus bridging the gap between Shi'ites and
Sunnis, Arabs and Kurds.[15] The Egyptian and Iraqi cases serve to highlight
that dislocative nationalism's reliance on pre-Islamic symbols was more
durable and less contested than Egypt's flirtation with Pharaonism or Iraq's
Mesopotamian identity. In fact, the symbolic reliance on the pre-Islamic past
became a permanent feature of dislocative nationalism.

In this chapter, I provide some answers as to why it was so, but first it should
be noted that prior to the Qajar period, views on pre-Islamic Iran were quite
different. John Malcolm confirms in *The History of Persia* that a nostalgic
longing for the pre-Islamic past was absent from traditional Iranian historiography: "Persian historians are alike disposed, from superstition and from
patriotism, to deem [the advent of Islam to Iran] one of the greatest miracles
by which God has manifested the truth of the Mahomedan religion."[16] That
being said, Iran also has a tradition of antinomianism where religious knick-
knack is openly mocked. Suffice it to think of the tales of Molla Nasr ed-Din,
or further back in time the writings of the fourteenth-century poet, satirist, and
lampoonist Obeyd Zakani. It has been claimed that this antinomianism could
be found in Sufi circles and culminated with Babism, which operated a break
with Islam.[17] However, this healthy skepticism toward established dogmas

should not be confused with the hostility toward Islam that appears in full force in Akhundzadeh's and Kermani's works.

As I discuss in chapter 1, the pre-Islamic past was usually evoked from a mythistorical perspective, such as that of the "kings of Ajam" tradition, of which the *Shāhnāmeh* is undoubtedly the most complete extant example. In the more rigorous historical works, pre-Islamic Iran constitutes only parts of universal or Islamic histories, rather than standing on its own. Additionally, the Achaemenids (and almost the Parthians) were entirely absent from this literature. Be that as it may, a close examination of sources shows that neither an explicit preference for that period of Iranian history nor the idea that it might have been more glorious or harbor more achievements than the Islamic period is found in writings in Persian until Akhundzadeh.[18] Before coming back to the availability of such sources, a detour by popular traditions is advisable to determine if the idea of archaism had a basis, outside of the literate few, in the social memory of ordinary people. Fortunately, in the case of Iran, we have testimonies of practices that will allow us to assess popular feelings even in the absence of written sources, which were the exclusive monopoly of the literate elites (*ahl-e qalam*).

The mythistorical tradition was highly popular among common individuals. Knowledge of the *Shāhnāmeh* stories was widespread in the Qajar era, even among illiterate villagers and tribesmen. Oral performance or "*Shāhnāmeh* reading" (*Shāhnāmeh khāni*) was an entrenched tradition that had kept the names of the epic's antique heroes alive. The heroic feats of Rostam, in particular, were read privately in family circles, especially in the indoors atmosphere of winter nights; publicly, such readings were the mainstream entertainment offered at traditional coffeehouses.[19] The lack of research into this oral tradition does not allow us to date it with precision. Some authors have claimed that it existed in the Safavid era when the *Shāhnāmeh* was read out aloud to combating troops to excite their fervor to defend the king's domain.[20] Malcolm also reports that during Aqa Mohammad Khan Qajar's campaigns, he "commanded a person to recite some verses from the Shah Nameh of Firdousee, to encourage the soldiers to heroic actions"; Malcolm adds that this "is a very common practice in Persian armies."[21] Regardless, the oral performance of epics can be safely considered an ancient practice, although perhaps with discontinuities in time and space. The presence of *Shāhnāmeh* narrators in the courts of the kings is also well documented.[22] Oral traditions are also recognized as an important source of ancient knowledge and legends; after all, Ferdowsi himself extensively relied on oral traditions in the writing of the

Shāhnāmeh in the tenth century AD.[23] *Shāhnāmeh* readings also certainly benefited from the advent of print, which increased the availability of such texts, although this claim should be tempered by the high illiteracy rates of Qajar Iran and a well-established oral tradition.[24]

Gobineau's travelogues written in the 1850s report on the practice of *Shāhnāmeh* reading among common folks. He claimed that even Iranian peasants had some knowledge of their past—in fact, far more so than did their French counterparts: "I have never met a man of even the humblest condition who did not know at least the main traits of these endless annals."[25] In his travelogues he describes at length—in a likely allusion to *Shāhnāmeh* reading—what he calls reunions of commoners, in which one or several individuals of usually humble extraction read aloud about history and myths. Gobineau concludes that "a nation which attaches such price to its antecedents evidently possesses a vital principle of tremendous energy."[26] He surmised that "a real Persian is infinitely more curious to learn about the deeds of Jamshid or Cyrus, than be edified by reading the life of the Prophet himself," indicating a greater interest in the remote past than in Quranic or Abrahamic narratives.[27] It can safely be assumed that this latter assumption proceeded from his own anti-Islamic bias, as one cannot deny the even greater liveliness of another tradition, that of the *taʿziyeh*, or Shiʿite passion play.[28] Moreover, the link he draws between knowledge of ancient myths and national consciousness is also a tenuous one, but this discussion should not detain us here.

In sum, if one is to believe Gobineau, whose accounts are usually reliable, the *Shāhnāmeh* tradition was known to commoners who took an intense interest in the fate of pre-Islamic heroes.[29] The question that remains is, to what extent can this inclination be considered to be related to the pre-Islamic frenzy that was starting to engulf some *literati*? For one thing, one can doubt that the masses of illiterate peasants and tribesmen, while listening to *Shāhnāmeh* readings, were in fact indulging in an exercise in memory retrieval or expressing their fondness for a historical period that they favored over that of Islamic Iran. These historicist subtleties were certainly lost to them, and it is highly improbable that they saw *Shāhnāmeh* reading as anything other than entertainment, the Qajar equivalent of bestseller novels and blockbuster movies. Radically different is the undertaking of an Akhundzadeh or a Kermani, who, in a typically nineteenth-century fashion—and a European one at it, were attempting to define the "essence" of the nation, its historical stage of purity and authenticity. Therefore, the archaistic frenzy cannot be explained by the preexistence of popular fondness for pre-Islamic heroes, although the liveliness of the mythistorical tradition may have provided models or created a receptive audience for it.

In Tavakoli-Targhi's view, the recovery of the pre-Islamic past can be attributed to the retrieval of the *dasātiri* texts, written in Persian in Mughal India around 1600 AD.[30] The *dasātiri* texts were produced by the *keyvānis*, who were a community of religiously seditious Iranians led by a Zoroastrian high priest named Azar Keyvan. The *keyvānis* took refuge in the tolerant India of Emperor Akbar to escape the Safavids' religious persecution. There they principally concerned themselves with the development of a new idiosyncratic mysticism. The result was a series of texts combining Islamic and Hindu with Zoroastrian spirituality, and in this process the *keyvānis* also — although only accessorily — attempted a recovery of distant memories of Iran's pre-Islamic past. Some *dasātiri* texts developed a new narrative and metamorphosed pre-Islamic Iran into an idealized and homogenous ethos of Zoroastrian purity. By their distinctive character, they raised interest among some orientalists, although this interest was often accompanied by skepticism. Malcolm, for instance, used two *dasātiri* texts, the *Dabestān-e mazāheb* and the *Dasātirnāmeh*, among his sources, although it is said that he found them to be of little value to his research.[31] Equally important, nationalist authors rarely mention *dasātiri* texts, and when they do, it is not in connection to the recovery of pre-Islamic memory. Akhundzadeh, for instance, refers to the *Dabestān-e mazāheb* to disdainfully affirm that Indians" "imagination in matters of religion is excessively fertile."[32] Conversely, their pages are covered in positive references to *farangiyāns* (Europeans). Only Jalal ed-Din Mirza seems to have used *dasātiri* texts as sources to depict pre-Islamic Iran.[33]

Although they conveyed an interesting and rare Iranocentric reading of history that may have added to the ongoing pre-Islamic frenzy or perhaps provided additional models, it seems that the impact of the *dasātiri* texts on the remodeling of history and the emergence of nationalist thought has been exaggerated. The *dasātiri* texts primordially engage with mysticism and spirituality and only incidentally with history. The *Dabestān-e mazāheb*, for instance, is a discussion of different religions and their respective doctrines. Its only interest in the present discussion lies in its account of the Parsis of India and their history, which can only indirectly be connected to the development of a pre-Islamic focus among nationalist literati. Additionally, in view of the large circulation of the *Shāhnāmeh* through manuscripts, print, and *Shāhnāmeh* reading, the *dasātiri* texts cannot be considered more significant in providing a heroic narrative of pre-Islamic Iran.

The availability of particular *dasātiri* texts does not seem to corroborate the thesis whereby they alone can account for the pre-Islamic frenzy either. The *dasātiri* text most relevant to pre-Islamic history is the *Shārestān-e chahār chaman*, which, inter alia, relates a discussion between Azar Keyvan and his followers on the respective merits of Persian and Arabic, concluding with a consensus on the superiority of Persian as a language and Iranians as a people.[34] Kermani briefly refers to it in his *A'ineh-ye sekandari* but dismisses it as an Indian source.[35] The *Shārestān* was not in wide circulation, even compared to other *dasātiri* texts. While Marashi stresses that the *Dabestān-e mazāheb*— largely concerned with religion and as such unrelated to historiography—went through seven editions between 1846 and 1904, the *Shārestān* went into press only once in the nineteenth century, with two additional editions in the early twentieth.[36] This is testimony to its limited circulation.[37] Oral circulation was an effective tool of dissemination in Qajar Iran, and the rarity of this text is not in itself sufficient to dismiss its impact. Yet, there were other sources with similar content that were more easily accessible. One such source was a fourteenth-century chronicle of the "kings of Ajam" tradition, Fazlollah Hoseyni Qazvini's *Tārikh al-Mo'jam fi āsār-e moluk-e 'Ajam*, which was reprinted as many as seven times between 1831 and 1891 alone, with three further editions in the early twentieth century.[38] The *Shāhnāmeh* itself saw twenty editions in the course of the nineteenth century, in both Iran and India.[39] Rather than influence the archaistic frenzy of incipient nationalists, it seems that the *dasātiri* texts found a wider audience among poets and played an important role in "reactivating" obsolete Persian terms and propagating *keyvāni* neologisms.[40] In fact, the increasing availability of the *dasātiri* texts and other local histories of the "kings of Ajam" tradition seems to be a result, rather than the starting point, of the pre-Islamic frenzy.

I have elsewhere stressed the influence of the Parsi traveler Manekji Limji Hataria on Jalal ed-Din Mirza and Akhundzadeh, and his efforts to publish texts conveying knowledge of the pre-Islamic past or Zoroastrianism (including *dasātiri* texts).[41] However, I also emphasized that he only consolidated a movement already in full swing, and that the texts he promoted found an audience because pre-Islamic frenzy was already strong among the literati. Manekji Limji Hataria (1813–1890) was a Parsi envoy from Bombay, sent to Iran on a philanthropic mission. He spent almost forty years in Iran working toward the amelioration of the condition of his fellow Zoroastrians, and his work culminated with Nasser ed-Din Shah's royal *farmān* (decree) abolishing the *jizya* tax, a traditional tax levied on non-Muslims for protection that had become the main instrument for the repression of Zoroastrians. This aspect of his life has been the object of several historical works.[42] The influence he exercised over Jalal ed-Din Mirza and Akhundzadeh, on the other hand, has been largely ignored by students of Qajar Iran.[43] Indeed, he was one of the close associates of Jalal ed-Din Mirza, and although he never met Akhundzadeh in person, they held a passionate correspondence. Due to his background as a Zoroastrian, he exerted significant influence over them and came to be seen as an "emissary of the Golden Age," endowed with special knowledge of Iran's past.[44] Kermani, on the other hand, who never met Manekji, had no lost love for the Parsi envoy. He accused him of being "ignorant" of Iranian customs.[45]

In a letter to Akhundzadeh, Jalal ed-Din Mirza emphasizes that Manekji is the "representative" of Zoroastrians and a *civilisé* (well-versed in European languages and ways). Jalal ed-Din Mirza also reported that Manekji had "no other thought but that of perhaps, through whatever means, free the people of Iran from their unwise beliefs—remnants of the Arabs—and lead them toward the right path."[46] Manekji reciprocated by telling Akhundzadeh that Jalal ed-Din Mirza was a "freethinking prince" who was "devoted to the ancients and the memory of our ancestors."[47] Jalal ed-Din Mirza's respect for Manekji and his knowledge was such that he included his *Tārikh-e Pārsiyān* (History of the Zoroastrians/Parsis) as an appendix to the first volume of the *Nāmeh*. Akhundzadeh pledged to Manekji that the publication of his *Maktubāt* would ensure that Zoroastrians would be loved and respected everywhere. The "sultans of Islam" will be "kinder to your kin than to their own brother and father." They "will regret that they did not know you until today and that throughout the history of Islam they have supported and admired Arabs, who are their enemies . . . who destroyed their country," rather than Zoroastrians who are "their brothers, who speak the same language, their compatriots, *the living memory of their glorious forefathers*, and their guardian angels" (my emphasis).[48]

Manekji is perceived as the living memory of Iran's past, as if he had just walked out of a time capsule. In another letter, Akhundzadeh's admiration for Manekji and his kin becomes more evident: "My wish is that . . . Iranians knew that *we are the children of the Parsis*, that our home is Iran, that zeal, honor, idealism, and our celestial aspirations demand that we favor our kin . . . rather than alien bloodthirsty bandits" (my emphasis).[49] It is revealing that Akhundzadeh calls Iranians the "children" of the Parsis. He accords Parsis a genealogical ascendancy that can only be explained by the fact that he considers them to be pure Iranians who have preserved the ancient religion, and are un-contaminated by Arabs and Islam. He then adds that "my appearance is that of a Turk, but I am of the Parsis' race."[50] It is here worthy of note that in spite of their inclination for Zoroastrianism, Jalal ed-Din Mirza and Akhundzadeh knew next to nothing about this religion. Akhundzadeh wondered if the Zoro-astrians of Yazd had their own language and script.[51] In a letter, he asks Manekji whether Zoroastrian priests are called *mowbed* (which indeed they are).[52] As far as Jalal ed-Din Mirza's knowledge of Zoroastrianism is concerned, the sec-tion of his *Nāmeh* dealing with Zoroastrianism was in fact written by no one else but Manekji himself.

That Manekji saw the possible generalization of the cult of pre-Islamic Iran to be potentially in favor of Zoroastrians' right, and in the interest of the com-munity's well-being is highly plausible. He may have considered the uproot-ing of Islam to be part of his mission, echoing ancient Zoroastrian apocalyptic poetry, which longed for a reversal of the advent of Islam: "We will bring down mosques, establish the fires, we will raze idol-worshipping and wipe it from the material world."[53] Manekji's historical perceptions echoed those of Jalal ed-Din Mirza or Akhundzadeh: "I grieve and deplore the land of Iran and the condition of Iranians" he once complained.[54] At a meeting with the Parsi benefactors in Bombay, he gave a long speech that became his *Rishāl-e ejhār-e shiyāt-e Irān* ("Essay on a description of a travel to Iran," published in Gujarati in 1865 and later translated into Persian[55]). An excerpt of his report—giving an account of the advent of Islam to Iran—is offered here to demonstrate the reso-nance with the works of dislocative nationalist authors:

> When the country went into the hands of the Muslims, hordes of Arabs, Mongols, Tartars and other barbaric tribes overran the country causing destruction and devastation everywhere. . . . These hordes were totally il-literate and uncultured and forced Islam upon the people at the point of the sword . . . men forgot their human characteristics and behaved like senseless brutes. . . . When the Arabs got their sway over Iran [the Zoroas-trians] were slaughtered mercilessly, their houses were burned down. . . . Rape, arson, fire, house-breaking and all other possible crimes were perpetrated by the Muslims. There was unspeakable cruelty[56].

Needless to say, it was neither Mongols nor Tartars that brought Islam to Iran (although such descriptions have been documented of the Mongols'—not

Arabs'—treatment of conquered people). In a fashion reminding of nationalist authors, Manekji presents the advent of Islam as a cataclysmic rupture
causing nothing less than the annihilation of Iranian civilization. In his
eagerness, and perhaps his disregard for historical accuracy, he throws the
Mongols into the lot.

In addition to his correspondence with nationalist authors, Manekji actively
pursued his aims by disseminating texts with a pre-Islamic and neo-Zoroastrian flavor. What follows is an overview of his publication efforts.[57] In the
1860s, his travelogue "Essay on a description of a travel to Iran" was translated
into Persian.[58] Before that, in 1857–58, he requested one of his close collaborators, Reza Qoli Khan Hedayat (1800–1872), a literary figure and courtier, to
produce a little-known volume called *Nezhād-nāmeh-ye pādeshāhān-e Irāni
nezhād*, or "The book of the Kings of Iranian descent," where it is claimed
that a number of Iranian and non-Iranian kings trace their origins to pre-
Islamic dynasties.[59] In 1877 he edited *Jāvidān kherad*, "a collection of moral
precepts of ancient sages." The *Āʿin-e Hushang*, a volume composed of four
translated Zoroastrian texts, one on the nature of God, one on man and the
prophet Zarathustra, one on immortality, and finally one on ethics, "purport-
ing to be derived from the words of Anushiravan [a Sasanian king] . . . was
edited with an introduction, appendix and marginal notes by Manekji" and
appeared in 1879.[60]

Finally, he encouraged Esmail Khan Zand Tuyserkani to write the
Farāzestān, published in 1894 and, according to one author, a "veritable rag-bag
of legends and myths from the [*dasātiri* texts]."[61] There was also the previously
mentioned *Tārikh-e Pārsiyān*, a mythistory of Zoroastrians that was added to
the first volume of Jalal ed-Din Mirza's *Nāmeh*. Manekji also encouraged
the publication and dissemination of the main *dasātiri* texts. In 1854 he
wrote the preface of the most relevant of them, the *Shārestān-e chahār chaman*.[62] Although he was not involved directly in the publication of *Dabestān-e
mazāheb* and *Dasātirnāmeh*, the two other important *dasātiri* texts, he actively
shared the Indian editions of these books with his friends and collaborators.[63]
Manekji disseminated other texts as well. He dispatched his travelogue and the
Āʿin-e Hushang to Akhundzadeh in Tbilisi and encouraged him to put his
hands on other *dasātiri* texts on several occasions.[64] Dastur Jamaspji Mino-
cherji, a prominent Parsi priest, seemed to corroborate the thesis that Manekji
perceived the diffusion of such texts to be in line with his mission of helping
Zoroastrians in Iran. In a letter to Akhundzadeh, the Dastur states: Manekji
"wants to print a number of ancient manuscripts, especially those in Persian

on the Zoroastrian religion and in so doing incline the hearts of Iranians toward their ancient creed."[65]

Yet Manekji's efforts to promote texts in Persian with echoes of the pre-Islamic past took place once archaism was already well under way. Indeed, all the texts that Manekji promoted, the *dasātiri* texts or the previously mentioned fourteenth-century text by Fazlollah Hoseyni Qazvini, were published or re-published after Jalal ed-Din Mirza's *Nāmeh*, and mostly even after Akhundza-deh's *Maktubāt*. The texts that Manekji promoted only consolidated an archaistic movement, which already had some traction. They do not explain its origins. They only testify to the success of this new outlook among Qajar literati. They provided local sources and models and offered a veneer of indig-enous authenticity, which has since then allowed Iranian historians to claim that an inclination for the pre-Islamic past is yet another primordial character-istic of the Iranian historical consciousness. I argue that such was not the case, and that the sources accounting for the original emergence of nationalist archaism lie clearly outside of Iran.

EUROPEAN VIEWS OF IRAN'S PAST

European scholarship on the "East" in the eighteenth and nineteenth centu-ries revealed that in the pre-Islamic period, Iran had witnessed great empires that had ruled over some of the largest territories recorded in antiquity. In this remote past, Iran had been the equivalent of modern European nations: a mighty world power. It is in the texts of nonspecialist European scholars such as Montesquieu or Johann Gottfried Herder, rather than in Iranian sources, that one can find the earliest traces of the discourse that reinterprets the ad-vent of Islam to Iran as a rupture. In a passage of the *Persian Letters* (1721) where antipathy toward Islam is palpable at every page, one of Montesquieu's fictional correspondents born in the Zoroastrian faith suggests that Zoroastri-anism is altogether nobler, more enlightened, and somewhat more natural for Persia than is Islam. Zoroastrianism is autochthonous, while Islam—which was imposed upon Persia "not through persuasion, but by conquest"—is alien.[66] It is also suggested that Zoroastrianism is the "oldest [religion] in the world," and that under its rule women enjoyed "sweet liberty" and "equality." The issue of authorial intention could have been raised of course as the *Persian Letters* are, according to Montesquieu himself, "a sort of novel."[67] However, he pushes the same points in the *Spirit of the Laws*: "The religion of the Ghebers [Zoroastrians] formerly caused the kingdom of Persia to flourish;

it corrected the bad effects of despotism: today the Mohammedan religion destroys that same empire (XXIV.11)."[68] He further insists in two other passages that Islam is a religion of the sword, disseminated and upheld through force (XXIV.4 and XXV.13).[69]

In the 1760s, the German Danish explorer Carsten Niebuhr, the only survivor of an ill-fated expedition to Arabia, reached Iran and drew minutely detailed sketches of Persepolis. According to Rudi Matthee, these sketches had great resonance in bringing about European views of pre-Islamic Iran within the broader context of the genealogy of human civilization.[70] Niebuhr's drawings would lead one of the pioneers of ethnic or cultural nationalism, Herder, to propose a new thesis, shifting the origins of human civilization from Greece and Egypt to "Asia" and Iran.[71] According to Hamid Tafazoli, who conducted painstaking research into Niebuhr and Herder's views of Iran, Herder offered in the process his descriptions of Persepolis in which the pre-Islamic ruins coalesced with his understanding of Iranian mythology and religions into a romantic narrative of humanity and civilization.[72] Herder attributed the end of that civilization he admired to the Islamic conquest, thus seconding Montesquieu in one of the earliest accounts of the advent of Islam to Iran as a rupture with deplorable consequences. According to Matthee, "Herder privileged ancient Iran; he hardly felt attracted to its Islamic past and heritage. Like most of his French Enlightenment colleagues, he was deeply ambivalent about Islam, considering it a contributing factor to the despotism that characterized government in the Middle East."[73]

Similarly, Malcolm stated in the early 1800s that ancient Iranians were "well advanced in all the arts of civilized life, and they enjoyed, under the rule of some of their ancient kings, a happiness and prosperity far beyond what they have ever since experienced."[74] Malcolm confirms (rather unscholarly) that this opinion was, already when he was writing his *History*, "so generally adopted, [that] it would appear presumption to doubt its correctness."[75] Indeed most other scholars of Iran had similar penchants for that period. George Rawlinson talked of pre-Islamic Iranians' "astonishing achievements."[76] It must be highlighted here that, although Malcolm conveyed the opinions of some of his fellow students of Iran, he himself did not have a particular preference for the pre-Islamic past and did not see the Islamic conquest as the end of a glorious era and the beginning of a deplorable one; rather, he saw continuity in despotism. For him, "though [Persia's] religion was completely changed, and the manners of its inhabitants much altered, the government continued essentially the same. . . . The tale of despotism, which is the only one they have to tell, is always the same."[77] Rather exceptionally, Malcolm's contempt for things Iranian was so thorough that it did not even spare the pre-Islamic period.

Nevertheless, most other scholars shared the view of rupture and a dark age following a bright one. These views clearly show the limits of the scientific character of the European scholarship on the "East" and the influence of various biases and assumptions in the development of historiography. European authors' overemphasis of the achievements of pre-Islamic Iran carries all the hallmarks of a general distaste for Islam on the part of European authors, which has little to do with science or historical facts but derives from cultural prejudice. The debate on European views of Islam should not detain us here, but the European scholarship that could have potentially served as model to dislocative nationalist authors should be reviewed.

According to Albert Hourani, in the eighteenth century, "the basic Christian attitude was still what it had been for a millennium: a rejection of the claim of Muslims that Muhammad was a prophet and the Qur'an the word of God, mingled with a memory of periods of fear and conflict, and also, a few thinkers and scholars apart, with legends, usually hostile and often contemptuous."[78] Malcolm's *History of Persia*, for instance, was tributary to this typical approach to Islam. He asserts confidently—and shockingly, for anyone with the slightest acquaintance of the history of medieval Islamic empires or more recent Ottoman, Safavid, and Mughal achievements—that there "is no example, during more than twelve centuries of any Mahomedan nation having attained a high rank in the scale of civilisation."[79] For him, as long as some nations of Asia were under the sway of Islam, they could possibly not enjoy the progress and prosperity of "the commonwealth of Europe," an idea that conjures up numerous times in the writings of Akhundzadeh and Kermani; the latter even expressly mentions Malcolm.[80]

This negative outlook on Islam was significantly cemented in the nineteenth century. By then the relationship between East and West became increasingly one of unequal power, and orientalist scholarship, or at least that segment of it developed by colonial envoys such as Malcolm tended to emphasize the indolence of Muslims and the inherent backwardness and inertia of their societies. Such societies, the argument went, should be ruled by Europeans—for the natives' own sake. This vision was well in place in European scholarship on the East over the period under study and has been famously analyzed in Edward Said's seminal *Orientalism* and subsequent literature. As Hourani has pointed out, however, one should be careful not to disregard those orientalists—Edward G. Browne and Louis Massignon, among others—who were opposed to the imperial endeavors of their countries and had significant sympathy for the Muslim masses.[81] The view of Islam and Muslims was—and arguably remains—depressingly essentialist. As the complexity of Muslim societies, stretching from one side of the planet to the other, would stagger any observer in search of digestible explanations, the temptation to essentialize Muslims to produce simplified accounts is irresistible. Islam then becomes a monolithic, all-encompassing phenomenon making sense of every aspect of the religious, social, cultural, economic, and political life of its adherents by reducing the diversity of the practices of Islam (or even absence of practice) into a handful of characteristics, such as indolence, backwardness, fanaticism, violence, and so on.

When it came to the historiography of the Islamic conquest of Iran, these European views of Islam were projected onto the events. Hence, even Browne—the prominent Cambridge Iranist whose *Literary History of Persia* would become one of the standards of the European scholarship of Iran and who, according to Hourani, had a great deal of sympathy for Iranians—wrote that "in the seventh century, the warlike followers of the Arabian prophet swept across Iran, overwhelming, in their tumultuous onslaught, an ancient dynasty and a venerable religion."[82] The depiction becomes then strikingly similar to the nationalist reading of Iranian history, in its vivid theatricality and pompousness and, of course, almost complete lack of reliance on actual historical sources (indeed, this passage does not contain one single reference): "Where for centuries the ancient hymns of the Avesta had been chanted, and the sacred fire had burned, the ery [eerie] of the *mu'ezzin* summoning the faithful to prayer rang out from minarets reared on the ruins of the temples of Ahura Mazda. The priests of Zoroaster fell by the sword, the ancient books perished in the flames. . . . Truly it seemed that a whole nation had been transformed."[83]

Use of the terms "eerie" or "ring out" when referring to the Islamic prayer here denotes the degree of Browne's antipathy toward Islam. For the rest, the vivid images of the end of a glorious age and the beginning of an altogether dark one can only remind one of Akhundzadeh, Kermani, and even Manekji's pages, and so does the entirely fallacious presumption that libraries had been destroyed. Some chapters later, Browne unambiguously offers the reasons of his distaste for Islam:

If the Arabs had not invaded Persia, slaying, plundering, and compelling, do you think that the religion of Muhammad would have displaced the

religion of Zoroaster? To us the great proof of the truth of Christ's teaching is that it steadily advanced in spite of the sword, not by the sword: the
great reproach on Islam, that its diffusion was in so large a measure due
to the force of arms rather than the force of argument. I sympathise with
your religion, and desire to know more of it, chiefly because the history of
its origin, the cruel fate of its founder, the tortures joyfully endured with
heroic fortitude by its votaries, all remind me of the triumph of Christ,
rather than the triumph of Muhammad.[84]

We have here the expression in clear terms of one of the main theological
foundations of hostility toward Islam in Christian Europe, as we can already
find traces of it as early as in St John of Damascus's *De Haeresibus* (676–749)
but also in Malcolm's *History of Persia*.[85] Hourani summarizes this religious
hostility in these terms: "Islam is a false religion, Allah is not God, Muhammad was not a prophet; Islam was invented by men whose motives and character were to be deplored, and *propagated by the sword*" (my emphasis).[86]
Browne's penchant for Zoroastrianism was just as much an expression of cultural bias: he admitted his ignorance about it but was well disposed toward it
because he associated it with Christianity. Of anti-Islamic feelings in orientalist writings, there is ample discussion in the next chapter; what matters here is
to place these views in the context of the reevaluation of the Islamic conquest
of Iran as a loss, a certain inclination toward the pre-Islamic past, and an
almost complete disregard for the achievements of Islamic Iran. The above
quotations suggest that from the eighteenth century onward, modern European
thinkers tended to be well disposed toward Zoroastrianism. It may have started
with the favorable picture painted by the seventeenth-century traveler Jean-
Baptiste Tavernier, who compared Zoroastrianism to Christianity.[87] The
combination of this sympathy for Zoroastrianism and the conventional antipathy toward Islam can partly explain their reading of the advent of Islam to
Iran. According to Nora Firby, who has investigated the perception of Zoroastrianism among early modern European travelers, this inclination toward
Zoroastrianism might have proceeded from other expedients as well:

Voltaire, Diderot, Holbach and other philosophes used religious polem-
ics in their anti-clerical struggle against the domination of the Church in
France. They hoped to find a non-Christian civilized society whose laws
were not based upon a revealed religion. China appeared such a society
to the 18th century rationalist. Ancient Persia seemed another. Voltaire

joined in the arguments about the nature of Zoroaster. There was, however, little recent information other than the accounts of Tavernier and
Chardin. Zoroastrianism was treated as a natural, not revealed religion
by Abbé Méhégan. Sylvain Maréchal in his Dictionnaire des Athées
included Zoroaster.[88]

As pointed out by Firby, this enthusiasm did not initially originate in genuine knowledge of Zoroastrianism but was rather instrumentalized within a
European (in this case French) religious polemic. This instrumentalization
acquired a life of its own, and actual knowledge of Zoroastrianism came to be
treated with skepticism: Voltaire, Denis Diderot, and even the orientalist Sir
William Jones scornfully dismissed the manuscript of the Zend-Avesta, which
the explorer and orientalist Abraham Hyacinthe Anquetil-Duperron brought
back from his voyage to India in the 1760s.[89] As a result, some inclination for
Zoroastrianism—informed or misinformed—persisted among many orientalist authors well into the twentieth century (in, for instance, Browne's writings)
and fed into the historiographical narrative surrounding the dramatic end of
Iran's glorious pre-Islamic past.

The legacy of classical historiography can provide another element to elucidate why many orientalists had more favorable views of Iran's pre-Islamic
past. Orientalist authors whose writings would inform Akhundzadeh and
Kermani had often been classicists before turning their attention toward the
"orient." Their surveys reached the orient through Rome and Greece, so to
speak. Such was the case of George Rawlinson, who started off teaching ancient
history at Oxford, and whose first major publication was his translation of the
Histories of Herodotus in 1858–1860. Classics were part of the cultural baggage
of the European literate classes throughout the nineteenth century and beyond, and historians, philologists, and archaeologists were of course particularly exposed to this tradition. This legacy involved, at least, a reading command of Latin and Greek and knowledge of the classical antiquities. Classicists
in this period could not escape the determining imprint of Edward Gibbon
and his monumental History of the Decline and Fall of the Roman Empire
(1776–1789), which loomed large over the entire field of ancient history. Gibbon
expressed in the clearest possible terms the views of many classicists before
and after him, for whom the classical age represented the climax of European civilization, later destroyed by what Gibbon termed "the triumph of
barbarism and religion" leading to the "dark ages."[90]

This view resonates with both the European scholarship of Iran and the
later writings of Iranian nationalism: a barbarous organized religion that in-

hibited science and progress took the place of a classical age of grandeur and enlightenment. Whatever these dark ages produced pales in comparison to that classical past of refinement, freethinking, and philosophy. It seems plausible that European historians who have evaluated the advent of Islam to Iran as a loss may have projected this Gibbonian view of European history upon the ancient East, even though it is hardly deniable that it was in the early centuries of Islam that science and erudition radiated from that part of the world. The assumption that the arson of fanaticism destroyed ancient Iranian books—as advanced by Browne, Manekji, and nationalist authors alike—can be similarly taken as an indication that European scholars nourished by classicism projected episodes of classical European or Christian history onto Iran. Such arson is, for instance, associated with the early history of Christianity, especially in the alleged destruction of the holdings of the Library of Alexandria by zealous Christians, but not of the Islamic conquest of Iran. As it is often the case with orientalism and nationalism, we step onto the realm of assumptions, rather than historical facts. It should be mentioned that Gibbon's *Decline and Fall* was partly translated into Persian by Mirza Reza Mohandes as part of a number of translations commissioned by Abbas Mirza as early as the second quarter of the nineteenth century.[91]

Both Akhundzadeh and Kermani boast about the scientific achievements of ancient Iranians, most of which they invent. Kermani at times seems to suggest that ancient Iran was as advanced as contemporary Europe because it allegedly produced trousers, chariots, and canons.[92] The period following the advent of Islam seems to be entirely devoid of any such scientific feat. Yet, in reality, it was during the first centuries of Islam that learned men from the Iranian plateau—but usually of Arabic expression—made a lasting impact on science, especially medicine and mathematics. Muhammad ibn Mūsā al-Khwarizmi's (AD 780–850) work introduced the decimal positional number system to Europe, and the terms "algebra" and "algorithm" are the results of his contribution to the field. Muhammad ibn Zakariyā al-Razi (Rhazes, AD 864–925), who first distinguished smallpox from measles and was dubbed "perhaps the greatest clinician of all times," introduced chemical preparations into the practice of medicine and remained the "undisputable authority on medicine" in Europe until the seventeenth century.[93] Abū al-Rayhān al-Biruni (AD 973–1048) introduced scientific method in fields as diverse as mechanics and mineralogy and is considered by some to be the "first anthropologist."[94] Ibn Sina (Avicenna, AD 980–1037), had a great impact on medicine as well as philosophy. His *Canon of Medicine* was used as a textbook in European universities until modern times. Many others could be mentioned.

The great Muslim Iranian historians Tabari and Beyhaqi left a deep imprint on their field and have not a single match in pre-Islamic Iran. That Akhundzadeh and Kermani wholly ignored the achievements of Iranian Muslim scholars may be taken as meaning that they replicated the European classicist view that antiquity was the age of science and advancement followed by a dark age in which religion inhibited progress. Although such views can hold some truth in a European context, they boldly run against historical facts when artificially transplanted onto the "East."

In view of this, I suggest that it was European sources that initially provided a prototypical new reading of Iranian history or a template decidedly revolving around the glories of the pre-Islamic period. Consider another passage from Malcolm and the conspicuous manner in which Akhundzadeh has replicated it in the first pages of his *Maktubāt*, which we discuss in chapter 2: we are told "in Grecian history [in Xenophon, to be precise], that ancient Persia was inhabited by a wise and enlightened race of men, who lived under a just government; and we read in Scripture, that the laws of the Medes and Persians were unchangeable."[95] The parallels to be drawn between the founding texts of Iranian nationalism and orientalist views of Iranian history—here the reference to the Greeks, the wisdom of Iranian kings, and the justness of their laws—are striking. It would be fanciful to claim that it might have been orientalist scholars who were in fact emulating texts of the kinds of Kermani. Orientalist scholars had nothing to learn from them and based all their works on ancient sources and the findings of their fellow European scholars. They would occasionally report and comment on contemporary Iranian writings like Browne did on Kermani, but with a degree of disdain—certainly not a desire for imitation.[96] Talking specifically of Kermani's work—this "literary curiosity," as he called it—Browne described it as "one unbroken diatribe against the Arabs, Islám and the post-Muhammadan dynasties of Persia" before mocking the author's "extravagant etymologies."[97] The work of the dislocative author is, according to Browne, "depressing to the last degree."

There is, however, one qualification to my argument on the European origins of the pre-Islamic frenzy. The inclination of European authors such as Montesquieu or Browne for Zoroastrianism was most probably informed by, in addition to the brief accounts of Chardin and Tavernier, the work of Abraham Hyacinthe Anquetil-Duperron (1731–1806), who introduced the European learned public to the Zend-Avesta and produced the first translation of the Zoroastrian sacred texts in French. Anquetil-Duperron's writings display some appreciation of the Zoroastrian faith and some admiration for Zarathustra, whom he considered "a sublime spirit."[98] Anquetil-Duperron's work did not emerge in the void but was extensively informed by two Zoroastrian priests, Dastur Darab and Dastur Kavus, thanks to whose training he acquired knowledge of Zoroastrian texts during his time in Surat among the Parsis of Gujarat from 1755 to 1761. In other words, Anquetil-Duperron's assessment of Zoroastrianism could be rooted in the Parsi teachings he received in Surat, rather than being the pure product of a European mind. In a discussion of orientalism's "genesis amnesia," Tavakoli-Targhi has convincingly argued that orientalist literature has portrayed Anquetil-Duperron and others like him as European "pioneers" who have unlocked knowledge about the East without any participation or input from the silent and passive Oriental.[99] To highlight the importance of local knowledge in the formation of orientalist understanding, Tavakoli-Targhi discusses the pivotal influence of his Parsi masters on the maturing of Anquetil-Duperron's erudition and the preexisting intellectual traditions of India's Parsis, without which Anquetil-Duperron would not have been able to achieve his work.

However, this is only one part of the story, and it should be emphasized that Anquetil-Duperron did not display hostility toward Islam but instead encouraged his fellow Europeans to use rationalism to reconsider their antagonism toward Islam.[100] Although the Indian origin of Anquetil-Duperron's views of Zoroastrianism should be acknowledged, it remains that the Iranian nationalist infatuation with pre-Islamic Iran stems from the discovery of European scholarship by Akhundzadeh, Kermani, and Jalal ed-Din Mirza before them. Once the adaptation of orientalist views had already taken place and archaism was firmly established within some circles, then Iranian literati rediscovered the local sources discussed earlier, including the *dasātiri* texts, which were linguistically and culturally more accessible to most of them. Local sources therefore followed, rather than initiated, the archaistic movement in Iran and allowed for the orientalist view of Iranian history to be articulated with local referents. What is remarkable in the transfer of European views of Iranian history to Iran itself is that ideas that would have seemed anathema to any Iranian only a few decades earlier started to find a foothold, although in a small circle at first.

SUBALTERNITY AND THE QUEST FOR DIGNITY

Dislocative nationalism's characteristic obsession with the pre-Islamic past at the expense of the equally eventful period following the advent of Islam did not have any precedent in an established Iranian narrative. It was informed by a proposition put forth in European sources and derived from assumptions and biases specific to European scholarship at the time. The prevalent European hostility toward Islam had a strong bearing over the narrative of invasion, destruction, and decay. It was previously rooted in theological considerations, chiefly the refutation of Islam's claims to holiness and the dismissal of the Prophet Muhammad as an impostor. The propagation of Islam through the sword was another criticism leveled at it, as we saw earlier. That Islam might have an inherent appeal, justifying its status as one of the world's major religions, was of course ignored altogether. Later, as we saw, new discourses emerged from the late eighteenth century onward, in which power inequality and essentialization loomed large. Orientalist scholars, by applying this new lens that still carried remnants of the old theological hostility toward Islam, came to naturally display favorable views of what they perceived to be non-Islamic in Iran: its pre-Islamic past and Zoroastrianism. In this process biblical sources praising Cyrus the Great certainly played an important role, but eighteenth-century texts by Herder, Montesquieu, and Anquetil-Duperron, among others, helped define new standards of interpretation. A racial element would become prominent later in the nineteenth century, suggesting that Iranians were racially related to Europeans but subdued by the contamination of that evil of all evils: Islam.

The classicist view of antiquity gained traction following the Renaissance and the recovery of ancient Greek and Latin texts, which came to serve as models for a new mode of production of knowledge. It ran in parallel to an increasing emphasis on reason (as opposed to the otherworldly Christian dogma) as the key to unlock the principles of nature and human society. Rationalism led to a growing attitude of skepticism toward religion among Enlightenment authors. God was now at best a "watchmaker god" who set the complex mechanism of the universe in place and then allowed it to function according to its own principles, refusing to intervene in its workings. In some cases such as Gibbon's, but also that of most Enlightenment *philosophes*, this changing outlook brought about a somewhat exaggerated degree of contempt for the Middle Ages, considered to be the antithesis of the scientific spirit of the "Elders," Romans and Greeks. This classicist reading of European history, with its categories, conventions, and preconceptions, was projected onto Iran's past, bringing about the historical narrative of Islamic rupture and decay with which the reader is now familiar. In fact, the historiography of pre-Islamic and Islamic Iran is illustrative of the subalternity of Iranian historians. This historiography represents an *external* reading of the Iranian past that is embraced and reproduced by local historians who in fact never took part in its elaboration. The logic and dynamics of that historiography are not theirs: they have simply adopted them.

Postcolonial authors led by Gayatri Spivak have emphasized since the 1980s that much of the historiography of the third world is made of a Western hegemonic discourse.[101] Thus, the local people—generally colonized—are not only politically subaltern but also intellectually dominated and passive. For example, the history of the British Raj has been traditionally produced using sources left behind by the colonizer, thereby silencing the local ordinary Indian whose history was being written (hence Spivak's aphorism "Can the Subaltern Speak?") Although we are not here concerned with a period of European colonialism, the problem of sources is every bit as relevant: Orientalists used Greek, Latin, and Biblical sources in addition to the works of fellow Europeans. They conveniently ignored what the inhabitants of the Iranian plateau ever had to say about the advent of Islam or their pre-Islamic past (I will come back to the case of Ferdowsi's *Shāhnāmeh*). However, I would like to digress from the conventional postcolonial interpretation whereby the historiography produced by Europeans was hegemonic and somewhat imposed itself on the subaltern. It seems to me that nationalist historians willingly and wholeheartedly *embraced* the European historiography of Iran because it could help them address a specific predicament. Their purpose was the recovery of Iran's dignity after the traumatic discovery by Qajar intellectuals that their country lagged behind Europe.

One has to imagine the state of mind of the literate few in the Qajar era, for whom the trauma of the encounter with Europe begged for a remedy. Despair transpires from many texts already quoted in this book, from Abbas Mirza and Qa'em Maqam Farahani to later nationalist authors. A cultural elite whose forefathers lived in complacency, confident in the superiority of the Persian language, its high culture, and—it is important to emphasize—Islam, was denied this comfort and thrown into a competition with an impregnable adversary. A palatable explanation could serve as a cure, albeit discursive and expedient. Theirs was a distressing quest for dignity, and while some advocated reform along modernist lines and developed concrete reform programs to drag Iran out of "backwardness," others, like Jalal ed-Din Mirza, Akhundzadeh, Kermani, and many more who followed, took the easier path of historicist narratives and intellectual shortcuts.

When Akhundzadeh encountered orientalist texts, one can imagine his delight to discover that it was the past of that same wretched land that European scholars praised to the sky. That it was the sacrosanct science of *farangiyān*

(Europeans)—those same who, according to him, were "knowledgeable" and "civilized" and who had brought about a "downpour of science"[102]—who offered such a flattering appraisal of Iran's past could only assuage the deeply affected minds of the Qajar literati. These views were not only pleasant, they were convenient, legitimate, and even indisputable (one will have to wait until the emergence of nativism in the 1960s to see Iranian authors adopt a critical stance against Western scholarship). Akhundzadeh and Kermani evoke Europe with awe. In their texts, Europeans were the only people spared by a harsh and unremitting harangue; they represented the highest possible degree of wisdom and human development. It is thus the extraordinary status of European scholarship combined with the tormented attempt on the part of the literati to make sense of Iran's ills that gave such an appeal to archaism and explains its later generalization in nationalist historiography (and indeed historiography *tout court*). In this quest for dignity, the orientalist view of Iran's past was immensely reassuring. Grandeur was cast as an inherent part of Iran's heritage and therefore its ontological destiny.

Yet it must be emphasized that in their adoption of the European view of pre-Islamic Iran, our authors used a great deal of creativity. The result was a complex hybrid product that was in many ways novel. Akhundzadeh and Kermani indigenized their accounts of pre-Islamic Iran by using the general framework of orientalist scholarship but placing familiar signposts borrowed from the mythistorical tradition and the "kings of Ajam" literature—hence the names of legendary heroes and kings that come up regularly. What was the purpose of this complex work of hybridization? Akhundzadeh's and Kermani's vision of a society that knows no poverty, ruled by quasi-divine faultless kings, where no death penalty is applied, and where prisoners of war are treated with clemency was meant to be an ideal, a utopia of sorts, dragged from a distant imaginary past to pose as a future objective for a mass ideology. Today historians of ancient Iran in fact emphasize continuities—political, institutional, cultural, and even religious—between pre-Islamic and Islamic Iran.[103] One would not, of course, judge Akhundzadeh and Kermani by the standards of today's scholarship; however, one is warranted to note that the two authors— undoubtedly purposefully—ignored Iranian sources available to them that contradicted their idealization of pre-Islamic Iran. Even a cursory glance at the chapters of the *Shāhnāmeh* treating that period reveals a stark contrast. Under Ferdowsi's pen, this period also knew despotic rulers devoid of the "divine grace" (*farr-e izadi*), thus indulging in wars, killings, and filicides before falling victim to regicide.

The fantasies and outlandish exaggerations of ancient Iran's achievements that one finds in Akhundzadeh's and Kermani's pages are meant to mutate that era into a Golden Age embodying the Iranian essence, an essence that they want as worthy and prodigious as possible. They also mean it to become an ideal toward which the nation can march in the future. I would like to come back here to John Breuilly's definition of nationalist ideology to propose the reasons behind Akhundzadeh's and Kermani's purposeful and far from accidental manipulation of this period of Iranian history. According to Breuilly, a nationalist ideology is a simplified version of philosophers' reflection on the predicaments of a particular society.[104] As the philosophers' response is often not immediately intelligible for large masses of people, they are simplified and come to be embodied in symbols and ceremonies in which everybody can partake: thus, a nationalist ideology can command mass mobilization. Many Qajar intellectuals were concerned to make their recipes for the regeneration of Iran understandable to the common man: this is why Malkam Khan, for instance, wrapped his philosophy in a religious language to which the ordinary people could relate. It seems as if Qajar intellectuals were aware of the necessity to produce a readily adoptable ideology (in Breuilly's sense) if their thought was to have any real impact. Similarly, Akhundzadeh and Kermani crafted a historicist narrative that commands authority because it is informed by European scholarship in its praises of the pre-Islamic past but is familiar to most Iranians in its form because it is indebted to the "histories of the kings of Ajam" genre (like the *Shāhnāmeh*). Most importantly, it provides the reader with the assurance that Iran was a great nation and Iranians an exalted people. The dignity is thus salvaged, and the two authors' insistence on the wretched state of contemporary Iran aims to somewhat awaken the nation and force them to toil and recreate the Golden Age.

The racial take on Iranian identity must now come up for scrutiny to shed further light on the ideological apparatus of nationalism as defined by Akhundzadeh and Kermani and its antagonistic view of the Arab "other."

4

OF LIZARD EATERS AND INVASIONS
THE IMPORT OF EUROPEAN RACIAL THOUGHT

A nation is a group of people united by a mistaken view of their past and a hatred of their neighbours.

— Karl Deutsch, 1969

DISLOCATIVE NATIONALISM'S INTENSE ARAB-HATRED HAS RARELY been adequately acknowledged, let alone analyzed, by scholarship.[1] The consistent approach within the literature sympathetic to nationalism has been either to sweep it under the rug, minimize its implication, or justify it. In his hagiographies of Akhundzadeh and Kermani, Fereydun Adamiyat, for instance, glosses over the nationalist authors' racial hatred, presents it as a "cultural and social phenomenon," and warns that if "some people simply disagree" with the opinions of these authors, this "only reveals their own intellectual deficiency."[2] In more serious academic circles, it has been acknowledged that Iranian nationalists have attempted to "dissociate Iran from Islam," but the reason of this dissociation and the sources used to conceptualize it have not been investigated.[3] Against this background, it is all the more important to stress that hatred of Arabs in the founding texts of Iranian nationalism is intense and often shockingly violent. Its rationale is also unusually out of touch with tangible geopolitical realities. At the time when Akhundzadeh and Kermani wrote, Arabs were not by any stretch of the imagination a threat to Iran. Arab nationalism had not yet taken definite shape, and even when it did, it never concerned itself with Iranians but with Ottomans in the first instance and, later, Western imperialism. This hatred is therefore not rooted in a concrete reality of physical threat as would be the case with the Korean suspicion of the Japanese, for instance, or that of the Irish for the English. Rather, the figure of the Arab serves a purpose similar to that of a voodoo doll: by cursing it, the nationalist imagination relieves the pains of Iran's decline into backwardness. The whole process really takes place in the realm of the imagination. As such, this hatred—and the term is an understatement—deserves serious investigation.

Arab-hatred has triggered a reformulation of the self and other in the nationalist imaginary. In particular, entrenched religious, cultural, or even linguistic practices have been in retrospect otherized, reinterpreted as Arab in origin, and therefore unsuitable for Iranians. The arbitrariness with which this view draws the boundary between Arabness and Iranianness is worthy of note, and so is the categorical refusal to take note of the large gray areas between the two. Indeed, although for most of history Arabs and Iranians were at least linguistically distinguished, centuries of active and arguably keen interaction within the multicultural Islamic space has engendered complex cultural practices that cannot be clearly defined as Arab or Iranian or even Turkish, as all three people have shared into them. How can one, for instance, neatly attribute a certain word to the Arabic language when Iranians and Turks have used it for more than a millennium, contributed to its definition, and even in some instances indigenized its meaning, pronunciation, or spelling? Equally problematic is the branding of a universal phenomenon such as Islam as part of the heritage of a particular people, when in fact a diverse group of devotees stretching across national boundaries have contributed to its theological, philosophical, and cultural content. When applied retrospectively to history, modern national categories can only create aberrations and inaccuracies because these categories are falsely neat whereas historical reality is always subtle if not blurry.

Jalal ed-Din Mirza did nurture hostility against Arabs, and he depicted them in his work as Iran's enemies.[4] Akhundzadeh, however, was one step ahead, as he already portrayed Iranians and Arabs as opposites. He praised the former's glories to the sky and demeaned the latter. Yet Akhundzadeh never clearly referred to race in its modern cultural-biological sense. It is really in Kermani's work that the modern idea of race and the distinction between Aryan and Semite start to appear. In Akhundzadeh and Kermani, Arabs and Iranians are not discussed as two groups that may not share the same language and cultural practices; they are seen as opposite, conflicting races. Both authors offer a description of their respective "nature," understood as immutable.[5] In texts quoted in chapter 2, ancient Iranians, before degenerating into some sort of miscegenated Iranian-Arabs, are described as having no short-comings and being free-minded, "respected," "virtuous," law-abiding, "cho-sen among all peoples," even-handed, dignified, and prosperous. Arabs, on the other hand, were and immutably are, "naked," "bare-arse," "hungry," des-potic, fanatic, "liars," "creators of tales," "thieves," "animal-like," "uncivi-lized," "savage," and their diet is composed of lizards. Iranian and Arab are irreconcilable, and their miscegenation can only produce a sordid despotic society such as that of Islamic Iran, whose glories and achievements, admired literature, traditions of mysticism, architectural feats, mathematical and med-ical discoveries, spiritual syncretism, and even political power in times like those of the Safavids are passed over in silence.

Given the nature of the topic, this chapter must take liberties with the chronological conventions of history writing and operate several temporal shifts; it does seem to be the best way to analyze the subject at hand.

DID FERDOWSI AND *SHUʿUBIS* LOATHE ARABS?

Dislocative nationalists have consistently contended that animosity toward Arabs is yet another ancient and perennial feature of Iranianness.[6] This is hardly surprising: nationalist thought being modern while concurrently preoccupied with the ancient past, it is generally prone to anachronism. It presumes that the inhabitants of the Iranian plateau in ancient times shared modern Irani-ans' identity—of course, exclusively couched in national and racial terms; ex-cluded local, religious, or tribal allegiances; and abided by the same modern prejudices and historicist constructs. Claims to antiquity derive from the un-critical projection of modern discourses and sentiments onto the ancient past. For all its retrospective nationalism, the allegation of antique hostility deserves some attention as it cannot be brushed aside by a simple reference to the mo-dernity of nationalism, which is itself subject to debate.

It is contended in nationalist ranks that Ferdowsi sang the glories of the pre-Islamic past and was an Iranian nationalist, opposed to Islam and hostile to Arabs.[7] Akhundzadeh and Kermani, who quoted at length from those verses of the *Shāhnāmeh* that seem to disparage Arabs, first formulated these claims, which were then taken up by an unbroken chain of loyal disciples down to this very day.[8] Although these verses ("From drinking camel milk and eating lizard / The Arab's fortune has reached the point / That he wishes for the Per-sian crown") seem to lend themselves to such a reading, a close and impartial

look at the *Shāhnāmeh* reveals a different picture. First, it should be emphasized that experts including Abolfazl Khatibi believe that this passage is a
later addition and was not included in the original *Shāhnāmeh* text.[9] Even
assuming that such was not the case, there are several other flaws in the dislocative nationalist claim. The speaker of the verses quoted is Rostam, son of
Farrokhzad, one of the *Shāhnāmeh*'s heroes. He was a Sasanian military commander, who for obvious reasons dreaded the victory of Islamic forces over his
own. Attributing these words to Ferdowsi himself amounts to a distortion of
sources: authorial intention cannot be attributed to the protagonists of a plot
in such a cavalier manner.[10] Who would claim that all the lines of Pierre
Bezukhov, Prince Andrei, and Natasha in *War and Peace* can be taken for a
reflection of Leo Tolstoy's personal opinions? The same authors that take
these verses at face value then go on to claim that Ferdowsi's personal profession of Islam should be ignored, that it is a false admission imposed upon him
by his "environment" (more below). Such an approach to the text should
rather be taken as suggesting that dislocative nationalist authors have consistently tried to force the *Shāhnāmeh* into their narrative, rather than analyze
its content with objectivity.

If there was a consistent disparaging of Arabs in Ferdowsi's work, one could
perhaps take these claims seriously. This is not the case, however, particularly
as shown in the Bahram Gur episode. Ferdowsi presents Bahram Gur as one
of the wisest kings of Iran. As a child, he was entrusted by his father to Monzer,
an Arab king who raised him to adulthood. This episode is narrated without
an ounce of animosity toward Arabs, quite the contrary. Yemen is favorably
described as a peaceful land where Arabs and Iranians coexist side by side. It
is suggested that, had Bahram Gur remained with his Iranian father, the
sinful King Yazdegerd, he would have grown into an unjust ruler himself. It is
his upbringing in Yemen in this Arabian court that made him into an upright
sovereign. The Arab Monzer in particular is depicted as a wise, generous, and
kind king. Dislocative nationalists have stood clear from quoting those passages because they do not serve their purpose.

Dick Davis, who published a much-praised English edition of the
Shāhnāmeh, has taken notice of other ambiguities in Ferdowsi's treatment of
Arabs:

> Although the poet is emphatic in his lament for the civilisation that was
> destroyed by the invasion, his depiction of the negotiations between the
> Arabs and the Persians seems at times weighted in the Arabs' moral favor.

It is difficult to read the scene in which the laconic and almost naked Arab envoy Sho'beh confronts the arrogant Persian commanders, resplendent in their golden armor, as anything but an indictment of the Persians. . . . In the ascetic unconcern of the Arab warrior Sho'beh it . . . brings home the virtues of spartan simplicity, the laconic uncluttered force that an attitude of *contemptu mundi* can bring with it. . . . In a brief scene of great richness and with consummate skill Ferdowsi sees and conveys both the glamor of the civilization that is dying and the valor of the new civilization that is emerging.[11]

Davis has also pointed out that the *Shāhnāmeh's* legendary sections (generally assumed to be Parthian in origin) and quasi-historical section (dating from Sasanian times) deal differently with the matter of "ethnic identity." The "details of the *Shāhnāmeh's* legendary narratives quickly dispose of any notions of ethnic purity as being a prerequisite of an Iranian identity," as the lineage of the kings and heroes that we are invited to admire can be traced as much to Iran as to demons or to Iran's traditional enemy of the pre-Sasanian period: Turan or Central Asia (and not Arabs, who were neither the only enemies, nor the traditional enemies, nor the eternal enemies).[12] The "paradigmatically perfect Iranian king" Key Khosrow descends from Afrasiyab the king of Turan ("the perpetual enemy of Iran"), the hero Rostam descends from the demon king Zahhak (the mythological snake man) through his Kabuli mother; similarly almost all the women named in this section are non-Iranians from "India, from Turan, from Rum, or from Hamaveran," but are shown in a positive light.[13] Moreover, if the foreign "gives birth to the poem's heroes" (Rostam, Sohrab, Siyavash, Key Khosrow), it is the Iranian—their own, as it were—that either directly destroys them or more obliquely ensures their destruction" (reference to the deaths of Rostam, Sohrab, Esfandiyar, Siyavash, Dara, and Yazdegerd III).[14] This is all rather surprising for an epic poem supposed to celebrate the national ethos and condone the racial Manichaeism of its modern admirers. That being said, the quasi-historical section does convey a more Sasanian version of Iranianness. In that section, miscegenation is regarded with suspicion (as in the cases of Hormozd and Shirui), and as far as foreign women are concerned, "they are much less welcome than they had been in the legendary narrative.[15]

This seems to point toward a less straightforward treatment of ethnicity in the *Shāhnāmeh*: it is trivial in the pre-Sasanian sources and becomes paramount in the sections that reflect Sasanian views—the views of the Sasanian elite and state, as it were. Therefore, all the passages that have traditionally been associated with some form of patriotism (such as the famous line "without Iran, my body would not exist," or *cho Irān nabāshad tan-e man mabād*) should not be so much attributed to Ferdowsi or to widespread popular feelings among the subjects of the Sasanians, but rather to a reflection of the Sasanian elite's worldview. It is thus essential to recognize that the *Shāhnāmeh* is a complex work reflecting multiple sources, rather than the expression of the personal convictions of a Ferdowsi, the zeitgeist of early Islamic Iran, or the timeless aspirations of all Iranians.[16]

A word should also be said of Zahhak, the serpent man whose origins go back to Avestan sources. As we saw, Zahhak is the ancestor of Rostam, and he is treated in some length in the *Shāhnāmeh*. He is an adaptable figure whose name, nature, and origins changed over time through re-associations that allow him to consistently remain the "other" to the Iranians, the embodiment of what is alien to them.[17] In the ninth century AD, Zahhak became Arabized in some sources, including the *Shāhnāmeh*. Yet, although it could be argued that the Zahhak episode of the *Shāhnāmeh* displays antipathy toward Arabs through its condemnation of Zahhak's nature, this claim should be to some extent qualified. In the *Shāhnāmeh* narrative (and let us bear in mind that it differs from other sources as it somewhat emphasizes the serpent man's foreign origin), the cause of the evil in him is not his lineage, even less race, but predominantly the spell that the devil has cast upon him, which manifests itself through the presence of two serpents on his shoulders—outgrowth of his own body—whose hunger must be satisfied through the daily offering of human brains. Moreover, in the *Shāhnāmeh* he does not invade Iran but is invited by its inhabitants to rid them of King Jamshid. His army is also made up of Iranians as much as Arabs (*tāzis*), and Kaveh the Blacksmith's main motivation to lead a rebellion against him, rather than some form of racial antipathy, is the fact that he has fed seventeen of his sons to Zahhak's serpents.

To demonstrate the permanence of hostility between Iranians and Arabs, nationalists also refer to a historical episode, that of the *shuʿubiyah*, a late-eighth and ninth-century AD literary controversy over the position of Arabs and non-Arabs within Islam. The *shuʿubiyah* has been refashioned into a nationalist awakening of Iranians against Arab oppression. Unsurprisingly, a European work is at the origin of this claim: *Muhammedanische studien* (Mohammedan Studies: 1889–1890) by Hungarian orientalist Ignaz Goldziher. Goldziher, whose influential works on Islam are classics, was writing in the midst of the nationalist fever in the Austro-Hungarian Empire. In a fashion

typical of so many nineteenth-century authors, he projected a modern interpretive perspective—European and nationalizing, in essence—onto the distant past and distant lands, presuming that all conflicts were necessarily about
flag and country.[18] Akhundzadeh and Kermani came too early to be aware of
Goldziher's work, but later dislocative nationalist authors made extensive use
of this view of the *shu'ubiyah* to argue that it was some form of nationalist
struggle. Jalal Homaei, though he was not a dislocative nationalist and was a
pious man, asserted in 1934 that "the greatest Iranian movement, which lastly
uprooted, and brought about the complete downfall of the Arab rule, was the
shu'ubiyah movement."[19] A close look at the *shu'ubiyah*, however, seems to indicate—as pointed out by Roy Mottahedeh—that

> [the movement's remains] provide very little evidence of any overt po-
> litical aspirations on the part of the *shu'ubis*. The *shu'ubiyah* was primar-
> ily a literary controversy, and if it was used on rare occasions by political
> movements with a noticeable "ethnic" (or regional) character like the Saf-
> farids, most *shu'ubis* were not political and were, as often as not, faithful
> servants of the caliphate.[20]

According to Mottahedeh, the bulk of the *corpus* of the *shu'ubiyah* was concerned "with points of honor and dishonor in the customs and past of the
Arabs and of the peoples they had conquered." As such, the polemic is

> a treasure trove of information on the curiosities of pre-Islamic life such
> as the nature of the *miswak*, the proto-toothbrush used by the pre-Islamic
> Arabs and Persians. . . . But anyone who hopes to find in a tract on the
> *shu'ubiyah* sentiments like: "I regret that I have but one life to give for my
> country" will . . . be severely disappointed. After reading countless discus-
> sions as to whether lizards were a food of choice to the ancient Arabs, or
> whether ancient Persians relished the brother-sister or mother-son mar-
> riages which were sanctioned by Zoroastrianism, it becomes clear that
> the central issues for the *shu'ubis* were not overtly political; that is, they
> were not primarily concerned with the creation of new governments.[21]

Mottahedeh and other scholars have therefore demoted the *shu'ubiyah* to a
peripheral issue and concluded that it says little about the questions that
"scholars have traditionally associated with it": it was not a "concerted movement with leaders, a program and spokesmen."[22] Richard Frye concurs and

suggests that the ethnic friction seen in the *shu'ubiyah* is not supported by the broader trends of this period either: "The elevation of literary diatribes to an almost cosmic conflict between two different cultures or approaches seems to me to be exaggerated . . . if the stakes had been so great the cleavage would have dominated the religious controversies . . . plus the political and social life of the caliphate, which it certainly did not."[23]

Moreover, the *shu'ubiyah* was restricted to a small literary elite in Baghdad, and all its actors were devout Muslims. None of them is known to have disparaged Islam. This should not be taken to mean that previously Omayyad ruling elites did not abuse their position as Arabs (which was a tribal category). It is incontrovertible that a large portion of the *shu'ubiyah* polemicists were people tracing their origins to a broadly Arab or Iranian heritage, calling each other names (they were not alone, as occasionally poets such as Abu Nuwas or a number of Mu'tazilite writers also disparaged Arabs in their writings[24]). But here we are neither dealing with a racist trope in the modern sense, which would consider races to be biologically, culturally, or psychologically distinct and incompatible, nor a nationalist uprising along racial lines. There was no attempt to categorize cultural or linguistic practices as "Arab" or "Persian" and argue their incompatibility. This is rather a classic case of ethnic stereotyping caused by rivalry between different groups competing for power within the same religious and political order. The very distinction between Arab and Iranian was far more obscured in premodern times. As noted by Frye:

> The impossibility of making clear divisions between Arabs and Persians during the Abbasid caliphate . . . is illustrated by an Arab poet praising the Persians, while Zamakhshari, the famous non-Arab philologist (d. 538/1144), as the last voice in the controversy bitterly attacked the *Shu'ubiya*. Al-Biruni, the great scholar of the Ghaznavid period, was proud of Iranian antiquities, but he praised the Arabic language. The Tahirids were Persian governors of [Khorasan] who were the first to rule independently of the caliphs, yet they were great patrons of Arabic. [Nasser Khosrow], a Persian poet and traveller said, in Persian, that the Arabs excelled the Persians in glory! The list of pro- and anti-Arabs is remarkable in that it includes Arabs and Iranians on both sides.[25]

Mottahedeh and Frye's findings seem to point to another direction, that people who may have called themselves Arabs or Iranians (*'Ajam*) were not as inherently antagonistic to each other as dislocative nationalists claim. There was occasional discord, but they lived in and served the same multicultural polity, in which the languages as well as administrative practices of all enjoyed a status, however different or competing. Most importantly, they rarely if ever openly questioned the Islamic faith. In fact, although the remaining Zoroastrians had been relegated to ghettoes, most heresies in the history of Islam were the result of syncretism between Islam and Zoroastrianism with both Iranians and Arabs at their heads. In sum, Ferdowsi or the Iranian *shuʿubiyah* authors can hardly be taken for the vanguards of some anti-Arab nationalist movement, and the very systematic and intense anti-Arab sentiments of Iranian nationalists do not stem from established and perennial Iranian customs and beliefs. It is therefore likely that Arab-hatred appeared later and had other sources.

ARABS, ISLAM, AND RACIAL ESSENTIALIZATION

Similarly to the cult of pre-Islamic Iran, the proposition that Iranians and Arabs are racially or culturally incompatible, the idea that Islam is the product of the "Semitic mind" only suitable to Arabs, and the claim that the advent of Islam amounted to an "Arab invasion" primarily aiming to force the Arabic language and culture—of which Islam was a part—upon the people of Iran had no currency in Persianate texts prior to the period under review. Nineteenth-century European scholarship on Iran, on the other hand, is replete with such assertions and imbued with racialism. With the development of natural sciences, racial theories emerged as a means to elucidate the reasons behind human diversity against the backdrop of the European overseas expansion and encounter with different peoples. It should be stressed that racial thinking in Europe was in a constant state of flux, and scientific consensus on a particular theory was always elusive.[26] However, simplified and uninitiated conceptions of racial difference and hierarchy were to be found in popularized writings on history, anthropology, and philology, including in works treating of the "East" and Islam. Orientalist authors used ideas of racial difference to shed light on the history of the "East," but their use of racial theories was not always fully informed or up to date. This had an implication for the even more simplified ideas that will filter through dislocative nationalism.

Akhundzadeh and Kermani had clearly consulted European orientalist texts, particularly those treating of Iran, although we do not know for certain which authors specifically. They never named their sources but rather vaguely referred to "the sages of Europe."[27] In the following I quote from a number of orientalist authors who either wrote about Iran or synthesized racial ideas that had some authority in their time, making it likelier that they directly or indirectly influenced Akhundzadeh and Kermani. The objective is to highlight the affinity between these orientalist texts with the core historicist dogma of dislocative nationalism.

Most orientalist authors racialized Islam into the progeny of the "Semitic mind," which they considered incapable of grasping complex ideas. The Semite's mind was characterized, in the words of Theodor Nöldeke, by "frightful exclusiveness and rigid fanaticism."[28] In his *Sketches From Eastern History* (1892), Nöldeke, who was primarily a Semitist but incidentally also an Iranist, builds on important previous works, especially that of Renan, and can thus be largely considered to express the consensus of the last few decades of the nineteenth century on these questions. Arabs' environment is argued to be "on the one hand, a lawless and highly-divided state of society, in which even the rudiments of political authority are hardly known (as among the ancient and modern Bedouins) and, on the other, unlimited despotism."[29] The racial essentialism that finds a distant echo in Kermani's writings is articulated in the confident language of European science to explain every aspect of the Arab's mind, for instance, his indolence: "As the Semite can hardly be induced, voluntarily, to submit to a strict discipline, he does not, on the whole, make a good soldier." The victories of the armies of Islam in the early centuries are thus attributed to an extraordinary factor, "the enthusiasm generated by a new national religion which promised a heavenly reward, and the allurements which the prospects of booty and of settlement in rich lands offered to the inhabitants of the sterile wilderness."[30]

Moreover—and in an extraordinary negation of empirical facts—the Semite "has only in a few cases contributed anything of importance to science"; according to Nöldeke the Arabs' speculation on "the freedom of the will and similar subjects, [was] very unsystematic and unscientific as long as it was only superficially affected by Greek thought."[31] However, he admits that Semites might have "at least made advances in some matters of detail," such as the mere invention of the alphabet, which he demeans by hesitating to call it "an achievement of science in the proper sense." His conclusion comes as no surprise: "the genius of the Semites is in many respects one-sided, and does not reach the level of some Indo-European nations"; they may have had some success in the past, but "this group of nations has long since passed its prime."[32]

The intimate complicity of these texts with the treatises of dislocative nationalism is made clearer by the use of racial concepts to differentiate Iranians and Arabs within a broader opposition between the Indo-European/Aryans and Semites. Iranians were considered Aryans on account of the linguistic similarities of the Persian language with Indian and European languages. I discuss the modalities of this racial assimilation more in detail in chapter 6. Following this logic, in an intriguing text published in 1852, Ernest Renan went so far as to consider the Iranians the vessels of Greek-European thought, animated by a racial sense of purpose that allowed them to consciously awaken Islam from its Arabian torpor. The fact that Iranians themselves never quite put it in those terms was left aside:

> Imprisoned as all Semitic people are in the narrow circle of lyricism and prophetism, the inhabitants of the Arabian peninsula never had the slightest idea of what can be called science or rationalism. It is when the Persian spirit, represented by the Abbasid dynasty, vanquished the Arab spirit, that Greek philosophy penetrated Islam. Although subjugated by a Semitic religion, Persia always maintained its rights as an Indo-European nation.[33]

It should be stressed that for Akhundzadeh and Kermani, who applied a far neater racial division than even Renan, labeling the Abbasid caliphate Iranian would have been anathema. Regardless of this subtle difference of views, for Renan the two races were endowed with two "perfectly recognizable individualities," so radically different that they represented the "two poles of mankind's movement," and their antagonism defined nothing less than the world in which we live.[34] Although one can occasionally find a handful of *shuʻubiyah* poems in which an Iranian disparages an Arab or vice versa, it is in these European texts that the innate opposition between Iranians and Arabs was for the first time expressed in systematic fashion, allowing Kermani and his nationalist heirs to appropriate it.

Historical interaction and blurred boundaries are refuted in Renan's contention that, to this day, Semites and Indo-Europeans are "perfectly distinct," as if they are from "two different species having nothing in common in the manner of thinking and feeling."[35] In a manner echoing the strategies of Akhundzadeh and Kermani, he uses the *Shāhnāmeh* as a proof of this. He deems Ferdowsi's epic poem to be similar to European mythologies while he believes that "Semites," obsessed by the simplicity of monotheism, are incapable of producing mythology.[36] Demeaning monotheism as "simplistic" is a leitmotiv in this literature. Similarly to dislocative nationalists, Renan daringly recast the compilation of the *Shāhnāmeh* and the emergence of Iranian dynasties in the tenth century AD as some form of nationalist rebellion against Arabs and Islam.[37] These ideas are almost literally appropriated by Kermani. He too celebrates Ferdowsi as a "reviver" of Iran's pre-Islamic heritage: "By composing the *Shāhnāmeh*, Ferdowsi resuscitated the Persian (*majus*) religion and the spirit of Jamshid, and has not allowed national pride to disappear from among the Iranians."[38] Moreover, Kermani also appropriates the proposition that monotheism is evidence of the Semitic mind's simplicity, when claiming that Iranians and Greeks had several gods "unlike Jews and Arabs, whose brains did not contain the latitude (*vos'at dāshtan*) for such poetic ideas."[39] Taken seriously, this argument would mean that polytheist pre-Islamic Arabs were also Indo-European. It should also be noted that most authoritative scholarship, even at the time of Kermani, regarded Zoroastrianism as both a dualistic and monotheistic religion but certainly not polytheistic.[40]

These quotations should not be taken as to mean that Renan and others were blind admirers of Iranians or considered them equal to Europeans. Far from it. Although Iranians were considered to be racially akin, they were still viewed as some debased variety. Gobineau, for instance, believed that the "Iranian nation" was composed of a Persian race under "heavy Semitic and Turkish influence."[41] As for Renan, although he praised the *Shāhnāmeh* in relation to its "Semitic" equivalents, he believed that it could "certainly not be compared to the masterpieces of Greek antiquity."[42] In his words, the *Shāhnāmeh* "is even inferior to the beautiful redactions of our medieval *chansons de geste* and the Indian Epics."[43] In fact, for Renan, the worth of the *Shāhnāmeh* is limited to its use for comparative "ethnographic mythology and psychology," allowing to study the difference between those races by way of comparing "racial" philological traditions.[44] One can find an echo of this dismissal of Iranians in Alfred Rosenberg, the Nazi ideologue who considered Iranians to be a typical case of racial bastardization (*Bastardierung*).[45]

Unfavorable assessment of "Semites" was intimately related to racialized views of Islam. The aversion of a Renan for Islam was intense: "[Islam] is the dreadful simplicity of the Semitic mind, shrinking the human brain, shutting it off from any delicate idea, any subtle feeling, any quest of the rational."[46] In works treating Iran specifically, such ideas were widespread, starting with Malcolm's *History of Persia*. In a typical fashion, Malcolm explained both backwardness and despotism by a simple all-encompassing reference to Islam, rather than by complex sociohistorical factors: "There is no example, during more than twelve centuries, of any Mahomedan nation having attained a high rank in the scale of civilisation. All who have adopted this religion, have invariably been exposed to the miseries of an arbitrary and unsettled rule."[47] Then follows a thesis that is startlingly—and certainly not coincidentally— similar to that of our dislocative nationalist authors: "The history of Persia from the Arabian conquest to the present day proves the truth of these observations: and while the same causes continue to operate, no material change in its condition can be expected."[48] The mere fact of Islam teleologically explains virtually every aspect of Iran's history in a period of more than a millennium, and as long as it is there, no change can happen. The reader is left with the impression that Iran before Islam was a land of liberty entirely devoid of despotism, or that any society that has not adopted Islam holds the beacon of progress.

The story of a young Iranian student in France not only substantiates the claim that nationalism's discourse on Arabs and Islam originated in European thought rather than proceed from local traditions but also illustrates the eagerness with which the Qajar elite, wrestling with the dilemma of backwardness, embraced such ideas. Hossein Qoli Aqa was dispatched to France in 1845 to learn infantry and artillery.[49] According to Gobineau, he was a brilliant student at the Saint-Cyr military academy and defended the Assemblée Nationale during the 1848 Revolution. Gobineau includes Hossein Qoli Aqa in what he calls "free-thinkers" (*libre penseurs*), a term he reserves for a particularly sharp minority among the *"asiatiques"* who had had the chance to be exposed to life in Europe. The ideas they would encounter there would have an impact on their worldview and modify to some extent their "Asiatic" racial predispositions. Gobineau stresses that they would "collect experiences, conceive impressions, and bring back home feelings that they would not have found elsewhere [i.e., in their home countries]."[50] As one of these free-thinking orientals, Hossein Qoli Aqa's views on Islam and Iran's past are of particular interest here: "His hatred for Islamism [i.e., simply Islam] knew no boundaries. He saw in this religion the import and the trace of Arab oppression over his country, and all his sympathy, all his love was for the creed of the *Guèbres* [Zoroastrians], under whom Persia had been so great."[51]

Gobineau leaves no doubt to his reader. Hossein Qoli Aqa acquired his hatred of Islam, the connection he draws between Islam and the Arabs' oppression, and the inclination he has for the pre-Islamic past and Zoroastrianism not in an immediate Iranian experience or in any Iranian source but in Europe, and this worldview could not have been acquired elsewhere:

[Hossein Qoli Aqa] was no exception, the Persians that I saw returning from Europe, all in a way or the other understood what we had taught them or showed them, or what they had seen or studied themselves, in a particular manner that is absolutely not ours. . . . Subsequently, their native ideas are deeply altered, but not in a European sense. Generally, their Muslim orthodoxy succumbs.[52]

Here Gobineau seems to be referring to the complex process that I called hybridization in the previous chapter. These Iranians with an experience of Europe would acquire knowledge, which then they would indigenize and transform to suit their own objectives, that of soothing the trauma of the encounter with Europe. They were concerned with making sense of Europe's advance and Iran's backwardness and—impressed to the highest possible degree by the immediate experience of life in mid-nineteenth-century Europe, itself imbued with the euphoria of scientific positivism—would readily accept any conclusion put forth by European scholarship. The contempt in which things Islamic were held there undoubtedly tempted these Iranians to shun, as far as European Aryanism assisted them in doing so, any connection to Islam and emphasize instead that pristine past and the creed of the Zoroastrians. They were not ready to broach a critical dialogue with Europe as equals to challenge some misconceptions or prejudices against Islam.[53] They could only submissively imitate, believing that Europe was an infallible oracle. In that sense again, they were subalterns; they made theirs the European racial view of Iranian history and traditional bias against Islam. This is in fact of little surprise. What is more surprising is that these ideas have survived in dislocative nationalist ranks to this day, when criticism of nineteenth-century European thinking on race and similar topics is not only possible but practically unanimous.

MISCEGENATION AND THE FIRE OF PURIFICATION

Racial theories of differentiation between Iranians and Arabs are not sufficient in themselves to fully elucidate the dislocative nationalist take on Iran's decline. The missing link is the idea that racial and cultural miscegenation (or mixing) causes degeneracy. Since the sixteenth century, wherever Europeans interacted with indigenous populations, theologians, philosophers, and colonial bureaucrats had tried to address the pressing dilemma of mixing. Legislations banning miscegenation or "interracial marriage" have been enacted in different historical periods and in various parts of the world, although—it should be stressed—not only by Westerners and not only in modern times. The most recent and studied examples, however, are South Africa under apartheid and the United States, where such bans were in force in some states until as late as 1967.

In European nineteenth-century racial thought, mixing between races was hotly debated. Polygenists, who believed that human races were in fact separate species, argued that the fruit of a mixed union was sterile, just as a mule would be. Later they had to concede that mixing could take place but contended that the fertility of mixed-race individuals would decline after a few generations. According to Robert Young, the idea of degeneration thus emerged as the polygenists' "retort to any apparent demonstration of the fertility of mixed unions" at a time of increased anxiety about keeping races separate to avoid a "raceless chaos."[54] Similarly to race itself, there has never been a scientific consensus on the results of miscegenation. However, aversion to racial miscegenation, itself to a degree tributary of the Romantic insistence (prominent in Herder's work[55]) on preserving the distinctive culture of a nation, was taken up by a number of philologists, historians, and orientalists who in turn claimed that miscegenation among populations brought about civilizational degeneration.

Gobineau provides a valuable illustration of these trends and their potential impact on Iranian nationalist authors. His opinions on miscegenation, expressed in his *Essay on the Inequality of Human Races* (1853–1855), rely extensively on the works of great anthropologists and physiologists of his time and, as such, embody the European perspectives that are of interest here.[56] It is a classic case of a view of history articulated around the interaction, or rather antagonism, between the different human races. As such, it sees racial miscegenation as the trend that will ultimately cause nothing less than the end of civilization. According to Gobineau, humans are biologically characterized by a form of racial instinct that predisposes them to reject interracial mixing. He calls this the "law of repulsion." The three white races that he calls—following the biblical terminology derived from the names of Noah's three sons—the Hamites, Semites, and Japhetites were at first pure. Yet the very characteristics of the white race, its "civilizing sociability and its expansion through conquests" engendered the reverse instinct in its ranks: the "law of attraction."[57] Proceeding from the principles of his "historical chemistry," the civilization of the white race is at danger of being degraded by amalgamation with inferior blood, leading to a degenerate race.[58] The Hamites and Semites were already engaged on the steep slope of degeneracy. The Aryan race had maintained its purity, but now its days were numbered too. One should note that by "Semite" he arguably meant Arabs, as he believed that the blood of Jews, that "chosen race," was unadulterated by inferior races.[59] Léon Poliakov considered Gobineau to be the "great harbinger of biological racism."[60] It should be noted that Gobineau was not entirely opposed to miscegenation and under specific circumstances even considered it to be beneficial; but this should not repudiate the point that aversion to miscegenation was widespread in scientific circles. The interested reader can refer to the works of the racial thinkers Robert Knox or J. C. Nott.[61]

A similar revulsion toward miscegenation can be observed in the writings of Akhundzadeh and Kermani. Dislocative nationalism cannot reconcile itself with the advent of Islam to Iran, not because Islam is any worse than Zoroastrianism or because Islamic Iran's history has fewer artistic or technical feats to boast about. In fact, there is a scholarly consensus that the two religions display more than one similarity, and it should be emphasized that it was the literature and scientific discoveries of early Islamic Iran that were passed down.[62] Rather, dislocative nationalists' issue with the advent of Islam is rooted in their reimagination of pre-Islamic Iran as an ethos of racial purity, and of Islam as a source of Semitic pollution. In the pages of Akhundzadeh the pre-Islamic "*mellat* (nation) of Iran" ruled by "the Kings of Iran" is contrasted with an Iran that has allegedly adopted the Arabs' cultural and religious practices and is ruled by despots on behalf of Arabs.[63] In their reappraisal of Iranian history and the reasons behind their country's backwardness vis-à-vis Europe, dislocative nationalists came to identify the advent of Islam (or what, since the twentieth century, has been racialized as "the Arab invasion") as an act of forced miscegenation: the adoption of another race's religion, hence the claim that Islam is not suited to the Iranians' temper. Akhundzadeh claims that his views on Islam were influenced by Voltaire, particularly his criticism of superstition and promotion of reason, and these contentions are taken at face value by people like Adamiyat. Yet the violence of Akhundzadeh's diatribes against Arabs that run in parallel to his admiration for another religion (Zoroastrianism) make clear that ideas of race and purity are central to his rejection of Islam.

Aversion to miscegenation is at the heart of dislocative nationalism. All the major tenets discussed so far—the exaggerated longing for the pre-Islamic past or the hatred of Arabs and Islam—proceed from it. The distinctive categorization of what is "Iranian" and what is "Arab" needed the import of European racial thought by Akhundzadeh and especially Kermani to become conceptually possible. Once this intellectual hybridization was completed, nationalists devised a project of regeneration aiming to eliminate things "Arab," however grossly or arbitrarily defined. A return to the sources of Iranianness became the antidote to virtually all the ills of Iranian society. Any cultural or religious case of miscegenation, particularly Islam and the Persian language's borrowings from Arabic, came to be seen with horror. This is a racial-historicist view of Iranianness that is identical to the Weltanschauung of Gobineau, Renan, George Rawlinson, Nöldeke, and later Edward G. Browne and Percy Sykes, to name just a few. Akhundzadeh's and Kermani's disparaging of the Shi'ite clergy, the religious practices of Iranians (for instance, Akhundzadeh's criticism of the Muharram procession described as Iranians mourning "an Arab" killed by "other Arabs") can all be seen as cases of horror at racial miscegenation.

The origin of the very idea that Iranians were forced by the sword to adopt the Arabs' culture and religion lies in orientalist texts. We have already discussed Browne's assessment of pre-Islamic Iran, Zoroastrianism, and the advent of Islam. Some of his passages are also relevant to the association of Islamization as a case of racial miscegenation: for Browne, there is clearly a racial clash, and he calls on vivid images of "the warlike followers of the Arabian prophet [sweeping] across Iran": "The priests of Zoroaster fell by the sword; the ancient books perished in the flames. . . . Truly it seemed that a whole nation had been transformed, and that henceforth the Aryan Persian must not only bear the yoke of the Semitic 'lizard-eater' whom he had formerly so despised, but must further adopt his creed, and almost, indeed, his language."[64]

In this quotation, one can recognize the vision of Akhundzadeh and Kermani, down to the very terminology, and two fundamental propositions. One is the unsubstantiated allegation that Iran's ancient books fell victim to the Arabs' criminal arson. The assumption that pre-Islamic literature was destroyed in its entirety by Muslim conquerors does not stand up to examination.[65] If there was a willingness to destroy what was considered un-Islamic, would it not be logical that Muslim conquerors burn the Zoroastrian books first? If that was the case, how can we explain that the largest surviving pre-Islamic corpus is precisely that of Avestan commentaries?[66] Moreover, there cannot have been just one library in the whole expanse of the empire. Books existed in various languages, particularly Syriac and Aramaic and, as in every similar situation, knowledge survives the destruction of books or else Iranian medical traditions would not have survived either. It is also useful to remember that the far more complete destruction brought about by Mongols in the following centuries did not obliterate preceding knowledge and literature. Finally, it suffices to look through the works of Arab historians, especially al-Masʿudi (856–956), or bibliographers such as Ibn al-Nadim (d. 995/998) to realize that as late as the tenth century AD, hundreds of common Pahlavi books were still available.

The second proposition is of course the racial incompatibility between Islam and Iran, which is here most prominent. The idea that an Iranian could not—in view of his racial characteristics—become a genuine Muslim is to be found in other passages from Browne:

> The change was but skin-deep and soon a host of heterodox sects born on Persian soil—Shiʿites, Sufis, Ismaʿilis, philosophers—arose to vindicate the claim of Arya thought to be free, and to transform the religion forced on the nation by Arab steel into something which, though still wearing a semblance of Islam, had a significance widely different from that which one may fairly suppose was intended by the Arabian prophet.[67]

These dehistoricizing views entirely elude the fact that the inhabitants of the Iranian plateau did not only espouse Islam but also celebrated it incessantly in their literature. A staggering number of genuine professions of faith scattered in the prose and verses of centuries of Islamic Iranian history is simply ignored.

Akhundzadeh and Kermani were more radical than their spiritual masters, and their rejection of Islam and Shiism was far more complete than even Browne's. Browne argued that Shiism and Sufism were somehow "racial" reactions against the Semites' creed, whereas for early dislocative nationalist authors even these spiritual traditions were but the remnants of the Arabs' subjugation of Iran's culture. Gobineau shared Browne's analysis; according to him, "gradually, a day arrived when the Sassanid religion more or less found itself resuscitated in Shiʿism. That day followed shortly on the advent of the Safavids, who thus in turn found themselves Sassanid Muslims of a sort."[68] This careless approach has been criticized recently by Geoffrey Nash, who marveled at "the aplomb with which the Frenchman elides the eight and a half centuries between the fall of the Sassanian dynasty (651) and the establishment of Safavid power in Persia (1502)."[69] Moreover, as Nash points out, this approach erases "many traces of Persia's Sunni and Sufi past . . . and—equally as important—the substantial Arab Shiʿih contribution that made the Safavids' project possible."[70]

Such strongly held belief that Iran and Islam are incompatible on racial grounds and unable to coexist led some scholars to frankly fanciful propositions. This brings us back to Ferdowsi and the claim that he allegedly hated Arabs and Islam. In another startling talk Renan gave in 1877 on the *Shāhnāmeh*, which he had read in Jules Mohl's French translation, and about which he had no expertise, he declared:

> Ferdowsi was hardly a Muslim. The fanaticism that surrounded him forced him to pay hypocritical homage to the Prophet; he discharged his duty as briefly as possible, in a fumbling and embarrassed manner behind which one can sense antipathy. In fact, he kept all his enthusiasm for Ali. Ali had become an outlet for the mystical and mythological needs of Persia. They would talk of him with a bombast bordering on madness. How to interpret these effusions toward a relative of the Prophet, the saintest of all Muslims? Covered up by such trick, the Persian heretic confided in his pantheistic dreams, what he thought of this Arab, whom deep inside he mocked. And he smiled inwardly, thinking of how well he just tricked the orthodox.[71]

This statement is mystifying in many ways. How can one be "hardly a Muslim" while devoted to Imam Ali, who, in addition to being the leader of Shi'ites and a prominent member of the house of the Prophet, was also the fourth "Rightly Guided Caliph" of Sunnis? On what grounds can one claim that Ferdowsi was hypocritical in his praise of Islam and the Prophet? Renan's bold assertion that Ferdowsi nurtured "pantheistic dreams," which he associates with the Aryan race—monotheism being, as mentioned, an invention of the simplistic Semites—is equally incongruous. These extravagant contradictions exclusively proceed from Renan's belief that Iranians and Arabs are racially distinct, and that an Iranian Muslim is—on grounds of racial miscegenation— an aberration. Later, in 1904, Nöldeke expressed similar opinions in his *National Epic of Iran*. This work was in time translated into Persian by Bozorg Alavi, a figurehead of the literary nationalist movement in the 1920s and the author of *Demon! . . . Demon . . .* , an apocalyptic short story about the Islamic conquest to which I return in due course. Nöldeke believed that Ferdowsi only expressed generally monotheistic ideas that were not Islamic in nature. Although Nöldeke's thesis is incomparably more balanced and empirical than Renan's, the German orientalist still assumed that "the poet [entertained] a decided aversion" against Arabs.[72] Nöldeke may have willingly ignored several sections of the *Shāhnāmeh*, certainly the Bahram Gur episode.

As a matter of fact, Ferdowsi gives all indications of being a devout Muslim, as noted by Mahmoud Omidsalar. He professes profound attachment to Shiism in the *Shāhnāmeh*'s preface—considered by experts to be an autobiography of sorts. Although the *Shāhnāmeh* was dedicated to Sultan Mahmud of Ghazni, a Sunni king, and although Shiism authorizes one to hide one's creed (the practice of *taqiyyeh*), Ferdowsi still solemnly and blatantly declares his adherence to Islam's minority faith.[73] This proclamation was not without risk as it could have brought about Mahmud of Ghazni's wrath. If he was as deceitful as Renan presumes, would he not have claimed that he was a Sunni, rather than be candid about his creed? Ferdowsi's commitment to Shiism is also confirmed by other accounts.[74] Moreover, it is quite indisputable that Shiism is a branch of Islam and not the expression of some racial antipathy toward Arabs, or else what are we to do of Sunni Iranians (who constituted the majority until the Safavids' enterprise of forced mass conversion) or of the significance of Shi'ite practices and traditions among the people of Mesopotamia and Mount Lebanon (today considered Arabs)? Omidsalar pointed out that Ferdowsi gave further clues about his religious convictions, for instance, in the sense of fault and remorse he expressed in relation to his consumption of wine, which he accompanied with the hope that the Almighty would forgive him. Why would he feel guilty of drinking wine if he did not believe that as a Muslim he was prohibited from its consumption?[75]

Ferdowsi in fact turns all assumptions of retrospective nationalism on their head because he did not see any contradiction between his compilation of ancient mythistories in Persian, the dedication of his poem to a Turkic prince, and his commitment to the Shi'ite variety of the Islamic faith. If truth be told, there is no trace of anyone having seen any contradiction between Iranianness and Islam in the entire body of literature in Persian until the rise of dislocative nationalist discourse. Omidsalar mentions the poet Mehyar ad-Deylami (d. AD 1037) as an example of the idiosyncrasies of the premodern period.[76] This poet conspicuously advertised his being Iranian and Zoroastrian, yet wrote in Arabic and later in his life converted to Shi'ite Islam. In one of his late poems in Arabic, one can read:

My people conquered the world by their courage
And trampled life and times under their feet
They rose as high as the sun
And hitched their abodes to the stars

And my father Kasra [lived] in his elevated castle
Is there a father similar to mine?'

Some verses further, ad-Deylami adds:

Truly, I received fatherhood from the best of fathers
And religion, from the best of prophets
And realized glory from one side to another:
The superiority of Iranians
And the religion of the Arabs.[77]

It is also in the context of aversion to miscegenation that one should see the nationalist concern with language purification. Gobineau's account of Hossein Qoli Aqa (the Iranian student at Saint-Cyr in the 1840s, discussed earlier) is here a case in point as he may be the first Iranian to be documented advocating linguistic cleansing. Hossein Qoli Aqa

> thought that in order to regenerate his country, they should purge the language from all Arabic phrases and words. . . . In sum for him, the only future and salvation for his country resided in the return, as complete as possible, to the things of the most ancient past, and what he imagined in his very approximate archaeological knowledge, to have been the religion and philosophy of his ancient forefathers.[78]

Gobineau's account of Hossein Qoli Aqa seems to be that of an archetypical dislocative nationalist. He longs for the distant past and is preoccupied with the idea of a return, which in his view can only be achieved through the overnight cleansing of Arabic loanwords, Islam, and often even the Arabic alphabet. This archetype also exhibits a particularly thin or manipulated historical knowledge of that pre-Islamic past, a fact that Gobineau does acknowledge.

The idea of the centrality of language within the national community had already infiltrated Iranian literati in the nineteenth century. For Kermani, a *mellat* (people, nation) is a community of language, and he advocated language reform.[79] Even before that, language reform had taken the shape of what the poet Yaghma Jandaqi called *pārsi negāri*—that is, the convention of writing Persian and avoiding use of Arabic loanwords—and had its parallels in Ottoman Turkey.[80] The concern with purifying the language of the community was one of the hallmarks of the thought of the German philosopher Johann

Gottlieb Fichte, among others. For Fichte, language embodied the soul of the nation, and purging the language was protecting it from foreign contamination.[81] The idea of the individuality of nations that must be preserved against undesirable mixing is already prominent in Fichte's take on languages, but dislocative nationalists' advocacy of language purification is more clearly crystallized around their aversion to racial miscegenation. In a letter to Akhundzadeh, Jalal ed-Din Mirza, who was also one of the proponents of this movement, linked *pārsi negāri* to his hatred of Arabs: "I came to realize that the language of our forefathers, similarly to the remainder of our knowledge, was lost to the *tāziyān*'s plunder, and there is currently nothing left of it."[82] Akhundzadeh had great admiration for Jalal ed-Din Mirza's endeavor, which he equated with his own attempts to rid "our people of the Arabs' alphabet."[83] It should be stressed that when it comes to language, Kermani adopted a different stance than Jalal ed-Din Mirza and Akhundzadeh. Indeed, although he loathed Arabs, Kermani did not support *pārsi negāri*, which he believed would produce a "dead and tasteless language": Kermani was instead in favor of integrating vocabularies and dialects from the Iranian provinces and countryside, a romantic nationalist endeavor that took place in mid-nineteenth-century Norway, of which he had perhaps heard.[84] It is also ironic that, in the views of the Kemalists, it was both the Arabic and Iranian imprints on the Turkish language that needed to be discarded to pave the way for modernization.

The history of language purification in Iran is eventful and the motivations behind it are not fully consistent.[85] Generations of Iranian nationalists devoted their energies to the elimination of Arabic and other foreign words—a project that will remain incomplete—while others opposed it vehemently.[86] In the early twentieth century, the authorities would import entire technical vocabularies from European languages to equip Persian for the age of centralized government, advanced technology, and the modern army. This linguistic transformation met some resistance. Some puritans advocated the production of local terms to replace these European lexicons. Others, who had fully internalized the racial distinctions discussed earlier, argued that as these were Indo-European terms they were compatible with the Persian language, whereas it is really the Arabic/Semitic words that should go, even though Persian-speakers may have used them for more than a millennium.[87]

The Pahlavi state established the *farhangestān-e Irān* or Iranian Academy in 1935, designed on the model of the Académie Française and aiming to direct the work of linguistic purification from a centralized state institution. Mohammad Ali Foroughi (Zoka ol-Molk; 1877–1942), prime minister of Reza

Shah, very reluctantly became the first head of the *farhangestān*, and he treaded a fine line between the proponents and opponents of language purification.[88] The success of the *farhangestān* was mitigated, and it gradually disappeared. Later, Mohammad Reza Shah Pahlavi and even the leaders of the Islamic Republic would create avatars of the *farhangestān* to continue the work of cleansing the Persian language. Nationalist publications of all sorts also advocated this route, especially the 1930s *Nāmeh-ye Irān bāstān* (The epistle of ancient Iran), edited by Abdorrahman Seif Azad, a pro-Pahlavi pro-Nazi nationalist. This newspaper's frontispiece announced its objective in the following terms: "to uplift Persia to [the] grandeur of ancient Iran."[89] This idea of return was associated in almost all issues with admonitions to purify the language. One article even insisted on altering the accent used to speak Persian— as if there was only one—because that too was but a relic of the enemies of Iran.[90] That these positions were informed by an anti-racial-miscegenation mindset is made clear when the author insists that language purification would require the return of "our Parsi brothers" from "exile." Like Akhundzadeh in his correspondence with Manekji, the Parsis are here seen as racially pure Iranians, uncontaminated by Arabs and Islam, who can guide Iran toward its own past; otherwise one would hardly understand how Gujarati-speaking Parsis could contribute anything to the purification of the Persian language.

Language purification goes hand in hand with forced Persianization as the principle of "purification" of the language is taken to the level of the "nation" in an attempt to dispose of those "alien elements" represented by the linguistic minorities. The nationalist hold over the minds of the promoters of forced Persianization and language purification even brought a few to support the eradication of their own kin's linguistic practices. Taqi Arani (1903–1940), for instance, a physicist and activist of Azeri origin who would later turn to communism, was a staunch supporter not only of language purification but also of the eradication of Azeri Turkish, his own mother tongue: "All well-wishing Iranians, especially the Ministry of Education, must do all they can to replace Turkish with Persian. They must send to Azarbayjan Persian school-teachers, Persian books, Persian journals, and Persian newspapers."[91] For him, it was the "Mongol invaders" who "had imposed their Turkic dialect on the local Aryan population"; he also advocated a "return" to the Sasanian times as an antidote to Iran's "backwardness."[92]

Similar cleansing ventures still have the wind behind them nowadays. Arabic loanwords continue to be replaced, endangering the continuity of Persian as a highly codified literary language and risking to bring about a generation of Iranians incapable of reading the great poets of the premodern era—ironically including Ferdowsi—without a dictionary. There is also a well-established habit to replace "F" with "P" in words where these two letters were inverted in response to the absence of "P" in the Arabic alphabet (ancient Espahān, for instance, came to be called Isfahan after the advent of Islam). Thus, the use of *pārsi* instead of *fārsi* when referring to the modern Persian language has become fashionable, and the promoters of such confusing nomenclature believe that by ridding the language of the post-Islamic "F," they somehow do their part in returning the nation into the pre-Islamic past. Even dictionaries refer on their cover page to *"pārsi"* rather than *"fārsi."* That "Parsi" is not and has never been the designation of the Modern Persian language but refers to the Zoroastrian community of India is lost in translation. One noteworthy and extremely resilient rumor has it that the Persian phrase *"pārs kardan"* (to bark) is the result of an Arab conspiracy to ridicule Iranians by associating their national designation with the dog's sound, hence the recurrent admonitions to avoid using this phrase. If true, this rumor would mean that the Arabs, whose language does not feature the letter "P" in the first place, have come up with this astonishingly cunning idea, and Persian-speakers have unquestionably adopted it as if they had no self-respect and no agency in the evolution of their own language. There is of course no evidence to support the altogether fanciful claim, but it demonstrates the topicality of the debate on language, foreign borrowings, and Arab-hatred.

The wholesale adoption of the European aversion to miscegenation is problematic in that it runs counter to what has arguably so far characterized Iranians—in other words, their capacity to integrate (*talfiq*) non-Iranian technical, cultural, religious, and even linguistic elements or practices that they found useful or appealing. This is of course not an Iranian specificity; exchange, mixing, and amalgamation are the stuff of history everywhere. As a matter of fact, dislocative nationalism itself is one such case of synthesis. There is no room here to list all such adoptions in the pre-Islamic period. One can still point to the scripts used to write both Old Persian and Middle Persian, which were influenced by that of Aramaic. Aramaic also served as the language of administration under the Achaemenids, and a variation of its script was used to write Pahlavi Parthian and Middle Persian until the Islamic conquest. Equally important, the Sasanians extensively relied on Roman technical know-how through the employment or enslavement of Roman engineers. In turn, this capacity to amalgamate led the inhabitants of the Iranian plateau to disproportionately influence the literature and sciences that developed within the large Islamic area and to produce many of the syncretisms that characterize Islamic theology.

Regarding the idea that pre-Islamic Iran was somehow (racially or other-wise) "pure"—in other words, homogenous—evidence to the contrary already existed in the nineteenth century. The idea runs counter to not only the ar-chaeological, philological, and historical findings of scholars working on this period but also to the spirit of ancient texts such as the *Shāhnāmeh*, which have never conveyed such ideas. In the classical Islamic age, Persian- and Arabic-speakers participated in poetry in both Arabic and Persian and drew on each other's literary heritage. The great twelfth-century poet Nizami Gan-javi (of Ganjeh), in his *Seven Beauties*, which tells the story of the Sasanian ruler Bahram Gur, who was raised among Arabs and who we have already touched upon in the context of his treatment by Ferdowsi, conveys ancient Arab legends (such as that of Layla and Majnun) and most importantly praises rather than condemns miscegenation. Indeed, the seven beauties in question are seven princesses from different kingdoms whom Bahram Gur takes as his brides. Similarly, *The Ebony Horse* tale in *One Thousand and One Nights* tells the story of a Persian prince rescuing his lover, the princess of Sanaa. Need-less to say, his being Persian and her Arabian origin are not referred to as constituting a case of an unusual, even less condemnable, union.

In spite of its defects, this racial view of Iranian history has proven highly tena-cious. The reason for this is twofold. First, blaming Iran's decadence on Arabs and Islam is convenient. Second, its origins lie in European scholarship, a scholarship that cannot be questioned by a nationalist ideology that has placed European science on a pedestal and has tied its own hands to evaluate or criti-cize it. This brings us to the question of dislocative nationalists' ambiguous relationship with Europe.

5
EUROPE, THAT FEARED YET ADMIRED IDOL

When I arrived in Paris in 1910, it came as a surprise to me that the streets were
not made of crystal.
> —Mohammad Ali Jamalzadeh, private conversation
> with Homa Katouzian, Geneva, 1976

THE POLITICIAN AND INTELLECTUAL HASSAN TAQIZADEH (1878–1970),
one of the brightest minds of twentieth-century Iran, famously said in the
pages of his newspaper, *Kāveh*, that "Iran must both in appearance and in reality, both physically and spiritually, become Europeanized (*farangi-ma'āb*) and
nothing else."[1] In a later clarification of this pronouncement, which came
after a storm of criticism, he confided to a friend what he had actually meant:

> By *apparent civilization* I meant such things as clean clothes, adequate
> housing and public health . . . and good manners . . . and . . . valuing
> time. And regarding *spiritual civilization*, I meant science, scholarship,
> foundation of universities, publication of books, improvement of the
> situation of women . . . and removal of corruption and bribery and still
> thousands of other spiritual, legal, moral and behavioral matters which
> would take another ten pages to enumerate. Unfortunately, we neither
> acquired the apparent civilization of Europe, nor its moral one. Of the
> apparent civilization, we did not learn anything except prostitution, gam-
> bling, sartorial aping and making ourselves up with imported material,
> and of real civilization, none other than rejecting the religions without
> having faith in any other moral idea or principle.[2]

In this quotation Taqizadeh refers to the modernist and nationalist project of emulating Europe. He criticizes the superficial mimicry that the heirs of Akhundzadeh and Kermani devised to reach that goal. Mimicry—as opposed to what Taqizadeh calls "physical and spiritual Europeanisation"—is central to the modalities in which dislocative nationalists understood the European Enlightenment projects of rationalism and secularism. Challenging the traditional reading promoted by Adamiyat that they are to be credited with the import of such ideas into Iran, I will argue that Akhundzadeh and Kermani had a superficial understanding of them. In fact, their approach was dogmatic, thus more akin to that of the Shi'ite clerics they tartly criticized; in their writings, "Europe" and "reason" simply replaced "Islam" and "the Sharia."

Closely related to the matter of adoption of enlightened European ideas is that of modernization, in the technical sense of the term, and the centralization of power that is its corollary. The sort of modernization that nationalist authors promoted in order to close the gap with Europe must be analyzed to reassess their standing in Iranian historiography as pivotal "modernizers." In the case of Kermani, his legacy does not allow us to take any definite conclusion because he did never address the matter in detail, but in the case of Akhundzadeh, his unwavering support for Russia's Caucasia wars, which is examined in the following, tends to confirm that a dogmatic, even despotic and brutal approach to modernization was embedded in dislocative nationalist aspirations to turn Iranians into Europeans. The urgency of finding a solution to Iran's embarrassing backwardness vis-à-vis Europe was such that it tempted nationalists to devise radical, even violent solutions to overpower tradition and religion and force Iran's way into modernity.

DENIGRATION OF IRAN, VENERATION OF EUROPE

Why did dislocative nationalist authors not derive any pride from the Iranian historical experience after the advent of Islam? Is there another explanation than those grounded in race and orientalism provided in the previous chapters? If one compares the Safavid with the Sasanian era, one must acknowledge that the former was an age of equal imperial splendor. Similarly to their pre-Islamic predecessors, the Safavids ruled over a sizable territory that, at its climax, included Baghdad and large parts of Caucasia and Central Asia. It was a military rival to both the Ottomans and the Mughals, its two fellow "gunpowder empires." Large numbers of Europeans flocked to Isfahan, the sumptuous imperial capital, lured by promises of trade and adventure. The extravagance of the court of "the Grand Sophy"—as they called the Safavid emperor—captivated the imagination of many of these European explorers as testified by their travelogues.[3] Needless to say, the Safavid period was also temporally much nearer and thus far better known than the pre-Islamic period, knowledge about which proceeded from either the highly mythologized "kings of Ajam" tradition or sketchy recent orientalist scholarship.

In fact, the proximity of the Safavid period was precisely the reason why dislocative nationalists could not equate it with either a glorious past or a desirable future. In so many ways, the Qajar and Safavid eras were similar, although the Qajar state was an exhausted version of its illustrious predecessor, pitted against a novel and impregnable enemy: modern European imperialism. The social, religious, and political structures of state and society were analogous in both eras. When diagnosing the deficiencies of Iran, modernists and nationalists each in their own way identified obstacles standing in the way of Iran's progress: the absence of modern military technology (Abbas Mirza), modern education and press (Amir Kabir), or the rule of law (Malkam Khan). For early dislocative nationalists it was the prevalence of illiteracy coupled with the use of the Arabic script (Akhundzadeh) or the pervasive Islamic culture of the population (Akhundzadeh and Kermani) that constituted the main impediments to progress and development. All of these obstacles represented gaps with Europe, rather than with any Iranian past. As almost all their texts show, modernists and nationalists alike did not aim to strengthen the Qajar state or revive the Safavid Empire. To varying degrees, they agreed that it was only emulation of Europe that could solve Iran's predicament. In a puzzling comparison typical of his writing, Kermani even stated that the Safavids' policy of imposing the Shi'ite creed on their subjects at the point of the sword did more harm to Iranians than the Mongol invasion did because the creed "impaired their brains."[4]

In this context, pre-Islamic Iran was a convenient golden age, and devising a return to it as the central narrative of dislocative nationalist ideology offered advantages that could not be overlooked. Afshin Marashi concurs in his assessment that ancient Iran presented endless possibilities for "invention and creative anachronism."[5] It was a malleable model that could simply be assumed to have witnessed every sort of achievement deemed necessary by a nationalist ideology, even in comparison with contemporary Europe. The historical remoteness of pre-Islamic Iran, the little extant knowledge of it, and the unanimous admiration of orientalists allowed dislocative nationalists to use it as a palimpsest to create a fanciful narrative that served their ideological objectives.

Part of this objective was the necessity to claim parity with Europeans, thus alleviating the complex of inferiority that Iran's traumatic encounter with Europe had engendered, the distressing discovery earlier in the nineteenth century that Europeans were ahead of Iranians and looked down upon them.

There is therefore more to Akhundzadeh and Kermani's dehistorization of pre-Islamic Iran than what we have previously said of it. They represented the achievements of the ancients, uncontaminated by Islam, as evidence of Iranians' natural high rank among the nations of the world, a status that remains unfulfilled by the fault of the "other," the Arab enemy. But this past was also calculated to be a reflection of Europe. In the *Maktubāt*, Akhundzadeh claims that ancient Iranians "were free inside the country and respected abroad." According to him, the government was efficient in a modern European sense: "in all cities bookkeepers were informed of the people's monies transferred to the government's treasury." The rule of law was upheld by all: "nobody transgressed another's rights," and "the army was subjected to a separate law."[6] Taxing was so equitable that peasants—these good citizens—voluntarily paid twice their dues. Ancient Iranians also enjoyed nothing less than free health care.[7] By attributing such modern achievements to ancient Iranians, Akhundzadeh does more than commit anachronism (which is standard practice among nationalists): by displacing both time *and space*, his narrative is both anachronistic and anatopistic, and the objective is to discursively match Europe's accomplishments.

Akhundzadeh's and Kermani's real muse—idealized beyond recognition, the model to emulate, the key to progress and prosperity—was very much Europe, more so than the times of Jamshid and Khosrow Parviz, to whom they refer. Kermani's admiration for Europe was such that he believed that corruption did not exist there; he claimed that even if presented with a bribe of 10,000 pounds, an English officer "would never agree to sell out his country's rights."[8] Encouraging Iranians to emulate Europeans was Kermani's main impetus to write his history of Iran, *Āʾineh-ye sekandari*. For him, "among Western peoples, especially those of France and England, one finds few individuals who are unaware of the events of their country and the reasons behind the progress and decline of the ancients" (let us remember that Gobineau claimed that Iranians were better informed of their past than Frenchmen).[9] Kermani's surreal medley of images of pre-Islamic Iran, too, is designed to pose as decently comparable to contemporary Europe. The result is an almost desperate attempt, through whatever subterfuge, to convince the reader that Iranians reached in the pre-Islamic past the same level of civilization as Europeans today, as in this fanciful passage where minor anecdotes and audacious inventiveness sit next to creative anachronism:

> Even frock and *pantalon* [trousers], which are the products of Europe's 4,000-years-old civilization, Iranians already possessed them in the first 4,000 years of their own civilization; and chariots that are now the outcome of Europe's progress were the norm on the streets and roads of Iran in the times of Jamshid [a mythical figure]. Canons and cannoneers, which today come out of the schools and industries of Paris, existed in the best condition in the court of the Kianids [a mythical dynasty].[10]

This passages echoes the Gibbonian view we touched upon that Medieval fanaticism put an end to the scientific spirit of the Ancients (although, as we saw in Iran's case, the golden age of scientific inquiry was really the early Islamic period). It is difficult to see what the starting point of Kermani's four-thousand-years-old European civilization is, but it is clearly intended to be juxtaposed to his frequent and no less mysterious claim that Iran's civilization, on the other hand, is eight thousand years old. These civilizational pedigrees— Iran's being twice as long—have been premeditated to offer a comparison between the two, Iran's older civilization being perhaps supposed to make up for its current backwardness. Kermani also claimed that ancient Iranians had invented mail, which is in fact accurate, and—more outlandishly—that they also invented the telegraph by way of communicating over long distances with smoke signals.[11] Even *électricité* was seemingly discovered in the land of Sasan. In Kermaniesque fashion, he goes on to claim that "one can assume from the term *keyhān* [cosmos, universe] that they knew about atoms and *bactériologie*."[12] Kermani's endeavor to prove that five thousand French words have Iranian origins can also be read in light of this inferiority complex toward Europe, this constant urge to prove that Iranians are capable of matching the feats of the European other. Akhundzadeh's approach was different, as he did not go so far as to claim that pre-Islamic Iran was in any way more advanced than nineteenth-century Europe. As a matter of fact, he compared Iran's past "splendor and felicity" with a "candle," contrasted to the "sun" of "contemporary Europe and America."[13]

In a remarkable paradox for a nationalist ideology, the founding texts of dislocative nationalism are intensely critical of Iranian civilization and culture in all its aspects. Even poetry in Persian is not spared. Notwithstanding the overt admiration that several generations of orientalists displayed for poetry in

Persian (suffice it to think of Italo Pizzi or Edward G. Browne), Akhundzadeh and Kermani adhered to this frankly perplexing idea that *poésie* in Persian is worthless, whereas in Europe it is one of the "main pillars of civilization and tools for progress."[14] Yet Kermani did not hesitate to quote verses at length from great Iranian poets, all of them post-Islamic, to support some of his assertions.[15] Browne found Kermani's denigration of poetry in Persian to be "ill-considered and unjustifiable: the noble mysticism of Jalálu'd-Dín Rúmí, the tender passion of Hafez, and the practical wisdom of Sa'dí will never be superseded so long as the Persian language is spoken and studied."[16] The reason for this unusual appraisal of poetry in Persian resides in Kermani's belief that a poem should only promote nationalistic feelings. Browne realized this when he attributed Kermani's "monstrous exaggeration" to a "demand for patriotic poetry" and considered "this passion for the Fatherland [to be] a new thing in Asia."[17]

Beyond poetry, nationalist authors despised in their entirety their countrymen's religious beliefs, customs, and cultural practices (to which language and script should be added in the case of Akhundzadeh). They were concerned with the destiny of Iran and the formation of a new identity but in a manner that cannot reconcile itself with any aspect of the actual, existing Iran. In their rather angry prose, only Europeans and ancient Iranians are spared. Europeans, their sciences, their laws, their systems of government, and their social mores are incessantly exalted. Both authors occasionally claim that even European infants are ahead of Iranians as they do not believe in Islamic superstitions (that one may find superstition among Europeans is passed over in silence). Equal to Europeans, ancient Iranians are praised, but these ancient Iranians are ahistorical products of the dislocative nationalist imagination, constructed solely for the purpose of being compared to Europeans. In fact, the reiteration of pre-Islamic achievements at times seems to be targeting a European audience: nationalist writing is exceedingly self-conscious, relentlessly persuading an imaginary European interlocutor that Iranians are no lesser people. I would go further by suggesting that nationalist authors feel patently embarrassed by Iran and their approach to the recent history of Iran, those "1,200 years" that have followed the advent of Islam, is an attempt at deletion. When Akhundzadeh advises Jalal ed-Din Mirza to omit in his history of Iran those Muslim rulers who in his opinion were *despotes*, he deliberately attempts to induce amnesia.[18] The purpose of their "historiography" is to dispose of post-Islamic Iran altogether. In other words, dislocative nationalism barters the historical Iran for an imaginary one.

This denigration of contemporary Iranians' cultural practices and way of life had parallels—although at a later date—in Kemalist Turkey. According to Cengiz Aktar, there was in the ideology of Kemalism "a hate of the people: they must be civilized in spite of themselves": "Consequently, what [was] lacking in them [could] only be made good through the perfection to be found in civilization, and not from any particular or local feature they might possess, and which did not exist anyway in the eyes of the elite."[19]

Another noteworthy aspect of nationalism's approach to European civilization is the authors' ambivalence toward—or rather silence about—European imperial encroachments. Outside of Europe, nationalism is associated with struggles of national liberation from external control or interference, although of course not exclusively. The nationalisms of the former colonies of Spanish America were early harbingers of these liberation struggles, which in due course would submerge all European colonies in Asia and Africa.[20] According to Partha Chatterjee, nationalism emerged in India as an ideology drawing boundaries between the domain of the national community and the colonial power, subsequently using this distinction to mobilize the population against colonialism.[21] Although Iran was never formally colonized, several Iranian movements endeavored to resist what they perceived as foreign encroachments; suffice it to think of the uproar caused by the Anglo-Iranian agreement of 1919, or Mosaddeq's successful struggle to nationalize Iranian oil.[22] It would seem almost axiomatic to state that generally nationalism resists foreign encroachments.

If that is the case, then the founding texts of dislocative nationalism are exceptional in their failure to display any anticolonial mindset. There is no call to put an end to British or Russian interference in Iran, although it is undeniable that later nationalists will be very much concerned with these matters (more in chapter 7). It is so much the case that Akhundzadeh's biographer, Adamiyat, had to resort to deception to portray Akhundzadeh as an anti-imperialist patriot. Adamiyat quotes a passage in which Jamal od-Dowleh (the other prince of the *Maktubāt*) declares, addressing Kamal od-Dowleh the Indian: "Although our king is a *despote*, we are still grateful to God that he is one of us."[23] In the epistolary exchange of the *Maktubāt*, Kamal od-Dowleh the Indian prince expresses Akhundzadeh's views, and the author uses Jamal od-Dowleh to hold the opposite position, something that Adamiyat himself recognizes elsewhere.[24] It is therefore deceitful to attribute authorial intention to Jamal od-Dowleh, and it is revealing that Adamiyat had to resort to such a trick to portray Akhundzadeh as an anticolonial liberator. In fact, Akhundzadeh served an imperial power—Tsarist Russia—throughout his life and supported its endeavor to subjugate Caucasia. Regarding Kermani, Adamiyat is slightly luckier as there is *one* passage in the author's corpus where he disapproves of "a people [who are] incessantly preoccupied with dominating and deceiving other peoples, and spend all their ambition and imagination in attaining this goal."[25] It must, however, be highlighted that this passage is rather unique and appears in *Hasht behesht* (The eight heavens, c. 1892), a book he coauthored with his companion Sheikh Ahmad Ruhi to offer a survey of Babi thought, rather than expound his own nationalist creed.[26] More often than not Kermani in fact celebrates "the even-handedness and mercy toward humankind" that is to be found in the "civilized nations of Europe."[27] Desperate to make his point, Adamiyat converts our authors' Arab-hatred into evidence of their preoccupation with the homeland and their wariness of foreign encroachments, a proposition that is very questionable in view of the previous chapters.[28]

HYBRIDIZATION AND DISCURSIVENESS

Akhundzadeh and Kermani have been promoted in partisan historiography as modernizers, liberators, patriots, freethinkers, and constitutionalists—in other words, thinkers who brought (European) modernity to Iran to save the country from the supposed backwardness and fanaticism of Islam.[29] These labels are particularly prominent in Adamiyat's work.[30] The question arises: what was the degree of Akhundzadeh's and Kermani's understanding of, and commitment to, the rationalist enlightened modernity that they claimed to promote? How sincere was their commitment to progress and reason, concepts that they invoked throughout their works?

Akhundzadeh seemed to have an appropriate grasp of certain civil liberties thanks to his readings of "the English sage John Stuart [Mill]," in particular, freedom of thought and freedom of speech, on which he expounds in some of his correspondence.[31] He firmly disapproved of physical punishment and mutilation (inexistent in Europe, according to him), for which he held the *despotes* responsible, and he rightly condemned violence against children.[32] In the *Maktubāt*, he also urged the Qajar princes to set up representative government in Iran.[33] Adamiyat rightly pointed out that Akhundzadeh preoccupied himself with civil liberties that, at the time, existed neither in Iran nor even in Russia, where he lived.[34] In specific contexts, his proposals could be sensible and practical steps toward reform and improvement. When Mostashar

od-Dowleh was temporarily appointed to head the Qajar judiciary, Akhundzadeh advised him not to allow clerics to edict court judgments, and to concen-
trate all judicial powers within the ministry.[35] He advocated to confine Iranian
clerics' prerogatives to religious affairs, just like "the priests of Europe"
('olamā-ye rowhani-e dowl-e yurupā), a sensible piece of advice in the context
of secularization. In sum, Akhundzadeh did advance some postures that we
could broadly consider "liberal."

Yet, these specific anecdotes aside, the overall vision of Akhundzadeh as
expressed in his nationalist writings is eminently unpractical, utopian, discursive, and violent. It cannot be implemented in a program of modernization.
One recurrent problem is the prevalence of his obsession with Arabs and
Islam, which often thwarts an otherwise laudable attempt to disseminate liberal
ideas among Iranian literati:

> [The King] must open houses of oblivion [masonic lodges, then seen as
> vanguards of modernity] set up assemblies, become like-minded and
> united with the people and pursue the same objective . . . legislate, estab-
> lish a Parliament . . . , which means that he should believe in *progrès* and
> march toward the *civilisé* circle . . . so that people consider him chosen
> [legitimate], love him . . . and become *patriotes*."[36]

The wish that the King altruistically implements modernization, in the
vein of the enlightened despots for whom Akhundzadeh professed admiration
(chiefly Frederick II of Prussia and the Tsar Peter the Great), is commendable.[37] The problem lies at the two ends of his line of reasoning. On one end,
he believes that the lack of modern government in Iran must be imputed to
religion and "people's absurd convictions," their propensity to believe any
prophet's tale of "jinns, the devil, angels, and miracles."[38] In view of the
earlier point on Akhundzadeh's horror at racial miscegenation, we can safely
infer that, through religious beliefs, he is in fact targeting the "alien" influence of Arabs, embodied in Islam (as he rarely if ever criticizes Zoroastrianism, Christianity, or any other organized religion). He assumes that it is this
influence that has brought about a prevalence of irrational and superstitious
behavior for which Iranians themselves, their traditions, or the permanence of
religious practices that in fact predate Islam are never to be blamed. Accord-
ingly, on the other end of the argument, he sees the solution in the simple
uprooting of these alien elements. For the king to be able to implement
the aforementioned project, literacy is indispensable. But this goal will not be

"easily achievable," without "changing and reforming the current script."[39] Again, the Arabs' influence is the main obstacle to Akhundzadeh's proposed solution: the elimination of what he refers to in ethnic terms as the "Arabs' script," it seems, will automatically solve the question of illiteracy (elsewhere, he calls it "the alphabet of Islam"[40]). In sum, it is the prevalence of racial miscegenation that renders *progrès* impossible. Eradicating Arab influence seems to be the solution to all Iran's ills in Akhundzadeh's mind.

Furthermore, his personal adherence to or understanding of some ideas associated with enlightened modernity seems to have been partial, if not insincere. He claimed, for instance, that men and women should be equal before the law, and Adamiyat rushed to praise him as "the pioneer" of gender equality "in the Islamic world."[41] Yet a close look at his correspondence shows a different picture. In a letter to Manekji, he mentions that he has a unique child called Mirza Rashid.[42] After telling Manekji about his son and his studies, he mentions in passing that "in addition to my only child, I also have a daughter." Then follows not a depiction of his daughter, but of her husband. There is not a single word about his wife in this letter. It is remarkable for a supposed supporter of women's rights to consider only his son as his true child, and his daughter as a lesser progeny who matters only thanks to her husband's achievements, while his wife should not be mentioned, perhaps because of a concern for honor. This pattern of contradiction between the promotion of women's rights and the actual behavior of its Iranian enthusiast is reminiscent of later policies enacted by one of Akhundzadeh's spiritual heirs: Reza Shah Pahlavi. The shah banned the veil in 1936 and allowed for recalcitrant women to be forcibly unveiled, abused, and sometimes physically mistreated. Dislocative nationalists who often condone despotic tendencies have presented this oppressive and arbitrary policy as one of the sovereign's most successful attempts to "free Iranian women." Yet, according to some authors, Reza Shah "treated his own three wives as his personal chattels."[43] His daughter Ashraf reported that "at home my father was very much a man of an earlier generation (I remember he ordered me to change my clothes 'at once' because I had appeared at lunch in a sleeveless dress)."[44] As late as 1978, his son, Mohammad Reza, suggested that "although women may be equal under the law, they were not equal in ability."[45]

In the same vein as Akhundzadeh, it is undeniable that some of Kermani's suggestions can be taken as relevant and potentially effective ways to ameliorate the lives of Iranians. According to Bayat, Kermani saw polygamy and seclusion of women as the source of many of Iran's moral and social issues.[46] He rightly lamented that women in Iran were "less valued than dogs in Europe."[47]

He criticized the full veil for "being an obstruction to full humanness, and a colossal impediment to obtaining education and culture."[48] For him, covering women distorts and exasperates the males' natural desires and pushes them toward lusting after the youths and other deviances.[49] He thoroughly criticized the attitude of holding things European in contempt, of considering Christians impure, and of believing that learning European languages and sciences was blasphemous.[50] He called for equality and for justice, for a more egalitarian society where it was not allowed that one starve "while another is so satiated that he is left wandering, not knowing what delicious food should be his next delight."[51] This latter quotation prompted Adamiyat to call him a "socialist" to emphasize the progressive nature of his thought or give it some vague veneer of intellectual recognition.[52]

Then again, in spite of these commending ideas, any workable program aiming to attain a fairer and more functional society is nowhere to be found in Kermani's pages. He calls for "a just and egalitarian law," yet he displays so much hatred for so many large groups of humans—Arabs, Jews, "Negroes" (*zangi*), not least contemporary Iranians, the clergy, the ruling elites, and so on—that this call for equality seems all too relative and selective.[53] One wonders who is left out from his invectives to benefit from a just society in Iran. Akhundzadeh's *Maktubāt* and Kermani's *Seh maktub* and *Sad khatābeh*, rather than programs of reform, are ideological texts revolving around a histori-cist discourse. They offer their Iranian readers concerned with their country's "backwardness" a reassuring narrative, relieving them of the embarrassment of Iran's underdevelopment. No precise program is offered as to how Iran should be ruled to improve the lot of the population apart from some occasional and vague talk of representative government or rule of law, which lacks the detail and depth of the treatises of a Mirza Ya'qub Khan on the same topic, for instance.[54] Rather than address concrete aspects of reform in the vein of a number of other modernists and constitutionalists including Malkam Khan, dislocative nationalist authors, in addition to their historicist narrative, offered solutions that defied rationality.[55] Their texts imply that as long as what their authors have arbitrarily and subjectively identified as Arab influence (in lan-guage, script, and so on) and Islamic religiosity were prevalent, *progrès* would be impossible. Therefore, only uprooting the Arabs' legacy will bring about change and modernity. There is a sincere belief that such project is desirable and achievable and will deliver the moon instantly.

Akhundzadeh and Kermani's approach to modernization stands in sharp contrast to the more reasoned and pragmatic thought of the modernist author Abdorrahim Talebof Tabrizi (1834–1911), for instance, who was influenced by

Islamic reformism. Talebof was another Iranian thinker writing out of Caucasia. According to Mehrdad Kia, his modernism was, similarly to Malkam
Khan, based on the

> establishment of a new political structure based on law and the introduc-
> tion of fundamental administrative reforms. But the creation of a mod-
> ern constitutional form of government was not equivalent to the rejection
> or destruction of Islam as a religion and a moral code. If only Islam could
> adjust itself to the changing demands of the modern world by accepting
> new ideas and laws imported from Europe, it could reinvigorate itself and
> become a religion of progress and enlightenment.[56]

Talebof maintained such pragmatic stance toward religion in Iran, although,
similarly to Akhundzadeh and Kermani, he did not live in Iran and was therefore not subjected to the censorship or pressures of the reform-wary court and
clergy. It should not be doubted that he held the Shi'ite clerics in low esteem,
like many of his fellow intellectuals who saw them as a hindrance to change.
Yet his distaste did not blind his political judgment as it did our authors'
(perhaps because he was a devout Muslim himself). This is even more
commendable in view of the uproar that his books caused among the Shi'ite
clerics who branded him a heretic.[57]

The nationalist authors' peculiar treatment of or commitment to certain
European ideas has been largely disregarded by Iranian historiography.[58] The
main cause behind this neglect has been conventional nationalist historiography's characterization of Akhundzadeh and Kermani with handpicked labels
borrowed from European intellectual history. This trend was perfected by
Adamiyat, who implied that Akhundzadeh and Kermani were, if not active
members, at least loyal disciples to, say, the European Enlightenment. Adamiyat claims that Akhundzadeh "is a representative of the philosophical and
scientific thought of the mid-nineteenth century," and then goes on to give a
description of European positivism (*'asr-e e'teqād beh 'elm*), which he sees as
the outcome of progress in natural sciences (*'olum-e tabi'i*) since the Enlightenment (*rowshanāyi*).[59] For him, the "foundations of these philosophical and
scientific movements are identically reflected in [Akhundzadeh's] work." In a
remarkably exaggerated claim, Adamiyat even considers Akhundzadeh to be
"the forerunner (*pishrow nashr*) of the Western scholarship of the second half
of the twentieth century" in his application of "scientific criticism" to Islamic
law.[60] For Adamiyat, Akhundzadeh believes in rationalism and in everything

that employs the scientific method and of course fits squarely into the "materialist" (*tafakkor-e māddi*) school.[61] Akhundzadeh has also been recently referred to as "the most significant representative of the Iranian Enlightenment
liberals."[62]

Similarly, Adamiyat claims that Kermani has played a crucial part in importing European ideas into Iran, "provided new principles as the foundations
of philosophical thinking," and furthered the idea that "philosophy (*hekmat*)
and science are not separate."[63] He takes at face value Kermani's claim that
"reason governs everything" to present his thought as part and parcel of the
European intellectual movements of rationalism (*esālat-e 'aql*) and empiricism
(*esālat-e tajrobeh*).[64] Adamiyat shuns his duty as a historian to verify whether
the author of *Seh maktub* ever applies this principle in his nationalist theorizing or his audacious treatment of history and etymology, and affirms that
Kermani is committed to "natural rights."[65] Adamiyat also elaborates on the
inclination that Kermani had for Jean-Jacques Rousseau, a thinker of equality
and universal rights, author of the *Discourse on Inequality* (1754), while not
reflecting on the seeming discrepancy of Kermani's concurrent espousal of
European scientific racism in its crudest form.[66] By the same token, Kermani's
contemporary editor sees him as a representative of "rationalism ('*aql gerāyi*)
and positivist scientism ('*elm gerāyi-e pozitivisti*)," having an "extraordinary
grasp of . . . modern sociology" and adhering to "socialist justice."[67]

The endeavor to portray Akhundzadeh and Kermani as genuine representatives of the European schools of thought that they claim to promote is problematic. First, it suggests that they brought ideas of representative government
and modernity to Iran, implying that they were the first authors toying with
such ideas and that, consequently, Iran owes them the "progressive" developments of that period, above all the Constitutional Revolution. Second, it
minimizes the ideas of other thinkers of the time, such as Malkam Khan,
"al-Afghani," and Talebof Tabrizi, partly because these three thinkers instrumentalized the language of Islam to further their modernist ideas, which is
nothing short of a crime of lese majesty, especially in the post-1979 variety of
nationalist historiography. These two ideas are particularly prominent in the
works of the amateur historian Ajudani.[68] Last, this reading obscures what the
writings of Akhundzadeh and Kermani really are: early attempts to syncretize
often contradictory European ideas with Iranian forms and content in order
to cement a nationalist ideology. Such an approach misses out on an analysis of the modalities in which political concepts are selected and adapted in
the pursuance of particular political aims. We may also be dealing with a

historiography so dependent on European models that it is incapable of coming up with its own categories to designate movements in Iranian intellectual history.

Maryam Sanjabi has made a laudable attempt to investigate the reasons behind Akhundzadeh's seemingly incomplete assimilation of European enlightenment and has identified the environment of nineteenth-century Russia, a society deeply affected by antirationalist romantic ideas, as an important factor. For her, the work of Akhundzadeh is situated on the "periphery of the western cultural domain" and is marked by a degree of naïveté.[69] In Adamiyat's generous appraisal, the hybridity of works such as the *Maktubāt* or *Seh maktub*, arguably their main interest from the perspective of intellectual history, is entirely overlooked. There is no doubt that there are traces of some Enlightenment ideas in these works, but what has been disregarded is the degree to which these ideas were filtered through traditional Iranian interpretive lenses to fit the ideological needs of dislocative nationalism.

Most importantly, what has been willfully ignored is that the thought of Akhundzadeh and Kermani is far more indebted to anti-Enlightenment, anti-egalitarian reactions *against* the ideals of the *philosophes* than the rationalism of the Enlightenment. Prominent among these is the very idea of the ethnic nation, which is a reaction against the cosmopolitanism of Enlightenment ideals. This communitarian, almost tribal current of thought culminated in racial theories that are omnipresent in dislocative nationalist writings.[70] This paradox is exemplified in Akhundzadeh's own admission of the influence that *both* Voltaire *and* Renan had on his antireligious stances.[71] In other words, Akhundzadeh does attempt to criticize religious fanaticism and superstition (along Voltairian lines), but he does so *also*, if not mainly, because he believes that Islam is incompatible with the Iranians' racial nature (an idea that conjures up in Renan's writings). Therefore, one could qualify these works in the following terms: early attempts to assimilate sometimes contradictory modern Western ideas—among which progress, rationalism, the nation and also the opposition between races—with traditional Iranian interpretive lenses *in order to* manage Iran's traumatic encounter with Europe.

Akhundzadeh's and Kermani's selection of Western ideas, which can at first glance seem haphazard, does in fact follow a consistent logic. In the context of a nationalist ideology, when taping into these ideas, Akhundzadeh and Kermani's priority was to reverse Iran's perceived backwardness, although in a discursive manner, in a form limited in its scope to a historicist narrative. In

Cyrus Masroori's words, "the typical Iranian intellectual of the nineteenth
century primarily and often exclusively understood, interpreted, and presented
the schools of European thought in terms of pragmatic political objectives."[72]
Masroori offers interesting insights into the "relationship between the formation and dissemination of political ideas and the intentions and pragmatic concerns of those who create and utilize them" and emphasizes the "contingency
in the reception and interpretation of 'foreign' ideas." Masroori therefore
emphasizes certain coherence in Kermani's work, which, unlike Bayat-
Philipp, he does not consider to be "confused" or "misinformed" but rather
pragmatically selective, syncretical, and designed to reach a particular
political objective.[73] For him, Kermani "borrowed" ideas from various authors
and "tailored" them "in manners he thought would best serve his purpose."[74]
I argue that his main purpose was to formulate a discursive way out of the dilemma of Iran's backwardness vis-à-vis Europe. In this context, it is indeed
important to take note of Masroori's recommendation and keep track of Kermani's "intentions and the context in which he wrote" when evaluating his
thought, as he was "a revolutionary at a time of crisis." But beyond political
objectives, it is undeniable that in his choice of European theories, Kermani—
in a manner identical to his predecessor—often adopted ideas that were contradictory if not antithetical to each other. It is also undeniable that Kermani
consistently failed to apply the scientific and rational standards he promoted
to his own nationalist writing.

The claim that Akhundzadeh and Kermani as enlightened intellectuals
(*rowshanfekr*) attempted to dethrone religion and in so doing paved the way
for the Constitutional Revolution and modernization is not supported by the
authors' own texts. In furthering such reading of the dislocative nationalist
authors, Adamiyat and others pursue a particular ideological objective, that of
transmuting Akhundzadeh and Kermani into models to be emulated, the nationalist equivalents of high-ranking Shi'ite clerics (aptly called "sources of
emulation" or *marāje'-e taqlid*). Reflecting over this largely successful enterprise brings us to one of the ironies of dislocative nationalism. In spite of all
the ado about science, rationalism, and *qertikā*, the founding texts of Iranian
nationalism bear far more resemblance to the preaching of the Shi'ite ulama
than to Hume's or Voltaire's treatises. Instead of enticing the Iranian reader to
apply critical thinking to presuppositions and superstitions, the *Maktubāt* and
Seh maktub and *Sad khatābeh* are ascriptive: they impose their own creed
in a vehement torrent of admonitions. While it is true that they attempt to
displace religious dogma in a counterhegemonic endeavor, in reality they

simply replace it with another dogma as rigid and totalistic as the previous one: the ideology of dislocative nationalism.

Parallels between religion and nationalism are seriously underexplored.[75] Some authors (Eric Hobsbawm and Benedict Anderson but also George Mosse) have observed this connection in various contexts, such as parallels between Nazi rituals and German Pietism (Mosse) or the tombs of unknown soldiers (Anderson).[76] Yet as nationalism theory is still generally marked by the works of Marxist-inspired modernists, more often than not this literature codes "nationalism" as modern and therefore secular, and religion is perceived as part of the heritage of the premodern world. World religions such as Christianity and Islam are also perceived as antithetical to nationalism because they are inherently universal in their reach and membership, whereas the nation is by definition limited, with "finite, if elastic, boundaries beyond which lie other nations."[77] Modernist orthodoxy therefore fails to take adequate notice of the modalities in which both religion and nationalism exploit symbols, develop systems of belief, draw narratives of people "chosen," celebrate heroes and prophets, and—put simply—have equal claims to sacredness. There are exceptions to this trend in the works of Adrian Hastings and Anthony D. Smith. For Smith, sacredness is really at the heart of nationalism. In his words, "the nation communes with and worships itself," and as noted by Breuilly, "nationalists celebrate themselves rather than some transcendent reality."[78] As early as 1915, Émile Durkheim had taken note of explicitly religious ceremonies and symbols in nationalist commemorations, comparing "Christians" celebrating the principal dates of Christ's life, Jews "celebrating the exodus from Egypt" with "a citizens' meeting commemorating the advent of a new moral charter or some other great event of national life."[79] That Western modernity got rid of religion and is intrinsically secular is of course an illusory simplification of a turbulent history, which is still in the making.

In the case of Iran, although Akhundzadeh's and Kermani's work attempted to relay some disparate ideas of European modernity, they remained prisoner of traditional frames of thought. Dogmatism changed shape but remained. The dislocative nationalist dogma is treated as sacred in a religious manner, and it commissions its own agents enforcing an official reading. The *Maktubāt* and *Seh maktub* and *Sad khatābeh* are the Holy Writs of dislocative nationalism (albeit less accessible due to continuous censorship); the narrative of the pre-Islamic past corresponds to that of the Lost Paradise; the Muslim is transmuted into the Infidel, the agent of Arab enmity in Iran; a dogma is cemented and rendered unquestionable by sanctioned exegesis (Adamiyat), sinning

against which earns the punishment of being called *vatan forush* (a traitor to
one's homeland); and soon monuments and sites of pilgrimage such as the
Ferdowsi shrine would be erected to complete the similitude.

DESPOTIC MODERNIZATION

Although dislocative nationalism—unlike modernism and later constitutionalism—does not as such offer a workable program of reform beyond vague
references to progress and the call to uproot Arab influence, we have in the
case of Akhundzadeh a historical illustration of his approach to modernization, allowing us to reassess his standing in nationalist literature as a modernizer and liberator. The nature of his work at the service of the Russian viceroyalty in Tbilisi at a time when the Tsarist Empire was "civilizing" the Muslim
populations of Caucasia is an overlooked aspect of his life that provides us
with invaluable insight into the ways in which his nationalist ideology aspired
to be implemented.[80] Akhundzadeh's career shows that his advocacy of modernization did not aim to gradually introduce reforms in order to drag Iran out
of its "backwardness" in a consensual or even humane manner. Rather, he
supported the imposition by brutal methods of what *he* considered to be a suitable form of modernity. A detour by the history of the Caucasia wars and
Akhundzadeh's role is here inescapable.

Akhundzadeh served as the dragoman of successive Russian viceroys from
1834 to his death in 1878, by which time he had reached the rank of colonel
in the Russian Army, an honor reserved for high-ranking officials regardless of any military involvement. In the 1830s and 1840s, Ivan Fyodorovich
Paskevich, the first viceroy Akhundzadeh served (and incidentally a relative
of Griboyedov, the Russian envoy slain in Tehran in 1829), undertook a violent suppression of Chechens. Before that Paskevich had been involved in
the second Russo-Iranian War, had defeated Qajar troops at Yelizavetpole in
1827, and was a signatory of the infamous Turkmenchay Treaty in 1828,
which stripped Iran of the remaining parts of Caucasia that Russia had not
already annexed and imposed capitulation rights in favor of Russian subjects. Paskevich thus played a prominent role in subjugating Qajar Iran and
imposing what were arguably the most humiliating peace terms the country
has signed.[81]

The manner in which Russians conquered Caucasia is crucial in exposing
Akhundzadeh's attitude toward modernization. According to some historians,
the tactics that Russians used would today "be described as mass terrorism

bordering on genocide."[82] The following comment by Platon Zubov, a Russian official specializing in the Caucasus, to Paskevich in 1834, the year Akhundzadeh started serving him, gives an idea of the outlook of the viceroy's entourage: "The only way to deal with this ill-intentioned people [the Chechens] is to destroy it to the last." The Tsar Nicholas I himself made the objective of Paskevich's appointment clear to avert any doubts: "the suppression once and for all of the mountaineers or the extermination of the recalcitrant."[83]

Akhundzadeh never expressed misgivings about Russia's enterprise in Caucasia. No doubt he knew exactly what was unfolding as Russia's actions were carried out in broad daylight and Akhundzadeh was an insider of the Russian viceroyalty. His own hometown had also been annexed by Russians in 1813; his family must therefore have witnessed the Russian Army's methods. Additionally, many Russian authors (chiefly Lermontov and Tolstoy) did express qualms about Russia's imperial expansion and the brutal massacres that accompanied it. Violence against Caucasia also had a history and did not start in 1834. Paskevich was only there to continue the work of his predecessor, the notorious Aleksey Petrovich Yermolov, whose strategy was limited to the indiscriminate and thoughtless use of violence. He was quoted as saying, "I desire that the terror of my name shall guard our frontiers more potently than chains of fortresses," and the techniques his general, Veliaminov, put forward are testimony to Russia's policies: "The enemy is absolutely dependent on his crops for the means of sustaining life. Let the standing corn be destroyed each autumn as it ripens, and in five years they would be starved into submission."[84] Incidentally, Yermolov too was involved in the Russo-Iranian wars. He is reported as treating Qajar court officials with arrogance and as having been one of the instigators of the second Russo-Iranian War.[85]

Dislocative nationalist historiography has kept quiet on this, and for good reason: the devil is in the detail. Akhundzadeh's inglorious work at the service of a government enemy of the Qajar state—an individual who played a role of significance in submitting and humiliating his country and also the administrative and military machinery that crushed with extreme brutality his own ethnic kin in Caucasia—has been swept under the rug. Not content with concealing these historical facts, Adamiyat brazenly turns Akhundzadeh into an opponent in disguise of the Tsarist regime. He assumes that Akhundzadeh not only associated himself to Russian Decembrist dissenters in Tbilisi but also claims that he was inspired by the Polish uprisings against Russia (which— keep in mind—were crushed by Paskevich his superior).[86] Adamiyat mentions that Akhundzadeh was suspended for one year and groundlessly—though cautiously—assumes that it may have been a result of "his friendship with Caucasian exiles and Armenian independentists."[87] He swiftly concludes that Akhundzadeh "had no affective bond with the Russian government," that that government was "the enemy of his love for freedom" (*āzādi khāhi*), and that he "hated" that "killing apparatus" (*dastgāh-e ādam koshi*). He also points—rightly—at the fact that the Russian secret police stormed Akhundzadeh's house upon his death, looking for subversive writings.[88] Adamiyat's extensive misrepresentation of facts should not come as a surprise anymore. His objective was to promote Akhundzadeh as a good patriot in what amounts to a minor case of historical revisionism.

That the tsar's secret police monitored Akhundzadeh's writing is hardly surprising. Surveillance in Tsarist Russia was high, and the authorities imprisoned and executed large numbers of people believed to be their critics. There is no explanation regarding Akhundzadeh's one-year suspension, if it did ever happen. However, there are mounds of evidence that Akhundzadeh was far from hating a government he loyally served for forty-four years. His correspondence bears no trace of shame, rather the contrary.[89] As Mehrdad Kia has pointed out, Akhundzadeh's plays unambiguously defend Russia's imperial expansion. In an 1852 play, Akhundzadeh linked the "struggle for freedom in love and marriage to the Russian attempts to modernize Transcaucasia."[90] In this play Akhundzadeh portrayed Russia as "a benevolent modernizing political and judicial system that sought to provide peace, security, and justice for all of its subjects." Many of his plays' plots revolve around the "irrational Oriental" confronted to enlightened Europeans, usually characterized by Russian soldiers, those same soldiers that were instructed to "exterminate the recalcitrant" or "destroy crops" to "starve the mountaineers into submission." According to Kia,

> Akhundzade presents Russia as the great educator, modernizer and liberator of Muslim society and Muslim women. . . . Akhundzade's glorification of Russian rule and his total rejection of traditional customs and practices among Muslims of Transcaucasia proved extremely effective as Russian propaganda. The Russians could emphasize a direct connection between the oppressive nature of Islamic practices and the inability of Muslims to enjoy political independence. The benevolent Russian government could introduce progress and modern civilization to such backward people . . . Akhundzade's work reaffirmed the Russians' sense of superiority and reassured the Tsarist state that it had the right to rule in the name

of introducing modern civilization, progress and human rights for Muslim women.[91]

Akhundzadeh's personal correspondence further confirms that he actively supported Russia's actions and believed that Muslims could only be "civilized" at the point of the sword. According to Kia, "Akhundzade stated in several of his personal letters that Russian rule was progressive because it introduced a new alphabet and a modern educational system," and that Russian occupation was a "blessing" for these "savages," adding that Tsarist Russia has taken the savages away from darkness into an era of enlightenment.[92]

Akhundzadeh was an important comprador intellectual serving the Russian Empire. Gen. Mikhail Vorontsov, one of the Russian viceroys in Tbilisi known for his campaigns against the Caucasian anti-Russian resistant and leader Imam Shamil, actively supported the composition and staging of Akhundzadeh's plays. Akhundzadeh later acknowledged his debt to Vorontsov in his autobiography.[93] The role Akhundzadeh played in the Caucasia wars was also celebrated during the Soviet era. Soviet authorities produced a movie about him (*Sukhi, Son of the People*, 1941) that was supposed, in Joseph Stalin's own words, to depict the "historically progressive significance of the unification of the Caucasus peoples with Russia" and the "vanguard role of the Russian intelligentsia."[94] Akhundzadeh's plays were staged again or inspired movies destined to promote modernization in Caucasia—the brutal Stalinist variety of it—by condemning Islam and traditional village life.

Akhundzadeh's support of the forced modernization of the people of Caucasia and indirect endorsement of the "extermination of the recalcitrant" is an indication of his approach to the very issue of modernization. No amount of violence was excessive enough if it were to "enlighten" backward and superstitious Muslims by giving them a modern European educational system and a new alphabet—to which Akhundzadeh accorded an exaggerated degree of importance. Any violence, any ruthless repression of traditional ways of life was thus justified if it were to drag an Islamic society out of its torpor. According to Cole, Akhundzadeh's attitude "may be a symptom of his own repressed guilt. . . . Only by coding all things European as 'progressive' and by coding Islam as essentially 'reactionary' could he have justified this holocaust [the Russian exactions in Caucasia]."[95] One can surmise that he also needed to somewhat compensate for his services to Russia and Paskevich (one could add *against* Iran) by blowing his nationalism out of proportion. For instance, rather than refer to the Russo-Iranian War as such, he called it "the war between

Paskevich and Nayeb os-Saltaneh" to reduce its significance to the level of a personal affair.[96] Sanjabi contends that "symptoms of dual loyalty" were typical of compradors like Akhundzadeh: "his anxiety about being rejected by his own people was bound to appear in criticism of his indigenous past," and in "a rejection of cultural values which resisted conciliation with that of the dominant power."[97] It should be said that in Kermani's case, his maelstrom of conflicting ideas and hodgepodge of invented facts allow no such supposition on his approach, although the anger and hatred that he exhibited for his contemporary countrymen did not presage a more humane form of "modernization."

The early Pahlavi state would reproduce the brutal and despotic approach to modernization that is embedded in Akhundzadeh's dislocative nationalism. Reza Shah's state imposed superficial mimicry of European sartorial habits through brutal means upon the population. Concurrently, it never allowed for accountability, equality, civil rights, and the rule of law—equally part of the baggage of European modernity—to take root in the country. The approval of an imaginary European interlocutor is of paramount importance to the adherent of this form of nationalism. This aspect is fully illustrated in the following anecdote. In 1935 Reza Shah ordered the European *chapeau* (felt hat) to become compulsory for all Iranian men, and he privately justified his decision in these words: "All I am trying to do is for us to look like [the Europeans] so they would not laugh at us."[98] He ordered the killing of several hundred protesters who opposed his sartorial regulation.[99] A British diplomat referred to this period of his rule by affirming that "the frenzy of western European window-dressing . . . increased to fever point."[100]

Yet it would be unpersuasive to claim that Akhundzadeh's support for Russia's Caucasia wars automatically turned the brutal imposition of European ways into a tenet of dislocative nationalism that the early Pahlavi state would just as automatically inherit. What is the missing link that can explain the similar approach of Reza Shah? In reality, it is not brutal modernization itself that is embedded in dislocative nationalism. Rather, this violent approach proceeds from the ideology's denigration of Iran's present state. What conceptually justifies that one forces a population to unconditionally and instantly surrender its way of life and value system is precisely the earlier mentioned contempt in which Iranian nationalists held contemporary Iran.

Keep in mind that the primary goal of dislocative nationalists' intellectual endeavor consisted of managing the trauma of the encounter with Europe. Nationalists devised a superficial emulation of Europe along with an extirpation of what they considered to be "alien"—particularly "Arab"—elements in Iran's culture as the only way to close the gap between Iran and Europe, thus saving Iran's dignity. As they saw the totality of the religious, cultural, and social practices of contemporary Iranians to be the result of some arbitrarily defined "Arab influence," none of it was worthy of preservation in their view. This outlook paved the way for the enthusiasts of dislocative nationalism to devise the eradication of traditional ways of life, which could certainly not be achieved without a degree of brutality. Dislocative nationalism's approach to modernization does therefore implicitly accept the use of force against "the recalcitrant," those whose behavior is seen as directly resulting in Iran's backwardness vis-à-vis Europe. Seen in this light, neither Akhundzadeh's active support of Russian exactions in Caucasia nor the repression that the Pahlavi state later unleashed on Iranians for matters of appearance and headgear should come as a surprise. They were seen as means to help Iran recover its rank among the nations of the world, and this recovery naturally demanded sacrifices. The dislocative nationalist project can be seen as a radical, even revolutionary thought aiming to create a rupture in Iranians' life.

6
ARYANISM AND DISLOCATION

As the Zoroastrian religion spread westward, Persia, Elymais, and Media all claimed for themselves the Aryan title.

— Max Müller, 1866

German diplomats found it amusing that every time they met Iranian officials, the question of the "shared" Aryan race would be brought up by the Iranian side in a casual attempt to break the ice.

— Kasra Naji, 2008

IN THE LATE 1940S, HASSAN TAQIZADEH LAMENTED THAT THE IRANIAN government "offers Iranian citizenship to foreigners, who reside in Iran for a few years," but refuses the "right to become Iranian" to "Arabic loanwords that have lived in Iran for a thousand years."[1] Referring to the concurrent habit of importing wholesale vocabularies from French and other European languages into Persian, he inferred this seeming inconsistency to the "calamity" of considering "this Aryan, that Semitic and that other Altaic."[2] A few decades later Mohammad Reza Shah (who in 1965 had himself titled *ariyāmehr*, "the light of Aryans," a title without any previous incidence in Iranian history[3]), privately confided to then British ambassador Sir Anthony Parsons that, as "Aryans," Iranians were in fact members of the European family and that it was a mere "accident of geography" that Iran found itself in the Middle East rather than among its fellow European nations.[4]

The three ideological aspects discussed over the previous chapters — pre-Islamic archaism, Arab-hatred, and hybridized-despotic approach to Europeanization — form the doctrinal backbone of dislocative nationalism. In the next decades and arguably down to this day, little would be added, little would be subtracted from this consistent and appealing ideological apparatus, which served its purpose with startling success. Relying on the sacrosanct science of *farangiyāns* (Europeans), it discursively cured the trauma of "backwardness" vis-à-vis Europe by blowing out of recognition Iran's past achievements and identifying an "other" to bear all the blame for Iran's perceived regression. The ideological stability of Akhundzadeh's and Kermani's nationalism is indeed remarkable, and although the Aryan discourse became prominent after the founding fathers' passing, some attention must be here devoted to its origins and implications. By retrieving European nineteenth-century racial thought and expressing it in the Persian language, Akhundzadeh and—even more so—Kermani paved the way for the reception of Aryanism in Iran. In other words, by presenting Iranians and Arabs as two not only separate but opposite and irreconcilable "races," they had already sowed the seeds of Aryanism that would in time become a central tenet of dislocative nationalism. Aryanism should therefore come up for scrutiny.

This chapter pursues a double objective: first, to provide evidence that the Aryan discourse is a modern European import by reviewing both its European sources and its first appearances in Iranian texts; and second, to demonstrate that it serves a particular purpose in the strategy of dislocation. Dislocated Iran is out of place in the Middle East, a claim clearly illustrated by Mohammad Reza Shah's statement that Iran's placement was an "accident of geography." The Iranian nation is adrift, a lost member of the European family. I could have said "Indo-European," but the reality is that the Indian connection of European Aryanism has been dropped by dislocative nationalism as it does not serve the ideology's strategies.

The Iranian variety of the Aryan discourse has for too long escaped serious analysis in spite of its relevance to any rigorous assessment of modern identity or political and historical thought in Iran. Such undertaking is all the more urgent in view of the resilience of this discourse in Iran and the refusal to recognize its scientific bankruptcy or even its inglorious historical legacy. Indeed, as a scientific concept, race has long since been abandoned by anthropologists and sociologists alike. As a political device, the Aryan discourse in the West has fallen into disuse since the discovery of Nazi Germany's death camps, except for a few publications of the most dubious scientific integrity, sometimes with evident racist and neo-Nazi leanings.[5] Nevertheless, Iranians continue to nonchalantly refer to the *nezhād-e āriyāyi* (Aryan race) and their alleged belonging to this racial family. Such claims are prominent even in scholarly production.[6] The two anecdotes at the opening of this chapter, although far—very far—from being exhaustive, give an idea of how deep the roots of what Léon Poliakov called *le mythe aryen* are in Iranian nationalist discourse, and of the sheer variety of contexts in which it is to be found.

Here the terms "Aryan" and "Indo-European" will mostly be used interchangeably. "Indo-European," "Aryan," and in some older sources "Japhethite" (in reference to a biblical parable tracing the origin of Europeans to Noah's son Japheth) do usually refer to the same ideational construct, although often using different lenses. At the beginning, "Aryan" gained the upper hand over "Indo-European" because it had a more appealing romantic charge, compared to "Indo-European," which had a cold scientific ring to it.[7]

THE ARYAN DAWN

The Aryan myth divides humankind into several races and regroups most Europeans, but also Iranians and Indians, under one racial banner.[8] The Aryan myth spans a long period in European intellectual history, from approximately the early nineteenth century to the end of World War II, and therefore its conceptual apparatus evolved considerably. It was initially only a philological device used to explain similarities between European, Iranian, and Indian languages. Yet it rapidly acquired a racial and political dimension. Aryanism's political charge, infused with romantic imagery, intensified over time, propagating claims that the Aryan race was bestowed with a special destiny—that of supremacy over what were now deemed to be the "others," the "inferior races." This glorification of the white man was a convenient justification for the imperial endeavors in which Europeans were engaged at the time. It is this racialist and politicized version of the Aryan myth and its extension into Iranian thought that is the subject of this chapter, although a detour by its more philological aspects is necessary to define the phenomenon.

The origin of the Aryan myth is usually associated with Sir William Jones's discovery in 1786 that Greek, Latin, Sanskrit, and Persian derived from common roots, although it should be stressed that many scholars had already taken notice of the similarities between European vernaculars and some Asian languages before Jones.[9] The term "Aryan" was coined by Abraham Hyacinthe Anquetil-Duperron. The French orientalist had lived in India from 1755 to 1761, had acquired some Persian, Sanskrit, and other languages of the East, and had published the first translation of the Zoroastrian Avesta in any European language. In a talk he gave in 1763, he came up with the first occurrence of the term *aryen* (French for Aryan) in any European language.[10] Anquetil-Duperron effectively Europeanized *ariya*, a term he found in the Avesta, fusing it with *arioi*, the term Herodotus used for Medes (which also occurred in Latinized versions), to coin a term to designate the people who produced the Avesta. It is interesting to note that the term "Aryan" was, from the beginning, derived from the ancient Iranian term *ariya*, a momentous coincidence that would lead to persistent confusions.

The key semantic evolution happened in 1819, when the young Friedrich Schlegel, a pioneering Romantic author, transformed the meaning of "Aryan" from a translation of *ariya* into a modern racial category, which immediately captured the imagination of his contemporaries. From then on, the term "Aryan," in this particular sense, became widespread in all of Europe.[11] There was always a degree of confusion between its modern racial use and ancient Vedic Indian or Avestic forms, creating one of history's less-researched malapropisms. In 1813 Thomas Young coined the term "Indo-European," and in 1823 Julius von Klaproth created a German variant: *"indogermanisch."*[12] The advantage of "Aryan" over "Indo-European" was its concision and its apparent correspondence to an actual ancient ethnonym. As mentioned, it was also more appealing to romantic fervor, "Indo-European" sounding somewhat too obtuse. Prominent figures of nineteenth-century philology and orientalism are associated with the evolution of Aryanism in Europe, the most important arguably being Max Müller (1823–1900), although it must be stressed that his work was linguistic and that he was mindful of keeping his distance from the racial interpretations of his theories.[13] Ernest Renan and Arthur de Gobineau, on the other hand, had more influence on the development of the *racial* definition of Aryan.

The force of the Aryan myth, and the reason partly explaining its extraordinary longevity in the face of scientific and discursive evolution, comes from its formulation in empirical terms. Most prophets of Aryanism upheld their views with such scientific assurance that little room was left for discussion. Consider this quotation from George Rawlinson, who happened to write extensively on Iran: "Ethnological science, we see, regards it as morally certain, as proved beyond all reasonable doubt, that the chief races of modern Europe, the Celts, the Germans, the Graeco-Italians and the Slavs, had a common origin with the principal race of Western Asia, the Indo-Persian."[14] Rawlinson holds this finding to be the outcome of advances in "modern inductive science, a result which it is one of the proudest boasts of the nineteenth century to have arrived at."[15]

Although wrapped in the language of science, the fundamentals of the Aryan myth were Romantic in nature, with three immediate consequences.

First, affinity between languages was immediately interpreted as racial kinship, race being conceptualized in a romantic fashion. Nothing is more disputable, as there are numerous examples of human groups speaking the language of other groups. There are of course the obvious cases of formerly colonized people having adopted the language of the colonizer in today's Africa, for instance, but history is replete with similar instances. Previously, the Bantu Expansion, a millennium-long migration of Bantu-speaking people, generalized the use of Bantu languages in Africa, including among non-Bantu ethnicities. Han Chinese also came to be spoken by non-Han people after a long process of cultural expansion. For Poliakov, this confusion of language and race was the original sin of the Aryan myth.[16]

Second, it was predominantly a genealogical endeavor. Aryanist authors' obsession with the quest of common genesis is well illustrated by their continuous attempts to localize the original home of Aryans. They assumed that there had been some primordial proto-Aryan (or proto-Indo-European) tribe from whom all subsequent descendants had sprung. Finding the proto-Aryan original home (or Urheimat), describing the cultural and "racial" features of the original Aryans, or coining their lost language became their main preoccupations. Using loosely connected clues and anecdotal facts, Aryanists offered audacious (if not outright fanciful) hypotheses on the proto-Aryan original home. India (or more generally Asia), the Caucasus, the Danube, and the Scandinavian peninsula all were at one time considered by some of these thinkers to be the cradle of Aryans. Iran too played its role in the Aryanist geography of origins as Anquetil-Duperron, Jones, and Herder all at some point suggested that Iran might be the birthplace of Aryans.[17] The fact that no evidence, ruin, tool, inscription, piece of art, or any other artifact left behind by the so-called proto-Aryans has ever been found did not prevent this quest to carry on unabated well into the twentieth century. Moreover, there is no trace of either a primordial tribe or their migrations in any European epic or oral tradition.[18] The appeal of genealogical pursuits was such that even the extreme fragmentation of opinions on the question of origins did not lead Aryanists to the conclusion that there were serious empirical flaws in their assumptions.

Third, the self-aggrandizement entrenched in romantic Aryanism and the horror at racial miscegenation brought about an obsession with racial purity. Racial anthropologists and phrenologists endeavored to define and separate racial categories, with their immutable physical and psychological characteristics. One race would be sensitive, creative, and innovative (Aryan), another would be decadent, inert, indolent, and submissive (most others). Cases of mixing were devoted a great deal of anxious attention. Excessive racial consciousness elevated the opposition between Aryan and Semite to the rank of founding principle of human history and hence draped the pervasive anti-Semitism of those days in the language of science. Ultimately, Nazi ideology brought the Aryan myth to its paroxysm. Obsession with racial purity reached such intensity that the road was paved for the next stage: extermination.

In the contemporary Western world, Aryanism is essentially relegated to history books or associated with Nazism. Racial anthropology and phrenology are discredited pseudo-sciences that are neither taught nor studied anywhere in the world, supplanted as they have been by social anthropology, genetic evolutionism, and biological history. The concept of "race," although still used in political discourses, especially in the United States, or controversial scientific works such as that of J. Philippe Rushton, is also receding. Genotypic or phenotypic variations are used to study hereditary and morphological differences between human groups or individuals, but they are not instrumentalized to demonstrate unchanging behavioral patterns or the superiority of a given group over others. Moreover, phenotypical variations are so gradual that, according to the American Anthropological Association, they "render any attempt to establish lines of division among biological populations both arbitrary and subjective."[19] This association officially discourages the use of the term "race."[20] In the scientific community, there is today a consensus on its socially constructed nature.[21]

Linguistically, the view of an Indo-European family of languages is widely held, although anything more than that is subject to fierce controversy. There is general agreement that these languages descend from a common prehistoric language or group of dialects spoken by one people whose descendants migrated and, due to military prowess, often conquered peoples in Europe and in West and South Asia, thus spreading linguistic features. Yet modern linguists do not believe that language has any relation to race, racial kinship, or cultural superiority. There are also minority views, such as those of the cultural invention of languages, accidental convergence, or borrowing. Such views—as yet controversial—are proliferating and challenging long-held beliefs in the common origin of Indo-European languages and their respective speakers. The linguist Merritt Ruhlen, for instance, dismisses the very concept of Indo-European distinction by arguing that "the notion that Indo-European is unrelated to any other [language] family is little more than a linguistic myth."[22] Similarly, other linguists claim that differences between Indo-

European languages, on the one hand, and those deemed "Semitic" or "Turkic" ones, on the other, have been overstated. A prominent and controversial linguist, Joseph Greenberg, proposed the concept of "Eurasiatic languages," a family regrouping all languages of northern Eurasia under one higher-order family that includes Indo-European languages as well as, for instance, Japanese. It is not the purpose of this chapter to instigate a technical discussion on linguistics and ethnology; here I simply highlight that Aryanism is held in disgrace, and the reason behind the similarities between Indo-European languages is still being debated. Generally, the idea of common origin is still a majority view, but it has no racial connotation anymore, and a common origin of languages does not necessarily mean a common origin of peoples.

IRAN AND THE ARYAN FLATTERY

In the course of the nineteenth century, the Aryanist discourse came to permeate the entire corpus of orientalist writing on Iran and India. Both countries were highly charged subjects for Aryanism and were often depicted as two of the most eventful stages of the struggle between races. The idea of racial antipathy was used to decipher military confrontations in the history of the area, as in this passage from George Rawlinson's influential *Origin of Nations* (1887):

> While the Aryan civilisations . . . were developing . . . in the extreme west of the Asiatic continent, . . . Asia Minor, the more central portion of the Continent—the Mesopotamian Plain, the great Iranic Plateau, and the Peninsula of Hindustan—was the scene of a struggle, not always peaceful, between three other types of human progress and advancement. Two of these were . . . Aryan, while one, the Assyrian, was of an entirely different character.[23]

The migrations and wars of Eastern antiquity were recast as racial endeavors, and the actors of these historical events were assumed to have been racially conscious and exclusively concerned with race mastery over others—this in spite of the absence of any trace of such thinking in historical sources. This view of history continued into the twentieth century, for instance, in the influential works of Percy Sykes (1867–1945) and in particular his *History of Persia* (1915): "The Semites had held sway in the Babylonian and Assyrian empires until they were succeeded by the Aryans of Media and Persia. They in their turn for five centuries were dominated by a Turanian race until, in the third century AD, the Aryans reasserted their supremacy."[24]

Other authors went as far as seeing an irrepressible Aryan racial instinct behind Iran's cultural production. French *iranologue* Henri Massé (1886–1969) endeavored to uncover the signs of such instinct and drew frankly fanciful parallels between Iranian and European literary traditions:

> The Indo-European character of the genius of Iran is much more mani-
> fest in epics (in general, not only the Shahnameh) than in other literary
> works that have been exposed to Muslim influence. To our epics of the
> French cycle relate the [*Shāhnāmeh*] and other Persian epics of the same
> cycle; to our *épopées courtoises* of the Breton cycle correspond the novelis-
> tic and marvelous epics of a Nizami.[25]

Such alleged similarity was not due to exchange or accident but to "racial instinct": according to Massé, "Since the dawn of history, the kings of Persia . . .
turned instinctively toward the West, toward their Indo-European brothers."[26]

These quotations could be multiplied indefinitely. But what matters here is that gradually the Aryan discourse started a new career among the *intelligen-tsias* of Iran, India, and elsewhere. According to Vasant Kaiwar, in India, European Aryanists and native collaborators constructed "the Aryan model of Indian history as a narrative of heroic invasions, migrations, and settlement of an Aryan stock . . . that not only founded kingdoms and empires but also de-
veloped a great philosophy and literature."[27] There the promotion of Aryanism from a philological concept to a political discourse was even swifter than in Europe.[28] Upper-caste Hindus used their alleged Aryanness to claim parity with Europeans while denying it to lower-caste Indians. Aryan racial theories also contributed to strong anti-Muslim sentiments within Hindu reviv-
alist ranks.

The Aryan myth provided an appealing model of history for nationalist ideologues in other parts of the world as well. Similarly to dislocative national-
ists, many of these ideologues were concerned with lifting their peoples to the level of European civilization. In Turkey, one such ideologue was Moïse Cohen, later renamed Munis Tekin Alp (1863–1961), a Jewish thinker from Salonika who seemed little bothered by the anti-Semitic proclivities of Aryanism. He asserted that Turks belonged to "the great Indo-European family." His allegations—unlike those of his fellow nationalists in Iran or India—did

not rely on any previous claim of European Aryanists but entirely proceeded from his own eagerness to portray Turks as Aryans. He praised the Turk's physical type, "his pink and blond complexion, his blue, gray, or azure eyes, his long and slim waistline, and his remarkable beauty."[29] He went on to add that "the Turks are pure Aryans and the word Aryan itself is of Turkish origin. The word 'ari' in fact means in the Turkish dialect ('Tchagatai'), pure, clean, and it is a word much used in the new Turkish language."[30] He further contended that Turks brought agriculture to Europe and founded nothing less than the Sumerian, Greco-Latin, and Chinese civilizations (one is reminded of Gobineau's mystifying allegation that Aryans created the Mexican and Peruvian civilizations[31]). By all means, Tekin Alp's thought was an aberration within already murky waters, and it shows how delusional Aryanist self-aggrandizement could become whenever its appeal was felt. "We are as good as Europeans" was certainly a common concern of both Iranian and Turkish intellectuals.

Before discussing Aryanism in Iran, it is crucial to first stress that in the entire corpus of Iranian literature there is no trace of the today ubiquitous Aryan race (*nezhād-e āriyāyi*) until the 1890s.[32] There are ancient occurrences of *ariya* in the Achaemenid and Sasanian periods and Hamza al-Isfahani used *ariya* as an alternative to Iran in the tenth century AD. But the definition of *ariya* was both more restrictive and fluid. The term had never been attached to anything even remotely resembling "race."[33] This leaves little doubt about the modernity of the concept on the one hand, and its European origin on the other. It was in fact Kermani who was the first Iranian to use the term "Aryan" in the 1890s. In *Seh maktub*, he equated the *majus* or ancient Zoroastrians to the "great Iranian people" and the "noble Aryan (*āriyān*) nation."[34] Similarly, in another work he mentions the "good Aryan people of good extraction."[35] A section in the introduction to his *Ā'ineh-ye sekandari* is called "The beginnings of Iran's history and the Aryan (*āreyan*) nation." As there was simply no equivalent of Aryan in Persian at the time, Kermani had to resort to the European term. He wrote *āriyān* or *āreyan*, which are transliterations of French *aryen*. At the time, Iranian authors had not yet merged the European neologism with the Avestic and Old Persian term "*ariya*." In similar fashion, Kermani referred to Semitic languages as *semetik*, rather than *sāmi*, which is the later indigenized version of the same term.[36] In *Ā'ineh-ye sekandari*, the vowels of *āreyan* are indicated, as is usually the case (at least in this work) when European terms are transliterated, and the actual French term, "*aryen*" is indicated in Roman characters.[37]

This leaves no doubt regarding the non-Iranian origin of the term. He also claims, in typically Kermaniesque fashion, that ancient Iranians were called "āreyan" (and not "ariya") because they worshiped fire and the sun, and this is the origin of the French world "orient."[38] He then attributes the foundations of civilization (boniyād-e ābādi) to these Iranian Aryans, hence subscribing—unsurprisingly—to the theory that Iran was the Aryan Urheimat. He continues by claiming that Germanic people trace their origin to his native Kerman and Zabol (Zhermān = Kermān)![39] The Aryan myth of common origins is laid in plain terms: "They say that Europe, Russian [sic], Rome . . . were initially of the same breed as Iranians and from there were scattered around the world."[40]

It took some time for other Iranian authors to catch up with Kermani's racialist enthusiasm. Slowly concepts of race and racial purity started to appear in historical commentaries, but no politicization was attempted yet. Taqizadeh's highly influential politico-cultural newspaper Kāveh, supported by German propagandists and published out of Berlin from 1916 through 1922, occasionally offered benignly racialist references to the "pure Iranian race."[41] References to Aryans appear but meant as the common ancestors of Iranians and Indians.[42] The New Year festival nowruz, we are told, was an ancient "Aryan ritual."[43] We also learn that ancient Iranians had a calendar system that predated Iranian history and therefore came from "the Aryan race." These initial Aryanist hints were philological rather than political in nature. In particular, one cannot claim that Kāveh was a publication with a racialist outlook: indeed, as the quotation at the beginning of this chapter shows, Taqizadeh had no kind words for the prophets of Aryanism in his country. Similarly benign allusions to ancient Aryans can be found in almost all books on Iranian history written at the time. One such book is noteworthy as it was written for high school pupils by a frequent Minister of Education, Issa Sadiq (1894–1978). In this book, he traced back the origins of Iran to two waves of Aryans that entered the Iranian plateau from the north.[44]

Works by another historian, Sadeq Rezazadeh Shafaq (1897–1971) demonstrate better awareness of contemporary European debates on the Aryan question. For instance, he imparted the theory much en vogue in the 1930s that the "Nordic race" originated in the Danube.[45] At its current stage, my research tends to confirm that he was the first Iranian author to translate the European term "Aryan" into "āriyā" (adj. āriyāyi), rather than merely transliterate it as "āriyān," like Kermani does. It is at this juncture, the term "āriyā" entered the modern Persian language.

More influential were the works of Hassan Pirniya. This patriotic historian was also a high-ranking politician who served six terms as a parliamentarian, twenty-four terms as a minister, and two terms as *ra'is ol-vozarā* (prime minister). His history volumes were some of the first in modern Iran to attempt to abide by the standards of European historical methodology. Yet, although the information he imparted was novel in Iran, his works were mainly compilations of orientalist literature. Like many historians of his generation, Pirniya failed to either add his own findings to or critically engage with European scholarship. This weakness did not prevent his work from having an important impact on Iranians' perception of their history: indeed, he sat on the commission tasked with the development of the first schoolbooks of the Pahlavi era.[46] Given the sheer importance of his historical work at the time, his impact on the type of identity that these schoolbooks instilled among young Iranians is not to be underestimated.

Of particular importance here is his *Tārikh-e Irān-e qadim* (History of ancient Iran; 1928), the first history textbook commissioned by the early Pahlavi state.[47] It comprises a chapter titled "Races—the White-Skinned Race—the Indo-European People," the content of which relies on "the science of race," that is, "the science of differentiating races, and the shapes and qualities of the people belonging to them."[48] The chapter entirely relies on European racial classifications of humankind into Aryans/Indo-Europeans, Semites, and so on, with a terminology borrowed from the common traditions of the Abrahamic faiths, in particular in its reference to the descendants of Noah's sons Japheth, Ham, and Shem, as a classificatory device. Pirniya also assumed that the ancestors of today's Aryans/Indo-Europeans lived in some ancient proto-homeland, and he imparted another opinion much held in the early twentieth century whereby this proto-homeland was the Scandinavian peninsula (hence the appellation "Nordic Race").[49] He therefore assumed that Iranians had migrated from Scandinavia!

According to Pirniya, "it is evident that the name Iran proceeds from [the Aryan people], since [Iranians] used to call themselves *āriyā*, which meant noble or loyal. The ancient name of Iran was *āyrān*, later altered to *ayrān*, *eyrān* and finally *irān*." He further claimed that "*ariyana vaej*" meant "the land of Aryans."[50] As we will see, all these claims are based on the conceptual and semantic confusion of "*ariya*" and "Aryan." Although Pirniya's tone was generally dispassionate, he did occasionally drift away from his rigorous academic pitch and indulge in racist prejudice. For instance, he referred to the "ugliness" and "racial and moral inferiority" of the original "pre-Aryan" inhabitants of

Iran (reference to the Elamites, of whom, it must be said, next to nothing was known at the time) and likewise claimed that, although initially Iranian Aryans had been behind their "Semitic neighbors," the Babylonians and Assyrians in terms of civilization, they were "morally superior" to them.[51]

Early Pahlavi-era schoolbooks, products of their own zeitgeist, duplicated Pirniya's views. An early textbook simply puts it this way: "The people of Iran are part of the Aryan race and their current language is Persian."[52] A geography manual traces the origin of Iranians back to "a group of people belonging to the Aryan race" who "called their homeland Iran."[53] These schoolbooks deliberately portrayed all other "people"—particularly Arabs but also Mongols—as non-Aryan invaders. This message was deeply ingrained in the minds of the first generation of Iranians educated by the Pahlavi state, making them particularly receptive to Aryanist propaganda.

By the beginning of World War I, more specific references to the alleged Aryan brotherhood between Iranians and Germans started to appear. Vahid Dastgerdi (1879–1942), a politically active poet, pamphleteer, and founder of the *Armaghān* (Gift) newspaper, was strongly averse to Russia and Britain and had fervent pro-German sympathies during the Great War. In a politically charged poem in tribute to "Germania," he called on Iranians to join the battlefield against the "ugly fox" (Britain) and "deceitful bear" (Russia), the underlying motivation being that "Iranian and German are united in race."[54] Most Iranians at the time shared his mistrust for *engelis-e por tadlis* (perfidious Albion) and *rus-e manhus* (ominous Russia), and as a result were naturally inclined toward Germany, which had never pursued imperial policies in the region. Germans were also popular in the Arab world for the same reasons. This inclination could also mean sympathy toward National-Socialism, and this sympathy could be reciprocated. In 1933 Seif Azad, an Iranian Nazi activist, started to publish the *Nāmeh-ye Irān bāstān* (The epistle of ancient Iran) journal. It has been claimed that this journal was published under direct supervision of the German Ministry of Propaganda.[55] According to one source, the actual editor of the journal was one Major von Vibran, a political cadre of the Nazi Party.[56] Although the numerous advertisements by German corporations (in particular Siemens-Schukkert) might be taken as an indication of German sources of financing, there is no evidence of any active role the Nazi Party would have taken in supporting or supervising the journal. Moreover, publication started in January 1933, one month before Adolf Hitler was sworn in as chancellor. This excludes an official initiation of the paper, although it does not rule out the involvement of Berlin's propaganda machine at a later stage. Be that as it may, the *Nāmeh-ye Irān bāstān*'s role as a conduit for Nazi propaganda, autonomous or supervised, can hardly be denied. One article reads as follows:

> Those with increased thought and creativity in imagination and action are known as the Aryan group, and those who content themselves with simplicity and whose thoughts remain to some extent stalled are called the Semitic group . . . [Aryans], in any place, at any time, and no matter how they are named, will carry out the same [creative] deeds. Iranian, German, English, French, these are the names of different kinds of Aryans, who have not renounced creativity in thought and deed, and are known for these qualities in the realm of science, although appellation, location and time have made them distinct.[57]

Elsewhere it is said of the swastika that it "was customary among Aryan tribes that comprised Germanic people and Iranians."[58] The author of the article finds it "truly delightful that the sign of Iran [allegedly the swastika] dating back two thousand years before Christ has become today a source of pride for Germans (who are of the same race and family as us)." The article goes on to claim that Iran is the "fatherland of all Aryans." Reporting a commemoration in Berlin where a fire-worship was staged, the newspaper affirms that the Aryan customs "that included igniting the holy fire has been renewed in the celebrations of the Nazis and not long will pass before all ancient Aryan customs, which are the same as those of ancient Iran, be revived in Germany." In yet another issue, Alfred Rosenberg, one of the main ideologues of the Nazi Party, is praised for allegedly advocating that National Socialist Germany should replace Roman and Greek law by "Aryan and Iranian."[59]

The journal is replete with such assertions of racial kinship and rarely misses an opportunity to praise Hitler's vision for his country. Germany's technical achievements and industrial progress, its objective of training the nation into sport, and even trivial pieces of news concerning Germany are given large coverage. The purpose of the *Nāmeh-ye Irān bāstān* is formulated on the front-page of every issue, where often the words "Iran" and "God" and Zoroastrian symbolism are combined with a swastika: the revival of pre-Islamic glory. This objective is pursued through incessant admonitions to purify the Persian language from foreign "non-Aryan" additions. Anti-Semitism is recurrent. The tone is nationalistic and self-serving to the highest possible degree, reviewing the glories and feats of ancient Iranians in the most grandiloquent terms. The journal enjoyed significant popularity among the pro-monarchy literate elites. The repeated advertisements selling past issues are witness to this success.

The idea of the Aryan brotherhood of Iran and Germany was also played up by Germans, who had a strong presence in Iran during the reign of Reza Shah Pahlavi, although a presence with ebbs and flows of its own due to British and Russian wariness. Germany played a prominent role in the industrialization of the country, and large numbers of German expatriates were established in the country, some of whom frequented the German social club Das Deutsches Haus in Tehran.[60] In 1934 the Deutsch-Persische Gesselschaft (German-Persian Society) was established to sponsor various forms of cultural exchanges between Iran and Germany.[61] There have been claims that in 1936 a special decree of the Reich cabinet exempted Iranians from the restrictions of the Nuremberg Racial Laws as "pure Aryans," but according to David Motadel, all foreigners were exempt from these laws, which were only directed against German Jews, and, moreover, this legislation never used the term "Aryan."[62] That being said, the theme of Aryan brotherhood was one aspect of Nazi propaganda toward Iran. According to George Lenczowski, who was then posted as a press attaché to the Polish Embassy in Tehran, the Nazis made great use

of the Aryan legend to encourage friendship between both nations. The adoption of the swastika as a symbol of the Nazi party was interpreted as pointing to the spiritual unity between the Aryans of the north and the nation of Zoroaster. . . . The German government presented Iran with a collection of books called the German Scientific Library, composed of 7,500 volumes. These carefully selected books were destined to convince Iranian readers of the cultural mission of Germany in the East and of the kinship between the National Socialist Reich and the "Aryan culture" of Iran.[63]

The Radio Berlin broadcasts in Persian were another channel used by the Germans to instill Aryanist ideas into Iran. The head of these programs was Bahram Shahrokh. Born to a prominent Zoroastrian family and son of Reza Shah's advisor, Keykhosrow Shahrokh, he had received his university education in Germany, where he acquired pro-Nazi sympathies and, according to one source, became a trainee of Joseph Goebbels (although this is dubious).[64] It is interesting to note that after the war, Mohammad Reza Shah appointed him to the post of director of news and propaganda, along with a number of members of the Nazi-inspired and pro-monarchy party, the Nationalist-Socialist Workers Party of Iran (known under the Iranian acronym SUMKA), who were given other key posts.

RECEPTION OF ARYANISM AND DISLOCATION

Dislocative nationalists do not acknowledge their debt to a modern racial theory formulated in nineteenth-century Europe.[65] Instead, they claim that the inhabitants of the Iranian plateau have been racially conscious of their Aryanness since time immemorial.[66] The name "Iran" and the recurrence of the word "*ariya*" in a number of pre-Islamic sources seem to corroborate this belief.[67] Although Aryan is a modernized and Europeanized version of ancient "*ariya*," I argue that the two terms are far from relaying the same meaning, and that the antique incidences of "*ariya*" can in no way be used to support the claims of modern Aryanism. The disconnection between ancient Iranian "*ariya*" and modern European "Aryan" has so far escaped serious investigation. To advocate a strict distinction between "*ariya*" and "Aryan," a detour by these ancient scriptures is necessary, and I hope the reader will forgive the liberty I take—once again—with chronology.

The term "*ariya*" and its variations occur several times in ancient sources. The Avesta refers to "*airyanem vaejah*." This is a location where mythistorical events take place, and is usually translated as "the *ariya* plain" or "expanse."[68] The Avesta mentions several other place-names containing "*ariya*" and describes several mythic heroes in relation to their being of the *ariyas*, like "the most swift-arrowed of all *ariyas*" (Arash) or "the hero of *ariyas*" (Key Khosrow). On the inscriptions of Naqsh-e Rostam, the descent of kings Darius and Xerxes is defined as "*hakhamanishiya; parsa, parsahya pucha; ariya, ariyachicha*" (an Achaemenid; a Persian, son of a Persian; *ariya*, of *ariya* stock). And in one inscription in Elamite at Bisotun, the Mazdean and Zoroastrian divinity Ahura Mazda is defined as "the God of *ariyas*," while in another, "*ariya*" is referred to as a language. Herodotus called the Medes "*arioi*," while before him Hellanicus believed that "*ariya*" was just another name for Persia.[69]

The Indian Rig Veda use another variety of "*ariya*" in similar senses, and the authors of the Vedic texts also defined themselves as *ariya*.[70] It is likely that the authors of the Avesta and the Rig Veda were culturally related as linguistic similarity between the two texts is striking, especially the oldest parts.[71] A comparative perspective should not detain us here as the debate on Sanskrit *ariya*'s meaning and its connection with the Iranian version still has some way to go.[72] Be that as it may, it has been argued based on these occurrences that *"ariya"* in the Iranian sources refers to a group of people sharing a common cultural and linguistic heritage, who defined themselves as *ariya* against *an-ariya*, or non-*ariyas*. Within this context, it is also claimed that the term "Iran" derives from *ariya* too. Indeed, by Sasanian times, *eran* meant "of the *ers*" or *ariyas*, while *eran shahr* was the official appellation of the Sasanian empire. This appellation was a Sasanian invention, a political device, as it were, to strengthen the legitimacy of the new empire by reference to the past. Be that as it may, the modern term "Iran" derives from *"eran"* and *"eran shahr,"* meaning once again "the land (or the expanse) of the *ariyas*."

The literature, both orientalist and nationalist, has been quite careless in deriving conclusions from these sources on the premodern existence of an Iranian nation, or the timeless racial consciousness of Aryans. Any reference to *"ariya"* in ancient sources is immediately taken as testimony of the primordial existence of a cultural or racial Iranian nation. The reality is that we know very little about what exactly *ariya* referred to. For instance, an Elamite inscription at Bisotun refers to *ariya* as a language rather than a people. We could, analyzing King Darius's declaration, infer that *"ariya"* is a sort of ethnonym meaning "the people," similarly, for instance, to "Hellen" or "Teuton." However, no evidence undermines the possibility that *"ariya"* was a more restricted category, such as a social class. If *"ariya"* is a socionym, we could then surmise that King Darius, by declaring that he is *ariya* of *ariya* stock, is simply emphasizing his nobility. This would square with the case made elsewhere that etymologically *"ariya"* meant "of good birth," denoting ideas of nobility and lordship (although this reading would not fully explain why the socionym comes *after* Darius's assertion of being a member of the ruling Achaemenid dynasty *and* a Persian).[73] Importantly, we cannot be certain that this appellation was applied beyond the elites, as the masses of peasants and artisans who were the subjects of the King of Kings have not left any written source behind. It is therefore impossible to ascertain whether *they* referred to themselves as *ariya* or not.

To complicate the matter, the meaning of *"ariya"* evolved and changed significantly throughout the pre-Islamic period. By the late Sasanian period (c. AD 500–651), *"ariya"* is neither a socionym nor an ethnonym, not even a linguistic or religious idea. In official Sasanian inscriptions, *"ariya"* is incontrovertibly a territorial and political concept without any cultural charge. Indeed, King Shapur I took the title of *shahanshah eran ud aneran*: King of *eran* and *aneran* (non-*eran*), of the *ariyas/ers* and the non-*ariyas/ers*. What is meant by *"eran"* and *"aneran"* is then explicated in another inscription at Naqsh-e

Rostam by the high-priest Kerdir. *Eran* is composed of Parthia, Susiane, Mesopotamia, Ray, Sakastene, Hyrcania, Khorasan, and Touran; *aneran* is composed of Antioch, Syria, Tarsos, Cilicia, Caesarea, Cappadocia, and Armenia.[74] In this definition, the *ariyas* (*eran*) are the people who had previously already been under Sasanian rule, and non-*ariyas* are the people who had recently integrated the imperial system following the conquests of King Shapur I. Both groups include widely diverse groups of peoples, languages, and cultural or religious practices. Furthermore, there are groups among the *ariyas* that Aryanist ethnology would consider "Semitic" (Mesopotamians), and groups that would be considered "Aryans" in the non-*ariya* group (Armenians).

The intermediary conclusion inferred from this analysis is that ancient *ariya* and modern Aryan do not refer to the same group of people. At the very least, what is irrefutable is that *"ariya"* is not a racial category. This would have been impossible simply because the division of humankind into biological or cultural categories is a modern European invention. The confusion between *"ariya"* and "Aryan" is a particularly acute case of anachronism, one that has distorted ancient sources and exploited them to confer credibility to the Aryan myth in Iran and elsewhere. Modern Aryan, although semantically derived from *"ariya,"* is a racial category born in the nineteenth century, and whose very conceptualization was only made possible with the advances of modern linguistics, racial anthropology, and comparative philology. It unites modern Indians, Iranians, and Europeans under one large racial cluster and endows them with biological, cultural, and psychological characteristics. Even regardless of the above analysis, the term *"ariya"* never referred to any inhabitant of the European continent (for instance, Romans or Greeks) and could occasionally include "Semitic" populations. The confusion of the two terms stems from the fact that an existing collective term with a fluid and changing signification (*ariya*) has been hijacked to describe a deterministic modern racial idea (Aryan).

In Europe, the analytical usefulness of the term "Aryan" started to be questioned as early as the 1940s. In 1941, when Nazis ruled Germany and civilians were about to be sent to death for failing to be Aryan, a German scholar, Hans Siegert, suggested that the use of the term "Aryan" should be abandoned altogether. According to Siegert, we have words at our disposal to mean Iranian, Indo-Iranian, Indo-European, and German-blooded, therefore there is no room for a word (Aryan) that "is ambiguous and lacks any . . . scientific clarity."[75] Moreover, the meaning of *"ariya"* remains largely contested, and experts regularly formulate new hypotheses. For instance, Jean Kellens has recently argued that only in the Iranian context is *"ariya"* an ethnonym (as opposed to the Vedic context, where it is not, according to him). Hence, it should be neither "reproduced as it is, nor adapted in any modern language," but rather translated, and the only valid translation is simply "Iranian": Kellens invites us to say "farewell to the term 'Aryan.' We have no reason to regret it: it comes with a lot of baggage."[76]

In this light, the idea that Iran means the "land of Aryans" (in the sense of the Aryan race) and that it was the Urheimat of the ancestors of Iranians, Indians, and all Europeans is not a defensible proposition. The definition of Iran as "the land of Aryans" was popularized by Müller, who in 1861 claimed that the term *"ariya"* found in the Zend-Avesta indicated both a people and a land, and that *"airyanem vaejah"* in fact meant the "Aryan seed," denoting the origin of Aryans.[77] Since then and to this day, Iran has been abundantly and erroneously referred to as the "land of Aryans" in popular and scientific writings alike.[78] The meaning of Iran as the "expanse (or land) of *ariyas"* is transmuted by its passage through modern Aryanism into a land populated by a particular race.[79]

Conceptually, the "land of Aryans" is the product of a period that believed in and advocated the homogeneity of populations within national boundaries—in other words, the congruence of nation and territory. The concept of the "land of Aryans" in nationalist writing and Pahlavi schoolbooks argues that Iran is a highly cohesive and primordial nation, contained as it was from its racially distinct neighbors. At best, it sweeps Iran's ethnic minorities under the Aryan carpet; at worst, it portrays them as non-Aryans and therefore alien.[80] This has been a consistent trend within Iranian Aryanism. Taqi Arani, the Berlin-educated Azerbaijani essayist who was an ardent nationalist (but later went on to found a Marxist-Leninist party) and an enthusiastic advocate of the purification of the Persian language, saw Azerbaijani Turkish to be an imposition of the Mongol invaders on Azerbaijan's Aryans and a language better stamped out.[81] This approach (to his own linguistic kin) assumes that Iran's territory is congruent with some Aryan nation, and that the adoption of non-Aryan loanwords and dialects must be eliminated to recover the nation's racial purity. It should hardly come as a surprise that in the same period, the early Pahlavi state was ruthlessly repressing Iran's linguistic minorities, nomads, and tribes.

Reality is very different from these assumptions of racial homogeneity. History is a long succession of migrations and synthesis through war, interaction, and amalgamation. All sources, written and material, including those accessible to Aryanists and dislocative nationalists, suggest that the Iranian plateau has always been home to a heterogeneous population, specifically due to its geographical situation at the crossroads of several migration and trading routes between Central Asia, the Middle East, and the Indian subcontinent. Most inscriptions in Persepolis and other sites are in several languages. The influence of Akkadians, Assyrians, Egyptians—people deemed "Semitic" in racial parlance—is prominent in the architecture of Achaemenid and Sasanian Iran.

It is very difficult if not impossible to reconstruct even an approximate image of the ethnic, linguistic, and cultural landscape of pre-Achaemenid Iran. We dispose of little material evidence, and whatever we have is usually open to multiple interpretations. A range of specialists (linguists, archaeologists, geneticists, historians) work on this material with mutually incomprehensible jargons and methodologies.[82] That Persian is one among many Iranian languages that have similarities with idioms of the Indo-European group is the only certainty, but using it to draw conclusions about ethnicity or migrations, to draw arrows on large maps, or to claim that Iranians are in some bizarre way more akin to Germans than to, say, Iraqis or Turks, defies common sense and empirical rigor. The results of comparative vocabulary analyses, the study of anonymous artifacts, and the attempts to use these frugal elements to construct a sweeping narrative of migration and kinship is scientifically not viable.

When Kermani, Rezazadeh Shafaq, and Pirniya introduced the modern European term "Aryan" ("āriyān," later "āriyāyi"), they infused ancient ariya with a new racial meaning. It is safe to assert that in modern Iran, nezhād-e āriyāyi, is not invoked as meaning Iran or Iranian or denote a community of language and culture between the various Iranian groups but almost always as evidence of Iranians' alleged racial bond with Europeans, or at the very least their opposition to Arabs/Semites. All the sources mentioned here are in this way indebted to European nineteenth-century racialist views. By confusing the ancient appellation "ariya" with modern "Aryan," a new strategy of racial demarcation from Arabs and Turks, and racial merger of Iranians and Europeans—in other words, a case of dislocation—was legitimized by reference to ancient sources.

The overview of the tenets of dislocative nationalism as offered in the previous chapters gives a clue as to why dislocative nationalist circles have been so receptive to Aryanism. Akhundzadeh and Kermani for the first time relayed the division of humankind along racial lines to an Iranian audience. But they did not refer to the terminology of Aryanism in unequivocal terms; Kermani did so only on a handful of occasions. It was the next generation of dislocative nationalists, more seasoned in racial thinking thanks to Akhundzadeh and Kermani, who fully exploited the potential of Aryanism to garb their ideology with the language of European science. Dislocative nationalists' complex of inferiority toward Europe could only uncritically embrace an ideational construct that defined Iranians as racially akin to Europeans. This made the reception and adaptation of Aryanism all the more swift and natural. Comforting nationalist thinkers in their easy way out of the historical dilemma of Iran's downfall, there is no wonder why Aryanism has become such a central element of the nationalist definition of identity. It is a comfortable belief without being a belief: it is a scientific theory. Not only that, it was developed in Europe. How can Europeans be wrong?

Thanks to its authority, Aryanism significantly strengthened the ideological apparatus of dislocative nationalism, its discursive nature, and its inherent racialism. It became the core element of an intellectual edifice that attempted to explain Iran's decay in the simplest terms possible: ancient Iran was magnificent because purely Aryan, then Iran's glory waned because the Arabs and later Mongols came, and in the future Iran has to blindly Westernize itself to become Aryan again. This discursive program, this vision of a future with an eye on an imagined past, brought about what I consider to be the feature that sets the nationalism of Akhundzadeh and Kermani apart from other ideologies: dislocation. Indeed, I have been referring to this concept throughout this book, but it is only this discussion of Aryanism that sheds definite light on its meaning. Dislocation is the attempt, through the historicist discourse of nation and race consolidated by the pseudo-scientific arsenal of Aryanism, to *dislodge* Iran from its Islamic and Eastern reality and artificially force it into a European one. As mentioned in the introduction, I do not aim here to reify Iran as essentially Islamic but simply suggest that Iran and Islam have some form of connection, whereas Iran's racial or cultural kinship with Europe can only be underpinned by Aryanist assumptions. Aryanism finally allowed Akhundzadeh's and Kermani's objective of imaginary dislocation to be fulfilled: Iran is now dissociated from Islam, and the grandeur of Europe can somewhat be claimed as ours too—all this with the apparent seal of approval of Europeans themselves. In one magical stroke, this ideational construct solves dislocative nationalists' anxieties rooted in a sense of inferiority toward Europe and their grappling with Iran's deficiencies.

Mohammad Reza Shah's claim that it was "an accident of geography" that Iran found itself in the Middle East is the clearest possible expression of dislocation.[83] In Mohammad Reza Shah's version, dislocation had been achieved thanks to his own leadership. In his mind, Iran was still situated on the Asian continent; however, it had nothing to do with Islam or the Middle East anymore. Iran was Europe's newly found cousin: as he once said, "yes, we are Easterners, but we are Aryans. This Middle East, what is it? One can no longer find us there. But Asia, yes. We are an Asian Aryan power whose mentality and philosophy are close to those of the European states, above all France."[84]

Testimony to the prevalence of dislocation in the early Pahlavi era is the modification of the international designation of Persia into Iran on Farvardin 1, 1314 (March 22, 1935). It is beyond doubt that *Iran* is a legitimate designation with a long history. However, the Pahlavi state's argument for this sudden change was altogether tainted with a dislocation syndrome. The government directive pertaining to the change from Persia to Iran read:

> From a racial point of view, as Iran was the original home of the *āriyan* [transliterated from French] race, it is natural that we should want to take advantage of this name, particularly since these days in the great countries of the world rumors around the Aryan race have arisen that indicate the greatness of the race and civilization of ancient Iran.[85]

I should add that this directive shows that in addition to racial considerations, anxiety about the sort of ideas that the term "Persia" might evoke in the minds of informed "foreigners" equally played a role in the international modification. It was naively believed that a new term would simply expunge the country from any preconception of backwardness and chaos, allowing Reza Shah's Iran to start on a new footing. The belief that one can evade empirical reality and history by changing a label has not entirely disappeared as many today promote in similar fashion a return to Persia in order to somehow cleanse the Iranian consciousness of the mischiefs of the Islamic Republic (hence the almost universal self-reference of American Iranians as "Persians").

It has been claimed that the initial idea of the international modification came from German officials who recommended the move to Iranian diplomats in Berlin.[86] Elsewhere, it is said that it was Ernst Herzfeld, a German archaeologist who had the shah's ear, who first suggested the international modification.[87] The official documents do confirm that the initial proposal emanated from Iran's imperial legation in Berlin, but it is not clear who exactly suggested it to the ambassador in the first instance.[88] Be that as it may, and as it appears from this directive, the appellation "Iran"—regardless of the legitimacy of its historical use—was perceived to be more suitable in portray-ing Iran as an Aryan nation, cousin of the so-adulated Europeans. The irony of dislocative nationalism is that it acts as a preservative for outmoded intel-lectual trends. It has effectively imprisoned its Iranian adherents in a racial-historicist worldview that belongs to nineteenth-century and early-twentieth-century Europe, in a way perpetuating intellectual "backwardness" vis-à-vis Europe, which has in the meantime subjected Aryanist assumptions to rigor-ous reconsideration and largely moved on.

7

THE ROAD TO OFFICIALDOM

An Asiatic nation's brain is not made like a European nation's brain.
—Arthur de Gobineau, 1866

If you want to understand Iran, you must read Gobineau.
—Fereydun Hoveyda, 1980

IT COULD BE ARGUED THAT BY PRESENTING AKHUNDZADEH AND Kermani as the initiators of dislocative nationalism, I am succumbing to what Skinner calls the "mythology of doctrines"—in other words, the anachronistic illusion that we can link a classical author to an ideology, the contours of which became apparent only after the author's death.[1] Indeed, the two authors never referred to dislocative nationalism in their writings, and never clearly stated that their intention was to enunciate a new ideology, nationalist or otherwise. However, I have so far tried to determine the two authors' intentionality by emphasizing their aims to bring about a new thinking among Iranians about their past and who or what to blame for their shortcomings. Akhundzadeh's and Kermani's texts and correspondence are replete with statements of this intention to change Iranians' outlook, for instance, Akhundzadeh's wish to make them realize that Arabs were "the enemies of their lives and possessions."[2] Other indications have been referred to in this book. It remains to be seen whether the two authors did indeed bring about a new thinking—or, in my view, a novel nationalist ideology. In other words, how and when did dislocative nationalism start to become a potent lens used to interpret the issues confronting society?

Akhundzadeh's plays—originally written in Azeri Turkish—were translated by Mirza Ja'far Qaracheh Daghi, Jalal ed-Din Mirza's secretary, and published between 1871 and 1874.[3] Akhundzadeh's *Maktubāt*, on the other hand, were not to be published during his lifetime, despite the author's relentless efforts. In 1874 a Russian translation by Akhundzadeh himself was rejected by all the publishing houses it was sent to.[4] One would have to wait until 1979, when the Iranian Revolution opened a propitious gap between the official censorship of the Pahlavi state and that of the Islamic Republic, to see a first edition of the *Maktubāt* published in Tabriz.[5] In Akhundzadeh's own time, in the absence of printed copies, only a handful of close friends to whom he sent manuscripts—as shown by his correspondence—read the *Maktubāt* and ensured its limited dissemination. It is beyond doubt that Kermani read one of these handwritten copies, his own *Seh maktub* being an overt tribute to, and often a paraphrase of, the *Maktubāt*. In addition to manuscripts, oral dissemination remained for a long time the main channel for the transmission of ideas in Qajar Iran, as printing houses were few and were subject to censorship. Most importantly, books were unaffordable for most people as paper was imported and fetched a high price.[6] It should also be remembered that the circle of Qajar intellectuals was limited to a handful of individuals, and this certainly increased the speed and scope of the oral circulation of ideas. Oral circulation also could take place in informal gatherings of intellectuals, modernist circles, groupings emulating the Freemason model (such as Malkam Khan's *farāmush khāneh*, or house of oblivion) or the constitutionalist *anjomans* (societies).

Unlike Akhundzadeh, Kermani's works were all written in Persian. Yet, similarly to his master's, many of his treatises must still be read as manuscripts held by various individuals and institutions.[7] Only a few of his historical works were published in the early decades following his death: his *Āʿineh-ye sekandari* was published in 1909, and his *Sālārnāmeh*, a history of pre-Islamic Iran, was released in 1937. A few of his essays were later published in the 1950s and 1960s (including *Hasht Behesht*, the Babi treatise he coauthored), but one had to wait until 2005 and 2007, respectively, to see the first print editions of his nationalist works, *Seh maktub* and *Sad khatābeh* (Frankfurt and Los Angeles).[8]

These limitations did not hamper the dissemination of Akhundzadeh's and Kermani's texts but simply obscured their authors. For instance, the newspaper *Tamaddon*, in a 1907 issue, paraphrased Akhundzadeh's description of the territorial expanse of pre-Islamic Iran (quoted in chapter 2), bordered by the Jayhun River, the Aral Sea, the Sutlej River between "Sind and Hindustan" and the Bosphorus, making it highly likely that the editors had read the

Maktubāt.[9] However, Akhundzadeh is not acknowledged, and his name appears nowhere in the article. These texts remained under the skin of the intelligentsia, eclipsed by modernism and constitutionalism until the chaos that succeeded the Constitutional Revolution. It is only then that dislocative nationalism started to gradually make an impression on Iranian intellectuals, who relayed its doctrine in their own works, generally without any reference to Akhundzadeh or Kermani. From the aftermath of World War I to the rise of the early Pahlavi state (approximately 1915 to 1925), one can clearly trace the gradual propagation of dislocative nationalism in politico-cultural pamphleteering. By the 1920s the ideology was solidly established among the elites. In particular, many of the bright young men who composed the inner circle of Reza Shah had joined the dislocative bandwagon and in time helped transform Akhundzadeh's and Kermani's doctrine into official state ideology. The startling rise of dislocative nationalism from the pages of obscure unpublished treatises to the corridors of power is the subject of this chapter.

GESTATION AND CONSTITUTIONALISM

Iran's long process of self-questioning—instigated by the traumatic encounter with Europe—came to age with the Constitutional era.[10] Most Iranian intellectuals had by then espoused one form or the other of modernism and were determined to create a rupture in Iranian history in order to drag the country out of stagnation. They also aimed to put an end to both the unlawful and disorderly exercise of power and the interference of Britain and Russia. Some Qajar princes and courtly officials, as well as the clergy who were wary of European influence in all its forms, put up tremendous resistance and attempted to at least partly maintain the status quo, although many princes and clergymen were also engaged in, or even led, revolutionary activities. Homa Katouzian reports a handful of anecdotes that give a vivid idea of the negative reception reserved for some superficial modernist attitudes during those days:

> Aref-e Qazvini, the nationalist poet and musician, had once entered a mosque in Qazvin, and been excommunicated (*takfir*) immediately because he was wearing a pair of Russian boots. Ali Akbar Davar, the future minister of justice and finance, had returned from Switzerland planning to hold a carnival in Tehran. Divan-Baigi, a future senator, had decided to change his name to Divan *de* Baigi, a decision that prompted a barrage

of abuse against him . . . from fellow modernists . . . who thought it was an insult to the Iranian sense of national self-respect.[11]

The Constitutional Revolution of 1906–1911 was the culmination of modernism in its pragmatic variety. The revolutionaries' main objective was to subject royal power to constitutional checks (*mashruteh sākhtan*) and make the state responsible before the people; according to Katouzian, it was a "Revolution for Law."

Yet, it has been argued that there was a nationalist aspect to this revolution as well.[12] Undoubtedly, Iranian constitutionalism was intensely concerned with imperialist influence in Iran and sought to put an end to it by limiting the royal prerogative to offer concessions. Additionally, Iran was an identifiable territorial state, however weak, and it was both the stage where the political struggle of the constitutionalists was unfolding and the object of their reform project. The congruence of state (*dowlat*) and people (*mellat*) was promoted and the constitutionalists aimed to implement their reforms within the territorial bounds of the Qajar state: nothing more, nothing less. Students of Iran have already noted the changing vocabulary of patriotism, which matured during the Constitutional Revolution and lends credence to this proposition.[13] The term "*mellat*" semantically evolved from the nineteenth century until the early Pahlavi era from meaning "community," one with religious connotations, to approximately "nation," in a Herderian, secular, and modern sense.[14] "*Vatan*" also evolved from meaning one's village, town, or province of origin to taking on the larger mantle of national home. Iran itself "was re-imagined to conform to the territorial realities of the 19th century."[15]

Edward G. Browne was the first author to offer a "nationalist" reading of the Constitutional Revolution. He remarked in his *Persian Revolution of 1905–1909* that "throughout their struggle [for a constitutional order] Persians have consciously been fighting for their very existence as a Nation, and in this sense the popular or constitutional party may very properly be termed 'Nationalists.'"[16] In his view, nationalism is essentially the resistance of people overseas seeking independence and autonomy from European imperial domination or from local rulers seen as puppets of the latter. Anti-imperialist struggles were positively viewed by European liberal idealists such as Browne. But there is more to his definition of nationalism, as he claims that there has been a division between—precisely—*mellat* defined as people/nation and *dowlat*, the state.[17] The constitutional struggle therefore aimed to align the interest of the nation and the state—in other words, bring about a modern nation-state (although confrontation between the two continued beyond the Revolution). He further asserts that the constitutionalists were "essentially patriotic" and stood "for progress, freedom, tolerance, and above all for national independence and 'Persia for the Persians.' "[18]

Following this line of reasoning, the Constitutional Revolution included a nationalist element, on account of its anti-imperialist outlook and some of its vocabulary. Janet Afary too seems to support the case for a semantic slide toward nationalism when she remarks that calls of "Long live Islam" and "death to 'Ain od-Dowleh" (the prime minister) soon were superseded by "Long live Iran."[19] Afary is right to point out that this semantic evolution from Islam to Iran was significant. It seemed to signal that confessional and regional belonging might be superseded by a sense of nationhood transcending these divides. At closer look, however, both claims can be qualified. It remains incontrovertible that the language of the Constitutional Revolution was largely religious, and the protagonists more often than not invoked religious symbols. As far as nationalist resistance to foreign interference was concerned, it was only a second objective, the main aim of the movement being to reform the state. The uproar against the projected 1919 Anglo-Iranian agreement in addition to—perhaps most importantly of all—the nationalization of oil by Mosaddeq in 1953, were much clearer cases of movements targeting Western imperial interests. In the case of oil nationalization particularly, the movement had an anti-imperialist objective that made it fit well into a form of anticolonial struggle.

A more convincing view would be to interpret the constitutional movement as a case of civic nationalism. The distinction between civic and ethnic nationalism was first formulated by Hans Kohn in his *The Idea of Nationalism* (1944) and remains to this day one of the most debated aspects of nationalism theory. Civic nationalism is usually embodied in liberal institutions to which citizens bound by common rational laws can belong, irrespective of ethnicity or religion. The United States, the United Kingdom, and the French Republic represent classic cases of civic nationalism. Ethnic nationalism, on the other hand, projects a more closed, ascriptive, and particularist definition of identity in cultural or even racial terms and is common in Eastern Europe (and also Germany, arguably, until recently).[20] Following this model, one could claim that the constitutional movement was a case of civic nationalism because its reforms were designed to be enacted within a particular Iranian state in its relationship with an Iranian territorial citizenry. Had the constitutional movement survived longer, the institutions it created—the constitution, the *majles* (parliament), and its embryo of bureaucratic and educational apparatuses—could have become the repository of a civic form of identity, heralding a sense of belonging to a legitimate (if not democratic) Iranian state, rather than a historicist and racial definition of the Iranian nation carrying with it the despotic tendencies described in chapter 5. Of course this is all counterfactual. As we will see, the constitutional movement lost its momentum and its gains, including institutional gains, and never attained the level of consolidation necessary to become the repository of any form of civic nationalism, or one that could at least be historically analyzed as such.

There are therefore at least two ways to look at the Constitutional Revolution through the lens of nationalism: consider that it included an important—although secondary—element of anti-imperialist resistance, or that it was an early form of civic nationalism. Yet some authors, chiefly Adamiyat and Ajudani, have argued that not only was the Constitutional Revolution "nationalistic" but it was also the fruition of Akhundzadeh's and Kermani's thought. This proposition is difficult to defend in view of the analysis of the tenets of dislocative nationalism as offered in the previous chapters. Although the Constitutional Revolution was carried out within a national frame, it owed nothing to the *Maktubāt* or *Seh maktub* and *Sad khatābeh*. No revolutionary is known to have considered Arabs as the culprits for Iran's misery, otherwise one would expect violence against Iran's Arab population (or their "agents," the Shiʻite clerics) to have taken place. There is no recorded trace of such violence, at least during that period. Uprooting Islam was not a demand of the constitutionalists either, as in fact religion played an important role in the language and even the logistics of the Revolution. Sit-ins (*bast*) and protests were held in mosques, which served as a nationwide network of popular assemblies disseminating revolutionary ideas and coordinating activities (in similar fashion than in the Islamic Revolution of 1979).

Claims that pre-Islamic Iran was a more fitting model for the country's future as opposed to Islamic Iran were also notably absent from the ideas that had currency on the streets of Tehran and Tabriz those days—and for good reason. One does not see how the discursive and historicist narrative of dislocative nationalism could have provided the constitutionalists with tangible political goals to aspire to. As a matter of fact, and according to Charles Kurzman, "constitutionalists frequently held up early Islamic history as a model for the contemporary Iranian nation, both privately and publicly. Virtually all of the movement's public documents, even when they chastised religious leaders, appealed to Islamic ideals and precedents."[21] Moreover, none of the

revolutionaries is known to have advocated alphabet reform or linguistic purification as the objective of Iranian constitutionalism. In terms of modern European ideas of, for instance, representative government, the prominence of
these ideas during the Constitutional Revolution was not in the slightest
owed to Akhundzadeh's and Kermani's thought, as these ideas had more articulate and less ambivalent promoters in Malkam Khan, Talebof, Mostashar
od-Dowleh, and others. Malkam Khan expressed them in pragmatic and ac-
tionable terms in his sizable work, first his early *Ketābcheh-ye gheybi* (The
booklet of the unseen, 1859) and later in his newspaper *Qānun* (Law, 1890–
1896). His devotee, Mostashar od-Dowleh, also wrote a book entitled *Yek ka-
lameh* (One word), and that one word "which would solve all the country's
main ills was thus dramatically revealed to be LAW."[22]

In spite of its laudable program, the Constitutional Revolution failed to deliver on its promises. So much so that some years later, Seyyed Mohammad
Reza Mosavat, a prominent constitutionalist, wrote to Hassan Taqizadeh that
the Iranian people will never forgive them for having participated in the Constitutional Revolution.[23] High hopes had been created, but the chaos that followed the establishment of constitutional government—largely due to the
weakness of the state, the onslaught of various rebellions, institutional dysfunc-
tion, and foreign intervention—brought the constitutional merry-go-round to
a juddering halt. According to Katouzian, "confusion between the *separation*
of powers and the *confrontation* of powers" paralyzed the newly elected
majles.[24] Inept governments followed each other at great speed, incapable
of implementing their policies, while parliamentary groups were caught in a
seemingly endless spiral of quarrels and discord. The interference of imperial
powers, especially Russia, whose officers supported the shah's 1908 coup and
cannonaded the *majles*, was another feature of the postconstitutional order. It
took the uprisings of Tabriz, Gilan, and that of Bakhtiyari tribesmen in Isfahan
in addition to pressure from Britain (and even Russia, at some later stage) for
the shah to yield and give in to constitutional government again. External interference culminated with the 1907 Anglo-Russian convention dividing Iran
into three zones, two recognized as Russian and British spheres of influence
and the third neutral. Internal instability was followed by the outbreak of the
hostilities of World War I, in which Iran effectively served as a theater for the
warring parties. British, Russian, and Ottoman troops moved unopposed in
the country and caused great suffering to the population.

In the years following World War I, Iranian intellectuals were left in disar-
ray. Constitutionalism had failed to deliver the moon, and many of them

turned their attention to alternative ideologies. They needed another panacea to replace law as the certain route to salvation. While socialist ideologies were starting to make an impression on Iran's intellectuals, it was also in those years that dislocative nationalism started its—at first timid but later inexorable— upsurge. This only furthers the point about the necessity to draw a line between dislocative nationalism and constitutionalism. Not only did the Constitutional Revolution owe nothing to the ideology of Akhundzadeh and Kermani, but in fact dislocative nationalism started a life of its own only once constitutional-ism had failed in the minds of most intellectuals. Constitutionalism competed with dislocative nationalism, rather than deriving from it. Dislocative nation-alism imposed itself in a process of gradual infiltration rather than a sudden wholesale adoption. Overall, the still unresolved trauma of Iran's encounter with Europe and the apparent failure of constitutionalism brought about an ideal environment for an ideological shift. If we upheld the thesis that the con-stitutional movement was a case of civic nationalism, then we could see here a typical situation in which ethnic nationalism rises from the ashes of civic nationalism, when people cannot see their way through political reforms. The transition from the Republic of Weimar to the National-Socialist state in Germany is one example. In other words, one can see such historical evolutions through the lens of ideological escapism. According to John Breuilly, when a "massive crisis has undermined the modern institutions of power," such transi-tion can take place and a "charismatic leader can emerge."[25] The charismatic leader of the transition in Iran was Reza Khan.

Before getting there, the uproar that followed the signing of the provisional Anglo-Iranian agreement of 1919, negotiated between Lord Curzon the Brit-ish Foreign Secretary and a "triumvirate" formed by Iranian Chief Minister Vosuq od-Dowleh and two cabinet ministers, must be reviewed to signal a momentous change in the intellectuals' stance toward European powers. By the provisions of the agreement, Britain committed—at Iran's cost—to provide the country with advisors to run its administration, military experts to build a new army, a loan of £2 million, and assistance to develop the country's rail-way infrastructure. The agreement was a direct result of the state of weakness and impending disintegration in which Iran found itself in the aftermath of World War I, and of the temporary withdrawal of Russia as a regional power due to the 1917 Revolution. The secrecy surrounding the negotiations, the (reluctant) payment of money by the British negotiators to their Iranian coun-terparts to secure the ratification of the *majles*, the disagreements between the different British ministries and the Government of India, and a sustained campaign against the agreement in France, Russia, and the United States caused such an uproar in Iran that the agreement was never ratified and later even annulled. The opponents to the agreement believed that it aimed to turn Iran into a British protectorate.[26]

By the end of the second decade of the twentieth century, Iranians had grown increasingly wary of imperial encroachments. The experience of World War I, with its stream of imperial machinations and resulting privations for Iranians leading to famine, had been essential in this process. So had been the withdrawal from the Iranian scene of now Bolshevik Russia, leaving Britain as the only possible target of rising anti-imperialist sentiments in Iran. The recent devolution of a mandate over Mesopotamia—a mainly Shi'ite land home to the sacred Shi'ite shrines of Najaf and Karbala, where many Iranians lived—to Britain made this danger look more immediate. Matters came to a head when the Bolsheviks landed their fleet in the Caspian port of Anzali, and British forces evacuated the area. This aggression could have been avoided if Lord Curzon had not effectively prevented Vosuq od-Dowleh from bargaining with the Bolsheviks. This episode annihilated whatever goodwill still existed in Iran for Britain, and the agreement.[27] The uproar against the 1919 agreement cut through Iran's society and political factions and provided an opportunity for patriotic exuberance and appeals to the "motherland" that, according to universal belief, had just been sold to Britain.[28]

There is no basis to claim that this uproar was expressed in dislocative nationalist terms. As a matter of fact, the enemy here being Britain rather than "backwardness" or "Islam," dislocative nationalism provided few ideological ammunitions to be fired at the agreement (although Aref-e Qazvini wrote in a poem "God condemn to everlasting shame / He who betrayed the land of Sassan"[29]). There were general concerns about Iran's independence, and one can imagine that anyone, regardless of political sympathies, could oppose an instrument perceived to surrender the country's sovereignty. What matters in terms of the history of dislocative nationalism is that a different approach to Europe and European powers imposed itself after these events and modified for good one particular aspect of the doctrine inherited from Akhundzadeh and Kermani. As mentioned in chapter 5, the founding fathers of dislocative nationalism were no anticolonial rebels, and their infatuation with France and Britain was such that they never openly criticized European imperial adventures overseas. Quite the contrary, in fact, as Akhundzadeh himself was a comprador intellectual serving the interests of tsarist Russia's southward expansion:

it should be remembered that the reviled 1828 Turkmenchay Treaty was signed by Akhundzadeh's first employer, Viceroy Paskevich.

Yet wariness of imperial encroachments reached such intensity in 1919 that it had a lasting impact on mainstream Iranian politics. All the intellectuals who had by then shown their sympathies for the discourse of dislocative nationalism became wholeheartedly opposed to European influence. This development had a noteworthy bearing on the ideological apparatus of dislocative nationalism and its relationship with Europe, as discussed in chapter 5. Although dislocative nationalists remained utterly infatuated with European achievements, unreservedly disdainful of contemporary Iran, and highly concerned with closing the gap with Europe through superficial mimicry, they also became hostile to Europe's political interference. A paradox was created as they used Europe as a model to imitate, but now they looked at European states with suspicion. This dichotomy would become more obvious in the writings of the next generations of dislocative nationalists, including Adamiyat, who attempted to portray Akhundzadeh and Kermani as anti-imperialist heroes fighting tooth and nail for their country's freedom. As the early Pahlavi state emerged from the ashes of the 1919 agreement, this dichotomy would become one of its characteristics: Westernization would be pushed to its extreme, accompanied with violence, but the Pahlavi rulers would always be personally wary of (particularly) British influence. Dislocative nationalism was evolving as the ideology that the founding fathers developed largely in their armchairs was now tested in the political arena. This evolution, although it largely preserved dislocative nationalism's discursive dimension, started to derive practical political objectives from its narrative. Keeping imperialism at bay became one of them.

DISLOCATIVE NATIONALISM AS AN ALTERNATIVE TO CONSTITUTIONALISM

Abolqasem Aref-e Qazvini (1882–1934) was one of the first intellectuals to retrieve the dislocative nationalism of Akhundzadeh and Kermani. He was a talented poet and musician, and he had been a constitutionalist, writing a number of songs and *ghazals*—a style of versification used in love and mystical poetry—to stir the ardor of his fellow revolutionaries. He is also credited with politicizing Iran's musical traditions during the revolution, singing the glories of the *vatan*, whose new meaning as "(national) homeland" he helped popularize.[30] During a brief sojourn in Baghdad and Istanbul around 1917,

Aref-e Qazvini wrote a few patriotic verses expressing his longing for Iran and his disillusionment with the aftermath of the Constitutional Revolution:

> Iran has become a ruin and home to bandits
> What can I do? Here is my refuge
> Although the love of homeland is killing me
> I am content with death, who is a well-wishing friend[31]

Similar patriotic utterances abound in his correspondence. In a letter to Reza-zadeh Shafaq, he attacks the supporters of the 1919 agreement as "worshippers of foreigners" who "proudly wear . . . their leashes."[32] An idealization of Iranians is manifest when he adds that "Iranians are noble (*sharif*) from every perspective, how can one consider oneself to be Iranian and sin through heart, eye or tongue?"[33] In another letter written in 1931, the influence of racialist ideas is obvious when he exclaims, "I am a pure-raced and pure-blooded (*pāk nezhād o pāk khun*) Iranian and if I have no historical proofs to offer, my love on the path of patriotism (*vatan parasti*) which nears madness, and my ever-increasing affection for the customs of Iranianness and national dignity should be enough."[34]

In yet another letter addressed to Zandokht Shirazi, a pioneer of the women's movement in Iran, he calls her his "Sasanian-raced sister of unique essence" (*yektā gowhar*).[35] In addition to actualizing the idea of a pure race, this curious appellation seems to lend credence to the entirely fallacious idea expressed by Kermani that Iranian women enjoyed better status in pre-Islamic times (whereas, in fact, apart from the ladies of the ruling classes, female Sasanian subjects fetched a price and belonged to their male next of kin).[36]

Dislocative nationalism is expressed in more conspicuous terms in an unnamed and undated poem that he probably wrote—like most of his poems—after World War I. According to Katouzian, Aref-e Qazvini's poems often ironically replicate the genres and stylistics of Shi'ite mourning ceremonies and passion plays:[37]

> Naught but death would relieve my pain,
> Alas that which would relieve my pain did not arrive,
> I am mourning Alexander's adventure in Iran,
> You wonder why at the Spring of Life he did not arrive . . .
> When the Arabs found their way into Iran and since,
> A word of happiness from the land of Sassan did not arrive . . .

That is why Aref has arrived wondering
Why the news of the total destruction of Tehran did not arrive.[38]

Aref-e Qazvini initiated the anti-Turkish component of dislocative nationalism. Given the centrality of racial thought in the ideology established by
Akhundzadeh and Kermani, one cannot consider this development to profoundly modify its general doctrinal outlook. Anti-Turkish sentiments were in
fact fully consistent with dislocative nationalism's racialist proclivities but were
also a reaction against the pan-Turkist claims that Azeri Iranians were part of
a larger Turkish community. This idea was first expressed by Ziya Gökalp
(1876–1924), one of the founding fathers of pan-Turkism who considered the
Turks of "Azerbaijan, Iran and Khwarizm" to belong to the "Turkmen unity."[39]
Pan-Turkism had muted success in Iran. Indeed, the harsh occupation of Azerbaijan by Ottoman troops during World War I, rather than convince local
inhabitants to join pan-Turkist ranks, in fact backfired and instigated the anti-
Turkish diatribes of Aref-e Qazvini as well as leading Azeris themselves, chief
among them Kasravi, Rezazadeh Shafaq, and Taqizadeh. Calls for Turkish
unity would briefly peak with the declarations of the pan-Turkist intellectual
Ruşeni Bey in 1923 that most of Iran belonged to Turks, and then subsequently
receded.[40] What is remarkable about Aref-e Qazvini's anti-Turkish verses is not
only his assumption that the Azeri language is somewhat unnatural and foreign in an "Aryan land," but also his incorporation of dislocative nationalist
clichés, especially when he invokes the spirit of Zarathustra or yet the land of
Ferdowsi:

The Turkish tongue has been hammered into the Azeri brain
Be serene, talk sweet, speak the language of Sa'di
In the land of Ferdowsi Tusi why do you ride the Turkish horse
Tread the path of purity, speak Persian, give up
This ugly and meaningless language[41]

Addressing his Iranian compatriots in Azerbaijan, Aref-e Qazvini summons
them to

Abstain from Turk and the Turkish language
Do not forget the [Persian] language
Zarathustra said, with water
Do not extinguish fire! Do not extinguish fire![42]

In another poem he added:

> The Turkish tongue is good for pulling out!
> It must be cut out of this country.[43]

Aref-e Qazvini had many powerful enemies and a frail health; he ended his life in solitary and destitute disenchantment.

Mirzadeh Eshqi (1893–1924) was another cultural figure of this period. After his disillusionment with constitutionalism around the period of World War I, his artistic and journalistic work became a major vehicle for the dissemination of dislocative nationalism. At a very young age in 1915 or 1916, he wrote an "opera," perhaps inspired by Turkish musical plays.[44] In this piece entitled "The Resurrection of the Rulers of Iran in the Ruins of Mada'en" (Al-Mada'in, in today's Iraq, where the ruins of the Sasanian capital Ctesiphon are located), all the main tenets of dislocative nationalism are manifested: the whining nostalgia of the pre-Islamic past, the scapegoating of Islam as the religion of racial "others" (here suggested in a veiled manner), and a violent denigration of contemporary Iran. Fascination with European modernity, as the tone and the format of the work show, is still present, but with the experience of World War I and the occupation of Iran unfolding, it is mixed with hostility toward the imperial designs of European powers. The author empathically announces that a visit to Ctesiphon's great arch of *tāq-e Kasra*, which he considers to be no less than the "cradle of world civilization," threw him into a sort of trance, and this opera was the result of "the tears that I shed on paper, in mourning our unfortunate ancestors."[45]

The opera opens with Eshqi himself sitting in the midst of Sasanian ruins, crying and lamenting what he believes is the destruction of that ancient ethos, and opposing—consistent with dislocative nationalism's habits—"the prestige, dignity and glory of ancient Iran" to the "wretchedness and abjectness of today's Iran."[46] The (fictitious) resurrected Sasanian princess Khosrow Dokht echoes Eshqi's desperation in seeing the ruined cemetery that symbolizes today's Iran:

> These ruins of a cemetery are not our Iran,
> These ruins are not Iran, where is Iran?[47]

Then appears Cyrus the Great, the founder of the Achaemenid dynasty (who is called by his Latinized denomination Cyrus/Sirus, rather than the

Persian *Kurosh*), who beats his forehead and expresses shame before chant-
ing the opera's hypnotic mantra that most of the resurrected protagonists
take up again after their appearances: "These ruins of a cemetery are not
our Iran / These ruins are not Iran, where is Iran?" Then it is Darius's turn
to resuscitate and grieve the loss of the realm's stretch that he had extended
to half the globe (*koreh-ye khāk*).[48] And then again Khosrow I (Anushiravān)
the celebrated Sasanian emperor appears, revealing a despondent counte-
nance, while Khosrow II (simply Khosrow) enjoins Iranians to rise again
from their misery.[49] This latter's beloved, Shirin, indignantly tells the audience that shame should have killed them, and finally she invokes the "fore-
going religion" and the spirit of its prophet Zarathustra.[50] The other protagonists
join her in her invocation, until Zarathustra himself materializes among
the ruins.

Zarathustra's monologue is designed to excite a particularly martial virility
in the audience by subtly referring to the imperial designs of Britain and
Russia.[51] Eshqi uses the revered ancient prophet to express his grief over the
powerlessness and passivity of Iran in the international conflict, which he
believes—or wants the audience to believe—is a scramble to divide up eastern
lands, including Iran. Iranians and other Asians are thus enjoined to rise up
against European domination. Zarathustra dramatically declares that the
seed of a brighter future is to be found in these dead people, suggesting
that a return to their glory is the key to all of Iran's ills.[52] Needless to say, we
are far from the political slogans and programs of the Constitutional Revolution. Eshqi's opera is unmistakably situated on dislocative nationalist territory, adorned with its distinctive romantic longing and historicist imagery,
its belief that a magical return to the things of that past will instantaneously
resurrect Iran to its former pomp and power. One can imagine that getting
rid of Islam and Arabic loanwords are part of the recipe, but one should not
expect a more workable blueprint. It is reported that at the first performance of Eshqi's opera, the audience wept, and in the words of Chehabi,
alluding to Shi'ite ritual mourning, "Iran had replaced the martyred Imam
Husayn."[53]

The field of music was not to be outdone. In the following years, concurrent with the rise of Reza Khan (later to become Reza Shah), the music of Col.
Ali-Naqi Vaziri (1887–1979) will become another conduit for ideas inherited
from dislocative nationalism. Vaziri, who was a military man trained in Western musical genres, became the principal creator of *soruds*, or patriotic
hymns.[54] This endeavor echoes Kermani's desire for "patriotic poetry," as noted

in chapter 5. Vaziri set forth his project in a 1925 lecture in which the influence of dislocative nationalism, transplanted to the cultural sphere, is evident. For him, the decadence of Iran's artistic heritage was to be blamed on the usual culprits. Referring to the high status of music in pre-Islamic Iran, he claimed that "two hundred years of Arab rule in Iran gave rise to passivism and disappointment in Iranian culture." Other "aliens" were not to be forgotten: "invasions by Turks, Mongols and Timurids left scars and sadness on Iranian culture." For him, the traditions of mourning, although they are clearly rooted in pre-Islamic practices, are nevertheless entirely attributable to those same invaders: "[Our music] is a reservoir of sad feelings, of memories of pain, suffering, imprisonment, and condemnation, of the influence of continued attacks by savage tribes, of mourning songs."[55] Needless to say, no poem or song of the traditional Iranian repertoire mourns any "invasion" or laments any "savage tribe."

Unlike Aref-e Qazvini and Eshqi's poetry and plays, Vaziri's work was already stepping onto the domain of the state in a period when dislocative nationalism had a solid foothold in the inner circle of Reza Khan. Vaziri founded Iran's first school of music. Later, his patriotic *soruds*, often inspired by or paraphrasing Ferdowsi, came to be taught to generations of Iranians mass schooled by the early Pahlavi state in order to, according to Vaziri, "imbue children with patriotism and to enhance public morality," or celebrate the monarchy, as in this *sorud*:

Our country is Iran
Its kings are Cyrus and Darius
O homeland, love of you is my way
Love of you is my faith and my religion[56]

Vaziri was to write a new national anthem in 1934 on the occasion of Reza Shah's state visit to Kemalist Turkey.[57]

The early Pahlavi state did not entirely monopolize dislocative nationalism, and at first literary works influenced by the ideology kept being produced. One such product of dislocative nationalism is an anthology of three short stories called *Anirān* (from Pahlavi "*aneran*" or "non-Iran"), written in 1931 by three major figures of twentieth-century Iranian literature: Shin Partow, Bozorg Alavi, and Sadeq Hedayat.[58] The common denominator of the three short stories is their plot: the invasion of Iran by foreign villains who are all driven by a common determination to destroy the country. Partow's story is entitled "The

Night of Excessive Drunkness" (*Shab-e bad masti*) and starts with an epigraph written by Kermani, which makes the author's intellectual affinities quite plain. The plot retells the story of the burning of Persepolis by Alexander the Great, with—according to Katouzian—"an elaborate, almost pornographic, tale of whores and orgies, which ends with the torching of the great structure."[59] The concluding sentence is worthy of notice: "The intemperance of one night destroyed the *Aryan city*, and arrested the march of world civilization for centuries" (my emphasis).[60] Hedayat's piece, entitled "The Mongol's Shadow" (*Sāyeh-ye Moghol*), is another fiction in which medieval Iranians are retrospectively modeled after modern dislocative nationalists. They all display a strong sense of racial unity and consider the Islamic conquest to have been a cataclysm for Iran, so much so that some protagonists hope that the Mongols will rid them of Arabs, until they find out that Mongols are in fact even crueler.

But it is Bozorg Alavi's story, *Div! . . . Div . . .* (Demon! . . . Demon . . .) that is of particular interest here. It starts with the following sentence: "Hot air, mounds of dust, excessive crowding and noise, the spectacle of dirty bodies, the smell of sweat emanating from coarse and filthy tunics (*'abā*); the groaning of Persian (*pārsi*) women, the tearful eyes of Arab women. This is a taste of the Kufa market, 1,000 years ago, or even more."[61] There follows a tale so overflowing with hateful racist clichés on Arabs—their desert mores, their supposed violence and squalor—and so generous with Iranians (all heroic and akin to modern dislocative nationalists), that it brings home the meaning of racial Manichaeism. The opening is one graphic, gory, and repulsive scene of rape and bloodshed, during which the Arab "demons" are described climbing on their camels like crawling insects, killing one another for the flesh of an Iranian slave girl.[62] Although the colorful terminology used to describe Arabs is directly borrowed from Akhundzadeh and Kermani, even Kermani's pages pale in comparison to Alavi's dehumanization of Arabs. The idea of decadence and rupture is omnipresent: "Camel's milk, camel's fur, . . . camel's feces, camel's bread, and camel's grudge [expression meaning enduring grudge], annihilated the age-long civilization of the Sasanians."[63] The plot revolves around the selflessness of a group of Iranians who agree to take care of a child born of an Iranian slave-woman and her Arab owner. The child, because of his Arab blood, cannot go against his demoniac nature and eventually betrays his foster kin. In fact the child has become worse than Arabs themselves: as we saw in chapter 4, "racial miscegenation" produces a "degenerate race" worse than the sum of its parts. The work is a fine, although unsophisticated, sample of

popular nineteenth-century European racial theories distilled through dislocative nationalism. Alavi later became an ardent communist and was exiled to
East Berlin.

Beyond his contribution to *Anirān*, Hedayat (1903–1951)—considered the
greatest writer of twentieth-century Iran—wrote a few plays early in his career
in which the same themes of an almost postapocalyptic Iran struggling against
dehumanized Arab brutes were developed. *Parvin, dokhtar-e Sāsān* (Parvin,
the Sasanian girl, 1928) is a play in three acts that tells the story of an Iranian
damsel whose fiancé is murdered by Arabs. The head of the Arab army displays sexual interest in her but she ultimately takes her own life in order not to
surrender her body to the enemy's lust (and, perhaps, allow for another case
of racial miscegenation to take place). The antagonism between Arab and
Iranian is, similarly to Alavi's play, exemplified by the Zoroastrian opposition
between the deity Ahura Mazda and the destructive spirit Ahriman.[64] A dialogue between the girl and the Arab translator summarizes Hedayat's views.
In a sentence that exemplifies the dislocative nationalist claim that the aim of
the "Arab invasion" was primarily about culture and identity, the translator,
referring to Arabic, tells her bluntly "This is the language you need to learn;
since the battle of Nahavand, your language and your religion are dead."[65] The
same recurring nomenclature of lizard-eater, desert-dweller, and camel-grazer
that one finds in the founding treatises of dislocative nationalism is reproduced
identically, and so is the belief that the books of ancient Iran perished in the
flames; Islam is equated with superstition while Zoroastrianism is, curiously,
equated with science (possibly in an application of the Gibbonian classicist
view to Iranian history); the idea endorsed by many orientalists that Islam is
illegitimate because spread through force (see chapter 3) is also replicated
mutatis mutandis.[66]

Hedayat wrote another play, *Māziyār* (Maziyar, 1933), about the rebellion
of the historical figure of the same name against the Abbasid caliphate, with a
"historical" introduction by Mojtaba Minovi, who happened to be a collector
of Kermani's manuscripts.[67] In their preface, the authors emphasize "the significance of Maziyar's uprising," which they describe as "a prime example of
nationalist Iranian resistance to Arab rule":

> Among the Iranian heroes and rulers . . . it was the House of Qaran [Mazi-
> yar's clan] who resisted most against the Arabs. Their Iranian education
> and their native gallantry would not allow them to be daunted by a bunch
> of snake-eating children of the devil (*mārkhārān-e ahriman-nezhād*). They

were reluctant to learn the language and customs of the Arabs even when they came into contact with them.[68]

This preface is a genuine product of dislocative nationalism and is self-serving to the highest possible degree, insisting, for instance, explicitly on Iranians' "racial and intellectual superiority."[69] Aversion to racial miscegenation reaches new heights, like in this passage where "Semitic filth" is indicted for Iranians' degeneration into a mixed race: "Cheating, treachery, theft, bribery and other vices contaminated Iranians, but were also salient features of the half Iranian and half Arab people."[70] We come full circle as the ultimate failure of Maziyar, betrayed by his kinsmen, is here blamed on the Iranians' transmutation into a degenerate mixed race. There are indeed a number of Iranian traitors in the play, some of whom are Jews, and they include the hero's half-brother (unsurprisingly a half Arab). According to Katouzian, the author's insistence to blame intercourse with Arabs for the hero's failure "is a serious technical weakness in view of the play's interpretative and ideological overtones" and a great many contradictions are created as a result.[71] Additionally, if Iranians are degenerate half-Arabs, how can one achieve the salvation that dislocative nationalists long for?

Last but not least, Hedayat wrote a satire called *Kārevān-e Eslām* (The caravan of Islam, 1930), in which he ridiculed every aspect of the Islamic faith. The work is composed of three fictional newspaper articles following the adventures of a handful of Islamic clerics who depart for Europe in order to proselytize. The work derides practices or attitudes found among Muslims (such as the Muslim prayer) in an identical fashion as a European Islamophobe would. This emphasizes dislocative nationalism's embarrassment with the current state of Iran as it brings about a high degree of self-consciousness vis-à-vis the opinion of Westerners. The result is a tendency to espouse Europeans' prejudices wholeheartedly, a tendency I have elsewhere called self-orientalization.[72] The clerics are filthy, backward, and superstitious, and end up on display at the Berlin zoo before succumbing to the wonders of Europe and becoming a bartender, croupier, and pimp and scorning Islam. They now claim that Islam is nothing more than "thievery and murder" (*chāpidan va ādam-koshi*), and equate "Islamic civilization" with "Arab civilization" in a noteworthy case of racial determinism in which "Arab" is associated—again and again—with "camel's milk, camel's feces, tunic (*'abā*), kebab, and lizard."[73] Generally, it is the cleric's duplicity that Hedayat targeted in this work, but there is also a passing attack on European imperialism, a fixture in post-1919 nationalist writing.[74] There are other works by Hedayat in which dislocative nationalism appears between the lines.[75]

THE RISE OF A NATIONALIST STATE

It is revealing that these first outbursts of dislocative nationalism were literary works. Undoubtedly, the discursive and historicist nature of the ideology was particularly well fitted for such types of expression. Nevertheless, its growing success after World War I and throughout the campaign against the 1919 agreement ensured its gradual permeation of Tehran's political culture as an alternative to the failed constitutionalist project. For a time, dislocative ideas could be found in the columns of elite newspapers and magazines, such as the aptly named *Irānshahr* magazine, published in Berlin by renowned intellectual Hossein Kazemzadeh in the period 1922–1927. In *Irānshahr* one could find familiar propositions such as the claim that the "imperialism" of "savage Arabs" in the early centuries of Islam "retarded the creative abilities of Iran's talented Aryan population."[76] Hardly any tenet of dislocative nationalism is absent from this one single quotation. In a 1924 article, Kazemzadeh claimed that the "Iranian soul" epitomized the "Aryan soul" and that it was thanks to the "advantages of the Indo-European race" that Iranians traversed "centuries of domination and savagery" and even "tamed" (*tarbiyat kardan*) other peoples with whom they came to contact.[77] In the same period of ideological unsettledness, we see Arani affirm yet again that if the country is to be "saved from backwardness and imperialism," we must cleanse "the language of foreign words" and revive "the ancient religion of Zoroaster" or yet "rebuild the centralized state of the Sassanids."[78] Some authors were actively using the Aryan myth to dislodge Iran from its empirical reality, and claim parity with their alleged racial kinsmen in Europe. Yet the speed at which dislocative nationalism became the official ideology of a new state is in many ways staggering.

By 1920 the country threatened to disintegrate, and the idea started to grow in the mind of a number of people, among them Seyyed Zia ed-Din Tabataba'i (1888–1969), a former constitutionalist and a prominent journalist, that a strong centralized government was the only way out of the crisis. After a process that should not detain us here, Seyyed Zia and a Cossack colonel (*mirpanj*) named Reza Khan (1878–1944) marched on Tehran with the blessing of Maj. Gen. Sir Edmund Ironside, the commander of the local British force, on February 21, 1921, and Seyyed Zia became prime minister.[79] In a prelude to the promotion of dislocative nationalism to officialdom, Eshqi wrote:

So as to renew the victory of the pure Sasanian race
The blessed and great Seyyed Zia ed-Din became chief minister.[80]

But before long, Reza Khan disposed of him, became minister of war, later prime minister, and finally in 1925 he deposed the last Qajar sovereign, founded the Pahlavi dynasty, and became Reza Shah.

Although Reza Khan was the muscle that allowed the coup, Seyyed Zia was its brain and ideologue. Reza Khan was a capable man and a charismatic military leader, but he was not particularly educated, just as most Cossack officers were not. Immediately after their ascension, Seyyed Zia and Reza Khan released two declarations (*bayāniyeh*), both undoubtedly written by Seyyed Zia, delineating the direction of their future government. The declarations were heavily patriotic in tone, invoking Iran the motherland at every page and scorning its internal and external enemies.[81] Naturally, the declarations oppose imperial interference as well as the 1919 agreement, as anti-imperialist feelings were strong and undoubtedly sincere. In his declaration, Seyyed Zia solemnly announced that "no nation, however strong and powerful, should be allowed to limit our freedom; we are free and we will remain free," before he dramatically announced the abrogation of the 1919 agreement.[82] Reza Khan's declaration too invoked "the sacred motherland" and warned against "foreign traitors."[83] Although these two declarations were highly patriotic, they do not contain any unambiguous trace of dislocative nationalism as analyzed in this book. Reza Khan even addressed his audience as "Muslims."[84]

Therefore, one cannot attribute Reza Khan's conversion to dislocative nationalism to Seyyed Zia. So when did that conversion happen and who was behind it? Hossein Makki, a politician who chronicled this period, tells us that when Reza became a Cossack, he was uneducated and knew nothing about the history of Iran.[85] When he reached the highest echelons of power, a "group of seven men" were convoked to the palace each day to instruct him about the country he was ruling. Prominent among the seven teachers was a Farajollah Bahrami (1878–1951), who had been Reza Khan's *chef de cabinet* from the aftermath of the 1921 coup until 1924, governor-general of Khorasan thereafter, and always a close advisor and confident until his fall from grace in 1927 and subsequent banishment.[86] Bahrami was knowledgeable about Iranian history and geography; he is credited with not only coaching Reza Khan into nationalist ideas but also with helping him articulate a reform program.[87] Among the topics covered at these daily reunions, particular emphasis was put on the history of Iran and the kings of the past, including episodes from the *Shāhnāmeh*, as Reza Shah was particularly fond of such stories.[88] One can imagine that he perceived himself to be the heir of the valiant kings whose praise the *Shāhnāmeh* sings, and perhaps these daily history lessons were not unrelated to his later megalomania and totalitarianism. Abdolhossein Sheikh ol-Molk Owrang, one of these seven teachers, reports that the king would shed tears upon hearing passages from Ferdowsi's masterpiece because, according to him in a passage that makes Owrang's ideological affinities plain, the king had before not known "this great poet of the land of Iran who resuscitated the Persian (*pārsi*) language."[89] Owrang conveys colorful anecdotes about these daily classes in which "the seven" would impart "patriotic stories" to the historically inquisitive king.[90]

One instance of crying occurred when Owrang told the story of Roxana (Rowshanak), daughter of Darius III, according to Ferdowsi (but in reality the daughter of a Sogdian ruler), and her marriage to Alexander the Great. It is here worthy of note that Alexander is celebrated as a great hero in Iranian sources and even indigenized in the *Shāhnāmeh* (as the child of an Iranian princess who married Philip of Macedon already expecting a son from her previous Iranian husband, hence giving birth to a fully Iranian Alexander). Similarly, in *dasātiri* sources, he is considered one of sixteen pre-Islamic Iranian sages.[91] However, in Owrang's description, Alexander is but another in a long series of foreign invaders whose sole purpose was to subjugate Iranians and destroy their culture and identity. This metamorphosis of Alexander, recent as it is, is yet another indication of the modernity of the core beliefs of dislocative nationalism. Be that as it may, Owrang went on telling how Iranians "lost everything they had," but particularly "the immense Iranian empire" and their beloved king, assassinated by "an alien man [Alexander]" who now wanted to marry the same king's daughter Roxana.[92] Upon hearing Owrang's somewhat distorted declamation of Ferdowsi's verses on the dreaded marriage, Reza Shah started to cry passionately for several minutes; Owrang remembers this episode with emotion and admiration.[93] Thereafter follows an equally emotional and patriotic declaration from the tearful king.

It is highly plausible, in view of the policies that Reza Shah will implement throughout the late 1920s and 1930s, and also in view of the success of dislocative nationalism among intellectuals those days, that he was converted to this ideology during these daily reunions. The tone that transpires from Owrang's memoirs, the overemphasis on historical narratives, past grandeurs, foreign invasions, and Ferdowsi are all characteristic of dislocative nationalism, and as such we are on different ideological ground than the generally patriotic declarations of Seyyed Zia and Reza Khan, which addressed "Muslims." We are also far removed from constitutionalism and its emphasis on individual freedom and the rule of law (ideas entirely absent from the discourse of the Pahlavi state and its supporters). Modernization and stability were being achieved in a despotic fashion at the expense of the people's rights and the constitutionalists' ideals, and the ideological backbone of this modernization was formulated in dislocative nationalist terms. Houchang Chehabi compares two songs that illustrate the ideological slide from democratic constitutionalism to the despotic dislocative nationalism of Reza Shah. The first is an early constitutionalist *sorud*:

> O youth of Iran, it's time for our freedom,
> The days of fun, merriment, and joy have arrived[94]

The second is an early Pahlavi *sorud*, in which "we look in vain for any references to freedom, equality, fraternity, or universal standards"; there is instead a cult of the monarchy and the idea of the regeneration of pre-Islamic Iran:

> Your guardian is the Pahlavi Shahanshah
> The kingdom of the Kianids [a pre-Islamic mythical dynasty] has been
>   strengthened by him
> From the bottom of your hearts yell out this cry:
> Long live for all eternity the name of Pahlavi![95]

It would be irrelevant to review all the policies that Reza Shah instigated in his modernization project, or even all the moves that the literature has traditionally deemed "nationalist," such as his drive to Persianize the ethnic minorities, or his helpful but excessively brutal pacification of volatile peripheries. A few policies that show the promotion of dislocative nationalism to officialdom need be discussed, however, to highlight the Pahlavi sovereign's implementation of ideas borrowed from Akhundzadeh and Kermani's ideology. As it will become clear, the transition from historicist narrative to political implementation was a leap into the unknown. It often translated into highly costly policies in terms of their execution, whose effectiveness or even relevance to a program of modernization can be legitimately doubted (sartorial regulations are a fine example).

It is almost universally claimed that Reza Shah built a modern state. It is, however, fair to say that he only built a centralized state. The label "modern" is an exaggeration in view of the arbitrariness of this state and some continuities with previous Iranian traditions of kingship. The early Pahlavi state was only modern in that it benefited from an army with a comprehensive system of conscription, which helped the ruler crush Iran's alternative (especially tribal) centers of local power. Reza Shah's achievement in this regard should be qualified as his army remained largely ineffective, politicized, and expensive to maintain, and it quite literally evaporated on the wake of the invasion of Iran by the Allied Forces in 1941.[96] The Pahlavi state also brought about a growing bureaucratic apparatus, the beginnings of mass schooling, and new means of transport and telecommunication. Unheard-of (and commendable) attention was given to the education of Iranian women. The state was concerned with shaping the collective memory of Iranians through education and propaganda. Yet this state also considerably failed to deliver on its promises of "modernity" as it quickly descended into arbitrariness and violence, disposed altogether of constitutionalism, participation, separation of powers, accountability, and civil rights. Reza Shah's state dominated Iranians as subjects who could choose between being forcefully guided toward the official understanding of "modernity" or being crushed. It did not treat them as modern citizens with their own legitimate say on these matters. Few were his supporters or collaborators who did not ultimately end in disgrace, exile, prison, or the graveyard (hence a sense of relief when he abdicated under Allied pressure in 1941). Even some die-hard dislocative nationalists fell victim to his repression, Eshqi being only one example (assassinated at the age of thirty-one). Iranians, who had fought to "condition" royal power to a constitutional framework, were offered stability and a particular form of progress but were denied participation in the affairs of the state and the security that can only be derived from the foreseeable nature of a system based on the rule of law.[97] Therefore, in many ways the early Pahlavi state also reproduced the premodern features of its predecessors. Reza Shah's main achievement was the realization of peace and stability, allowing economic development to take place in a country that had endured too much chaos, and one should also highlight the early Pahlavi state's relative reluctance to use torture as a method for obtaining confessions. Yet this was achieved at a high price, especially in the case of the tribes and the nomads, victims of a senseless repression of their way of life.

Nevertheless, he did build a state, and dislocative nationalism became an integral part of its ideological outlook. First, state resources were mobilized to emphasize the greatness of Iran's pre-Islamic history as opposed to its more recent past. One outlet for this archaistic endeavor was a propaganda that aimed to draw a parallel between the Pahlavi state and pre-Islamic kings (as in the above-quoted *soruds* for instance). In 1925 the *majles* adopted the solar *"shamsi"* calendar. Although this latter also took the *hijrah* (i.e., the migration or flee-ing of Prophet Muhammad from Mecca to Medina) as its starting point, it was a solar instead of lunar calendar, thus dislodging Iran from the time of Islamic liturgy. Most importantly, it revived the twelve months of the ancient Zoroas-trian calendar. The project of purifying the Persian language from Arabic loanwords, the other grand ambition of dislocative nationalism within the broader project of returning the nation to its pre-Islamic glory, was effectively institutionalized when the *farhangestān-e Irān* or Iranian Academy, molded on the model of the Académie Française, was founded in 1935. Ultimately a fail-ure, the *farhangestān's* work was never fully consistent. It did attempt to purify foreign loanwords (against significant resistance), but it occasionally targeted European loanwords as well. I mention it in passing as it is not an unequivo-cal manifestation of dislocative nationalism.[98]

As Talinn Grigor points out, "Under the Pahlavis, a systematic process of discrediting the recent past . . . in order to recuperate antiquity (Achaemenid and Sassanian culture) was to serve as a link to modernity."[99] As she goes on to explain, the early Pahlavi state consistently relied on pre-Islamic aesthetics in the state's repertoire of symbols, especially in its use of architecture. The *anjo-man-e āsār-e melli*, or the Society for National Heritage, was founded in 1921 by a group of intellectuals and officials whose names have already appeared in this book due to their sympathies for dislocative nationalism: Hassan Pirniya, Mahammad Ali Forughi, Keykhosrow Shahrokh, and Issa Sadiq (but also Hassan Taqizadeh, Said Nafisi, and Ali Asghar Hekmat).[100] The *anjoman* en-deavored to build a number of shrines dedicated to ancient poets, thus posing them as secular alternatives to *emāmzādehs* (Shi'ite shrines), with striking parallels.[101] In Afshin Marashi's words, the state's objective was "to construct a counterdiscourse to prevailing forms of the sacred."[102]

The most illustrative case is the shrine erected to Ferdowsi's memory in the early 1930s, a modern structure inspired by pre-Islamic forms.[103] It was built as a symbol "for a modern Aryan nation on a march to a bright future" in a fas-cinating case of "propaganda architecture."[104] Although the *anjoman's* project was at first a private matter, and funds were raised privately, the early Pahlavi state soon threw its support behind the Ferdowsi mausoleum. In fact, the whole matter became a state affair and Reza Shah himself inaugurated the monument at the Ferdowsi millennial celebrations in 1934, an event given extraordinary coverage in the state media amid the publication of new state-sponsored editions of the *Shāhnāmeh*. The nationalist myths surrounding

Ferdowsi (see chapter 4), largely drawn from Theodor Nöldeke's *The Iranian National Epic*, were popular among the members of the *anjoman*.[105] Issa Sadiq, for instance, whose Aryanist writings were mentioned in the previous chapter, wrote a biography of Ferdowsi, elevating him to a champion of Iranian nationalism who revived "the glory of ancient Persia."[106] Ferdowsi had also by then been reappropriated as a closet Zoroastrian, as dislocative nationalists could decidedly not reconcile themselves with the great poet's profession of Shi'ite Islam.[107] Consistent with this belief, the shrine designed by French archaeologist and architect André Godard amalgamated a number of pre-Islamic and Zoroastrian symbols into its structure. As Grigor describes it:

> The most striking decorative element at the center of the main façade is the icon of the Zoroastrian Good Spirit; a faithful copy from Persepolis' Hall of One Hundred Columns or that of The Throne Hall. This is framed in four pairs of engaged columns as at Hatra [a Parthian city in today's Iraq], crowned with bull-headed capitals. . . . [Inside,] the bronze chandelier, a gift from Tehran's Zoroastrian Society, hung over the grave.[108]

The resemblance with the tomb of Cyrus the Great is the natural outcome of the *anjoman* members' belief that "since Ferdowsi's 'service to the history and culture of Iran' was 'like' that of Cyrus, then the 'shape' of his resting place ought to resemble to that of Cyrus at Pasargadae."[109] Ferdowsi was flanked with a mausoleum as if he had been an Achaemenid king or a Zoroastrian priest. In other words, he was forced into a category to which he did not belong so that he could find his place in the pantheon of dislocative nationalism and serve as a national hero.

Second, Reza Shah had fully internalized the contradiction between being hostile to external interference and adulating all things European. A number of his close collaborators were dismissed or jailed because the sovereign suspected them of having had contacts—however inconsequential—with foreign legations.[110] Yet a number of his policies derive from a high level of self-consciousness vis-à-vis an imaginary European interlocutor. "What will Europeans think of us" was a question that obsessed dislocative nationalists, rooted as it were in the feeling of deficiency (traumatic encounter) coupled with a complete stigmatization of Iranians' way of life. It translated into a degree of self-hatred, for which dislocation was the antidote: transforming Iran from what it was into France, England, or Germany. Discursively, the Aryan myth did the job, but the early Pahlavi state also had an obsession with mere appearance. It therefore imposed policies of superficial mimicry so that Iranians would look European. Akhundzadeh and Kermani's wish to erase Iran's shameful contemporary reality and emulate Europe in the most extensive manner possible was reflected in the demands of Minister of Court Abdolhossein Teymourtash to "erase everything" and "start over again."[111]

By the late 1920s the military was unleashed on the nomadic populations of Iran with the explicit objective of obliterating their way of life and culture. Besides being a threat to centralization, the nomads were perceived to be "hostile to modernity, archaic and outmoded."[112] They embarrassed dislocative nationalists when dealing with Europeans, as they were attempting, in Stephanie Cronin's words, to "incubate a society homogeneous and Europeanized in appearance and modern in modes of cultural expression."[113] Thus, they were forcibly settled. According to Katouzian, this policy entirely proceeded from ideology:

> Sedentarization could never be justified on rational grounds, as it led to widespread death, destruction and hardship, while at the same time it was economically harmful since it led to a sharp decline in the country's livestock production, comparable to the effects of Stalin's forced collectivization of Soviet agriculture in the same period.[114]

Cronin also highlights the despotic and punitive character of the sedentarization program: "The main method employed to enforce settlement was the simple expedient of using the army to block the migration routes, the government taking no other practical steps, for example, the provision of agricultural training, implements or seed, to aid the conversion of the nomads into peasants."[115]

One *majles* deputy at the time stated that "the way they settled the tribes was the way of execution and annihilation, not education and reform," adding that this violence "sapped the strength of the Iranian society and weakened the hope of national unity."[116] Contrary to nationalist assumptions, the settlement of the tribes was not necessary in terms of modernization or the outcome of the pacification of Iran's peripheries: it was political and a matter of perception.[117] It was directly rooted in dislocative nationalists' keenness to show Europeans that Iran was a modern country—modern in the sense that one did not witness nomads living in tents and migrating with their livestock, wearing exotic outfits.

Aryanism is a handy device when it comes to imagining Iran's nomadic tribes as lying somewhat outside the nation, as internal others that need to be policed. In that sense, although forced sedentarization is not today pursued as violently as it was under Reza Shah, there is some degree of continuity in the perception of nomads from the 1920s into the current period. As recently as 2011, an article in the state-sponsored English-language daily *Tehran Times* offered the following description of Iran's nomadic tribes: "Most the tribes of central Iran are from pure Aryan stock, while other tribes such as the Arabs of Khuzestan and Khorassan, the Turkish tribes of Quchan, the Qashqai tribes, the Shahsevan and Afshar tribes of Azarbaijan and the Turkmans are remnants of races that have passed through Iran at various periods of history."[118] The article refers to other nomadic populations (in particular Kurds and Lurs) as "the original invaders who, in the first millennium BC, swept down from Central Asia and settled in various parts of the Iranian Plateau." The idea of nomadism, invasion, and racial difference is casually and innocuously invoked in order to place Iran's nomads outside the racial frame of reference of the nation, portraying them as a curiosity of foreign origin, descending from alien invaders. This article is remarkably antediluvian in its tone and conceptual content, once again highlighting the vivacity of dislocative nationalism in today's Iran. One is reminded of old European racial anthropological taxonomy when, we are told, the Lur tribes "are probably the most intact tribes of Iran, retaining their robustness, virility and tall stature."[119]

Going back to the early Pahlavi state's obsession with appearance, unprecedented sartorial regulations also came to be devised for the entire population and despotically implemented without any attempt to seek a national consensus. The objective was the standardization and Europeanization of the Iranians' appearance, which, according to Chehabi, "had a deep and at times traumatizing effect on [their] lives."[120] First, in 1927 the Pahlavi hat, which was inspired by the French army's *képi*, was imposed on all male citizens— who heretofore wore a variety of headdresses. Muslim and non-Muslim clerics in benefit of an aptly named "turban license" could be exempt. In 1928 all males became legally bound to wear a European suit. All other attires were outlawed through the whole country. When Reza Shah came back from his state visit to Turkey, he became determined to accelerate his Westernization policies to catch up with Iran's Kemalist neighbor. By then sartorial regulations were not enacted by the *majles* but promulgated as decrees and were also subject to the sovereign's whims and volte-faces: after having imposed the Pahlavi hat a few years earlier, now he suddenly decided that it was European chapeaux (felt hats) that all Iranian males should wear.[121] These expensive items that all men had to wear were mass imported, mainly from Europe. Reza Shah justified this new fancy with these words: "All I am trying to do is for us to look like [the Europeans] so they would not laugh at us."[122] On another occasion he declared to a number of *majles* deputies that "we do not want those others to think that they are superior to us because of a minor difference in head covering."[123] One can hardly express a complex of inferiority in clearer terms. Some even saw sartorial regulations as a way to achieve the main project of dislocative nationalism: returning the nation into the pre-Islamic past. An official of the early Pahlavi state hailed the imposition of the European chapeau and claimed that it was in fact "the ancestral headdress of Iran," stating that during the Sasanian period the "Iranians had worn similar brimmed hats."[124] The claim is of course preposterous; the degree of blind infatuation with pre-Islamic Iran was such that any policy, however arbitrary, could be justified by reference to that period. We will come back to the human cost of this "modernization" program.

Third, there was a consistent drive to dislodge Iran from its Islamic reality and underscore Iranians' Aryanness—that is, their racial difference with Arabs and kinship with Europeans. Aryanism was hammered into the minds of Iranians through the history and geography textbooks used in state schools. As far as Reza Shah's moves against religious practices were concerned, they were dislocative in two different but interrelated manners. Considering Islam as "a source of backwardness," Reza Shah cracked down on the clergy and simply outlawed the most visible ceremonies and behaviors associated with the Shi'ite faith. In 1929 all the public rituals performed during the Muharram processions were simply prohibited: the mourning ceremonies (*rowzeh khāni*), the passion plays (*ta'ziyeh*), and the procession marches in their entirety. Newspapers close to the government attacked these religious practices, although they arguably remained as popular as ever, even though they were now performed in people's backyards. According to one author, Iranians "adjusted themselves to a double life of public secularism and private religiosity; it might even be argued that Reza Shah's coercive policy of declericalization increased the religious zeal and fervour of the population."[125] One can only be struck by the reversed parallel with post-1979 Iran. Reza Shah also willingly violated the sanctity of mosques and holy places. In repressing the Gowharshad protest in Mashhad (more below), he unleashed his army on the protesters at what was a sacred pilgrimage site. This contempt for the sacredness of Islamic spaces was unprecedented in the annals of Iranian history, as these spaces had always been used by protesters who would take sanctuary (or *bast*) in them, to be safe from the crown's fury. Reza Shah also famously walked into a shrine in Qom with his boots on and "personally manhandled a number of seminarians and clerics" and even caned one of them because they had criticized his female relatives for wearing light chadors.[126]

The other strategy pursued by the early Pahlavi state in its relentless moves against popular religion—and its continuous concern about what Europeans would think of us—was the policy of unveiling in 1935–1936. It was first implemented within the bureaucracy and the royal family. Meetings were held in protest in the historic Gowharshad mosque adjoining the shrine of Imam Reza in Mashhad, a holy place and pilgrimage site for Shi'ites. The shah's forces violated the sanctity of the shrine and put an end to the protest; shot into the crowd, wounding and killing a large number of people, who were later buried in mass graves; and arrested others.[127] The trustee of the shrine, an important public figure, was executed. Such was the determination of Reza Shah to uproot Islam and give his country the modern look that he assumed would be more palatable to Europeans.

Finally, in 1936 the order was out to enforce a strict policy of unveiling on all Iranian females, ensuring that they would look like the "civilized women of the world."[128] One group of women were the notable exception: prostitutes. This was "an attempt to turn the symbol of virtue into a symbol of vice."[129] Policemen were given contradictory orders to avoid violence, yet clear the streets of veiled women:[130] many veiled women (including those wearing simple headscarves) were physically assaulted, insulted, and their veils were torn apart in public. "Emancipation" had at long last come to Iran. Faced with such humiliating treatment, large numbers of women retreated into seclusion until Reza Shah's abdication in 1941 and the subsequent end of sartorial totalitarianism. It is undeniable that Reza Shah's repression of the veil left deep scars on the collective psyche of Iranians and immensely contributed to his unpopularity. As Chehabi points out, veiling mores had gradually relaxed: the mask that many women wore under their chadors, for instance, had almost disappeared by itself, counterfactually suggesting that further relaxation could have happened naturally, if not for Reza Shah's impatience to give Iranians the appearance of Europeans overnight.[131] That Iranian women could become modern while being sufficiently empowered to decide about their own clothing never occurred to Reza Shah and his supporters, as their conception of modernity—identical to that of Akhundzadeh, praising the Russian "modernization" of Caucasia—was not only seriously flawed and superficial but despotic and violent. However, this should not erase the fact that other measures, mainly in the domain of education and civil law, did in fact improve the lot of Iranian women. Previously their position had been, according to testimonies, worse than anywhere else in the region.[132]

The link between these policies and dislocative nationalism is made clear in the justifications provided in the writings of Ali Akbar Siyasi (or Siassi), a long-serving rector of the University of Tehran and the minister of education after Reza Shah's abdication. He was one of the founders of the Young Iran Club (Kolub-e Irān-e Javān), an organization whose members were young dislocative nationalists who had recently earned their degrees in French and German universities and were ardent supporters of Reza Shah. Their intense anticlericalism brought them into an alliance with the members of New Iran (Irān-e Now), another party of devotees of Reza Shah. According to British diplomatic wires, Irān-e Now was set up "on Fascist lines" with the shah as its honorary president (and such members as Minister of Court Teymourtash and Ali-Akbar Davar, who reformed Iran's judiciary).[133] Reza Shah was not particularly touched by all this fervor: he disbanded Irān-e Now because he "was not in favour of party politics."[134]

In his book based on his doctoral dissertation presented at the University of Paris, Siyasi offers a comprehensive case for complete Westernization in which denigration of contemporary Iran (hence, its worthlessness for preservation) is fanatical and praise for Reza Shah's rule ubiquitous. Other dislocative nationalist ideas are recurrent: there is a complete reification of the discourse on "Arab domination," an anachronistic nationalization of Iran's history (Safavids were nationalists), and Siyasi displays significant admiration for Gobineau's racialist views on Iran.[135] There is also a startling denial of the multiethnic and multilingual character of Iran.[136] Sartorial regulation is justified on two accounts. First, it supposedly gives all Iranians a sentiment of unity, whereas before their outfits differentiated between regions and tribes. Second, imitating Europeans clothing will, in Siyasi's words, help Iranians "adopt their ideas."[137] Siyasi—somewhat prematurely—praises Reza Shah for having brought about "the end of the mullahs' hegemony and the death of religious power."[138] His assessment of Islam becomes clear in this characteristic passage where he discusses the relationship (or lack thereof) between Iran and Imam Ali: "Upright man, saint, martyr, he has perhaps been all these and even more; but *he was only an Arab* and as such I am not interested in him; for anything that is not of my motherland, anything that is not *irani* (Persian) *cannot be of any interest* to me" (my emphases).[139] This passage is fascinatingly paradoxical.

Ironically, an Iranian should not take interest in "anything that is not *irani*" but should comprehensively emulate Europeans (the core argument of the book).

Siyasi's approach can only be fully grasped in light of dislocative nationalism, in particular the horror inspired by racial miscegenation, and the idea of Aryan kinship with Europeans. That we dress like Europeans is acceptable because we are Aryans, but we cannot revere Imam Ali because he was of another race. Siyasi also strongly advocates alphabet reform in these now familiar terms: "This script, although more than a thousand years old, is not Persian. It was imposed on Persia by Arabs concurrently with Islam." He therefore stresses "its essentially foreign nature," and his other arguments for alphabet reform are identical to Akhundzadeh's (the Arabic script is the main cause of illiteracy in Iran, etc.).[140] He ignores, like all those advocating alphabet reform on the basis of the "foreign nature" of the Arabic script, that all the scripts ever used on the Iranian plateau were borrowed from neighboring cultures to the west, and the argument of forcible adoption runs counter common sense, for when has a script ever been imposed on a people? The Arabic script is by far the best of the lot, hence its adoption by Persian-speakers. In Sasanian times, the script used to write Pahlavi consisted of only twelve signs used for writing over twenty sounds (vowels and consonants) and involved an extensive use of heterograms, practically putting reading and writing outside the reach of the common people and granting it an elite status, limited to a class of professional scribes. This may explain the swift adoption of the far more adequate Arabic alphabet.

Siyasi has an interesting Aryanist solution to the alphabet dilemma. Unlike Akhundzadeh, but in compliance with his own core argument, it is the Latin alphabet that he promotes rather than a new script created for the Persian language. For him, Aryans can adopt other Aryans' script in order to go back home. Aryanism is the ideological backbone of Siyasi's views, as it is for many who supported or collaborated with the early Pahlavi state. Siyasi's work concludes on this telling formulation: in order to modernize Iran, one must "clear up the Persian soul *from this impurity* and allow it to shine from the sparkle peculiar to the Aryan genius" (my emphasis).[141] This represents the application in the policy sphere of dislocative nationalism's main discursive program as it appears in Akhundzadeh's and Kermani's work: uproot whatever there is of "the Arabs' influence" and Iran will transmute into Europe, and the problem of backwardness will be magically solved.

8
TRIUMPH

O Cyrus! Sleep in peace,
for we are awake.
—Mohammad Reza Shah Pahlavi, 1971

IN 1934 A LARGE CELEBRATION WAS SET UP FOR THE MILLENNIAL
of Ferdowsi's birth. Although the location of the original tomb of the great
poet has never been determined with any certainty, a large shrine inspired by
the tomb of Cyrus the Great, heavy in pre-Islamic and Zoroastrian symbolism, was built in Tus as part of the millennial celebration.[1] Afshin Marashi has
rightly highlighted the correspondence between Ferdowsi's shrine and Nora's
concept of *lieu de mémoire*: a totem of collective memory is a universal ingre-
dient of nationalism.[2] An unprecedented international conference was organized in Tehran, followed with the inauguration with great pomp of the
shrine in Tus in presence of the shah and the Ferdowsi luminaries of the
time. The lucky guests exchanged gifts, attended performances and readings, and visited neo-Achaemenid administrative buildings in Tehran.[3] During the inauguration ceremony, Reza Shah "delivered one of the few official
public speeches of his career," announcing that "the establishment of this
structure" is "a measure of our appreciation and gratitude for the pains which
Ferdowsi bore to revive the language and history of this nation."[4] British diplomatic wires reported that the "imposing mausoleum" consumed the "attention of the Persian government . . . to the exclusion of almost all other
businesses."[5] Although celebrations surrounding a poet's anniversary may seem

trivial, it was not so for the early Pahlavi state. According to Marashi, the ubiquity of references to Ferdowsi in the Pahlavi state's symbolic repertoire demonstrates the centrality of this project to Reza Shah's drive to establish his legitimacy on secular "national memory."[6] Indeed, the mausoleum started to appear on the Iranian currency and stamps, several statues of Ferdowsi were erected throughout the country, and streets and squares were named after him.

In sum, the Pahlavi sovereign was eager to establish his legitimacy in terms of cultural and linguistic nationalism.[7] The new Iranian state paid homage to the hero who, according to dislocative nationalist myth, saved the language and culture of Iran from the onslaught of its non-Aryan enemies, the Arabs. The centrality of Ferdowsi in this nationalist narrative was such that its proponents failed to take note that Rudaki used the same modern Persian idiom of which Ferdowsi was supposed to have been "the reviver" almost a century earlier. The Pahlavi state reconnected itself to the pre-Islamic age through Ferdowsi and—as is always implicitly suggested when the *Shāhnāmeh* is invoked—*against* Arabs and their essentialised religion, culture, and language. The remodeling of Ferdowsi into a modern dislocative nationalist, feeding on European scholarship in the vein of Renan (an author whose knowledge of the *Shāhnāmeh* and Iranian history was close to nil) and Nöldeke, could not reconcile itself with either the poet's profession of Shi'ite Islam or the sometimes contradictory treatment of ethnicity appearing in his poem (due to the multiplicity of his sources rather than his personal opinion; see chapter 4).

The 1934 celebrations were echoed abroad in the United Kingdom, Germany, France, the United States, and the Soviet Union, where Ferdowsi's millennial was marked with exhibitions of manuscripts here and public speeches there. Of the many declarations emanating from the four corners of the Western world celebrating Ferdowsi's work or the commemoration in Tus, some resonated with the Pahlavi state's rationale for these celebrations. Referring to the mausoleum, the president of the American Institute of Persian Art and Archaeology observed that the objective of the institute was to pay "respect and affection for the *brilliant race* that could create such notable monuments" (my emphasis).[8] Even more tellingly, in Paris, where Ferdowsi celebrations took place in December 1934 under the chairmanship of President Albert Lebrun, a French scholar imparted ideas propagated by Renan and later Massé (see chapters 4 and 6), that Ferdowsi, this "emulation of Homer," was "one of us," the "purest of the Indo-European genius," and that with him "we discover the secret affinities with that of our time and race and hence we remember the ancient relation between France and Iran."[9] One can imagine the exuberance of the shah and his entourage when they read these declarations. They must have felt that they had finally reached one of the main objectives of their policies—to obtain from Europeans, whose opinion was absolutely paramount, that Iranians were racially superior to those wretched Semites, and were akin to the French and the Germans. These Europeans were now even appropriating Iran's cultural achievements as part of Europe's heritage, on a par with Homer. As flattering as such statements might have been for Iran's ruling elite, it must be said that they found little echo—if at all—beyond the confined pale of a handful of Iran experts.

One can assess the full significance of the Ferdowsi celebrations, beyond a self-proclaimed interest for culture, literature, or heritage, only in light of the dislocative nationalist objectives pursued. That a shrine was built although the actual body was never found and, most tellingly, that the Pahlavi state throughout 1934 was almost exclusively concerned with the inauguration of a monument and an international academic conference, all this at considerable cost, shows the degree to which the sovereign and his circle prioritized the direct connection between pre-Islamic glories and the Pahlavi state that they tried to bring about via Ferdowsi. This line of argument must of course consider other concurrent policies, the change in the country's international designation, the sartorial repression, and the forced settlement of the nomads. But such assessment should also account for certain retreats, as it is well understood that an ideology cannot be applied in its totality, however strong the zeal of its exponents. The Pahlavi state, for instance, did not withdraw or ban the teaching of Arabic or religion in schools. Hedayat's "The Caravan of Islam" (see chapter 7) was censored, and—importantly—the criminal and civil codes of the early Pahlavi state remained largely Islamic in inspiration.[10] Moreover, and as pointed out by Chehabi, after the unveiling policies of 1936, Reza Shah's government attempted to alleviate criticism from the ulama by turning against the religious minorities: they forced out all Baha'i officers from the army, and Jews from the government bureaucracy.[11] In spite of these concessions, the extent to which some of the most decisive of early Pahlavi policies were directly informed by the dislocative nationalism of Akhundzadeh and Kermani is remarkable. The ideological fanfare of these policies stands in sharp contrast to the constitutionalism of earlier days and the struggle for law and freedom.

The rule of Reza Shah's son, Mohammad Reza Shah (r. 1941–1979), is largely marked by moderation in continuity. As evoked earlier, this latter considered Iran's situation in the Middle East to be "an accident of geography" because he believed Iran belonged to the fellowship of Aryan nations.[12] This idea of geographical accident is to be classified among the most explicit expressions of dislocative nationalism. The shah's choice of the entirely new title *āriyāmehr* ("the light of Aryans") in 1965 makes plain the ideological imperatives at work. The 1971 celebrations surrounding the 2,500th anniversary of the "Persian Empire" marked, in a far more ostentatious manner than his father's Ferdowsi millennial celebrations, the climax of the pre-Islamic legitimation during his reign. Pharaonic sums were spent on the festivities that the shah and the queen hosted for sixty-two heads of state or their representatives as well as a large number of foreign and Iranian guests. Among the festivities was a son et lumière show in the ruins of Persepolis glorifying pre-Islamic history and all the clichés attached to it (territorial expanse and Iran being the cradle of civilization, for example).[13] A parade of the Iranian armies throughout the ages (in full period outfit) was staged to emphasize the alleged continuity of the Iranian monarchy. To further accentuate the spiritual and temporal connection between the Achaemenid kings and Mohammad Reza Shah, the royal retinue and the guests embarked on a choreographed pilgrimage to the tomb of Cyrus the Great in Pasargadae. The shah delivered a highly solemn speech to the memory of the founder of the "Persian Empire," aiming to establish—at long last—Iran's high rank among nations by bringing back to life its glorious past:

O Cyrus! Great King, King of kings, Achaemenid King, King of the land of Iran. I, the Shahanshah of Iran, offer thee salutations from myself and from my nation. At this glorious moment in the history of Iran, I and all Iranians, children of the empire thou founded 2,500 years ago, bow our heads in reverence before thy tomb, and cherish thy undying memory. At this moment, *when the new Iran renews its bond with ancient pride,* we all salute thee as the immortal hero of the history of Iran, the founder of the most ancient monarchy of the world, the great freedom giver, the precious child of mankind.

O Cyrus! We have gathered in front of thy tomb today, to tell thee: sleep in peace, for we are awake! And to guard thy honored legacy, we always will be. . . .

During these 2,500 years, every span of this land's expanse has been watered with the blood of the valiant and the self-sacrificing, so that Iran can remain alive and proud. Many have come to this land to vanquish it, but all have departed, and Iran has remained. . . .

After twenty-five centuries, today as in thy gratified time, the name of Iran is admixed with ample respect and praise throughout the universe. Today, as in thy time, on the chaotic stage of this world, Iran is the messenger of freedom, humanity, and the guardian of the greatest ideals of mankind. The beacon that thou ignited has never been extinguished in the eventful storms of the past 2,500 years, and is today more alight and radiant than ever in this luminescent land. . . .

Cyrus! . . . Sleep in peace, for we are awake! And we always will be." (my emphasis)[14]

The National Film Board of Iran produced an official documentary about the event, entitled *Flame of Persia* (1971, directed by Shahrokh Golestan). The script is narrated by no less than Orson Welles, and alongside its commentary of the celebrations, it aims to convince, yet again, the imaginary Western interlocutor that Iran is no lesser nation. Comparisons are offered in passing, particularly with Britain, to further the point: we are told that "Cyrus, King of kings" was the "champion" of "human liberties," "long before Magna Carta" (reference to the myth whereby the Cyrus's cylinder is a charter of human rights; see chapter 3).[15] Without any apparent reason, we are taught that Iran is "five times the size of Great-Britain." The idea that the history of Iran is nothing less than a succession of invasions conjures up incessantly: we are told that "Alexander the Great, the conqueror, . . . reduced" Persepolis "to a shell," and that "conquerors trampled on its heritage, but through golden ages the spirit of Persia has always triumphed." There is also a minor case of historical revisionism when it is observed that "there were no slaves in the Persian empire."[16] Finally, the return of Iran among the greatest nations is signaled by the metaphor "the sleeping beauty is now awake," and the film concludes with a long shot of the Cyrus Cylinder and the statement "it was here that the rights of men were first made law." In sum, through the celebrations, the shah seems to be telling the world "my father proved that we were your peers; but I say that we are better." He also made up for the brutal nature of his regime by trumping up human rights as part and parcel of the Iranian monarchy. Whether the expenses, the security crackdown surrounding the events, and the resentment it caused among most Iranians were worth the message is another question. In any case among the secular opponents to the current regime, there is today an almost fanatical nostalgia surrounding this event and the ideas it conveyed, which can be easily observed in comments on the Internet.

The shah finished his father's job of dislodging Iran from liturgical Islamic time. While keeping the solar calendar that was established in 1925, he modified the beginning point of this calendar from the Prophet Muhammad's hijrah to Cyrus the Great's supposed accession to power. Thus, in AD 1976, Iranians were catapulted from 1355 of the hijrah to 2535 of the imperial era. The shah was in fact one step ahead of most dislocative nationalists because for him dislocation had already taken place, or was a given. He once privately observed that his ambition was to "raise ourselves to the level of a great world power," rather than to be a mere regional leader.[17] He did not moan about the lost glory of pre-Islamic Iran anymore because he was convinced, especially after the 1971 celebrations, that he had managed to revive that glory and, not only that, that he was leading the country to a future that surpassed ancient Iranians' achievements. His idea of Iran's future was articulated in his 1977 book *Beh su-ye tamaddon-e bozorg* (Toward the great civilization): "It is the civilization in which the best elements of human knowledge and thought are employed in order to secure the highest level of material and spiritual living for every member of the society."[18] Fereydun Hoveyda sardonically described the "Great Civilization" as "a combination of Cyrus the Great and of economic and social development."[19] The shah believed that in "the next 12 years," we will "reach the present level of progress of Western Europe."[20] This was all hubris and delusion, as Iran was far from having sufficiently developed at the time: few of its villagers had access to electricity, clean water, or education. Freedom of speech and assembly were nonexistent. Be that as it may, his confidence that he had achieved the dislocative nationalist goal of returning the nation to its previous splendor, while reaching the level of development of the great nations of this world was such that he had in fact become critical of the West and its "immoral lifestyle."[21]

Yet it must be emphasized once again that espousal of an ideology cannot be total. Indeed, although the shah was keen to curb the powers of the clergy, his approach to Islam was more ambiguous and certainly less harsh than his father's.[22] For instance, he would go on pilgrimages to the holy shrines of Najaf and Karbala in Iraq in 1953, several times to the shrine of Imam Reza in Mashhad and the shrine of *emāmzādeh Dāvud* in Tehran, and even flew to Mecca to perform the hajj. He also believed that he was protected by popular saints and figures of Shi'ite Islam, such as (in his own words) "Imam Ali's exalted son Abbas," or "the Lord of Time, the Twelfth Imam."[23] He once wrote in a language not lacking in reverence that his father "named all of his sons after the Imam Reza [the eighth Imam of the Shi'ite pantheon]—with a first

name by which they were distinguished—because he had a particular veneration for this descendant of *our sainted Ali*" (my emphasis).[24] He would relate
visions and apparitions and claim that his life was "protected" by divine forces,
but—always wary of what the Western reader might think—he would justify
his beliefs by arguing that many Westerners, too, have "faith in non-material
things."[25] As a child he was saved from death by typhoid after Imam Ali visited
him in a dream and told him to drink a beverage; "The next day, the crisis of
my fever was over."[26] Furthermore, Ansari argues that he, and not Khomeini,
was the promoter of religious and empathetic rule, and that, more wary of
communism than religion, he occasionally instrumentalized Shiism.[27] Yet
this should not be taken for an argument that Islam had any role in his ideology or the identity that the Pahlavi state crafted for itself.

What better demonstration of the influence of dislocative nationalism than
his preoccupation with history and narratives—in other words, with the historicist discursiveness so typical of the thought of Akhundzadeh and Kermani?
The 2,500th celebrations are ample evidence of the prominence of historicism
in his definition of his country's identity and his own place in the world, and
his willingness to instrumentalize the past for purposes of legitimation. His
Answer to History (1980), in a most unusual manner for a head of state's political statement, starts with a historical overview with many familiar themes:
"The founder of this Empire, Cyrus, deserves to be called 'The Great' because
he founded it on tolerance and justice. As a conqueror he should be considered the first advocate of human rights."[28] He also equated the "Sassanid
Renaissance" with "the European one 1,200 years later" in the recurring com-
petition with Europe that started in Kermani's texts; the shah claimed that
Iranians developed "the Shi'ite doctrine" in order not to submit themselves to
Arab Sunnism, an assertion that proceeds from the racialist assumptions of a
Gobineau, a Renan, or a Browne (see chapter 4).[29] He does, however, acknowl-
edge that "Irano-Islamic cultural centers" developed with "the golden age of
Persian poetry," but he considers nomadism to be "much at odds with the true
spirit of Persia," thus relaying another modern idea without any precedence in
Iranian sources, that of the alien origin of Iranian nomads.[30] He denigrated
Arabs in public, although a degree of racial Manichaeism is implicitly suggested in this book: diplomacy set boundaries on what a sovereign who aimed
to be the leader of the Middle East could say. In the following passage, he does
demean what he believed were Iran's Turkish adversaries (some of whom have
in fact contributed in no insignificant amounts to Iranian civilization or competed with it on a par) but he is cautious to refer to them with ethnonyms that

are not used by any people in his time. He also wonders why racially akin Indo-Europeans have not automatically been each other's allies:

> The Persian Empire was the first barrier against the savage or half-savage nomads who swept in from the steppes or the Asian mountains. The Scythians, the white Huns, the Seljuqs, and the Ottomans were contained for centuries at the price of Persian blood. The Indo-Europeans of the Eastern Roman Empire showed no gratitude. They thought only of profiting of our difficulties in the East. . . .[31]

A word must be said of Mosaddeq and his drive to confront the remnants of British imperialism in Iran. Mosaddeq became prime minister following a democratic process in 1951, helped nationalize Iranian oil away from the Anglo-Iranian Oil Company that same year, and was later overthrown in a notorious coup d'état. Because the nationalization of oil that he instigated hurt British economic interests, the literature coding all extra-Western nationalisms as anticolonial struggles and all anticolonial moves as nationalist has portrayed Mosaddeq as the personification of Iranian nationalism, while Mohammad Reza Shah was, due to the partly CIA-fomented coup that brought him back to his throne in 1953, rebranded a "lackey" of the United States or Britain, or both.[32] However, as Katouzian's work has shown, Mosaddeq's most important objective was democratic government, as he had remained faithful to the ideals of the Constitutional Revolution.[33] The nationalization of natural resources was for Mosaddeq a prerequisite to a genuine democratic regime. Complete independence was the first step toward democratic government. According to Katouzian, Mosaddeq and his colleagues believed that, "so long as a large and powerful foreign company owned the country's most important modern industry, effectively controlled one of its provinces, and interfered in its politics to defend and promote the company's own interest, it was not possible to establish either sovereign or democratic government."[34]

Mosaddeq was ultimately brought down by a combination of forces opposing him—"the shah, landowners, army generals, the Tudeh (communist party), leading ulama, Britain and America."[35] If emphasis is put on his democratic (or at least liberal) credentials, one could argue that Mosaddeq's nationalism was of a civic type, one that could be embodied in a pluralist state and its legitimate laws and institutions. Alternatively, one could call him a constitutional nationalist. This designation stresses both his political affinity with the constitutionalist values of 1906 and his commitment to the Iranian community whose sovereignty over an important national asset he restored. However, it is worth noting that Mosaddeq was not a dislocative nationalist. He kept professing his Shi'ite faith in public, even during his trials; he invoked Imam Hussein in his speeches before the *majles*; and he never waved the Aryanist flag. He never adhered to a historicist narrative, did not indulge in racial narcissism, never claimed that the Sasanian period was akin to the Garden of Eden, and did not espouse all-out Westernization. Quite the contrary, he was a pragmatic man, pursuing the tangible political objectives of Iranian constitutionalism: freedom, independence, and a state of law.

In the late Pahlavi period, dislocative nationalism experienced ebbs and flows among the intellectuals. A few monuments of dislocative nationalism were produced during Mohammad Reza Shah's reign. Arguably the most popular of these (to this day) is Abdolhossein Zarrinkub's *Do qarn sokut* (Two centuries of silence, 1957), which has been reprinted many times and has shaped the historical consciousness of Iranians for decades.[36] Zarrinkub's main objective was to demonstrate through a historical work that the "Arab invasion" was a disaster of cataclysmic magnitude for Iran. Through a dislocative nationalist lens, Zarrinkub sees this event as essentially cultural and argues that, during the first two centuries of Islam, Iranians were on the verge of forgetting their language and identity and sinking into oblivion as a result of the domination of Arabs (hence the title: two centuries of silence). Although Zarrinkub's work is infinitely more serious and scholarly than Akhundzadeh's and Kermani's—at least in appearance—and although he uses a large number of historical sources in Persian and Arabic, the ideological purpose underlying his endeavor is identical to his spiritual heirs: apply racial Manichaeism to the history of Iran to dissociate Iran from Islam, and portray Arabs as the implacable enemies of Iranians' identity and culture. Attention is given to Iranian heroes such as Afshin and Maziyar, who rebelled against the caliphate, but in Zarrinkub's pages they rebelled against "Arab rule," in a complete racialization of history that ignores the cultural amalgamations that took place over that period and arguably gave birth to a great literary and scientific renaissance in Iran.

The first pages offer what is by now a hackneyed description of the Arabs in their desert. For several pages there is not a single reference to a historical source. Zarrinkub's description of Arabs abounds with subjective judgmental terms, from "greedy" (*haris*) to "savage-like" (*vahshi guneh*).[37] Again and again we are told that the aridity of the climate in the Arabian Peninsula explains why "since time immemorial, civilization and culture did not shine there," an assertion that runs in the face of the archaeological richness of this area.[38] As is the case with Kermani and even Adamiyat, the degree of contempt shown for the desert and the lifestyle that it apparently engenders makes one wonder how far the author has traveled in Iran. Indeed, almost 20 percent of the country's territory is covered in one of the most barren deserts in the world, and the rest is fairly arid. This discrepancy might be taken to argue that the roots of this contemptuous discourse on the Arab desert-dweller are to be found in European, rather than Iranian, prejudices.

But to really take a measure of the influence of dislocative nationalism in Iranians' Weltanschauung, one must turn to the responses that intellectuals formulated against Zarrinkub's thesis from a broadly Shi'ite Islamic perspective. As Kamran Aghaie's research has shown, even these responses, although emanating from the other end of the political spectrum, remained prisoners of an Aryanist frame of thought. One such response came from Morteza Motahhari (1920–1979), a prominent cleric and later Shi'ite revolutionary dubbed "the chief ideologue of the Islamic Revolution."[39] He wrote *Khadamāt-e moteqābel-e Eslām va Irān* (The contributions of Islam and Iran to each other) as a direct riposte to Zarrinkub's thesis. In this book Motahhari perceptively characterizes nationalism as a divisive ideology of European origin.[40] He goes on to argue that the basis of nationalism should be "shared suffering" and that Iranians voluntarily espoused Islam, which is a universal religion rather than the cultural product of one specific people; he also refutes the idea that there is an Iranian variant of Islam. Yet to some extent he does reify Aryanism by conceding that the heritage of pre-Islamic Iran could "identify [Iranians] more closely with Europeans as fellow Aryans."[41]

Aghaie goes on to analyze a completely different and more interesting rebuttal by another important ideologue of the Islamic Republic to Zarrinkub's work that even more overtly espouses Aryanist myths. In his *Bāzshenāsi-ye hoveyyat-e Irān-e Eslāmi* (The rediscovery of the identity of Islamic Iran), Ali Shariati (1933–1977), dubbed (again) "the main ideologue of the Iranian Revolution,"[42] argues that Aryans are a "rational, introspective, tolerant, relativistic, and spiritual" calm race (*nezhād-e ārām*) and Semites are an "emotional, irrational, intolerant, materialistic, harsh, and sensual" rash race (*nezhād-e tond*), and he turns history into a clash between these two.[43] For him, the two first centuries of Islam were a period during which Iranians were busy "Aryanizing" a "Semitic" religion.[44] At the end of the process, while remaining "Aryans by race and culture," they became Muslims nevertheless. Shariati also reifies the advent of Islam as a rupture while accusing

Arabs of having perverted Islam.[45] In sum, Shariati espouses many of the assumptions of dislocative nationalism while upholding a broadly Shi'ite revolutionary stance. It is fascinating to observe the influence of dislocative nationalism in twentieth-century Iranian intellectual history. Dislocative nationalism is so dominant that even in the opposite camp sediments of this ideology are to be found in unexpectedly conspicuous fashion. Or one may claim, in Motahhari's case, that these ideas were so entrenched that he was impelled to give in to Aryanism as a concession.

In spite of the predominance of dislocative nationalism, Mohammad Reza Shah's increasingly megalomaniac obsession with Cyrus the Great caused some fatigue among intellectuals in the 1960s and 1970s, especially after the 2,500th celebration. This lassitude brought about what Mehrzad Boroujerdi calls "the tormented triumph of nativism," and—at long last—a thorough "critique of Western colonialism, machinism, and humanism."[46] With significant delay over their Turkish or Egyptian peers, only by the 1960s did Iranian intellectuals start to free themselves from the spell of Europe and engage in a critical dialogue with it, albeit one that was almost as fanatical as their predecessors' reverence and sometimes somewhat excessive in its anti-imperialism and third-worldism. This was the time of Jalal Al-e Ahmad's virulent criticism of *gharbzadegi* ("Westoxication," alternatively translated as "West-struckness" or "Occidentosis") in 1962.[47] *Gharbzadegi* refers to the uncritical and pathological infatuation of secular nationalists with things European; this infatuation had, in Ale-e Ahmad's view and that of other intellectuals, gradually replaced "backwardness" (as Iran's main sociohistorical problem) with alienation.[48] According to Boroujerdi, intellectuals such as Al-e Ahmad or Abolhossein Jalili viewed "a systematic critique of the West" as "a prerequisite to their own process of identity formation."[49] In other words, nativism was one step toward the maturity of Iranian intellectual production, but it was also a reaction against some aspects of dislocative nationalism, particularly Aryanism.

The Islamic Revolution of 1979 marked the pinnacle of disaffection with dislocative nationalism. Talk was now of the political aspirations of the Islamic *umma*, and of Iran's position in leading this universal group by exporting its revolution and taking on the arrogance of "imperialist powers," especially the Great Satan (the United States). Thanks to the nativists and Ali Shariati in particular, an ideology combining opposition to foreign interference and socialist ideals wrapped in the language and symbols of Shi'ite Islam mobilized frustration with the Pahlavi monarchy into a powerful revolutionary movement. Yet it is interesting to note that with resentment with the rule of the clergy

mounting throughout the 1980s, we started to witness by the 1990s a dislocative nationalism return with a vengeance. Akhundzadeh and Kermani's ideology has now taken on the mantle of opposition to the Islamic Republic and
the "dictatorship of the Mullahs." Just as Akhundzadeh perceived the clergy
and the *despotes* as the servants of the Arab cause in Iran (that of destroying
Iran's culture and identity), modern-day dislocative nationalists are convinced
that the mullahs of the Islamic Republic are somewhat of Arab descent (*'arab
zādeh*) and inherently hostile to what they perceive as genuine Iranianness.
Now again, as before, some authors refer to the racial characteristics of Iranians and their alleged incompatibility with Islam—supposed to be the religion
of the racial other—and point to the Islamic Republic and its human rights
abuses as proof of this. Anyone who has visited Iran has heard some Iranians
curse Arabs, who "brought Islam to this Aryan land 1,400 years ago," for the
misery that the Islamic Republic has brought down upon them, in eccentric
distortions of reality, facts, and history as well as a systematic effort to eschew
collective responsibility for domestic events. Now as before, external "others"
are convenient targets to be blamed for Iranians' shortcomings. One would
surely have heard some Iranians oppose the state's support for Palestinians
because "Palestinians are Arabs" and as such are to be blamed in some ludicrous
way for the Islamic Republic and its excesses. Anyone with access to social
networks popular with Iranians has had a taste of the liveliness and virulence
of dislocative nationalism in some segments of Iranian society (especially the
diaspora), the renewed cult of the Pahlavi monarchy, the revived hatred for all
things Islamic, and the reappearance of pre-Islamic symbolism that now more
than ever—and in a most redundant fashion—adorns restaurants, grocery
shops, publishing houses, and websites of all sorts. Any sober criticism is vehemently attacked as support for the "regime of the mullahs" and Islamic fundamentalism in general. But in an ironic twist, the regime in Tehran itself is not
entirely insensitive to the popularity of ancien régime ideologies: when confronted with issues of legitimacy, presidents of the Islamic Republic themselves have tapped into the ideological clichés of dislocative nationalism.
Akbar Hashemi Rafsanjani's government invested large sums of money into
a *Shāhnāmeh* congress in 1990, which he inaugurated himself with a solemn
speech, and which was thoroughly covered by the state media in ways reminding of the Ferdowsi millennial celebrations of 1934. Recently the Ahmadinejad government stirred controversy with an "Iranian doctrine" in which Cyrus
the Great, among other themes dear to dislocative nationalists, was instrumentalized to strengthen the ex-president's patriotic credentials.

However, pundits, pseudo-intellectuals, agitators, and armchair dissidents are not to be undone. New publications with strong dislocative nationalist overtones appear every year. The greater number of these recent publications is startling when compared to the literary works of the early Pahlavi era or the history treatises of the same period. Anyone familiar with dislocative national-ist literature can notice that these publications are highly repetitive, merely recycling the works of Akhundzadeh, Kermani, and their heirs. There is some-thing new, however, and this is their generally appalling quality and their outlandish claims. Any inaccuracy, any nonsensical theory is admissible as long as it fits into the strategy of discursively soothing the reader's concerns with the state of the country, fundamentalism having replaced backwardness as the main malady of modern Iran. Some authors today attempt to establish Aryan calendars or claim that ancient Iranians had space-faring ships.[50] We have come full circle as these new publications have abandoned the little methodological soundness that one could find in Pahlavi-era dislocative treatises and returned to the preposterous inventiveness of a Kermani. This is all the more ironic for our time, as Iranians have never been as literate as today, and empirical data has never been as readily accessible.

Among the most influential authors, one can refer to Shoja'ed-Din Shafa (1918–2010). Shafa held numerous cultural offices during Mohammad Reza Shah's reign. According to his obituary, he was the shah's cultural advisor, is suspected of having written some of the shah's speeches (including the famous "Sleep in peace, for we are awake") and having suggested both the 2,500th an-niversary and the imperial calendar.[51] He is also believed to have been the ghost-writer of *Toward the Great Civilization*.[52] If true, this would mean that he was behind the shah's most conspicuous dislocative nationalist moves. Shafa spent the last few years of his life criticizing the regime of the Islamic Republic, then Islam, and finally all Abrahamic faiths, as if in an endeavor to indict increasingly broader phenomena for Iran's Islamic Revolution. Shafa's obituary points out that his latest books "are not as sound as his pre-revolutionary works" and rightly stresses that when it comes to matters relating to the post-1979 order, Shafa "sacrificed learned writing for fanatic anger (*khashm-e mote'asebāneh*)." This statement could be applied to all contempo-rary dislocative nationalists on all matters related to Iran, history, Islam, the Islamic Republic, and Arabs. This obituary prompted a barrage of abuses against its author in several websites for failing to glorify dislocative national-ism and its champions. Writing for the BBC, the author was also portrayed as a "lackey of Britain."

Shafa's *Pas az 1,400 sāl* (After 1,400 years), which solemnly announces under its title "What every Iranian of the third millennium must know about the verities of the 1,400-years-long Islamic history of his country," is a 1,000-page indictment of Islam. Shafa quotes Akhundzadeh and Kermani one after the other, with reverence.[53] According to him, "Our ancient Iran was the first and greatest victim of the novel imperialism of the desert."[54] Again and again and again we are told of camel-grazers spreading out of the desert to drink the blood of Iranians, to turn the supposedly "life-worshiping" foundations of Iranian civilization into a culture of death and mourning (which in fact clearly has, as mentioned before, pre-Islamic roots) and bring about—in a remarkable historical shortcut—the Islamic Republic.[55] It is the most complete rehashing of by now threadbare dislocative nationalist banalities, a racialist flight from reality with simplistic polarizations aiming to deny the agency of Iranians in their own history. Freed of any responsibility in conducting their own affairs, Iranians are instead portrayed as the eternal victims of the machinations of others who apparently have no concerns of their own apart from conspiring against the Persian language and Iranians' identity.

CONCLUSION
THE FAILURE OF DISLOCATIVE NATIONALISM

DISLOCATIVE NATIONALISM WAS ESTABLISHED IN THE FOUNDATIONAL treatises of Akhundzadeh and Kermani and went on to become the official ideology of the Pahlavi state, with particular bearing on domestic policies during the reign of Reza Shah. Yet, in spite of its implementation, dislocative nationalism is not a reform program concerned with practical political and social objectives. It is a discursive flight from the empirical reality of Iran, an ideational construct designed to treat the suffering caused by the discovery two centuries ago that Europeans were more advanced than us. As such, it is akin to a medication concocted to treat the symptoms of a persistent case of collective post-traumatic disorder, but which fails to address the root-causes of the malady itself. Indeed, the ideas of Akhundzadeh and Kermani, and their implementation under the Pahlavis, have failed to close the gap with the nations of the West or generate the modern state and society that most Iranians aspired to. Two main reasons explain this failure.

First, dislocative nationalism's outlook is excessively romantic. One can of course justifiably doubt that romanticism, referring to a current of thought born in modern Europe, can be applied to Iranian dislocative nationalism. Yet I suggest that it is a fitting description, mainly on two premises.[1] First, if we refer to romanticism as a philosophical reaction against the rationalism of the

Enlightenment, then dislocative nationalism is certainly irrational and similarly displays a predisposition for instinctive and emotional impulses. Second, if romanticism refers to the atavistic exaltation of the ethnic community, then again dislocative nationalism could suitably fall under this heading. It is a romantic thought since, rather than deal with state–society relations, it invokes and weeps upon an ethereal imagery of a bygone golden age. Rather than dispassionately analyze the practical shortcomings of the Iranian state in terms of legal, institutional, or administrative needs, it promotes the eradication of what it has arbitrarily defined as racially alien—especially Arab—influence over the culture, mores, even language of Iranians while concurrently advocating out-and-out Westernization. Dislocative nationalism naively believes that such eradication, coupled with the superficial imitation of Europeans, will automatically solve the issue of backwardness and return the nation to its original state of racial purity and, hence, splendor and power (following Gobineau's argument that only a pure race can attain the highest spheres of civilization). Its obsession to see the origin of all Iran's ills in racial miscegenation prevented it from seeing the more pressing practical issues to be addressed: for instance, the effort and capital diverted to brutally repress religious practices under Reza Shah or throw a costly birthday party for the "Persian Empire" in 1971 could have been used toward more immediate social and economic needs, which would have also presented Pahlavi policies under a more favorable and legitimate light.

The second reason lies in dislocative nationalism's despotic tendencies. Dislocative nationalism is a poor representative of the Enlightenment's values of universality and freedom, contrary to what an Adamiyat would have us believe. Its ideological apparatus was, in crucial ways, indebted to the "counter-Enlightenment" and its adulation of the racial community, a very dubious ground in which to grow a democratic, law-abiding, modern state that would enjoy the support of the population it governs.[2] More crucially, dislocative nationalists considered the customs, practices, religious beliefs, language, even appearance of the country's inhabitants to be just as many signs of backwardness, or the heritage of the Arabs and other invaders: dislocative nationalism had identified these elements for elimination. It is inconceivable that such a contemptuous and authoritarian approach to Iranians' way of life could lead to the creation of a state that would respect their diversity and rights and would treat them like citizens. Dislocative nationalism was meant to violate their moral and physical integrity as individuals to force them into its own shallow understanding of European modernity. The early Pahlavi state did so by treating them like the subjects of some medieval polity to be shaped at will, yet intruding in their private lives through means that only a modern state could yield. The militaristic assault on popular religion, sartorial traditions, linguistic minorities, and nomads could only alienate large segments of society and undermine the legitimacy of that very state and its ideology. This lack of legitimacy in turn partly explains why the abdication of Reza Shah was welcomed with a sigh of relief rather than popular protest. Such rigid and dogmatic ideology could not attract and retain the goodwill of Iranians beyond dislocative nationalists themselves: it was too uncompromising. It was therefore unsuited to delivering a modern state that would enjoy legitimacy and the support of a majority of the population. The resentments it engendered certainly played a role in the ultimate demise of the Pahlavi state, although many other complex forces were at work in the events of 1978–1979.

It is often claimed that ethnic nationalism in Iran succeeded in "holding together" a complex country where centrifugal forces are at work. This is unconvincing: ethnic minorities and nomads have been to a large extent alienated by dislocative nationalist policies, which have been implemented with equal zeal by the Pahlavi state and the Islamic Republic. It must be stressed that prominent Azeris starting with Akhundzadeh have disproportionately contributed to the development and expansion of the ideology and have at times even advocated the annihilation of the Azeri language (Arani). But beyond minorities, many a religious Iranian has also been estranged: the dislocative nationalist endeavor to dissociate Iran from Islam created a deep fracture between the enthusiasts of pre-Islamic Iran and those Iranians attached to the Islamic, especially Shi'ite, heritage. Among mainstream Iranians today, one can see two large groups that one could call the devotees of Cyrus the Great and the disciples of Imam Hussein, who have very different readings of Iranian history and identity.[3] Since this fracture has been artificially created by Akhundzadeh, Kermani, and Jalal ed-Din Mirza before them, every attempt at fusing these two aspects of Iranian identity has failed (the most recent example being Ahmadinejad's ill-fated flirting with Cyrus the Great, see chapter 3). This tension and competition is, again, one among many aspects of the Islamic Revolution in 1979: Imam Hussein took his revenge over Cyrus the Great. Yet one must also recognize that the frontiers between ideologies are blurred and that individuals can blend various elements of different doctrines, often in a contradictory fashion. This is illustrated by Ali Shariati's nativist Shi'ite response to Abdolhossein Zarrinkub's *Two Centuries of Silence*, which relied on the Aryan myth to formulate its arguments. Sediments of dislocative nationalism in various quantities are to be found in virtually any ideology with a significant following in Iran.

I suggest that dislocative nationalism's startling success, its very real appeal to large segments of Iranian society even today, and the influence of its historicist and racialist vision beyond its own ranks indicate that it is the dominant ideology of modern Iran. Ever since discursive, ethnic, and authoritarian nationalism triumphed over the pragmatic objectives of constitutionalism, ever since dislocative nationalism became the official ideology of Pahlavi Iran, it has been the main paradigm defining and interpreting Iran, its history, and the identity of its people. However successful the ideologies of the Left or Shi'ite political movements have been, they have either failed to challenge dislocative myths or have selectively adopted them.

I hope that my study of dislocative nationalism in Iran will be a useful contribution to nationalism theory, particularly in showing that the Eurocentrism of the field can be a serious limitation in the development of a sufficiently diverse spectrum of analytical models. The Europe-based models of civic nationalism, ethnic nationalism, *ethnies*, and so on, are undoubtedly useful; however, one has to move beyond the perception of nationalism in the extra-Western world as simply derivative of European models, or generally limited to their anticolonial dimension, if one is to uncover additional useful models. I tried to show that dislocation, which I have analyzed as a fundamental characteristic of Akhundzadeh's and Kermani's nationalism, can be just one such useful model that can assist the investigation of other forms of historicist nationalism inside, outside, or on the fringes of the Western world. As far as the study of nationalism in the extra-Western world is concerned, I hope dislocation will stimulate research on forms of nationalism beyond anticolonialism. Indeed, dislocative nationalism cannot be assimilated to an anticolonial form of resistance; rather than free the nation from European hegemony, dislocative nationalists' first aim was to *become* Europe.

I hope that my work has supported the understanding that there can be—and usually is—more than one nationalist ideology within the same state–national structure. The multiplicity of nationalist ideologies, their interactions and divergences, has already been noted by several authors, although it would certainly benefit from increased scrutiny and theorization. Breuilly, for instance, has argued that nationalism tends to take a sequence of ideological forms (liberal, republican, civilizational, cultural/linguistic, racial/ethnic).[4] The earlier forms do not give way to the later ones but coexist and interact with them. In Iran, besides dislocative nationalism, other forms of nationalism coexist. One can refer to the nationalist aspects of constitutionalism, of Moss-adeq's oil nationalization movement, and there is also a very real form of na-tionalism embedded in the Islamic Republic's worldview that is begging for academic analysis. What I believe sets dislocative nationalism apart is, on the one hand, its appeal and dominance and, on the other hand, its level of ideo-logical development. More than any other form of nationalism in Iran, disloca-tive nationalism benefits from ideological treatises stabilizing and cementing its dogmas; most importantly, as one element of the official ideology of the Pahlavi state, it was for half a century disseminated through educational cur-ricula, state symbols, propaganda, and sanctioned historiography.

In spite of my complaint against the enduring Eurocentrism of the field of nationalism theory, one must acknowledge that dislocative nationalism is over-whelmingly influenced by ideas born in Europe. Besides the general charac-teristics of nationalism (best expressed in Gellner's definition of nationalism as "a political principle, which holds that the political and the national unit should be congruent"[5]), some of the core beliefs of dislocative nationalism first appeared in European scholarship. It was in texts such as those of Montes-quieu and Herder, possibly informed by European accounts of the Avesta and Zoroastrianism (by Tavernier, Anquetil-Duperron, and others) that one first finds the idea that the advent of Islam amounted to a rupture in the country's history. The infatuation with pre-Islamic Iran was a result of European orien-talists' hostility toward Islam, not a sentiment shared by the inhabitants of the Iranian plateau. The differentiation of Iranians and Arabs as racial groups deemed incompatible and opposite is also clearly rooted in the racialist in-terpretations of William Jones's discovery of the Indo-European family of languages. The view of Ferdowsi as a national poet who saved the Persian language from the onslaught of Arabic and who loathed Islam and Arabs is also found in European texts, particularly Renan's and most importantly Nöldeke's. The assumption that Arabs were animated by genuine racial an-tipathy against Iranians, their identity, and their language, so much so that they aimed to annihilate the Persian language (whereas, as we know, they in fact used Persian and propagated it in the East) is nowhere to be found in premodern Iranian texts, not even in *shuʿubiyah* tracts. Browne, on the other hand, articulated these views, and they can also be found in earlier orientalist accounts. No premodern Iranian source is known to have racialized the advent of Islam to Iran as an "Arab Invasion." In addition to antipathy toward Islam, the other distorting lens that European scholarship used to assess the history of Iran seems to have been inspired by the Gibbonian view of antiquity as an age of science and progress, and the Middle Ages as one of religious fanaticism and barbarity.

Although of European origin, these ideas were nevertheless not simply imitated by the ideologues of Iranian nationalism. They were filtered through Iranian mythistorical and poetic forms, selected and sometimes significantly manipulated to serve the strategy of dislocative nationalism: discursively address the trauma of the encounter with Europe. Once this process of hybridization completed, dislocative nationalism was petrified into a rigid dogma akin to a religious creed. This rigidity has prevented dislocative nationalism from evolving since its inception. In this context, one of the main interests presented by modern-day dislocative nationalists for the scholar of ethnicity and nationalism is the modalities in which they have preserved, down to this very day, items of nineteenth-century European thought that have long since passed their prime. Although it could be retorted that racial thinking, for instance, is still lively in the West under new forms, it has at least been subjected to analysis and questioning and is largely discredited in academia. In Iran, on the other hand, the Aryan race is a lively discourse that has never been systematically reassessed.[6] Testimony to this intellectual paralysis is the Iranians' general attachment to the European historiography of Iran as developed in the nineteenth and early twentieth century through the lens of the perennial nation and race. Popular understandings of history and nation are in a state of suspended animation. Any visitor to an Iranian bookshop would be puzzled to see contemporary editions of not only Sykes, Browne, and Gobineau but even Malcolm's *History of Persia*, originally published in 1815. It is also fairly easy for anyone willing to pay a surplus to acquire the censored monuments of dislocative nationalism through illegal channels, in dark alleys, or—increasingly—for free on the Internet. In contrast, more recent critical reassessments of Iranian historiography produced these past few decades by scholars of Iran are more difficult to find (if they are translated at all, in the case of works produced abroad), as if there was a general aversion to reexamine past assumptions. That they are couched in a language that only specialists may understand is of course part of the problem. When such critical reassessments of nationalist myths do occasionally appear, the author is automatically accused of being an Iran-hater, a lackey of Britain or the United States, or—all at the same time—an agent of the Islamic Republic, an Arab-lover, a fundamentalist, and so on. Any of these authors has received myriad letters and emails of verbal abuse from dislocative nationalists who, like most highly ideologized individuals, do not have a particular inclination for civilized and logical argumentation. No amount of rational evidence can weaken the quasi-religious and dogmatic convictions that they would uphold at any price.

In sum, present-day Iranian dislocative nationalists are bringing into the twenty-first century worldviews that belong to another time. Some of the doctrinal articulations underlying their creed have been thoroughly discredited in the West itself, and their historical assumptions do not stand up to an examination that would be even perfunctorily impartial and rational. This is noteworthy and paradoxical for an ideology overtly concerned with "backwardness." Its dogmatic rigidity in fact perpetuates backwardness by imprisoning its defendants in an antiquated mindset. Their outmoded view of history and identity is rooted in a traumatic encounter with Europe that is now two hundred years old. It is high time to reassess defective, racialist, historicist, and romantic takes on the Iranian nation, and come to terms with the complexity of Iran and its very deep connections with neighboring peoples.

I entertain the hope that a form of civic nationalism based on the voluntarist submission to a set of laws and institutions considered to be just by all the residents of Iran regardless of their stance toward religion, history, or their belonging to an arbitrarily defined "race" or even linguistic community will supersede dislocative nationalism. Contrary to Shafa's hope, Iranians of the third millennium need not be told to naively blame all unpalatable events unfolding in their country to one essentialized and monolithic "Islam," or be encouraged toward racial hatred or simplistic flights from reality. Rather, they need to give their assent to open and independent institutions that embody a civic identity that is not ascriptive. Only then will Iran put "backwardness"—the one enshrined in the nineteenth-century ideas of dislocative nationalism—behind and finalize its tormented entry into its own variety of modernity. The heritage of the Constitutional Revolution can be a useful guide in this new adventure. Alas, at the time when these lines are being written, this seems to be a very distant prospect.

NOTES

Note on Transliteration and Spelling

1. Marshall G. S. Hodgson, *The Venture of Islam: Conscience and History in a World Civilization* (Chicago: University of Chicago Press, 1974), 8.

Introduction

1. Kasra Naji, *Ahmadinejad: The Secret History of Iran's Radical Leader* (London: I. B. Tauris, 2008), 179–80.
2. See Norman Davies's introduction to *Europe: A History*, new ed. (London: Pimlico, 1997).
3. Benedict Anderson, *Imagined Communities: Reflections on the Origin and Spread of Nationalism*, rev. ed. (London: Verso, 2006), 6.
4. A good overview is provided in Carter V. Findley, *Turkey, Islam, Nationalism, and Modernity: A History, 1789–2007* (New Haven: Yale University Press, 2010), chap. 4 and esp. 5.
5. Kevin Robins, "Interrupting Identities: Turkey/Europe," in *Questions of Cultural Identity*, ed. Stuart Hall and Paul Du Gay, 61–86 (London: Sage, 1996), 67.
6. Dorothy Matilda Figueira, *Aryans, Jews, Brahmins: Theorizing Authority Through Myths of Identity* (Albany: State University of New York Press, 2002); see also Thomas R. Trautmann, *Aryans and British India* (Berkeley: University of California Press, 1997).

7. See Ellison's review of Amiri Baraka's "Blues People" in *The Collected Essays of Ralph Ellison* (New York: Modern Library, 1995); and Albert Murray, *The Omni-Americans: New Perspectives on Black Experience and American Culture* (New York: Outerbridge & Dienstfrey, 1970).

8. On these matters, see Daniel Matlin, "Blues Under Siege: Ralph Ellison, Albert Murray, and the Idea of America," in *Uncertain Empire: American History and the Idea of the Cold War*, ed. Joel Isaac and Duncan Bell, 195–222 (New York: Oxford University Press, 2012), esp. 216.

9. Stephen Howe, *Afrocentrism: Mythical Pasts and Imagined Homes* (London: Verso, 1998).

10. Quentin Skinner, "Meaning and Understanding in the History of Ideas," *History and Theory* 8, no. 1 (1969): 3–53.

11. Karl Marx and Friedrich Engels, *Selected Correspondence, 1846–1895, with Explanatory Notes* (Moscow: International Publishers, 1942), 511.

12. John Breuilly, *Nationalism and the State*, 2nd ed. (Manchester: Manchester University Press, 1993), 54.

13. Ibid.

14. To be fair, Anderson too criticizes the eurocentrism of the field and emphasizes the forerunning role of nationalisms in Spanish America. However, the social processes he refers to, print-capitalism and vernacularization, remain specific to European history.

15. See, for instance, Fereydun Adamiyat, *Andishehā-ye Mirzā Āqā Khān-e Kermāni* [Life and thought of Mirza Aqa Khan Kermani] (Tehran: Tahuri, 1346/1967), 264 and 113–14. For a more recent example, see Hamid Ahmadi, "Unity Within Diversity: Foundations and Dynamics of National Identity in Iran," *Critique: Critical Middle Eastern Studies* 14, no. 1 (2005): 127–47.

16. Mohammad Tavakoli-Targhi, "Review, Mostafa Vaziri's Iran as Imagined Nation: The Construction of National Identity," *International Journal of Middle East Studies* 26, no. 2 (1994): 316–18.

17. Mohammad Tavakoli-Targhi, "Refashioning Iran: Language and Culture During the Constitutional Revolution," *Iranian Studies* 23, no. 1–4 (1990): 77–101.

18. See, in particular, Mohammad Tavakoli-Targhi, "Contested Memories: Narrative Structures and Allegorical Meanings of Iran's Pre-Islamic History," *Iranian Studies* 29, no. 1–2 (1996): 149–75; and Mohammad Tavakoli-Targhi, *Tajadod-e bumi va bāz andishi-ye tārikh* [Vernacular modernity and the rethinking of history] (Tehran: Nashr-e Tārikh-e Irān, 1381/2002).

19. Adamiyat, *Andishehā-ye Mirzā Fath'ali Ākhundzādeh*; and *Andishehā-ye Kermāni Mirzā Āqā Khān-e Kermāni*.

20. Mangol Bayat, "Mirza Aqa Khan Kirmani: Nineteenth Century Persian Revolutionary Thinker," PhD diss., University of California, Los Angeles, 1971; Cyrus Masroori, "European Thought in Nineteenth-Century Iran: David Hume and Others," *Journal of the History of Ideas* 61, no. 4 (2000): 657–74; Cyrus Masroori, "French Romanticism and Persian Liberalism in Nineteenth-Century Iran: Mirza Aqa Khan Kirmani and Jacques-Henri Bernardin de Saint-Pierre," *History*

of Political Thought 28, no. 3 (2007): 542–56; Juan R. I. Cole, "Marking Boundaries, Marking Time: The Iranian Past and the Construction of the Self by Qajar Thinkers," *Iranian Studies* 29, no. 1–2 (1996): 35–56; Mehrdad Kia, "Mirza Fath Ali Akhundzade and the Call for Modernization of the Islamic World," *Middle Eastern Studies* 31, no. 3 (1995): 422–48; and Maryam B. Sanjabi, "Rereading the Enlightenment: Akhundzada and His Voltaire," *Iranian Studies* 28, no. 1–2 (1995): 39–60.

1. THE PALEONTOLOGY OF IRANIAN NATIONALISM

1. Mohammad Tavakoli-Targhi, *Refashioning Iran: Orientalism, Occidentalism, and Historiography*, St. Antony's series (New York: Palgrave, 2001), 2.

2. See, for instance, Stuart Hall, "The West and the Rest," in Stuart Hall and Bram Gieben, *Formations of Modernity* (Oxford: Polity Press in association with Open University, 1992).

3. For a detailed overview of the causes of this conflict, see Maziar Behrooz, "Revisiting the Second Russo-Iranian War (1826–28): Causes and Perceptions," *Iranian Studies* 46, no. 3 (2013): 359–81.

4. For a detailed study, see Laurence Kelly, *Diplomacy and Murder in Tehran: Alexander Griboyedov and Imperial Russia's Mission to the Shah of Persia* (London: I. B. Tauris, 2002).

5. George N. Curzon, *Persia and the Persian Question* (London: Longmans, Green & Co., 1892), 480.

6. See, for example, Nikki R. Keddie, *Religion and Rebellion in Iran: The Tobacco Protest of 1891–1892* (London: Cass, 1966).

7. The Qajar shahs' trips to Europe have been often negatively viewed as wasteful enterprises. For a different take highlighting the important considerations at stake, see David Motadel, "Qajar Shahs in Imperial Germany," *Past & Present* 213, no. 1 (2011): 191–235.

8. Abdul-Hadi Hairi, *Nakhostin ruyāruyihā-ye andishegarān-e Irān bā do ruye-ye tamaddon-e burzhuāzi-e qarb* [The early encounters of Iranian thinkers with the two-sided civilization of Western bourgeoisie] (Tehran: Amir Kabir, 1367/1988), 132–33.

9. This subject is discussed at length in Bernard Lewis, *The Muslim Discovery of Europe* (New York: Norton, 1982), esp. chap. 2 and 3.

10. Rudi Matthee, "Facing a Rude and Barbarous Neighbor: Iranian Perceptions of Russia and the Russians from the Safavids to the Qajars," in *Iran Facing Others: Identity Boundaries in a Historical Perspective*, ed. Abbas Amanat and Farzin Vejdani (New York: Palgrave Macmillan, 2012), 101.

11. Ibid., 103–5.

12. Rudi Matthee, "The Imaginary Realm: Europe's Enlightenment Image of Early Modern Iran," *Comparative Studies of South Asia Africa and the Middle East* 30, no. 3 (2010), 452.

13. John Malcolm, *The History of Persia, from the Most Early Period to the Present Time* (London: J. Murray, 1829), 1:55.

14. Arthur Comte de Gobineau, *Trois ans en Asie; de 1855 à 1858* (Paris: B. Grasset, 1923), 5–6.

15. Monica M. Ringer, *Education, Religion, and the Discourse of Cultural Reform in Qajar Iran*, Bibliotheca Iranica. Intellectual Traditions series no. 5 (Costa Mesa, CA: Mazda Publishers, 2001), 53.

16. Rudi Matthee, "Between Aloofness and Fascination: Safavid Views of the West," *Iranian Studies* 31, no. 2 (1998), 226–27.

17. Rudi Matthee, "Suspicion, Fear, and Admiration: Pre-Nineteenth-Century Iranian Views of the English and the Russians," in *Iran and the Surrounding World: Interactions in Culture and Cultural Politics*, ed. Nikki R. Keddie and Rudi Matthee, 121–45 (Seattle: University of Washington Press, 2002).

18. Ringer, *Education*, 1, quoting Pierre Amédée Jaubert, *Voyage en Arménie et en Perse fait dans les années 1805 et 1806* (Paris: Pélicier, 1821), 175–77.

19. See Abbas Amanat, "'Russian Intrusion into the Guarded Domain': Reflections of a Qajar Statesman on European Expansion," *Journal of the American Oriental Society* 113, no. 1 (1993): 36–37.

20. Quoted in ibid., 43.

21. Ibid., 48. It must be said that blaming defeat and other disasters to some occult force was a habitual approach of Qajar historians. See Firuz Kazemzadeh, "Iranian Historiography," in *Historians of the Middle East*, ed. Bernard Lewis and P. M. Holt (Oxford: Oxford University Press, 1962), 430. Julie Scott Meisami claims that this tradition runs deeper; see Meisami, *Persian Historiography to the End of the Twelfth Century* (Edinburgh: Edinburgh University Press, 1999), 285.

22. Arthur Comte de Gobineau, *Les Religions et les philosophies dans l'Asie Centrale*, 2nd ed. (Paris: Didier et cie, 1866), 130.

23. This flawed understanding had a correspondence in the way early modern European travelers initiated orientalist scholarship in the early modern period. The different intellectual framework they used to scrutinize the "Orient" could not fully grasp its reality.

24. Cyrus Masroori, "European Thought in Nineteenth-Century Iran: David Hume and Others," *Journal of the History of Ideas* 61, no. 4 (2000), 660.

25. Mostafa Vaziri, *Iran as Imagined Nation: The Construction of National Identity* (New York: Paragon House, 1993), 179. Note that the first newspaper in Persian was Mi'rat ol-Akhbār, published for the first time in 1822 in India.

26. Gobineau, *Les Religions et les philosophies*, 130.

27. Edward Granville Browne, *A Year Amongst the Persians* (London: Adam and Charles Black, 1893), 97–98.

28. The ulama and the monarchy were generally not tolerant of European ideas. A translation of Descartes, for instance, was burned in 1853. See Masroori, "European Thought," 663.

29. Stephanie Cronin, "Building a New Army: Military Reform in Qajar Iran," in *War and Peace in Qajar Persia: Implications Past and Present*, ed. Roxane Farmanfarmaian (London: Routledge, 2008).

30. It must be added that in his otherwise stellar record of accomplishment, Amir Kabir's violent dealing with the Babi insurrection is a serious stain.

31. Cronin, "Building a New Army," 49.

32. Mehrdad Kia, "Constitutionalism, Economic Modernization and Islam in the Writings of Mirza Yusef Khan Mostashar od-Dowle," *Middle Eastern Studies* 30, no. 4 (1994), 755.

33. See Abdolhossein Nava'i, *Sharh-e hāl-e Abbās Mirzā Molk Ārā* (The life of Abbas Mirza Molk Ara), 2nd ed. (Tehran: Bābak, 1361/1982), 175.

34. Statement by Sir Henry Drummond Wolff, British Minister to Tehran. See Firoozeh Kashani-Sabet, *Frontier Fictions: Shaping the Iranian Nation, 1804–1946* (Princeton, NJ: Princeton University Press, 1999), 77.

35. Chris Paine and Erica Schoenberger, "Iranian Nationalism and the Great Powers: 1872–1954," *MERIP Reports*, no. 37 (1975), 3–4, citing Jean-Baptiste Feuvrier, *Trois ans à la cour de Perse* (Paris: F. Juven, 1899), 350.

36. T. C. W. Blanning, *The Culture of Power and the Power of Culture: Old Regime Europe 1660–1789* (Oxford: Oxford University Press, 2003), 259.

37. Joep Leerssen, "Literary Historicism: Romanticism, Philologists, and the Presence of the Past," *Modern Language Quarterly* 65, no. 2 (2004): 234–35.

38. Ibid., 226, 233, and 238.

39. There are also a few examples of such conserved epics in Europe. One could mention the Icelandic sagas.

40. Sadeq Rezazadeh Shafaq, *Tārikh-e adabiyyāt-e Irān barāy-e dabirestānhā* [Literary history of Iran for high school students] (Tehran: Amir Kabir, 1342/1963), 95. This is also paraphrased in Azar Nafisi, Foreword to *Shahnameh: The Persian Book of Kings* (New York: Penguin, 2007), x.

41. On the oral traditions, see Dick Davis, "The Problem of Ferdowsî's Sources," *Journal of the American Oriental Society* 116, no. 1 (1996): 48–57; and Kumiko Yamamoto, *The Oral Background of Persian Epics: Storytelling and Poetry* (Leiden: Brill, 2003).

42. See Davis, "Ferdowsî's Sources."

43. On this see Tavakoli-Targhi, *Refashioning Iran*, chap. 5.

44. See Muhammad Ibn Jarir Tabari, *The Sasanids, the Byzantines, the Lakhmids, and Yemen* (Albany: State University of New York Press, 1999), 268.

45. Julie Scott Meisami, "The Past in Service of the Present: Two Views of History in Medieval Persia," *Poetics Today* 14, no. 2 (1993): 267.

46. Tavakoli-Targhi, *Refashioning Iran*, 78.

47. In particular, Bertold Spuler. For a detailed account of historiography in Mongol Iran, see Bertold Spuler and Ismail Marcinkowski, *Persian Historiography and Geography: Bertold Spuler on Major Works Produced in Iran, the Caucasus, Central Asia, India and Early Ottoman Turkey* (Singapore: Pustaka Nasional, 2003), chap. 5.

48. Opinion held by David O. Morgan and Jan Rypka; see Charles Melville, "Historiography; iv. Mongol Period," in *Encyclopædia Iranica*, ed. Ehsan Yarshater; New York: Bibliotheca Persica, 2004, 12:349.

49. Mohammad Tavakoli-Targhi, *Tajadod-e bumi va bāz andishi-ye tārikh* [Vernacular modernity and the rethinking of history] (Tehran: Nashr-e Tārikh-e Irān, 1381/2002), 11. For a different take on the time of Muslim historiography, see Meisami, *Persian Historiography*, esp. 11 and 284.

50. Tavakoli-Targhi points out that starting with Marvi's *ʿAlam ārā-ye Nāderi*, Iranian historians blended dynastic history with that of the land of Iran and therefore expanded the object of historical narration. Yet we are still far from a modern *völkisch* concern. See Tavakoli-Targhi, *Tajadod-e bumi*.

51. John Stevens, Preface to *The History of Persia* (London: Printed for Jonas Brown, 1715). Stevens's book is a translation of some of Teixeira's writings into English.

52. A. K. S. Lambton, "Major-General Sir John Malcolm (1769–1833) and 'The History of Persia,'" *Iran Journal* 33 (1995): 103.

53. Malcolm, *History of Persia*, 1:6.

54. Ibid., 2:218.

55. Ibid., 2:391. As pointed out by Tavakoli-Targhi, Malcolm's assertion that the Iranian "Oriental" is fundamentally stagnant and unchanging is identical to the "Hegelian postulate of the fundamental similarity of the ancient and contemporary Persian mode of life." Tavakoli-Targhi, *Refashioning Iran*, x.

56. Malcolm, *History of Persia*, vol. 2, chap. 23.

57. Ibid., 1:v.

58. Fath ed-Din Fattahi, *Safarnāmeh-ye Mirzā Fattāh Khān Garmrudi beh Orupā* [Mirza Fattah Khan Garmrudi's Europe travel diary] (Tehran: Chāpkhāneh-ye Bānk-e Bāzargāni-e Irān, 1347/1968), 919. See Tavakoli-Targhi, *Tajadod-e Bumi*, 17.

59. Rüdiger Schmitt, "Grundriss der Iranischen Philologie," in *Encyclopædia Iranica*, ed. Ehsan Yarshater; New York: Bibliotheca Persica, 2003.

60. Jalal ed-Din Mirza Qajar, *Nāmeh-ye Khosrovān* [the Book of Sovereigns], 3 vols. (Tehran: Mohammad Taqi & Ali Qoli Khan Qajar, 1868–1871), 1:4.

61. Marashi and Amanat concur on this point. See Afshin Marashi, *Nationalizing Iran: Culture, Power, and the State, 1870–1940* (Seattle: University of Washington Press, 2008), 56–64; and Abbas Amanat, "Jalal ed-Din Mirzā va nāmeh-ye khosrovān" [Jalal ed-Din Mirza and the Book of Sovereigns], *Iran Nameh* 17, no. 1 (1999): 23.

62. Jalal ed-Din Mirza published three volumes of the *Nāmeh* but died before writing the fourth volume, which was supposed to cover the period between the Safavid and Qajar dynasties. See Jalal ed-Din Mirza to Akhundzadeh, undated letter, in Hamid Mohammadzadeh and Hamid Arasli, eds., *Mirzā Fathʿali Ākhundof: alefbā-ye jadid va maktubāt* [Mirza Fathali Akhundov: The new alphabet and the Maktubāt] (Baku: Nizami, 1963), 373.

63. Qajar, *Nāmeh-ye Khosrovān*, 1:9 and 234 for instance.

64. In ibid., 2:57–58.

65. In ibid., 2:67.

66. Marashi, *Nationalizing Iran*, 59.

67. Qajar, *Nāmeh-ye Khosrovān*, 1:9–10. Regarding Jalal ed-Din's sources, see Amanat, "Jalāl ed-Din Mirzā," 23–29.

68. For a criticism of Iranian national historiography, see Vaziri, *Iran as Imagined Nation*, 151–67; Fereydun Adamiyat and Thomas M. Ricks, "Problems in Iranian Historiography," *Iranian Studies* 4, no. 4 (1971): 132–56; and Hamid Enayat, "The Politics of Iranology," *Iranian Studies* 6, no. 1 (1973): 2–20.

69. Mirza Aqa Khan Kermani, *Seh maktub* [Three letters], ed. Bahram Choubine (Frankfurt: Alborz, 2005), 233–34.

70. On the evolution of the word *vatan*, see Kashani-Sabet, *Frontier Fictions*, 49–52; and Mohammad Tavakoli-Targhi, "From Patriotism to Matriotism: A Tropological Study of Iranian Nationalism, 1870–1909," *International Journal of Middle East Studies* 34, no. 2 (2002): 217–38.

71. Eric J. Hobsbawm, *On History* (London: Weidenfeld & Nicolson, 1997), 5. For more on European national histories, see Stefan Berger, Mark Donovan, and Kevin Passmore, *Writing National Histories: Western Europe Since 1800* (London: Routledge, 1999).

2. AKHUNDZADEH AND KERMANI: THE EMERGENCE OF DISLOCATIVE NATIONALISM

1. Partha Chatterjee, *The Nation and Its Fragments: Colonial and Postcolonial Histories*, Princeton Studies in Culture/Power/History (Princeton: Princeton University Press, 1993).

2. For a similar position, see Partha Chatterjee, *Nationalist Thought and the Colonial World: A Derivative Discourse?* (Minneapolis: University of Minnesota Press, 1993), 40–41.

3. See his short autobiography in Fath'ali Akhundzadeh, *Maktubāt: Nāmehā-ye Kamāl od-Dowleh beh Shāhzādeh Jamāl od-Dowleh* [Maktubat: Letters from Kamal od-Dowleh to Prince Jamal od-Dowleh], ed. Bahram Choubine (Frankfurt: Alborz, 2006), esp. 452.

4. Ibid., 279; regarding Renan, see also Akhundzadeh to Mirza Yusuf Khan, March 29, 1871, in Hamid Mohammadzadeh and Hamid Arasli, eds., *Mirzā Fath'ali Ākhundof: Alefbā-ye Jadid va Maktubāt* [Mirza Fathali Akhundov: The new alphabet and the Maktubāt], (Baku: Nizami, 1963), 212–13.

5. Adamiyat mentions two sources, I. Andronikov and L. Klimovitch. See Fereydun Adamiyat, *Andishehā-ye Mirzā Fath'ali Ākhundzādeh* [Life and thought of Mirza Fath'ali Akhundzadeh] (Tehran: Khārazmi, 1349/1970), 38.

6. Hamid Algar, *Mirza Malkum Khan: A Study in the History of Iranian Modernism* (Berkeley: University of California Press, 1973), 12. Mostashar od-Dowleh too was careful not to offend religious sentiment when he called for the reform of Iran's system of law. See Mehrdad Kia, "Constitutionalism, Economic Modernization and Islam in the Writings of Mirza Yusef Khan Mostashar od-Dowle," *Middle Eastern Studies* 30, no. 4 (1994): 762–63.

7. See Nikki R. Keddie, *An Islamic Response to Imperialism: Political and Religious Writings of Sayyid Jamal ad-Din "al-Afghani"* (Berkeley: University of California Press, 1983), 89.

8. Tadeusz Swietochowski, *Russian Azerbaijan 1905–1920: The Shaping of National Identity in a Muslim Community* (Cambridge: Cambridge University Press, 2004), 24.

9. Mehrdad Kia, "Women, Islam and Modernity in Akhundzade's Plays and Unpublished Writings," *Middle Eastern Studies* 34, no. 3 (1998): 5.

10.	The Rev. A. Duff's address to the General Assembly of the Church of Scotland, quoted in Mohammad Tavakoli-Targhi, "Historiography and Crafting Iranian National Identity," in *Iran in the 20th Century: Historiography and Political Culture*, ed. Touraj Atabaki (London: I. B. Tauris, 2009), 16.

11.	See Hamid Algar, "Malkum Khān, Ākhūndzāda and the Proposed Reform of the Arabic Alphabet," *Middle Eastern Studies* 5, no. 2 (1969): 118.

12.	Akhundzadeh, *Maktubāt*, 276–77.

13.	Ibid., 320.

14.	Akhundzadeh to Mirza Ja'far Qaracheh Daqi, March 25, 1871, in ibid., 460.

15.	Ibid., 291.

16.	Kermani, on the other hand, had some scant knowledge of the Achaemenids. See Mirza Aqa Khan Kermani, *Ā'ineh-ye sekandari* [Alexandrian mirror] (Tehran [?], 1326/1909), 3 and 171 et seq.

17.	Akhundzadeh, *Maktubāt*, 291–92.

18.	Akhundzadeh to Jalal ed-Din Mirza, May 20, 1871, in Mohammadzadeh and Arasli, eds., *Alefbā-ye Jadid va Maktubāt*, 220.

19.	Akhundzadeh, *Maktubāt*, 291–92.

20.	Ibid., 292.

21.	Ibid., 293–94.

22.	Compare between Akhundzadeh, *Maktubāt*, 291 and 293.

23.	Ibid., 293.

24.	Ibid., 290.

25.	Ibid., 294.

26.	Ibid.

27.	Ibid.

28.	Ibid., 295–96. I am grateful to Homa Katouzian for his help in translation.

29.	Ibid., 303–4, 307–9.

30.	Ibid., 311.

31.	Ibid., 312–313, 321.

32.	Ibid., 324.

33.	Ibid., 337.

34.	Ibid., 332.

35.	Ibid., 368–69.

36.	Ibid., 381.

37.	Ibid., 412.

38.	Ibid.

39.	Akhundzadeh to Mirza Ja'far Qaracheh Daqi, March 15, 1871, in ibid., 458.

40.	Akhundzadeh to Jalal ed-Din Mirza, September 1870, in Mohammadzadeh and Arasli, eds., *Alefbā-ye Jadid va Maktubāt*, 175.

41.	See Akhundzadeh to Jalal ed-Din Mirza, June 15, 1870, in ibid., 172.

42.	Akhundzadeh to Manekji (through Jalal ed-Din Mirza), May 20, 1871, in ibid., 222–23.

43.	For more on Akhundzadeh's and Jalal ed-Din Mirza's correspondence with Manekji and its archaistic overtones, see Reza Zia-Ebrahimi, "An Emissary of the Golden Age: Manekji Limji Hataria and the Charisma of the Archaic in Pre-Nationalist Iran," *Studies in Ethnicity and Nationalism*, 10, no. 3 (2010): 377–90.

44. For a full (if slightly outdated) list of his writings, see Mangol Bayat-Philipp, "Mirza Aqa Khan Kirmani: A Nineteenth Century Persian Nationalist," *Middle Eastern Studies* 10, no. 1 (1974): 55–57.

45. Sorour Soroudi, "Mirza Aqa Khan Kermani and the Jewish Question," in *Muslim-Jewish Encounters: Intellectual Traditions and Modern Politics*, ed. Ronald L. Nettler and Suha Taji-Farouki (Amsterdam: Harwood Academic, 1998), 149.

46. This point is made by both Adamiyat and Bayat-Philipp. See Fereydun Adamiyat, *Andishehā-ye Mirzā Āqā Khān-e Kermāni* [Life and thought of Mirza Aqa Khan Kermani] (Tehran: Tahuri, 1346/1967); and Bayat-Philipp, "Mirza Aqa Khan Kirmani."

47. He came to the point of criticizing Babism. See Mirza Aqa Khan Kermani, *Seh maktub* [Three letters], ed. Bahram Choubine (Frankfurt: Alborz, 2005), 308–9.

48. See, for instance, Adamiyat, *Andishehā-ye Kermāni*, 14–25. Adamiyat himself relies on another source for his assertions, but he does not treat it critically.

49. Bayat-Philipp, "Mirza Aqa Khan Kirmani," 37.

50. Ibid., 39.

51. On this reading of his legacy, see Cyrus Masroori, "French Romanticism and Persian Liberalism in Nineteenth-Century Iran: Mirza Aqa Khan Kirmani and Jacques-Henri Bernardin de Saint-Pierre," *History of Political Thought* 28, no. 3 (2007): 542–56.

52. Kermani, *Seh maktub*, 127.

53. Ibid., 123, 124, 127.

54. See, for instance, ibid., 271, 278, 305, 317, 326, 327, and 394.

55. Regarding religious continuities, see, in particular, Shahrokh Meskoob, *Sug-e Siyāvosh: Dar marg va rastākhiz* [The Sug-e Siyavosh, in death and resuscitation] (Tehran: Khārazmi, 1350/1971); and Henry Corbin, *En Islam Iranien: Aspects spirituels et philosophiques* (Paris: Gallimard, 1971). For cultural and political continuities, see Richard N. Frye, *The Heritage of Persia* (London: Weidenfeld and Nicolson, 1962).

56. Kermani, *Seh maktub*, 128.

57. Ibid., 139.

58. Ibid., 142–44.

59. Mirza Aqa Khan Kermani, *Sad khatābeh* [One hundred lectures], ed. Harun Vohouman (Los Angeles: Ketab Corp., 1386/2007), 281. On his idea of the locality of religion (thence the non-universality of it), see Mangol Bayat-Philipp, "The Concepts of Religion and Government in the Thought of Mirza Aqa Khan Kirmani, a Nineteenth-Century Persian Revolutionary," *International Journal of Middle East Studies* 5, no. 4 (1974): 388–89.

60. Soroudi, "Mirza Aqa Khan Kermani and the Jewish Question," 156.

61. Kermani, *Seh maktub*, 213 and 216.

62. Ibid., 205.

63. Ibid., 265.

64. Ibid., 304.

65. Ibid., 129–30.

66. Ibid., 137.

67. Kermani, *Sad khatābeh*, 75.

68. Kermani, *Seh maktub*, 180–81. On the translation of "*zangi*" into "Negro," see Shihan de Silva Jayasuriya, "Identifying Africans in Asia: What's in a Name?" *African and Asian Studies* 5 (2006): 277. Kermani also calls them "savage." See Kermani, *Seh maktub*, 308.

69. See Soroudi, "Mirza Aqa Khan Kermani and the Jewish Question," 151n7 and 154.

70. Kermani, *Sad khatābeh*, 76.

71. In the *Nouveau dictionnaire d'histoire naturelle* of Jean-Joseph Virey, for instance. For quotations, see Léon Poliakov, *Le mythe Aryen: Essai sur les sources du racisme et des nationalismes*, new exp. ed. (Brussels: Editions Complexe, 1987), 206.

72. Kermani, *Seh maktub*, 269.

73. Quoted in Bayat-Philipp, "Mirza Aqa Khan Kirmani," 48.

74. Kermani, *Sad khatābeh*, 245.

75. Ibid., 246.

76. Kermani, *Seh maktub*, 283–84. There is more anti-Semitism, 293–98. It must be highlighted that his attitude toward Jews was complex. See Soroudi, "Mirza Aqa Khan Kermani and the Jewish Question."

77. Kermani, *Sad khatābeh*, 56.

78. Kermani, *Seh maktub*, 396.

79. Ibid., 386–87.

80. Ibid., 402–3.

81. Kermani, *Sad khatābeh*, 85–86, 96–98.

82. Kermani, *Ā'ineh-ye Sekandari*, 14.

83. See, for instance, Kermani, *Sad khatābeh*, 74.

84. Kermani, *Seh maktub*, 223.

85. Kermani, *Sad khatābeh*.

86. Bayat-Philipp, "Mirza Aqa Khan Kirmani": although she maintains that Kermani genuinely searched for the truth and had blind faith in science, ibid., 38; and Soroudi, "Mirza Aqa Khan Kermani and the Jewish Question."

87. Mehrdad Kia, "Mirza Fath Ali Akhundzade and the Call for Modernization of the Islamic World," *Middle Eastern Studies*, 31, no. 3 (1995): 442–48; and Kia, "Women, Islam and Modernity." See also Maryam B. Sanjabi, "Rereading the Enlightenment: Akhundzada and His Voltaire," *Iranian Studies* 28, no. 1–2 (1995): 39–60; Juan R. I. Cole, "Marking Boundaries, Marking Time: The Iranian Past and the Construction of the Self by Qajar Thinkers," *Iranian Studies* 29 (1996): 35–56; Afshin Marashi, *Nationalizing Iran: Culture, Power, and the State, 1870–1940* (Seattle: University of Washington Press, 2008), 66–75; and Homa Katouzian, *Sadeq Hedayat: The Life and Legend of an Iranian Writer* (London: I. B. Tauris, 1991), 5–8.

88. Adamiyat, *Andishehā-ye Ākhundzādeh*, 120.
89. Kermani, *Sad khatābeh*, introduction by Harun Vohouman, 25, 23 and 29.
90. Ibid., 24 and 25.
91. Akhundzadeh, *Maktubāt*, introduction by Bahram Chubine, 7, 171, and 207.
92. Ibid., 179.
93. Mashallah Ajoudani, *Mashruteh-ye Irāni* (Iranian constitutionalism), partly censored Iranian edition (Tehran: Akhtarān, 1382/2003), 219.
94. See Shojaʿed-Din Shafa, *Pas az 1,400 Sāl* [After 1,400 years] (2003), 21–22.
95. Cyrus Masroori, "Mirza Yaʿqub Khan's Call for Representative Government, Toleration and Islamic Reform in Nineteenth-Century Iran," *Middle Eastern Studies* 37, no. 1 (2001), 95.
96. See six hundred pages of hagiographic praise in *Bokhārā: Majaleh-ye Farhangi Honari* [Bukhara: A Persian Review of Culture, Art and Iranology] 11 no. 65 (April–May 2008).
97. There are other works on Akhundzadeh in Russian, Turkish, German, and English. See, in particular, H. W. Brands, *Azerbaiganisches Volksleben und modernistische Tendenz in den Schauspielen Mirza Feth-Ali Ahundzades* (Leiden: Brill, 1975); and M. Rafili, *M. F. Akhundov, Zhizn' i Tvorchestvo* (Baku: Azerbaĭdzhanskoe gos. izdvo, 1957).
98. For an exception, see Houchang E. Chehabi, "The Paranoid Style in Iranian Historiography," in *Iran in the 20th Century: Historiography and Political Culture*, ed. Touraj Atabaki, 155–76 (London: I. B. Tauris, 2009).
99. Ali Asghar Haj Seyyed Javadi, "Ādamiyat, pedar-e ʿelm-e tārikh-e Irān" [Adamiyat, the father of the science of history in Iran], *Bokhārā: Majaleh-ye Farhangi Honari* 11, no. 65 (April–May 2008): 195–201. Even Ali Ansari praises him as a historian "with a professionalism that would have been familiar to Western practitioners of the discipline": Ali M. Ansari, *The Politics of Nationalism in Modern Iran* (Cambridge: Cambridge University Press, 2012), 143–44.
100. On his propensity to misquote sources, see Chehabi, "The Paranoid Style in Iranian Historiography," 162–63; for partisan authors considering these misquotations as "mistakes," see Ajoudani, *Mashruteh-ye Irāni*, 330–31.
101. Adamiyat, *Andishehā-ye Kermāni*, 264. Also refer to Adamiyat, *Andishehā-ye Ākhundzādeh*, 113–14.
102. Adamiyat, *Andishehā-ye Kermāni*, 266.
103. Adamiyat, *Andishehā-ye Ākhundzādeh*, 129, 134, and 154.
104. Ibid., 119.
105. Cosroe Chaqueri, "Ravesh shenāsi-e tārikhi-e Fereydun Ādamiyyat" [Fereydun Adamiyat's historical methodology], *Bokhārā: Majaleh-ye Farhangi Honari* 11, no. 65 (April–May 2008): 307.
106. Adamiyat, *Andishehā-ye Ākhundzādeh*, 120.
107. Ibid.
108. Akhundzadeh to Jalal ed-Din Mirza, May 20, 1871, in Mohammadzadeh and Arasli, *Alefbā-ye Jadid va Maktubāt*, 221 and 225.
109. Adamiyat, *Andishehā-ye Ākhundzādeh*, 120–21.

110. Ruth Benedict's work, for instance, had been published almost three decades earlier. See Ruth Benedict, *Race and Racism* (London: Routledge, 1942).

111. See, for instance, Chehabi, "The Paranoid Style in Iranian Historiography," 162–64.

112. Adamiyat, *Andishehā-ye Ākhundzādeh*, 119.

113. Ibid., 120.

114. Ibid.

115. Ibid., 121.

116. Adamiyat, *Andishehā-ye Kermāni*, 2, 241, and 244.

117. Iraj Parsinejad, *A History of Literary Criticism in Iran, 1866–1951* (Bethesda, MD: Ibex Publishers, 2002), 77, quoting Mohammad Taqi Bahar, *Sabkshenāsi yā tārikh-e tatavor-e nasr-e Fārsi* [Stylistics or the history of change in Persian prose], vol. 3 (Tehran: Amir Kabir, 1337/1958), 373.

118. Adamiyat, *Andishehā-ye Kermāni*, 149.

119. Ibid., 156.

120. Touraj Daryaee, *Sasanian Persia: The Rise and Fall of an Empire* (London: I. B. Tauris in association with the Iran Heritage Foundation, 2009), 87.

121. For a more detailed discussion of the Mazdakite revolt, see Patricia Crone, "Zoroastrian Communism," *Comparative Studies in Society and History* 36, no. 3 (1994): 447–62.

122. Daryaee, *Sasanian Persia*, 89.

123. Kermani, *Seh maktub*, 268; Browne concurs in calling Mazdak "the earliest philosohpical Communist"; see Edward Granville Browne, *The Persian Revolution of 1905–1909* (Cambridge: Cambridge University Press, 1910), xiv.

124. Kermani, *Sad khatābeh*, 186–87.

125. One should add that he recognizes elsewhere that pre-Islamic Iran's rulers were despotic, although despotism increased after Islam. See Kermani, *Ā'ineh-ye Sekandari*, 120–24.

126. Kermani, *Seh maktub*, 181.

127. See quotation in Bayat-Philipp, "Mirza Aqa Khan Kirmani," 47; see also Bayat-Philipp, "The Concepts of Religion and Government," 396–97. On Kermani's "pan-Islamist" activities, see Nikki R. Keddie, "Religion and Irreligion in Early Iranian Nationalism," *Comparative Studies in Society and History* 4, no. 3 (1962): 286 et seq.

128. Quoted in Bayat-Philipp, "Mirza Aqa Khan Kirmani," 52.

129. Kermani, *Ā'ineh-ye sekandari*, 608.

130. Adamiyat, *Andishehā-ye Kermāni*, 122.

131. Ibid., 123.

132. Programmatic modernism did not prevent Malkam Khan from cooperating with Akhundzadeh on a project of alphabet reform. Nevertheless, my distinction between them is justified in view of Malkam Khan's philosophy of reform.

133. Mangol Bayat, "Āqā Khan Kermānī," in *Encyclopædia Iranica*, ed. Ehsan Yarshater; New York: Bibliotheca Persica, 1986.

134. Kermani, *Seh maktub*, 405.

135. Akhundzadeh, *Maktubāt*, 276–77, 320.

3. Pre-Islamic Iran and Archaistic Frenzy

1. Stéphane Foucart, "Rois de l'Entre-deux-Fleuves. Mésopotamie 6—Cyrus le Tai-seux, Vers 550–529 avant J.-C.," *Le Monde*, August 19, 2007.
2. "Motahhari Criticizes Ahmadinejad for Praising Cyrus," *Tehran Times*, September 19, 2010.
3. Golnaz Esfandiari, "Historic Cyrus Cylinder Called 'A Stranger in Its Own Home,'" in *Persian Letters: Notes of an Iran Watcher* (Prague: Radio Free Europe, 2010).
4. Ibid.
5. Talinn Grigor, *Building Iran: Modernism, Architecture, and National Heritage under the Pahlavi Monarchs* (New York: Periscope, 2009), 12.
6. Ali Gheissari, *Iranian Intellectuals in the 20th Century* (Austin: University of Texas Press, 1998), 19.
7. Juan R. I. Cole, "Marking Boundaries, Marking Time: the Iranian Past and the Construction of the Self by Qajar Thinkers," *Iranian Studies* 29, no. 1–2 (1996): 43–45, 53.
8. Grigor mentions a few of them in *Building Iran*, 10.
9. Quoted by Alexis Politis, "From Christian Roman Emperors to the Glorious Greek Ancestors," in *Byzantium and the Modern Greek Identity*, ed. David Ricks and Paul Magdalino, 1–4 (Aldershot: Ashgate, 1998), 3.
10. Quoted in ibid.
11. Henrik Mouritsen, "Modern Nations and Ancient Models: Italy and Greece Compared," in *The Making of Modern Greece: Nationalism, Romanticism, and the Uses of the Past (1797–1896)*, ed. Roderick Beaton and David Ricks, 43–52 (Farnham: Ashgate, 2009), 48.
12. Anthony D. Smith, *Chosen Peoples: Sacred Sources of National Identity* (Oxford: Oxford University Press, 2003), 204.
13. Israel Gershoni, "Imagining and Reimagining the Past: The Use of History by Egyptian Nationalist Writers, 1919–1952," *History and Memory* 4, no. 2 (1992): 14.
14. Ibid., 20.
15. Amatzia Baram, "A Case of Imported Identity: The Modernizing Secular Ruling Elites of Iraq and the Concept of Mesopotamian-Inspired Territorial Nationalism, 1922–1992," *Poetics Today* 15, no. 2 (1994): 279–319.
16. John Malcolm, *The History of Persia, from the Most Early Period to the Present Time* (London: J. Murray, 1829), 1:133.
17. Abbas Amanat and Farzin Vejdani, "Jalal-al-Din Mirza," in *Encyclopædia Iranica*, ed. Ehsan Yarshater, vol. 14 (New York: Bibliotheca Persica, 2008).
18. The *dasātiri* texts might be an exception, and this question is addressed in this section.
19. Mohammad Mirshokraei, "Shāhnāmeh khāni az did-e mardom shenāsi" [Shāhnāmeh reading from an anthropological perspective], *Honar va Mardom* 14, no. 165–66 (1355/1976): 57.
20. Hossein Lassan, "Shāhnāmeh khāni" [Shānāmeh reading]," *Honar va Mardom*, no. 159–160 (1354/1976): 12.
21. Malcolm, *History of Persia*, 2:191.

22. See Mohammad Tavakoli-Targhi, "Historiography and Crafting Iranian National Identity," in *Iran in the 20th Century: Historiography and Political Culture*, ed. Touraj Atabaki (London: I. B. Tauris, 2009), 7, 8, and related notes.

23. Kumiko Yamamoto, *The Oral Background of Persian Epics: Storytelling and Poetry* (Leiden: Brill, 2003).

24. As highlighted in Afshin Marashi, *Nationalizing Iran: Culture, Power, and the State, 1870–1940* (Seattle: University of Washington Press, 2008), 60.

25. Arthur Comte de Gobineau, *Trois ans en Asie; de 1855 à 1858* (Paris: B. Grasset, 1923), 2:9.

26. Ibid., 2:9–10.

27. Ibid., 2:8. It is doubtful that an ordinary Qajar subject had ever heard of Cyrus the Great as no knowledge of the Achaemenids had survived.

28. On this topic, see Kamran Aghaie, "Religious Rituals, Social Identities and Political Relationships in Tehran under Qajar Rule, 1850s–1920s," in *Religion and Society in Qajar Iran*, ed. Robert Gleave (London: RoutledgeCurzon, 2005).

29. Gobineau's comments need to be stripped of their Eurocentrism, racism, and treated for what they are: an amateur's observations. Travelogues are generally the only sources that we have for information on the lives of the common people, as local sources are not concerned with them. For a discussion of the influence and validity of Gobineau's Iranian travelogues, see Arthur Comte de Gobineau, Daniel O'Donoghue, and Geoffrey Nash, *Comte de Gobineau and Orientalism: Selected Eastern Writings* (New York: Routledge, 2009), esp. the introduction.

30. See Mohammad Tavakoli-Targhi, *Tajadod-e bumi va bāz andishi-ye tārikh* [Vernacular modernity and the rethinking of history] (Tehran: Nashr-e Tārikh-e Irān, 1381/2002); Mohammad Tavakoli-Targhi, "Contested Memories: Narrative Structures and Allegorical Meanings of Iran's Pre-Islamic History," *Iranian Studies* 29, no. 1–2 (1996): 149–75.

31. Malcolm, *History of Persia*, 1:6 and 1:183–84; see also M. E. Yapp, "Two British Historians of Persia," in *Historians of the Middle East*, ed. Bernard Lewis and Peter Malcolm Holt (Oxford: Oxford University Press, 1962), 346.

32. Fathʿali Akhundzadeh, *Maktubāt: Nāmehā-ye Kamāl od-Dowleh beh Shāhzādeh Jamāl od-Dowleh* [Maktubat: Letters from Kamal od-Dowleh to Prince Jamal od-Dowleh], ed. Bahram Choubine (Frankfurt: Alborz, 2006), 382.

33. Abbas Amanat and Farzin Vejdani, "Jalāl-al-Din Mirzā," in *Encyclopædia Iranica*, ed. Ehsan Yarshater, vol. 14 (New York: Bibliotheca Persica, 2008).

34. Tavakoli-Targhi, *Tajadod-e Bumi*, 19.

35. Mirza Aqa Khan Kermani, *Āʾineh-ye sekandari* [Alexandrian mirror] (Tehran [?], 1326/1909), 36–37.

36. Marashi, *Nationalizing Iran*, 60–61. Tavakoli-Targhi only mentions three editions: see Tavakoli-Targhi, "Historiography and Crafting Iranian National Identity," 15.

37. The *Shārestān* was published by Matbaʿi Mozaffari in Bombay (1854, 1909, and 1911).

38. See Ahmad Ashraf, "Iranian Identity; iii. Medieval Islamic Period," in *Encyclopædia Iranica*, ed. Ehsan Yarshater (New York: Bibliotheca Persica, 2006), 523.

39. Tavakoli-Targhi, "Historiography and Crafting Iranian National Identity," 7, citing Iraj Afshar, *Ketābshenāsi-e Shāhnāmeh* [Bibliography of the Shahnameh] (Tehran:

Anjoman-e Āsār-e Melli, 1347/1968); and Javad Safinezhad, *Shāhnāmehā-ye Chāpe Sangi* [Shahnameh lithographies], Mirās-e Farhangi 14 (Winter 1996): 21–24.

40. Tavakoli-Targhi, "Historiography and Crafting Iranian National Identity," 15.

41. Reza Zia-Ebrahimi, "An Emissary of the Golden Age: Manekji Limji Hataria and the Charisma of the Archaic in Pre-Nationalist Iran," *Studies in Ethnicity and Nationalism* 10, no. 3 (2010): 377–90.

42. See, for instance, these three publications: Mary Boyce, "Manekji Limji Hataria in Iran," in *K. R. Cama Oriental Institute Golden Jubilee Volume*, ed. N. D. Minochehr-Homji and M. F. Kanga (Bombay: K. R. Cama Oriental Institute, 1969); Marzban Giara, Ramiyar P. Karanjia, and Michael Stausberg, "Manekji on the Religious/Ritual Practices of the Iranian Zoroastrians: An English Translation of a Passage from His Travel Report in Gujarati (1865)," in *Zoroastrian Rituals in Context*, ed. Michael Stausberg (Leiden: Brill, 2004); and Monica Ringer, "Reform Transplanted: Parsi Agents of Change Amongst Zoroastrians in Nineteenth-Century Iran," *Iranian Studies* 42, no. 4 (2009): 549–60.

43. There are two exceptions: Marashi, *Nationalizing Iran*, 61–63; and Michael Stausberg, *Die Religion Zarathustras: Geschichte-Gegenwart-Rituale*. Band 2. (Stuttgart: Kohlhammer, 2002).

44. Zia-Ebrahimi, "Emissary of the Golden Age."

45. Kermani, *Āʾineh-ye sekandari*, 576.

46. Jalal ed-Din Mirza to Akhundzadeh, undated (probably 1871), in Hamid Mohammadzadeh and Hamid Arasli, eds., *Mirzā Fathʿali Ākhundof: Alefbā-ye jadid va Maktubāt* [Mirza Fathali Akhundov: The new alphabet and the Maktubāt] (Baku: Nizami, 1963), 375.

47. Manekji to Akhundzadeh, March 22, 1871, in ibid., 387.

48. Akhundzadeh to Jalal ed-Din Mirza, May 20, 1871, in ibid., 222–23.

49. Akhundzadeh to Manekji, July 29, 1871, in ibid., 249.

50. Ibid.

51. Akhundzadeh to Jalal ed-Din Mirza, May 15, 1870, in ibid., 172.

52. Ibid.

53. Touraj Daryaee, *Sasanian Persia: The Rise and Fall of an Empire* (London: I. B. Tauris in association with the Iran Heritage Foundation, 2009), 93–94, quoting "Abar madan i Wahram i Warzāwand," 22–23. For more on Zoroastrian apocalyptic literature, see Michael G. Morony, *Iraq After the Muslim Conquest*, Princeton Studies on the Near East (Princeton: Princeton University Press, 1984), 302 et seq.

54. Manekji to Akhundzadeh, July 14, 1871, in Mohammadzadeh and Arasli, *Mirzā Fathʿali Ākhundof*, 396.

55. See Khanbaba Moshar, *Fehrest-e ketābhā-ye chāpi-e Fārsi* [Catalogue of printed books in Persian], 2nd ed. (Tehran: Arzhang, 1350/1971), 278.

56. Manekji Limji Hataria, *Rishāl-e ejhār-e shiyāt-e Irān* [Essay on a description of a travel to Iran] (Bombay: Union Press, 1865), serialized and reproduced in "A Millenium of Misery," J. Patel, ed., *Parsiana Journal*, Bombay, September 1990.

57. Marashi has also investigated Manekji's publications. See Marashi, *Nationalizing Iran*, 61–63.

58. One catalogue indicates that it was published in the lunar year 1280, correspond-
     ing to Gregorian 1863. However, this seems unlikely as the Bombay speech on
     which the book is based was given in 1864. Moshar, *Fehrest*, 278.

59. C. A. Storey, *Persian Literature: A Bio-Bibliographical Survey* (London: Luzac,
     1927), vol. 1, part 1, p. 239; See Marashi, *Nationalizing Iran*, 63n147.

60. Edward Edwards and British Museum, Dept. of Oriental Printed Books and Man-
     uscripts, *A Catalogue of the Persian Printed Books in the British Museum* (London:
     British Museum, 1922), 378; and Moshar, *Fehrest*, 94.

61. Storey, *Persian Literature*, vol. 1, part 1, p. 246.

62. Edwards and British Museum, *Catalogue*, 146.

63. He sent them to Akhundzadeh, for instance. See Mohammadzadeh and Arasli,
     Alefbā-ye Jadid va maktubāt, 406 and 430.

64. Various letters in ibid., 336, 395, 397, 405, 406, 430, and 432.

65. Dastur Jamaspji to Akhundzadeh, December 29, 1876, in ibid., 434.

66. Montesquieu, Margaret Mauldon, and Andrew Kahn, *Persian Letters* (Oxford:
     Oxford University Press, 2008), letter 65, esp. p. 91.

67. Ahmad Gunny, *Images of Islam in Eighteenth-Century Writings* (London: Grey
     Seal, 1996), 129.

68. Montesquieu et al., *The Spirit of the Laws* (Cambridge: Cambridge University
     Press, 1989), 467.

69. Ibid., 462 and 490.

70. Rudi Matthee, "The Imaginary Realm: Europe's Enlightenment Image of Early
     Modern Iran," *Comparative Studies of South Asia Africa and the Middle East* 30,
     no. 3 (2010): 451; see also Josef Wiesehöfer, *Ancient Persia: From 550 BC to 650 AD*,
     trans. Azizeh Azodi (London: I. B. Tauris, 1996), 230–31.

71. Johann Gottfried Herder, *Persepolis: Eine Muthmassung* (Gotha: Ettinger, 1787).
     See also Johann Gottfried Herder, *Outlines of a Philosophy of the History of Man*,
     trans. T. Churchill, Second ed., 2 vols. (London: J. Johnson, 1803), 475–86.

72. On Herder's interpretation, see Hamid Tafazoli, *Der Deutsche Persien-Diskurs: Zur
     Verwissenschaftlichung und Literarisierung des Persien-Bildes im Deutschen Schrift-
     tum, von der Frühen Neuzeit bis in das Neunzehnte Jahrhundert* (Bielefeld: Aisthe-
     sis, 2007), 374–419.

73. Matthee, "The Imaginary Realm," 451.

74. Malcolm, *History of Persia*, 1:548.

75. Ibid.

76. George Rawlinson, *The Five Great Monarchies of the Ancient Eastern World, or,
     the History, Geography and Antiquities of Chaldaea, Assyria, Babylon, Media, and
     Persia*, 4 vols. (London: John Murray, 1862), 349.

77. Malcolm, *History of Persia*, 2:144–45.

78. Albert Hourani, *Islam in European Thought* (Cambridge: Cambridge University
     Press, 1991), 136.

79. Malcolm, *History of Persia*, 2:451.

80. See Kermani, *Āʿineh-ye sekandari*, 121.

81. Hourani, *Islam in European Thought*, 56. Although in the case of Browne it was
     sympathy for Iranians coupled with radical Islamophobia; his dissociation of Iran

and Islam also augurs aspects of dislocative nationalist thinking. For his opposition to intervention in Iran, see Edward Granville Browne, *The Persian Revolution of 1905–1909* (Cambridge: Cambridge University Press, 1910), xii and xiii.

82. Edward Granville Browne, *A Year Amongst the Persians* (London: Adam and Charles Black, 1893), 123.

83. Ibid.

84. Ibid., 305.

85. Malcolm, *History of Persia*, 1:135.

86. Hourani, *Islam in European Thought*, 10.

87. Nora Kathleen Firby, *European Travellers and Their Perceptions of Zoroastrians in the 17th and 18th Centuries*, vol. 14, *Archäologische Mitteilungen aus Iran* (Berlin: D. Reimer, 1988), 54, 55 and 174.

88. Ibid., 156.

89. Ibid., 160 and 164.

90. Edward Gibbon and Alexander Chalmers, *The History of the Decline and Fall of the Roman Empire* (London: T. Cadell, 1837), 1220.

91. Fereydun Adamiyat, *Andishehā-ye Mirzā Āqā Khān-e Kermāni* [Life and thought of Mirza Aqa Khan Kermani] (Tehran: Tahuri, 1346/1967), 152n1.

92. Mirza Aqa Khan Kermani, *Sad khatābeh* [One hundred lectures], ed. Harun Vohouman (Los Angeles: Ketab Corp., 1386/2007), 54–55.

93. By G. Sarton, mentioned in B. Lee Ligon, "Biography: Rhazes: His Career and His Writings," *Seminars in Pediatric Infectious Diseases* 12, no. 3 (2001): 266.

94. Akbar S. Ahmed, "Al-Beruni: The First Anthropologist," *RAIN*, no. 60 (1984): 9–10.

95. Malcolm, *History of Persia*, 1:549.

96. See, for instance, Edward Granville Browne and Mohammad Ali Khan "Tarbiyat" of Tabriz, *The Press and Poetry of Modern Persia: Partly Based on the Manuscript Work of Mirza Muhammad Ali Khan "Tarbiyat" of Tabriz* (Cambridge: Cambridge University Press, 1914), xxxvi.

97. Edward Granville Browne, *Materials for the Study of the Bábí Religion* (Cambridge: Cambridge University Press, 1918), 222–23. Adamiyat has of course not missed the opportunity to criticize Browne for these comments; see Adamiyat, *Andishehā-ye Kermāni*, 58.

98. Quoted in Firby, *European Travellers*, 162.

99. Mohammad Tavakoli-Targhi, *Refashioning Iran: Orientalism, Occidentalism, and Historiography*, St. Antony's series (New York: Palgrave, 2001), 20–23.

100. Siep Stuurman, "Cosmopolitan Egalitarianism in the Enlightenment: Anquetil Duperron on India and America," *Journal of the History of Ideas* 68, no. 2 (2007): 268.

101. Gayatri Chakravorty Spivak, "Can the Subaltern Speak? Speculations on Widow-Sacrifice," *Wedge*, no. 7–8 (Winter–Spring 1985): 120–30.

102. Mirza Aqa Khan Kermani, *Seh maktub* [Three letters], ed. Bahram Choubine (Frankfurt: Alborz, 2005), 321, 323, and 227.

103. On this topic, see Fred McGraw Donner, *Muhammad and the Believers: At the Origins of Islam* (Cambridge: Belknap Press of Harvard University Press, 2010): esp. chap. 3; and Daryaee, *Sasanian Persia*, 32.

104. John Breuilly, *Nationalism and the State*, 2nd ed. (Manchester: Manchester University Press, 1993), 54.

4. Of Lizard Eaters and Invasions: The Import of European Racial Thought

1. Katouzian and Marashi have referred to it; see Homa Katouzian, *Sadeq Hedayat: The Life and Legend of an Iranian Writer* (London: I. B. Tauris, 1991), chap. 5; and Afshin Marashi, *Nationalizing Iran: Culture, Power, and the State, 1870–1940* (Seattle: University of Washington Press, 2008), 71–75.

2. Fereydun Adamiyat, *Andishehā-ye Mirzā Fathʿali Ākhundzādeh* [Life and thought of Mirza Fathʿali Akhundzadeh] (Tehran: Khārazmi, 1349/1970), 120.

3. Mohammad Tavakoli-Targhi, *Refashioning Iran: Orientalism, Occidentalism, and Historiography*, St. Antony's series (New York: Palgrave, 2001), 96.

4. See, for instance, his letter to Akhundzadeh, undated, in Hamid Mohammadzadeh and Hamid Arasli, eds., *Mirzā Fathʿali Ākhundof: Alefbā-ye jadid va maktubāt* [Mirza Fathali Akhundov: The new alphabet and the Maktubāt] (Baku: Nizami, 1963), 376.

5. Kermani expressly mentions their "different nature." See Mirza Aqa Khan Kermani, *Seh maktub* [Three letters], ed. Bahram Choubine (Frankfurt: Alborz, 2005), 287, 301, and 305.

6. Such ideas are also to be found in more recent and serious scholarship. For an example, see Ali M. Ansari, *The Politics of Nationalism in Modern Iran* (Cambridge: Cambridge University Press, 2012), 145 and 148.

7. Kermani, *Seh maktub*, 135–39; Fathʿali Akhundzadeh, *Maktubāt: Nāmehā-ye Kamāl od-Dowleh beh Shāhzādeh Jamāl od-Dowleh* [Maktubat: Letters from Kamal od-Dowleh to Prince Jamal od-Dowleh], ed. Bahram Choubine (Frankfurt: Alborz, 2006), 295–96.

8. See Azar Nafisi, Foreword to *Shahnameh: The Persian Book of Kings* (New York: Penguin, 2007). In only three pages, Nafisi relays all the most common nationalist myths regarding the Shāhnāmeh.

9. Abolfazl Khatibi, "Beythāye ʿArab setizāneh dar Shāhnāmeh" (Anti-Arab verses in the Shāhnāmeh), *Nashr-e Dānesh* 21, no. 3 (1384/2005).

10. Renowned *Shāhnāmeh* expert Mahmoud Omidsalar has a similar view and believes that the letter from Rostam, son of Hormozd, to his brother Farrokhzad derives from ancient Sasanian sources. Therefore, again, they cannot be imputed to Ferdowsi. See Mahmoud Omidsalar, "Irān, Eslām va rowshanfekrān-e ʿāmi" [Iran, Islam and public intellectuals], *Fars News Agency*, 17.07.1389 / October 9, 2010.

11. Abolqasem Ferdowsi and Dick Davis, *Shahnameh: The Persian Book of Kings*, new ed. (New York & London: Penguin, 2007), xxi and xxxii.

12. Dick Davis, "Iran and Aniran: The Shaping of a Legend," in *Iran Facing Others: Identity Boundaries in a Historical Perspective*, ed. Abbas Amanat and Farzin Vejdani (New York: Palgrave Macmillan, 2012), 39.

13. Ibid., 39–41.

14. Ibid., 41–42.

15. Ibid., 46.

16. For a similar take on the nationalist distortions of the Shāhnāmeh, see Mahmoud Omidsalar, *Iran's Epic and America's Empire: A Handbook for a Generation in Limbo* (Santa Monica: Afshar Publishing, 2012).

17. Martin Schwartz, "Transformations of the Indo-Iranian Snake-Man: Myth, Language, Ethnoarcheology, and Iranian Identity," *Iranian Studies* 45, no. 2 (2012): 275.

18. For a critique, see Roy P. Mottahedeh, "The Shuʿubiyah Controversy and the Social History of Early Islamic Iran," *International Journal of Middle East Studies* 7, no. 2 (1976): esp. 163.

19. This doublespeak (traditional and nationalist) is typical of men of his generation. See Jalal ed-Din Homaei, *Shuʿubiyeh* (Isfahan: Sāʾeb, 1363/1984), 2.

20. Mottahedeh, "The Shuʿubiyah Controversy," 162.

21. Ibid.

22. Ibid.

23. Richard N. Frye, *The Golden Age of Persia: The Arabs in the East* (London: Weidenfeld and Nicolson, 1988), 122.

24. Books written on the topic at the time bore titles such as "The Superiority of the Persians" or "The Vindication of the Persians in the Face of the Arabs." See Ignaz Goldziher and S. M. Stern, *Muslim Studies* (New Brunswick, NJ: Transaction Publishers, 2006), 153.

25. Frye, *The Golden Age of Persia*, 122.

26. Michael Banton, *Racial Theories*, 2nd ed. (Cambridge: Cambridge University Press, 1998); and Robert Young, *Colonial Desire: Hybridity in Theory, Culture, and Race* (London: Routledge, 1995).

27. Mirza Aqa Khan Kermani, *Sad khatābeh* [One hundred lectures], ed. Harun Vohouman (Los Angeles: Ketab Corp., 1386/2007), 245.

28. Theodor Nöldeke, *Sketches from Eastern History* (London: Adam and Charles Black, 1892), 7.

29. Ibid., 11.

30. Ibid., 14–15.

31. Ibid., 17.

32. Ibid., 20.

33. Ernest Renan, *Averroès et l'Averroïsme: Essai historique*, 4th ed. (Paris: Calmann-Levy, 1882), 90–91.

34. Ernest Renan, *Mélanges d'histoire et de voyages* (Paris: Calmann Lévy, 1878), 8–9.

35. Ibid., 9–10.

36. Ibid., 137.

37. Ibid., 139–40.

38. Mirza Aqa Khan Kermani, *Āʾineh-ye Sekandari* [Alexandrian mirror] (Tehran [?], 1326/1909), 577–78.

39. Ibid., 116.

40. For recent takes on this matter, see Gherardo Gnoli, "Dualism," in *Encyclopædia Iranica*, ed. Ehsan Yarshater (New York: Bibliotheca Persica, 1996); and James W.

Boyd and A. Donald, "Is Zoroastrianism Dualistic or Monotheistic," *Journal of the American Academy of Religion* 47 (1979): 557–88.

41. Arthur Comte de Gobineau, *Trois ans en Asie; de 1855 à 1858* (Paris: B. Grasset, 1923), 2:20.

42. Renan, *Mélanges d'histoire et de voyages*, 143.

43. Ibid.

44. Ibid., 142.

45. David Motadel, "Iran and the Aryan Myth," in *Perceptions of Iran: History, Myths and Nationalism from Medieval Persia to the Islamic Republic*, ed. Ali M. Ansari (I. B. Tauris, 2013), 127.

46. Renan, *Mélanges d'histoire et de voyages*, 22.

47. John Malcolm, *The History of Persia, from the Most Early Period to the Present Time* (London: J. Murray, 1829), 2:451.

48. Ibid., 2:453.

49. Monica M. Ringer, *Education, Religion, and the Discourse of Cultural Reform in Qajar Iran*, Bibliotheca Iranica. Intellectual Traditions series no. 5 (Costa Mesa, CA: Mazda Publishers, 2001), 48.

50. Arthur Comte de Gobineau, *Les Religions et les philosophies dans l'Asie Centrale*, 2nd ed. (Paris: Didier et cie, 1866), 133–35.

51. Ibid., 133–34.

52. Ibid., 134. Gobineau here claims that the antipathy Iranians developed against Islam in a European environment was of no great consequence as he believed that Islam was being questioned in Iran too. Here he seems to contradict himself as a few pages earlier he claimed that Iranians tended to mock Islam to please the European traveler in a hypocritical rather than sincere way. See ibid., 119.

53. One exception was "Al-Afghani" who publicly rebutted some of Renan's views. See Nikki R. Keddie, *An Islamic Response to Imperialism: Political and Religious Writings of Sayyid Jamal ad-Din "al-Afghani"* (Berkeley: University of California Press, 1983).

54. Young, *Colonial Desire*, 15 and 24.

55. Johann Gottfried Herder, *Outlines of a Philosophy of the History of Man*, trans. T. Churchill, 2nd ed., 2 vols. (London: J. Johnson, 1803).

56. Léon Poliakov, *Le mythe Aryen: Essai sur les sources du racisme et des nationalismes*, New exp. ed. (Brussels: Editions Complexe, 1987), 266.

57. Ibid.

58. Ibid., 266–67.

59. Ibid., 267–68.

60. Ibid., 270.

61. For an overview, see Young, *Colonial Desire*, 14 and 15.

62. On the similarities, see Frye, *The Golden Age of Persia*, 101; Touraj Daryaee, *Sasanian Persia: The Rise and Fall of an Empire* (London: I. B. Tauris in association with the Iran Heritage Foundation, 2009), 56–57; and Homa Katouzian, *The Persians: Ancient, Medieval, and Modern Iran* (New Haven: Yale University Press, 2009), 70.

63. See, for instance, Akhundzadeh, *Maktubāt*, 291–92.

64. Edward Granville Browne, *A Year Amongst the Persians* (London: Adam and Charles Black, 1893), 123.

65. For a twentieth-century treatment of this theory, see Abdolhossein Zarrinkub, *Do qarn sokut* [Two centuries of silence], 7th ed. (Tehran: Jāvidān, 2536/1977 [1957]), 96–98.

66. Daryaee, *Sasanian Persia*, 108–9.

67. Browne, *A Year Amongst the Persians*, 123.

68. Quoted in Arthur Comte de Gobineau, Daniel O'Donoghue, and Geoffrey Nash, *Comte de Gobineau and Orientalism: Selected Eastern Writings* (New York: Routledge, 2009), 9.

69. Ibid.

70. Ibid.

71. Renan, *Mélanges d'histoire et de voyages*, 140–41.

72. This article first appeared in volume 2 of the famous *Grundriss der Iranischen Philologie*, later translated by L. Bogdanov. See Theodor Nöldeke, *The Iranian National Epic*, trans. L. Bogdanov (Bombay: K. R. Cama Oriental Institute, 1930), 55–56. This text was translated into Persian by Bozorg Alavi, a prominent nationalist novelist.

73. There are several other indications of Ferdowsi's attachment to Shiism. See Omidsalar, "Irān, Eslām va Rowshanfekrān-e ʿĀmi."

74. See "Religion," in Djalal Khaleghi-Motlagh, "Ferdowsi, Abu'l-Qāsem; i. Life," in *Encyclopædia Iranica*, ed. Ehsan Yarshater (New York: Bibliotheca Persica, 1999).

75. Omidsalar, "Irān, Eslām va Rowshanfekrān-e ʿĀmi."

76. Ibid.

77. Quoted in ibid.

78. Gobineau, *Les religions et les philosophies dans l'Asie Centrale*, 134.

79. Kermani, *Seh maktub*, 396 and 388 et seq.

80. Mohammad Tavakoli-Targhi, "Historiography and Crafting Iranian National Identity," in *Iran in the 20th Century: Historiography and Political Culture*, ed. Touraj Atabaki (London: I. B. Tauris, 2009), 16 and 18.

81. John Breuilly, *Nationalism and the State*, 2nd ed. (Manchester: Manchester University Press, 1993), 60.

82. Jalal ed-Din Mirza to Akhundzadeh, undated, in Mohammadzadeh and Arasli, eds., *Alefbā-ye Jadid va Maktubāt*, 373.

83. Ibid., 374–77; and Akhundzadeh to Jalal ed-Din Mirza, June 15, 1870, in Mohammadzadeh and Arasli, eds., *Alefbā-ye Jadid va Maktubāt*, 172; for more details on the question of alphabet reform, refer to Hamid Algar, "Malkum Khān, Ākhūndzāda and the Proposed Reform of the Arabic Alphabet," *Middle Eastern Studies* 5, no. 2 (1969): 116–30.

84. Mehrdad Kia, "Persian Nationalism and the Campaign for Language Purification," *Middle Eastern Studies* 34 (1998): 14.

85. Those interested in the topic can refer to ibid.; and John R. Perry, "Language Reform in Turkey and Iran," *International Journal of Middle East Studies* 17, no. 3 (1985): 294–311.

86. Mohammad Qazvini and Hassan Taqizadeh were among them. See Kia, "Persian Nationalism," 18–25.

87. For a critique of this view, see Hassan Taqizadeh, *Khatābeh-ye Āqā-ye Seyyed Hasan Taqizādeh dar mozu'e akhz-e tamaddon-e khāreji va āzādi, vatan, mellat, tasāhol* [Seyyed Hasan Taqizadeh's lectures on the subject of grasping foreign civilization, freedom, country, nation, tolerance] (Tehran: Chāpkhāneh-ye Mehregān, 1339/1960), 36–37.

88. See Mohammad Ali Forughi, *Payām-e man beh farhangestān* [My message to the academy], 3rd ed. (Tehran: Enteshārāt-e Payām, 1354 [1975]); and an analysis of it in Kia, "Persian Nationalism," 22–25.

89. Frontispiece, *Nāmeh-ye Irān bāstān*, July 29, 1933.

90. See, for instance, "Barāye bāzgasht-e farr va shokuh-e bāstāni" [For a return to the dignitiy and glory of antiquity], *Nāmeh-ye Irān Bāstān*, July 29, 1933.

91. Quoted in Ervand Abrahamian, "Communism and Communalism in Iran: The Tudah and the Firqah-i Dimukrat," *International Journal of Middle East Studies* 1, no. 4 (1970): 298.

92. Ervand Abrahamian, *Iran Between Two Revolutions* (Princeton: Princeton University Press, 1982), 156–57.

5. EUROPE, THAT FEARED YET ADMIRED IDOL

1. Hassan Taqizadeh, *Kāveh*, January 22, 1920. Translated by Homa Katouzian, "Seyyed Hasan Taqizadeh: Three Lives in a Lifetime," *Comparative Studies of South Asia, North Africa and the Middle East* 32, no. 1 (2012): 195–213.

2. Hassan Taqizadeh, *Zendegi-ye tufāni: Khāterāt-e Seyyed Hasan Taqizādeh* [Tempestuous life: The memoirs of Seyyed Hasan Taqizadeh], ed. Iraj Afshar, 2nd ed. (Tehran: 'Elmi, 1372/1993), 672–73; quoted and translated in Katouzian, "Taqizadeh."

3. For an overview of these, see Roger Stevens, "European Visitors to the Safavid Court," *Iranian Studies* 7, no. 3–4 (1974): 421–57.

4. Mirza Aqa Khan Kermani, *Seh maktub* [Three letters], ed. Bahram Choubine (Frankfurt: Alborz, 2005), 205.

5. Afshin Marashi, *Nationalizing Iran: Culture, Power, and the State, 1870–1940* (Seattle: University of Washington Press, 2008), 55.

6. Fath'ali Akhundzadeh, *Maktubāt: Nāmehā-ye Kamāl od-Dowleh beh Shāhzādeh Jamāl od-Dowleh* [Maktubat: Letters from Kamal od-Dowleh to Prince Jamal od-Dowleh], ed. Bahram Choubine (Frankfurt: Alborz, 2006), 291.

7. Ibid., 292.

8. Mirza Aqa Khan Kermani, *Sad khatābeh* [One hundred lectures], ed. Harun Vohouman (Los Angeles: Ketab Corp., 1386/2007), 227.

9. Mirza Aqa Khan Kermani, *Ā'ineh-ye sekandari* [Alexandrian mirror] (Tehran [?], 1326/1909), 13.

10. Kermani, *Sad khatābeh*, 54–55.

11. Kermani, *Ā'ineh-ye sekandari*, 110 and 112.

12. Ibid., 114–15.

13. Akhundzadeh, *Maktubāt*, 291.

14. Kermani, *Seh maktub*, 228.

15. See, for instance, his quotations from the Masnavi of Jalal ed-Din Rumi (Mowlana), in Kermani, *Sad khatābeh*, 347 and 357. There is in fact two degrees of contradiction in Kermani's reliance on the Masnavi. It is not only poetry, it is Sufi—that is, religious of the mystical type.

16. Edward Granville Browne and Mohammad Ali Khan "Tarbiyat" of Tabriz, *The Press and Poetry of Modern Persia: Partly Based on the Manuscript Work of Mirza Muhammad Ali Khan "Tarbiyat" of Tabriz* (Cambridge: Cambridge University Press, 1914), xxxvi.

17. Homa Katouzian, *The Political Economy of Modern Iran: Despotism and Pseudo-Modernism, 1926–1979* (London: Macmillan, 1981), 103–7.

18. Akhundzadeh to Jalal ed-Din Mirza, May 20, 1871, in Hamid Mohammadzadeh and Hamid Arasli, eds., *Mirzā Fath'ali Ākhundof: Alefbā-ye jadid va maktubāt* [Mirza Fathali Akhundov: The new alphabet and the Maktubāt], (Baku: Nizami, 1963), 221–25.

19. Quoted in Stuart Hall and Paul du Gay, eds., *Questions of Cultural Identity* (London: Sage, 1996), 70.

20. For an overview of Spanish America, see Benedict Anderson, *Imagined Communities: Reflections on the Origin and Spread of Nationalism*, rev. ed. (London: Verso, 2006): chap. 4.

21. For more on this, see Partha Chatterjee, *The Nation and Its Fragments: Colonial and Postcolonial Histories*, Princeton Studies in Culture/Power/History (Princeton: Princeton University Press, 1993).

22. For more on these topics, see Homa Katouzian, *State and Society in Iran: The Eclipse of the Qajars and the Emergence of the Pahlavis* (London: I. B. Tauris, 2006), chap. 5; and Homa Katouzian, *Musaddiq and the Struggle for Power in Iran*, rev. pbk. ed. (London: I. B. Tauris, 1999).

23. Fereydun Adamiyat, *Andishehā-ye Mirzā Fath'ali Ākhundzādeh* [Life and thought of Mirza Fath'ali Akhundzadeh] (Tehran: Khārazmi, 1349/1970), 116–17.

24. Ibid., 225.

25. Fereydun Adamiyat, *Andishehā-ye Mirzā Āqā Khān-e Kermāni* [Life and thought of Mirza Aqa Khan Kermani] (Tehran: Tahuri, 1346/1967), 247–48.

26. Mangol Bayat-Philipp, "Mirza Aqa Khan Kirmani: A Nineteenth Century Persian Nationalist," *Middle Eastern Studies* 10, no. 1 (1974): 56–57.

27. Kermani, *Seh maktub*, 323.

28. See, for instance, Adamiyat, *Andishehā-ye Ākhundzādeh*, 119–21.

29. For one recent example (2008) of Kermani being called "great pioneer of freedom," see Mohammad Ebrahim Bastani-Parizi, "Fereydun Ādamiyyat va andishehā-ye Mirzā Āqā Khān-e Kermāni" [Fereydun Adamiyat and the thoughts of Mirza Aqa Khan Kermani], *Bokhārā: Majaleh-ye Farhangi Honari* 11, no. 65 (April–May 2008), 562.

30. See, for instance, Adamiyat, *Andishehā-ye Ākhundzādeh*, 19, 108 and 136.

31. Quoted in ibid., 142.

32. Akhundzadeh, *Maktubāt*, 312–13.

33. Ibid., 326.

34. Adamiyat, *Andishehā-ye Ākhundzādeh*, 143.

35. Akhundzadeh to Mosta'sher od-Dowleh, March 25, 1871, in Mohammadzadeh and Arasli, *Alefbā-ye Jadid va Maktubāt*, 199.

36. Akhundzadeh, *Maktubāt*, 326.

37. See ibid., 311; and Mohammadzadeh and Arasli, *Alefbā-ye Jadid va Maktubāt*, 95.

38. Akhundzadeh, *Maktubāt*, 326.

39. Ibid., 325.

40. Akhundzadeh to Manekji, in Mohammadzadeh and Arasli, *Alefbā-ye Jadid va Maktubāt*, 339.

41. Adamiyat, *Andishehā-ye Ākhundzādeh*, 143–44; see also 223–25.

42. Akhundzadeh to Manekji, undated, in Mohammadzadeh and Arasli, *Alefbā-ye Jadid va Maktubāt*, 339–40.

43. Katouzian, *Political Economy*, 127.

44. Ashraf Pahlavi, *Faces in a Mirror: Memoirs from Exile* (Englewood Cliffs, NJ: Prentice-Hall, 1980), 24–25; quoted in Houchang E. Chehabi, "The Banning of the Veil and Its Consequences," in *The Making of Modern Iran: State and Society Under Riza Shah, 1921–1941*, ed. Stephanie Cronin (New York: RoutledgeCurzon, 2003), 200.

45. Interview with Oriana Fallaci, quoted in Ali M. Ansari, *The Politics of Nationalism in Modern Iran* (Cambridge: Cambridge University Press, 2012), 173n200.

46. Bayat-Philipp, "Mirza Aqa Khan Kirmani," 42.

47. Kermani, *Sad khatābeh*, 306.

48. Ibid., 320.

49. Ibid., 324.

50. Ibid., 330 and 343.

51. Ibid., 180.

52. Adamiyat, *Andishehā-ye Kermāni*, 241, 250, and 252.

53. Kermani, *Sad khatābeh*, 180.

54. Paradoxically, Mirza Ya'qub Khan did not advocate the liberation of women. See Cyrus Masroori, "Mirza Ya'qub Khan's Call for Representative Government, Toleration and Islamic Reform in Nineteenth-Century Iran," *Middle Eastern Studies* 37, no. 1 (2001): 92–93 and 98.

55. It must be highlighted that Malkam Khan too considered the current alphabet used in Iran to be an impediment to progress.

56. Mehrdad Kia, "Nationalism, Modernism and Islam in the Writings of Talibov-i Tabrizi," *Middle Eastern Studies* 30, no. 2 (1994): 210.

57. Ibid., 203.

58. For two noteworthy exceptions, see Cyrus Masroori, "French Romanticism and Persian Liberalism in Nineteenth-Century Iran: Mirza Aqa Khan Kirmani and Jacques-Henri Bernardin de Saint-Pierre," *History of Political Thought* 28, no. 3 (2007): 542–56; and Maryam B. Sanjabi, "Rereading the Enlightenment: Akhundzada and His Voltaire," *Iranian Studies* 28, no. 1–2 (1995): 39–60. See also Katouzian, *Political Economy*; Mehrdad Kia, "Mirza Fath Ali Akhundzade and the Call

for Modernization of the Islamic World," *Middle Eastern Studies* 31, no. 3 (1995): 442–48; and Bayat-Philipp, "Mirza Aqa Khan Kirmani."

59. Adamiyat, *Andishehā-ye Ākhundzādeh*, 172.

60. Ibid., 173.

61. Ibid., 174 and 181.

62. Cyrus Masroori, "European Thought in Nineteenth-Century Iran: David Hume and Others," *Journal of the History of Ideas* 61, no. 4 (2000): 666.

63. Adamiyat, *Andishehā-ye Kermāni*, 75.

64. Ibid., 81–82.

65. Ibid., 118.

66. Ibid., 157.

67. Kermani, *Sad khatābeh*, introduction by Harun Vohouman, 24 and 27.

68. Mashallah Ajudani, *Mashruteh-ye Irāni* [Iranian constitutionalism], partly censored Iranian edition (Tehran: Akhtarān, 1382/2003).

69. Sanjabi, "Rereading the Enlightenment," 40 and 42.

70. For more on these topics, see Zeev Sternhell, *The Anti-Enlightenment Tradition*, trans. David Maisel (New Haven: Yale University Press, 2009); and Michael Banton, *Racial Theories*, 2nd ed. (Cambridge: Cambridge University Press, 1998).

71. Akhundzadeh, *Maktubāt*, 279; see also Akhundzadeh to Mirza Yusuf Khan, March 29, 1871, in Mohammadzadeh and Arasli, *Alefbā-ye Jadid va Maktubāt*, 212–13.

72. Masroori, "European Thought," 671.

73. Masroori, "French Romanticism and Persian Liberalism," 542–43.

74. Ibid., 545.

75. For a similar perspective, see Barbara-Ann J. Rieffer, "Religion and Nationalism," *Ethnicities* 3, no. 2 (2003): 216.

76. Marashi, *Nationalizing Iran*, 112.

77. Anderson, *Imagined Communities*, 7.

78. Anthony D. Smith, *Nations and Nationalism in a Global Era* (Cambridge: Polity, 1995), 155; and John Breuilly, *Nationalism and the State*, 2nd ed. (Manchester: Manchester University Press, 1993), 64.

79. Émile Durkheim and Karen E. Fields, *The Elementary Forms of Religious Life* (New York: Free Press, 1995), 429. For a study of the Durkheimian in Smith, see Siniša Malešević, *Identity as Ideology: Understanding Ethnicity and Nationalism* (Basingstoke: Palgrave Macmillan, 2006), chap. 5.

80. Only two authors have taken note of this aspect of Akhundzadeh's life. Juan R. I. Cole, "Marking Boundaries, Marking Time: The Iranian Past and the Construction of the Self by Qajar Thinkers," *Iranian Studies* 29, no. 1–2 (1996): 35–56; and Sanjabi, "Rereading the Enlightenment."

81. He had also suppressed the Polish Uprising of 1830–1831 and the Hungarian Revolution of 1848–1849, among other feats.

82. Robert Seely, *Russo-Chechen Conflict, 1800–2000: A Deadly Embrace* (London: Frank Cass, 2001), 34.

83. Both quoted in John B. Dunlop, *Russia Confronts Chechnya: Roots of a Separatist Conflict* (Cambridge: Cambridge University Press, 1998), 18.

84. Both quoted in Seely, *Russo-Chechen Conflict*, 33–34.

85. See Maziar Behrooz, "Revisiting the Second Russo-Iranian War (1826–28): Causes and Perceptions," *Iranian Studies* 46, no. 3 (2013): esp. 367–68 and 370.

86. Adamiyat, *Andishehā-ye Ākhundzādeh*, 24–25.

87. Ibid., 27.

88. Ibid., 28.

89. For one example, see Akhundzadeh to Mostowfi ol-Mamalek, September 1868, in Mohammadzadeh and Arasli, *Alefbā-ye Jadid va Maktubāt*, 104–5.

90. Mehrdad Kia, "Women, Islam and Modernity in Akhundzade's Plays and Unpublished Writings," *Middle Eastern Studies* 34, no. 3 (1998): 9.

91. Ibid., 11–12.

92. Ibid., 24.

93. See Sanjabi, "Rereading the Enlightenment," 43.

94. Quoted in Michael G. Smith, "Cinema for the 'Soviet East': National Fact and Revolutionary Fiction in Early Azerbaijani Film," *Slavic Review* 56, no. 4 (1997): 673, 657, and 659.

95. Cole, "Marking Boundaries," 41.

96. Akhundzadeh to Mirza Mohammad Ja'far, March 25, 1871, in Mohammadzadeh and Arasli, *Alefbā-ye Jadid va Maktubāt*, 205.

97. Sanjabi, "Rereading the Enlightenment," 47.

98. From Mokhber ol-Saltaneh's memoirs, quoted in Katouzian, *State and Society in Iran*, 336.

99. Hamideh Sedghi, *Women and Politics in Iran: Veiling, Unveiling, and Reveiling* (Cambridge: Cambridge University Press, 2007), 85.

100. Quoted in Chehabi, "The Banning of the Veil and Its Consequences," 198.

6. Aryanism and Dislocation

1. Hassan Taqizadeh, *Khatābeh-ye Āqā-ye Seyyed Hasan Taqizādeh dar mozu'e akhz-e tamaddon-e khāreji va āzādi, vatan, mellat, tasāhol* [Seyyed Hasan Taqizadeh's lectures on the subject of grasping foreign civilization, freedom, country, nation, tolerance] (Tehran: Chāpkhāneh-ye Mehregān, 1339/1960), 36.

2. Ibid., 37.

3. Ansari reports that the title was coined by a scholar of ancient Iran named Mohammad-Sadeq Kia. Ali M. Ansari, *The Politics of Nationalism in Modern Iran* (Cambridge: Cambridge University Press, 2012), 174n203. Ansari also points out that "this title exemplified the way in which the new ideologues of Iranian nationalism were out of step with international trends in intellectual life" (174).

4. Private discussion between Anthony Parsons and Homa Katouzian, 1987, conveyed to the author by Homa Katouzian, August 18, 2009.

5. Lincoln gives an overview of these publications. See Bruce Lincoln, "Rewriting the German War God: Georges Dumézil, Politics and Scholarship in the Late 1930s," *History of Religions* 37, no. 3 (1998): 188n4.

6. The same situation is prevalent within Hindu nationalist circles in India. The interested reader can refer to two excellent publications: Gérard Fussman, "Entre fantasmes, science et politique: L'entrée des Aryas en Inde," *Annales. Histoire, Sciences Sociales* 58, no. 4 (2003); and Thomas R. Trautmann, *Aryans and British India* (Berkeley: University of California Press, 1997).

7. Stefan Arvidsson, *Aryan Idols: Indo-European Mythology as Ideology and Science* (Chicago: University of Chicago Press, 2006), 21.

8. Iran and India were by turns seen as either the idealized native soil of Aryans or as home to degenerate mixed-raced people. For an example, see Arthur Comte de Gobineau, *Trois ans en Asie; de 1855 à 1858* (Paris: B. Grasset, 1923), 2:20.

9. On Jones, see Léon Poliakov, *Le mythe Aryen: Essai sur les sources du racisme et des nationalismes*, new exp. ed. (Brussels: Editions Complexe, 1987); and Arvidsson, *Aryan Idols*. On other scholars, see Konrad Koerner, "Observations on the Sources, Transmission, and Meaning of 'Indo-European' and Related Terms in the Development of Linguistics," in *Papers from the 3rd International Conference on Historical Linguistics*, August 22–26, 1977, Amsterdam Studies in the Theory and History of Linguistic Science, Series 4, ed. J. Peter Maher, Allan R. Bomhard, and E. F. K. Koerner, 153–80 (Amsterdam: John Benjamins, 1982), 154–55.

10. The talk was published in 1768 in *Histoire de l'Académie Royale des inscriptions et belles-lettres*, vol. 31, partly quoted in Hans Siegert, "Zur Geschichte der Begriffe 'Arier' und 'arisch'," *Wörter und Sachen* 4 (1941–1942): 86.

11. Arvidsson, *Aryan Idols*, 20–21.

12. See Siegert, "Zur Geschichte der Begriffe 'Arier' und 'arisch'," 75–79. On the different uses of these terms, see Koerner, "Observations on the Sources."

13. See, for instance, Korner, "Observations on the Sources," 170–71.

14. George Rawlinson, *The Origin of Nations* (New York: Charles Scribner's & Sons, 1881) 176.

15. Ibid.

16. Poliakov, *Mythe Aryen*, 217.

17. Arvidsson, *Aryan Idols*, 52.

18. Ibid., 295.

19. "American Anthropological Association Statement on 'Race,' May 17, 1998," http://www.aaanet.org/stmts/racepp.htm.

20. See ibid.

21. Michael Banton's works are key in this regard. See Michael Banton, *The Idea of Race* (London: Tavistock, 1977); and Michael Banton, *Racial and Ethnic Competition*, Comparative Ethnic and Race Relations series (Cambridge: Cambridge University Press, 1983). Also see "Race," in *Encyclopedia of Race and Ethnic Studies*, ed. Ernest Cashmore (London: Routledge, 2004).

22. Merritt Ruhlen, *On the Origin of Languages: Studies in Linguistic Taxonomy* (Stanford, CA: Stanford University Press, 1994), 9.

23. Rawlinson, *The Origin of Nations*, 86–87.

24. Percy M. Sykes, *A History of Persia*, 3rd ed. (London: Macmillan, 1951), 1:501.

25. Henri Massé, *Firdousi et l'épopée nationale* (Paris: Perrin, 1935), 1–2.

26. Ibid., 5.

27. Vasant Kaiwar, "The Aryan Model of History and the Oriental Renaissance: The Politics of Identity in an Age of Revolutions, Colonialism and Nationalism," in *Antinomies of Modernity: Essays on Race, Orient, Nation*, ed. Vasant Kaiwar and Sucheta Mazumdar, 13–61 (Durham, NC: London: Duke University Press, 2003), 24.

28. This fundamental text of Indian nationalism provides a good illustration: Surendranath Banerjea, "The Study of Indian History," in *Nationalism in Asia and Africa*, ed. Elie Kedourie, 225–44 (London: Frank Cass, 1974). For a detailed study of the topic, see Trautmann, *Aryans and British India*.

29. Tekin Alp, "The Restoration of Turkish History," in *Nationalism in Asia and Africa*, ed. Elie Kedourie (London: Frank Cass, 1974), 214.

30. Ibid., 219.

31. Mentioned in Michael Banton, *Racial Theories*, 2nd ed. (Cambridge: Cambridge University Press, 1998), 63.

32. Katouzian has reached similar conclusions. See Homa Katouzian, "Problems of Political Development in Iran: Democracy, Dictatorship or Arbitrary Government?" *British Journal of Middle Eastern Studies* 22, no. 1–2 (1995): 16–17.

33. It is useful to note that although "*nezhād*" is an ancient word that often occurs in literature, its contemporary use is unmistakably that of "race" in the modern European sense.

34. Mirza Aqa Khan Kermani, *Seh maktub* [Three Letters], ed. Bahram Choubine (Frankfurt: Alborz, 2005), 269.

35. Quoted in Mangol Bayat-Philipp, "Mirza Aqa Khan Kirmani: A Nineteenth Century Persian Nationalist," *Middle Eastern Studies* 10, no. 1 (1974): 48.

36. Kermani, *Seh maktub*, 387.

37. See, for instance, Mirza Aqa Khan Kermani, *Ā'ineh-ye sekandari* [Alexandrian mirror] (Tehran [?], 1326/1909), 26.

38. Ibid.

39. Ibid., 29.

40. Mirza Aqa Khan Kermani, *Sad khatābeh* [One hundred lectures], ed. Harun Vohouman (Los Angeles: Ketab Corp., 1386/2007), 56.

41. Oskar Mann, "Kāveh va derafsh-e kāviyāni" [Kaveh and his standard], *Kāveh*, January 24, 1916, 3.

42. Moreover, Taqizadeh defines "Aryans" as people living in Central Asia in prehistoric times that gave birth to Indians and Iranians, and explicitly rejects the use of the word to refer to all Indo-Europeans as "sometimes can be seen in Iranian newspapers and books." See Hassan Taqizadeh (?), "Khiyālāt-e gunāgun" [Various beliefs], *Kāveh*, October 3, 1921, 111.

43. Hassan Taqizadeh, "Nowruz-e Jamshidi" [Jamshidian Nowrouz], *Kāveh*, April 18, 1916, 2.

44. Issa Sadiq, *Tārikh-e farhang-e Irān* [Cultural history of Iran] (Tehran: Enteshārāt-e Dāneshgāh-e Tehrān, 1336/1957), 31. This 1957 publication is based on a schoolbook first published in 1316/1937.

45. Sadeq Rezazadeh Shafaq, *Tārikh-e adabiyyāt-e Irān barāy-e dabirestānhā* [Literary history of Iran for high school students] (Tehran: Amir Kabir, 1342/1963), 5–6.

46. Afshin Marashi, *Nationalizing Iran: Culture, Power, and the State, 1870–1940* (Seattle: University of Washington Press, 2008), 99.

47. Ibid., 101.

48. Hassan Pirniya, *Tārikh-e Irān-e qadim: Az āqāz tā Enqerāz-e Sāsāniyān* [History of ancient Iran: From the beginnings to the fall of the Sasanians] ([Tehran?]: Khayyām, [1928?]), 8.

49. Ibid., 8–10.

50. Ibid., 12.

51. Ibid., 14 and 16.

52. Vezārat-e Farhang [Ministry of Culture], *Ketāb-e chahārom-e ebtedāyi* [4th grade textbook] (Tehran: Motabaʿeye Rowshanāyi, 1310/1931), 276.

53. Vezārat-e Maʾāref [Ministry of Education], *Joqrāfiyā-ye panj qatʿeh barāy-e tadris dar sāl-e sheshom* [Geography in five parts for teaching at sixth grade], 6th ed. (Tehran: Chāpkhāneh-ye Farhang, 1316/1937), 87.

54. Quoted by Homa Katouzian, Introduction to *Qiyām-e Sheikh Mohammad Khiyābāni* [The revolt of Sheikh Mohammad Khiyabani] by Ahmad Kasravi, ed. Homa Katouzian (Tehran: Nashr-e Markaz, 1376/1998), 39–40.

55. Miron Rezun, *The Soviet Union and Iran: Soviet Policy in Iran from the Beginnings of the Pahlavi Dynasty Until the Soviet Invasion in 1941* (Alphen aan den Rijn: Sijthoff & Noordhoff; Genève: Institut Universitaire de Hautes Études Internationales, 1981), 319.

56. See ibid., esp. n24.

57. "Mā Cherā Bartarim?" [Why are we superior?], *Nāmeh-ye Irān bāstān*, October 14, 1933.

58. Jalal Al Ahmad, "Cheguneh dar Ālmān jashnhā va ādāb-e Āriyāyi va Irāni az now zendeh mishavad" [How Aryan and Iranian celebrations and customs are revived in Germany], *Nāmeh-ye Irān bāstān*, November 3, 1933.

59. "Tahqiqāt-e ʿelmi va tārikhi beh khāmeh-ye yeki az siyāsiyun-e bozorg-e doniyā, rāje' beh Irān-e kohan" [Scientific and historical research into ancient Iran, authored by one of the most important politicians of the world], *Nāmeh-ye Irān bāstān*, April 14, 1934.

60. George Lenczowski, *Russia and the West in Iran, 1918–1948: A Study in Big-Power Rivalry* (New York: Cornell University Press, 1949), 162.

61. Ibid., 159. On the German-Persian Society, see also note dated Mordad 1, 1313 (July 23, 1934). Sāzmān-e Asnād-e Melli-ye Irān, Prime Ministry Records (nakhost vazir), Foreign Ministry (ʿomur-e khārejeh), File 102012, Folder 3201.

62. David Motadel, "Iran and the Aryan Myth," in *Perceptions of Iran: History, Myths and Nationalism from Medieval Persia to the Islamic Republic*, ed. Ali M. Ansari, 119–46 (I. B. Tauris, 2013), 134–35.

63. Lenczowski, *Russia and the West in Iran*, 161.

64. Massoud Kazemzadeh, "The Day Democracy Died," *Khaneh* 3, no. 34 (2003).

65. What follows is a slight departure from my previous research on the topic (Reza Zia-Ebrahimi, "Self-Orientalization and Dislocation: The Uses and Abuses of the 'Aryan' Discourse in Iran," *Iranian Studies* 44, no. 4 [2011]: 445–72). I argued then that *"ariya"* was an ethnonym.

66. For instance, Fereydun Adamiyat, *Andishehā-ye Mirzā Āqā Khān-e Kermāni*
    [Life and thought of Mirza Aqa Khan Kermani] (Tehran: Tahuri, 1346/1967),
    264.

67. For the sake of simplicity, here I use one single transliteration, *ariya*, although in
    reality the Sanskrit, Avestic, and Old Persian versions of the term slightly differ.

68. See, for instance, H. W. Bailey, "Iranian *Arya-* and *Daha-*," *Transactions of the Phil-
    ological Society* 58, no. 1 (1959): 94; and Emile Benveniste, "L'Eran-vez et l'origine
    légendaire des Iraniens," *Bulletin of the School of Oriental Studies, University of
    London*, 7, no. 2 (1934): 264–74.

69. For more details, refer to H. W. Bailey, "Arya," in *Encyclopædia Iranica*, ed. Ehsan
    Yarshater (New York: Bibliotheca Persica, 1987).

70. Kellens believes that the Sanskrit *"ariya"* cannot be unequivocally taken for an eth-
    nonym, whereas Avestic *"ariya"* can. See Jean Kellens, "Les Airiia ne sont plus des
    Aryas: Ce sont déjà des Iraniens," in *Aryas, Aryens et Iraniens en Asie Centrale*, ed.
    Gérard Fussman, Jean Kellens, Henri-Paul Francfort, and Xavier Tremblay, 233–
    52 (Paris: Collège de France, 2005), 240–42.

71. Rüdiger Schmitt, "Aryans," in *Encyclopædia Iranica*, ed. Ehsan Yarshater (New
    York: Bibliotheca Persica, 1987).

72. Excellent publications address this aspect of the topic. See, for instance, Gérard
    Fussman, Jean Kellens, Henri-Paul Francfort, and Xavier Tremblay, *Aryas, Aryens
    et Iraniens en Asie centrale*, Publications de l'Institut de civilisation indienne (Paris:
    Collège de France, 2005). See in particular the Kellens's article in this volume,
    "Les Airiia ne sont plus des Aryas," 233–52.

73. Bailey, "Arya."

74. See Michael Back, "Die Sassanidischen Staatinschriften," in *Acta Iranica* 18—
    Textes et Mémoires VIII (Tehran and Liège: Bibliothèque Pahlavi, 1978); and Zeev
    Rubin, "Res Gestae Divi Saporis: Greek and Middle Iranian in a Document of Sa-
    sanian, Anti-Roman Propaganda," in *Bilingualism in Ancient Society: Language
    Contact and the Written Word*, ed. J. N. Adams, Mark Janse, and Simon Swain,
    267–97 (Oxford: Oxford University Press, 2002).

75. Siegert, "Zur Geschichte der Begriffe 'Arier' und 'arisch'," 99.

76. Kellens, "Les Airiia ne sont plus des Aryas," 242.

77. Friedrich Max Müller, *Lectures on the Science of Language: Delivered at the Royal
    Institution of Great Britain in April, May and June 1861*, 5th rev. ed. (London: Long-
    mans Green, 1866), 268. Before him, no direct hint was made to such definition of
    Iran: Anquetil-Duperron for instance, believed that *airyanem vaejah* meant "l'Iran
    pur." Quoted in Siegert, "Zur Geschichte der Begriffe 'Arier' und 'arisch'," 86.

78. Examples abound, even in highly influential and serious scholarly works, for in-
    stance: Edward Granville Browne, *A Literary History of Persia: From the Earliest
    Times Until Firdawsí* (London: T. Fisher Unwin, 1909), 4; and Richard N. Frye,
    Persia, rev. ed. (London: Allen & Unwin, 1968), 13.

79. For a similar take on this topic but from a slightly different perspective, see Mo-
    stafa Vaziri, *Iran as Imagined Nation: The Construction of National Identity* (New
    York: Paragon House, 1993), 75–81.

80. For more on race and minorities, see Rasmus Christian Elling, *Minorities in Iran: Nationalism and Ethnicity After Khomeini* (New York: Palgrave Macmillan, 2013), 22 and 130.

81. Mehrdad Kia, "Persian Nationalism and the Campaign for Language Purification," *Middle Eastern Studies* 34, no. 2 (1998): 1133. Men of Arani's generation could amalgamate several outlooks with radically different ideological origins (in this case nationalism and communism).

82. See the wise warnings of Fussman, "Entre fantasmes, science et politique," 785–788 and 813.

83. Private discussion between Anthony Parsons and Homa Katouzian, 1987, conveyed to the author by Homa Katouzian, August 18, 2009.

84. In *Kayhan International*, September 19, 1973, quoted in Mangol Bayat-Philipp, "A Phoenix Too Frequent: Historical Continuity in Modern Iranian Thought," *Asian and African Studies* 12 (1978): 211.

85. Note dated Dey 3, 1313 (December 24, 1934). Sāzmān-e Asnād-e Melli-ye Irān, Prime Ministry Records (nakhost vazir), Foreign Ministry ('omur-e khārejeh), File 102012, Folder 3201.

86. Homa Katouzian, *The Persians: Ancient, Medieval, and Modern Iran* (New Haven: Yale University Press, 2009), 217–18.

87. Talinn Grigor, *Building Iran: Modernism, Architecture, and National Heritage Under the Pahlavi Monarchs* (New York: Periscope, 2009), 73.

88. Notes dated Mordad 1 and 5, 1313 (July 23 and August 19, 1934). Sāzmān-e Asnād-e Melli-ye Irān, Prime Ministry Records (nakhost vazir), Foreign Ministry ('omur-e khārejeh), File 102012, Folder 3201.

7. THE ROAD TO OFFICIALDOM

1. Quentin Skinner, "Meaning and Understanding in the History of Ideas," *History and Theory* 8, no. 1 (1969): 3–53.

2. Akhundzadeh to Manekji (through Jalal ed-Din Mirza), May 20, 1871, in Hamid Mohammadzadeh and Hamid Arasli, eds., *Mirzā Fath'ali Ākhundof: alefbā-ye jadid va maktubāt* [Mirza Fathali Akhundov: The new alphabet and the Maktubāt] (Baku: Nizami, 1963), 222–23.

3. Hamid Algar, "Āḵūndzāda," in *Encyclopædia Iranica*, ed. Ehsan Yarshater (New York: Bibliotheca Persica, 1985).

4. Leah Feldman brought to my attention that the Russian translation available at Alyazmalar (manuscript archive) in Baku bears Akhundzadeh's signature (shelf mark: F. 2 s. v. 21), but Algar claims that the translation was by Adolf Bergé. See ibid.

5. Fath'ali Akhundzadeh, *Adabiyāt-e mashruteh: Maktubāt-e Mirza Fath'ali Ākhundzādeh* [Constitutionalist literature: Mirza Fath'ali Akhundzadeh's Maktubat] (Tabriz: Ehiyā, 1357/1979).

6. Cyrus Masroori, "European Thought in Nineteenth-Century Iran: David Hume and Others," *Journal of the History of Ideas* 61, no. 4 (2000): 660.

7. A list of his writings and where they are located—although slightly outdated—is provided in Mangol Bayat-Philipp, "Mirza Aqa Khan Kirmani: A Nineteenth Century Persian Nationalist," *Middle Eastern Studies* 10, no. 1 (1974): 55–57.

8. Some sources mention a 1987 edition, probably samizdat, of *Seh maktub.* See Shoja'ed-Din Shafa, *Pas az 1,400 sāl* [After 1,400 years] (2003), 22.

9. Quoted in Firoozeh Kashani-Sabet, *Frontier Fictions: Shaping the Iranian Nation, 1804–1946* (Princeton: Princeton University Press, 1999), 105.

10. On the Constitutional Revolution, see Ahmad Kasravi, *History of the Iranian Constitutional Revolution,* trans. Evan Siegel (Costa Mesa, CA: Mazda Publishers, 2006); Nazem ol-Eslam Kermani, *Tārikh-e bidāri-e Irāniyān* [History of Iranian awakening], 5th ed. (Tehran: Agāh, 1376/1997); Mangol Bayat, *Iran's First Revolution: Shi'ism and the Constitutional Revolution of 1905–1909* (New York: Oxford University Press, 1991); Janet Afary, *The Iranian Constitutional Revolution, 1906–1911: Grassroots Democracy, Social Democracy, and the Origins of Feminism* (New York: Columbia University Press, 1996); and Vanessa Martin, *Islam and Modernism: The Iranian Revolution of 1906* (London: I. B. Tauris, 1989).

11. Homa Katouzian, *Sadeq Hedayat: The Life and Legend of an Iranian Writer* (London: I. B. Tauris, 1991), 67.

12. See, in particular, Kashani-Sabet, *Frontier Fictions,* chap. 4, n. 2.

13. See Mohammad Tavakoli-Targhi, "Refashioning Iran: Language and Culture During the Constitutional Revolution," *Iranian Studies* 23, no. 1–4 (1990): 77–101; and Kashani-Sabet, *Frontier Fictions,* 91 et seq.

14. See Homa Katouzian, "Darbāreh-ye mellat, melli, melligerā va nāsionālism" [Regarding the terms mellat, melli, melligerā and nationalism], in *Estebdād, demokrāsi va nehzat-e melli* [Arbitrary rule, democracy and the popular movement] (Tehran: Nashr-e Markaz, 1388/2009), 38–51.

15. Tavakoli-Targhi, "Refashioning Iran," 78.

16. Edward Granville Browne, *The Persian Revolution of 1905–1909* (Cambridge: Cambridge University Press, 1910), xix and xx; for other cases of authors who have considered the Constitutional Revolution to be "nationalist," see Bayat, *Iran's First Revolution,* 3–5.

17. Browne, *The Persian Revolution,* xix.

18. Ibid., xx.

19. Afary, *The Iranian Constitutional Revolution,* 54.

20. For a criticism of the civic/ethnic distinction, see Rogers Brubaker, *Ethnicity Without Groups* (Cambridge: Harvard University Press, 2004), chap. 6.

21. Charles Kurzman, "Weaving Iran into the Tree of Nations," *International Journal of Middle East Studies* 37, no. 2 (2005): 152.

22. Homa Katouzian, *The Persians: Ancient, Medieval, and Modern Iran* (New Haven: Yale University Press, 2009), 175.

23. Iraj Afshar, ed. *Nāmehā-ye Tehrān* [Letters from Tehran] (Tehran: Farzān, 1385/2006), 111.

24. Katouzian, *The Persians,* 189.

25. John Breuilly, "Max Weber, Charisma and Nationalist Leadership," *Nations and Nationalism*, 17, no. 3 (2011): 492.

26. For more on this topic, see Homa Katouzian, "The Campaign Against the Anglo-Iranian Agreement of 1919," *British Journal of Middle Eastern Studies* 25, no. 1 (1998): 5–46; and Nasrollah S. Fatemi, "Anglo-Persian Agreement of 1919," in *Encyclopædia Iranica*, ed. Ehsan Yarshater (New York: Bibliotheca Persica, 1987), especially the bibliography provided.

27. Katouzian, "The Campaign Against the Anglo-Iranian Agreement," 23 et seq.

28. For examples of patriotic poems written at the time, see ibid., 10.

29. See quotation in ibid., 10.

30. Houchang E. Chehabi, "From Revolutionary Tasnif to Patriotic Surud: Music and Nation-Building in Pre-World War II Iran," *Iran* 37 (1999): 144 and 145.

31. Abolqasem Aref-e Qazvini, *Kolliyāt-e Divān-e 'Āref-e Qazvini* [The complete divan of Aref-e Qazvini], ed. Abdorrahman Seif Azad, 6th ed. (Tehran: Amir Kabir, 2536/1977), 212.

32. Aref Qazvini to Rezazadeh Shafaq, undated, in Abolqasem Aref-e Qazvini, *'Āref-e Qazvini, shā'er-e melli-ye Irān* [Aref-e Qazvini, Iran's national poet], ed. Seyyed Hadi Ha'eri (Kurosh) (Tehran: Jāvidān, 1369/1990), 532.

33. Ibid., 535.

34. Aref Qazvini to Adel Kal'atbari, February 27, 1931, in ibid., 558.

35. Aref Qazvini to Zanddokht Shirazi, undated, in ibid., 563.

36. Touraj Daryaee, *Sasanian Persia: The Rise and Fall of an Empire* (London: I. B. Tauris in association with the Iran Heritage Foundation, 2009), 59–60.

37. Homa Katouzian, *State and Society in Iran: The Eclipse of the Qajars and the Emergence of the Pahlavis* (London: I. B. Tauris, 2006), 80.

38. Aref-e Qazvini, *Kolliyāt*, 262–63; translated by Katouzian, *State and Society in Iran*, 80–81.

39. Quoted in Touraj Atabaki, *Azerbaijan: Ethnicity and the Struggle for Power in Iran*, rev. ed. (London: I. B. Tauris, 2000), 45. On this topic, see also Touraj Atabaki, "Recasting Oneself, Rejecting the Other: Pan-Turkism and Iranian Nationalism," in *Identity Politics in Central Asia and the Muslim World*, ed. Willem van Schendel and Erik Jan Zürcher, 65–84 (London: I. B. Tauris, 2001).

40. See Kaveh Bayat, "Āshnāyi bā pāntorkism va ta'sir-e mājarā-ye Rowshani Beyg bar ān" [Getting to know Pan-Turkism and the impact of the Ruşeni Bey episode], in *Irān: Hoveyyat, meliyyat, qowmeyyat* [Iran: Identity, nationhood, ethnicity], ed. Hamid Ahmadi (Tehran: Mo'aseseh-ye Tahqiqāt va Towse'eh-ye 'Olum-e Ensāni, 1383/2004).

41. Aref-e Qazvini, *Kolliyāt*, 427.

42. Ibid., 390.

43. Ibid., 384. Translated by Katouzian, *State and Society in Iran*, 81.

44. Chehabi, "From Revolutionary Tasnif to Patriotic Surud," 145.

45. Mirzadeh Eshqi, *Kolliyāt-e mosavvar-e Mirzādeh-ye 'Eshqi* [Illustrated complete works of Mirzadeh Eshqi], ed. Ali Akbar Moshir-Salimi (Tehran: 1322/1943), 262.

46. Ibid., 264.

47. Ibid., 265. Translated by Houchang Chehabi, in Chehabi, "From Revolutionary Tasnif to Patriotic Surud," 145.

48. Eshqi, *Kolliyāt*, 267.

49. Ibid., 267–68.

50. Ibid., 269.

51. Ibid., 271.

52. Ibid., 272.

53. Chehabi, "From Revolutionary Tasnif to Patriotic Surud," 145.

54. Ibid., 147.

55. Quoted in ibid.

56. Quoted in ibid., 148.

57. Ibid., 149.

58. See Katouzian, *Sadeq Hedayat*, 71 et seq.

59. Ibid., 72.

60. Ibid.

61. Bozorg Alavi, *Div! . . . Div . . .* [Demon! . . . Demon . . .], new ed. (Tehran: Amir Kabir, 1357/1978), 5.

62. Ibid., 5–6.

63. Ibid., 7.

64. Sadeq Hedayat, *Parvin, dokhtar-e Sāsān* [Parvin the Sasanian girl], ed. Mohammad Ali Sheikh Olia Lavasani, online ed., www.sadegh-hedayat.mihanblog.com, 18.

65. Ibid., 24.

66. Ibid.

67. Bayat-Philipp, "Mirza Aqa Khan Kirmani," 383.

68. Mojtaba Minovi and Sadeq Hedayat, *Māziyār* (Tehran: Amir Kabir, 1342/1963), 10. Translated by Katouzian, *Sadeq Hedayat*, 74.

69. Minovi and Hedayat, *Māziyār*, 12.

70. Ibid.

71. Katouzian, *Sadeq Hedayat*, 75.

72. Reza Zia-Ebrahimi, "Self-Orientalization and Dislocation: The Uses and Abuses of the 'Aryan' Discourse in Iran," *Iranian Studies* 44, no. 4 (2011): 445–72.

73. Sadeq Hedayat, *Kārevān-e Eslām* [The caravan of Islam], ed. Bahram Choubine, online ed. (Paris: Organisation des mouvements nationalistes des universitaires, chercheurs et intellectuels Iraniens, 1381/2002), 19.

74. Ibid.

75. See Katouzian, *Sadeq Hedayat*, chap. 5.

76. *Iranshahr*, December 1924, 41–42, quoted in Talinn Grigor, *Building Iran: Modernism, Architecture, and National Heritage under the Pahlavi Monarchs* (New York: Periscope, 2009), 10.

77. Hossein Kazemzadeh Iranshahr, *Chahār asar-e arzandeh az taʻlifāt-e Irānshahr* [Four valuable works of Irānshahr] (Tehran: Eqbāl, 1353/1974), 12.

78. Taqi Arani, in *Mahnāmeh-ye mardom*, June 1960, 1, quoted in Ervand Abrahamian, *Iran Between Two Revolutions* (Princeton: Princeton University Press, 1982), 156; and Grigor, *Building Iran*, 10.

79. Interested readers can refer to Katouzian, *State and Society in Iran*: chap. 8 and 9; and Nikki R. Keddie, *Qajar Iran and the Rise of Reza Khan, 1796–1925* (Costa Mesa, CA: Mazda Publishers, 1999).

80. Eshqi, *Kolliyāt*, 303–4.

81. For the full texts of the declarations, see Hossein Makki, *Tārikh-e bist sāleh-ye Irān* [Twenty years of Iran's history], vol. 1 (Tehran: 'Elmi, 1374/1995), 245–51 and 254–56.

82. Ibid., 249.

83. Ibid., 254.

84. Ibid., 255.

85. Hossein Makki, *Tārikh-e bist sāleh-ye Irān* [Twenty years of Iran's history], vol. 6 (Tehran: Nāsher, 1362/1983), 161.

86. See ibid., 163; and Mehrdad Amanat, "Bahrāmī, Faraj-Allāh," in *Encyclopædia Iranica*, ed. Ehsan Yarshater (New York: Bibliotheca Persica, 1989).

87. Mehrdad Amanat, "Bahrāmī, Faraj-Allāh."

88. Makki, *Tārikh*, 6:162–63.

89. Reported by Sheikh ol-Molk Owrang, in ibid.6:175–76, see also 6:179–80.

90. See ibid., 6:176.

91. Mohammad Tavakoli-Targhi, *Refashioning Iran: Orientalism, Occidentalism, and Historiography*, St. Antony's series (New York: Palgrave, 2001), 87.

92. Makki, *Tārikh*, 6:179.

93. Ibid., 6:180.

94. Chehabi, "From Revolutionary Tasnif to Patriotic Surud," 148.

95. Ibid.

96. On Reza Shah's military, see Stephanie Cronin, "Riza Shah and the Paradoxes of Military Modernization in Iran, 1921–1941," in *The Making of Modern Iran: State and Society Under Riza Shah, 1921–1941*, ed. Stephanie Cronin, 37–64 (London: RoutledgeCurzon, 2003).

97. For a different take, presenting Reza Shah as a "product of the Constitutional Movement," see Ali M. Ansari, *The Politics of Nationalism in Modern Iran* (Cambridge: Cambridge University Press, 2012), 65–76.

98. For more on this, refer to Mehrdad Kia, "Persian Nationalism and the Campaign for Language Purification," *Middle Eastern Studies* 34, no. 2 (1998): 9–36; and John R. Perry, "Language Reform in Turkey and Iran," *International Journal of Middle East Studies* 17, no. 3 (1985): 295–311.

99. Grigor, *Building Iran*, 12.

100. It should be emphasized that Forughi, for one, never espoused racialist views. See Ansari, *Politics of Nationalism*, 105.

101. Grigor points out for instance that Ferdowsi's shrine came to be called *ferdowsi-yeh*, similarly to the *hoseyniyehs*, spaces where a number of Shi'ite rituals are performed during the Muharram commemorations. See Grigor, *Building Iran*, 67.

102. Afshin Marashi, *Nationalizing Iran: Culture, Power, and the State, 1870–1940* (Seattle: University of Washington Press, 2008), 113.

103. On the shrine and the millenial Ferdowsi celebrations in 1934, see Grigor, *Building Iran*, 46–81; and Marashi, *Nationalizing Iran*, 110–32. Primary sources can be found in Makki, *Tārikh*, vol. 6.

104. Grigor, *Building Iran*, 9.

105. Marashi concurs; see Marashi, *Nationalizing Iran*, 124.

106. Grigor, *Building Iran*, 49, quoting Issa Sadiq, *Ferdowsi: His Life, his Personality, and his Work* (Tehran: Society for the Protection of National Monuments, 1945), 1–3.

107. Grigor, *Building Iran*, 54.

108. Ibid., 63.

109. Ibid., p. 62, quoting Society for National Heritage, *Kārnāmeh*, no. 131: 30.

110. Katouzian, *State and Society in Iran*, 272.

111. Grigor, *Building Iran*, 11, quoting British Minister of the Foreign Office, OF 371, 12293/E3909, Clive, August 26, 1927, Tehran.

112. Stephanie Cronin, *Tribal Politics in Iran: Rural Conflict and the new State, 1921–1941* (London: Routledge, 2007), 2. See this work for an in-depth analysis of this topic.

113. Ibid., 1.

114. Katouzian, *The Persians*, 213.

115. Cronin, *Tribal Politics in Iran*, 36–37.

116. Soltan Ali Soltani, quoted in Katouzian, *State and Society in Iran*, 326.

117. Cronin, *Tribal Politics in Iran*, 2.

118. "Iran's Nomadic Tribes," *Tehran Times*, August 5, 2011.

119. Ibid.

120. Houchang E. Chehabi, "Staging the Emperor's New Clothes: Dress Codes and Nation-Building under Reza Shah," *Iranian Studies* 26, no. 3–4 (1993): 209.

121. Ibid., 215.

122. From Mokhber ol-Saltaneh's memoirs, quoted in Katouzian, *State and Society in Iran*, 336.

123. Quoted in Chehabi, "Staging the Emperor's New Clothes," 225.

124. Ibid., 226.

125. Ali Rahnema, *An Islamic Utopian: A Political Biography of Ali Shari'ati* (London: I. B. Tauris, 2000), 5.

126. Chehabi, "Staging the Emperor's New Clothes," 213.

127. Houchang E. Chehabi, "The Banning of the Veil and Its Consequences," in *The Making of Modern Iran: State and Society Under Riza Shah, 1921–1941*, ed. Stephanie Cronin (New York: RoutledgeCurzon, 2003), 199.

128. This is a quotation from a representative of the Kermanshah provincial authorities but is very much representative of the general approach of the Pahlavi elite. Quoted in Chehabi, "Staging the Emperor's New Clothes," 226.

129. Chehabi, "The Banning of the Veil and Its Consequences," 201–2.

130. Ibid., 202.

131. Ibid., 196.

132. For this alternative view, see Shireen Mahdavi, "Reza Shah Pahlavi and Women: A Re-Evaluation," in *The Making of Modern Iran: State and Society Under Riza Shah, 1921–1941*, ed. Stephanie Cronin (London: RoutledgeCurzon, 2003), esp. 193.

133. Touraj Atabaki and Erik Jan Zürcher, *Men of Order: Authoritarian Modernization Under Atatürk and Reza Shah* (London: I. B. Tauris, 2004), 70–71.

134. Katouzian, *The Persians*, 209.

135. See, for instance, Ali Akbar Siassi, *La perse au contact de l'Occident: Étude historique et sociale* (Paris: Ernest Leroux, 1931), 18–19.

136. Ibid., 204.

137. Ibid., 204–6.

138. Ibid., 200.

139. Ibid., 208.

140. Ibid., 228 and 230.

141. Ibid., 230.

8. Triumph

1. Talinn Grigor, *Building Iran: Modernism, Architecture, and National Heritage Under the Pahlavi Monarchs* (New York: Periscope, 2009), 49–57.

2. Afshin Marashi, *Nationalizing Iran: Culture, Power, and the State, 1870–1940*, 1st ed. (Seattle: University of Washington Press, 2008), ch. 4.

3. Grigor, *Building Iran:* 70.

4. Ibid., 70–71. The speech is quoted in Marashi, *Nationalizing Iran*, 130.

5. Grigor, *Building Iran*, 172, quoting British Minister of the Foreign Office, E 6749/47/34, A. C. Trott, November 5, 1934, Tehran.

6. Marashi, *Nationalizing Iran*, 131.

7. The reader intersted in linguistics manifestations of nationalism in Iran can refer to Shahrokh Meskoob, *Iranian Nationality and the Persian Language* (Washington, DC: Mage Publishers, 1992).

8. Grigor, *Building Iran*, 70.

9. Ibid., 73.

10. Homa Katouzian, *Sadeq Hedayat: The Life and Legend of an Iranian Writer* (London: I. B. Tauris, 1991), 78; and Homa Katouzian, *The Persians: Ancient, Medieval, and Modern Iran* (New Haven: Yale University Press, 2009), 215.

11. Houchang E. Chehabi, "The Banning of the Veil and Its Consequences," in *The Making of Modern Iran: State and Society Under Riza Shah, 1921–1941*, ed. Stephanie Cronin (New York: RoutledgeCurzon, 2003), 203.

12. Private discussion between Anthony Parsons and Homa Katouzian, 1987, conveyed to the author by Homa Katouzian, August 18, 2009.

13. See Shahrokh Golestan, *The Flame of Persia*, 60 min. Iran: Edāreh-ye Koll-e Omur-e Sinamā'i-ye Keshvar [Iran National Cinema Board], 1971.

14. *Rastākhiz* newspaper, October 10, 1977.

15. Golestan, "The Flame of Persia."

16. It is undeniable that slavery existed: it was underdeveloped in the Achaemenid age but highly regulated in the Sasanian. The *Mādayān i hazār dādestān* (Book of a thousand judgements), which was a Sasanian law book, regulated the treatment of slaves. See Maria Macuch, "Barda and Barda-Dāri; i. In the Achaemenid Period,"

in *Encyclopædia Iranica*, ed. Ehsan Yarshater (New York: Bibliotheca Persica, 1989).

17. Reported by Asadollah Alam, quoted in Katouzian, *The Persians*, 270.

18. Quoted in ibid., 271.

19. Quoted in Tim Kirby, "The Last Shah," documentary series (United Kingdom: BBC, 1995).

20. Quoted in Ali M. Ansari, *Modern Iran Since 1921: The Pahlavis and After* (London: Longman, 2003), 191.

21. Ibid., 190.

22. Ansari believes that it was due to his "acute lack of self-confidence." Ali M. Ansari, *The Politics of Nationalism in Modern Iran* (Cambridge: Cambridge University Press, 2012), 146.

23. Quoted in Gholam R. Afkhami, *The Life and Times of the Shah* (Berkeley: University of California Press, 2009), 26. According to this author, the shah's sincerity is indisputable.

24. Mohammad Reza Pahlavi, *Answer to History* (New York: Stein and Day, 1980), 55–56.

25. Ibid., 57–60.

26. Ibid., 57.

27. Ansari, *Politics of Nationalism*, 180–81.

28. Pahlavi, *Answer to History*, 36.

29. Ibid., 38.

30. Ibid., 39. See also Stephanie Cronin, *Tribal Politics in Iran: Rural Conflict and the New State, 1921–1941* (London: Routledge, 2007), 17.

31. Pahlavi, *Answer to History*, 37–38.

32. Examples of Mosaddeq as the personification of Iranian nationalism abound in the writings of Nikki Keddie, L. P. Elwell-Sutton, and Fakhreddin Azimi. See also Richard W. Cottam, *Nationalism in Iran* (Pittsburgh: University of Pittsburgh Press; London: Feffer and Simons, 1979); and Abbas Milani, *The Persian Sphinx: Amir Abbas Hoveyda and the Riddle of the Iranian Revolution: A Biography* (London: I. B. Tauris, 2000), for instance 17 and 236.

33. Homa Katouzian, *Musaddiq and the Struggle for Power in Iran*, rev. pbk. ed. (London: I. B. Tauris, 1999), x.

34. Ibid.

35. Ibid.

36. See also Abdolhossein Zarrinkub, "The Arab Conquest of Iran and its Aftermath," in *The Cambridge History of Irani*, vol. 4: *The Period from the Arab Invasion to the Saljuqs*, ed. Richard Nelson Frye (Cambridge University Press, 1975).

37. Abdolhossein Zarrinkub, *Do qarn sokut* [Two centuries of silence], 7th ed. (Tehran: Jāvidān, 2536/1977 [1957]), 13.

38. Ibid., 12.

39. Kamran Aghaie, "Islam and Nationalist Historiography: Competing Historical Narratives of Iran in the Pahlavi Period," *Studies on Contemporary Islam*, published by the Center for Islamic Studies, Youngstown State University, 2, no. 2 (2000): 30,

citing Hamid Dabashi, *Theology of Discontent: The Ideological Foundations of the Islamic Revolution in Iran* (New York: New York University Press, 1993), 148.

40. Ibid., 31.

41. Ibid., 33.

42. Ervand Abrahamian, *Radical Islam: The Iranian Mojahedin* (London: I. B. Tauris, 1989), 103.

43. Quoted in Aghaie, "Islam and Nationalist Historiography," 41.

44. Ibid., 42.

45. Ibid., 43–44.

46. Mehrzad Boroujerdi, *Iranian Intellectuals and the West: The Tormented Triumph of Nativism* (Syracuse, NY: Syracuse University Press, 1996), 132.

47. For an English translation, see Jalal Al-e Ahmad, R. Campbell, and Hamid Algar, *Occidentosis: A Plague from the West* (Berkeley, CA: Mizan Press, 1984).

48. Boroujerdi, *Iranian Intellectuals and the West*, 132.

49. Ibid., 133.

50. Hassan Abbasi, *Tārikh-e āriyāyi va hoveyyat-e melli* [Aryan history and national identity] (Paris: Homā, 7018 of the Aryan calendar/1996); and Omid Ataei Fard, *Shegeftihā-ye bāstāni-e Irān* [The ancient wonders of Iran] (Tehran: Ashiyāneh Ketab, 1380/2001).

51. Mehrdad Farahmand, "Shojā' ed-Din Shafā: Hekāyat-e din setizi az diyār-e Qom" [Shoja'ed-Din Shafa; Anti-religious accounts out of Qom], *BBC Persian*, April 18, 2010.

52. Milani, *Persian Sphinx*, 312–13.

53. Shoja'ed-Din Shafa, *Pas az 1,400 sāl* [After 1,400 years] (2003), 21 and 22, for instance.

54. Ibid., 30.

55. Ibid., 31.

CONCLUSION: THE FAILURE OF DISLOCATIVE NATIONALISM

1. I am grateful to Homa Katouzian for his input.

2. For definitions, see Zeev Sternhell, *The Anti-Enlightenment Tradition*, trans. David Maisel (New Haven: Yale University Press, 2009).

3. See Mohammad Tavakoli-Targhi, *Refashioning Iran: Orientalism, Occidentalism, and Historiography*, St. Antony's series (New York: Palgrave, 2001), chap. 5.

4. John Breuilly, "On the Principle of Nationality," in *The Cambridge History of Nineteenth-Century Political Thought*, ed. Gareth Stedman Jones and Gregory Claeys, 77–109 (Cambridge: Cambridge University Press, 2011).

5. Ernest Gellner, *Nations and Nationalism* (Ithaca, NY: Cornell University Press, 2006), 1.

6. There is a controversial publication, Alireza Asgharzadeh, *Iran and the Challenge of Diversity: Islamic Fundamentalism, Aryanist Racism, and Democratic Struggles* (Basingstoke: Palgrave Macmillan, 2007), esp. chap. 3; for a critique, see Rasmus Christian Elling, *Minorities in Iran: Nationalism and Ethnicity After Khomeini* (New York: Palgrave Macmillan, 2013), 167 et seq.

BIBLIOGRAPHY

Abbasi, Hassan. *Tārikh-e āriyāyi va hoveyyat-e melli* [Aryan history and national identity]. Paris: Homā, 7018 of the Aryan calendar/1996.

Abrahamian, Ervand. "Communism and Communalism in Iran: The Tudah and the Firqah-i Dimukrat." *International Journal of Middle East Studies* 1, no. 4 (1970): 291–316.

——. *Iran Between Two Revolutions*. Princeton: Princeton University Press, 1982.

——. *Radical Islam: The Iranian Mojahedin*. London: I. B. Tauris, 1989.

Adamiyat, Fereydun. *Andishehā-ye Mirzā Āqā Khān-e Kermāni* [Life and thought of Mirza Aqa Khan Kermani]. Tehran: Tahuri, 1346/1967.

——. *Andishehā-ye Mirzā Fath'ali Ākhundzādeh* [Life and thought of Mirza Fath'ali Akhundzadeh]. Tehran: Khārazmi, 1349/1970.

Adamiyat, Fereydun, and Thomas M. Ricks. "Problems in Iranian Historiography." *Iranian Studies* 4, no. 4 (1971): 132–56.

Afary, Janet. *The Iranian Constitutional Revolution, 1906–1911: Grassroots Democracy, Social Democracy, and the Origins of Feminism*. New York: Columbia University Press, 1996.

Afkhami, Gholam R. *The Life and Times of the Shah*. Berkeley: University of California Press, 2009.

Afshar, Iraj, ed. *Nāmehā-ye Tehrān* [Letters from Tehran]. Tehran: Farzān, 1385/2006.

Aghaie, Kamran. "Islam and Nationalist Historiography: Competing Historical Narratives of Iran in the Pahlavi Period." *Studies on Contemporary Islam*, Published by the Center for Islamic Studies, Youngstown State University, 2, no. 2 (2000): 20–46.

——. "Religious Rituals, Social Identities and Political Relationships in Tehran Under Qajar Rule, 1850s–1920s." In *Religion and Society in Qajar Iran*, ed. Robert Gleave, 373–92. London: RoutledgeCurzon, 2005.

Ahmad, Jalal Al. "Cheguneh dar Ālmān jashnhā va ādāb-e Āriyāyi va Irāni az now zendeh mishavad" [How Aryan and Iranian celebrations and customs are revived in Germany]. *Nāmeh-ye Irān Bāstān*, November 3, 1933.

Ahmadi, Hamid. "Unity Within Diversity: Foundations and Dynamics of National Identity in Iran." *Critique: Critical Middle Eastern Studies* 14, no. 1 (2005): 127–47.

Ahmed, Akbar S. "Al-Beruni: The First Anthropologist." *RAIN*, no. 60 (1984): 9–10.

Ajoudani, Mashallah. *Mashruteh-ye Irāni* [Iranian constitutionalism], partly censored Iranian edition. Tehran: Akhtarān, 1382/2003.

Akhundzadeh, Fath'ali. *Adabiyāt-e mashruteh: Maktubāt-e Mirza Fath'ali Ākhundzādeh* [Constitutionalist literature: Mirza Fath'ali Akhundzadeh's Maktubat]. Tabriz: Ehiyā, 1357/1979.

——. *Maktubāt: Nāmehā-ye Kamāl od-Dowleh beh Shāhzādeh Jamāl od-Dowleh* [Maktubat: Letters from Kamal od-Dowleh to Prince Jamal od-Dowleh]. Ed. Bahram Choubine. Frankfurt: Alborz, 2006.

Al-e Ahmad, Jalal, R. Campbell, and Hamid Algar. *Occidentosis: A Plague from the West*. Berkeley, CA: Mizan Press, 1984.

Alavi, Bozorg. Div! . . . Div . . . [Demon! . . . Demon . . .]. New ed. Tehran: Amir Kabir, 1357/1978.

Algar, Hamid. "Ākūndzāda." In *Encyclopædia Iranica*, vol. 1, ed. Ehsan Yarshater. New York: Bibliotheca Persica, 1985.

——. "Malkum Khān, Ākhūndzāda and the Proposed Reform of the Arabic Alphabet." *Middle Eastern Studies* 5, no. 2 (1969): 116–30.

——. *Mirza Malkum Khan: A Study in the History of Iranian Modernism*. Berkeley: University of California Press, 1973.

Alp, Tekin. "The Restoration of Turkish History." In *Nationalism in Asia and Africa*, ed. Elie Kedourie, 207–24. London: Frank Cass, 1974.

Amanat, Abbas. "Jalāl ed-Din Mirzā va nāmeh-ye khosrovān" [Jalal ed-Din Mirza and the Book of Sovereigns]. *Iran Nameh* 17, no. 1 (1999).

——. "'Russian Intrusion into the Guarded Domain': Reflections of a Qajar Statesman on European Expansion." *Journal of the American Oriental Society* 113, no. 1 (1993): 35–56.

Amanat, Abbas, and Farzin Vejdani. "Jalāl-al-Din Mirzā," in *Encyclopædia Iranica*, vol. 14, ed. Ehsan Yarshater. New York: Bibliotheca Persica, 2008.

Amanat, Mehrdad. "Bahrāmī, Faraj-Allāh." In *Encyclopædia Iranica*, vol. 3, ed. Ehsan Yarshater. New York: Bibliotheca Persica, 1989.

Anderson, Benedict. *Imagined Communities: Reflections on the Origin and Spread of Nationalism*. Rev. ed. London: Verso, 2006.

Ansari, Ali M. *Modern Iran Since 1921: The Pahlavis and After*. London: Longman, 2003.

——. *The Politics of Nationalism in Modern Iran*. Cambridge: Cambridge University Press, 2012.

Aref-e Qazvini, Abolqasem. *'Āref-e Qazvini, shā'er-e melli-ye Irān* [Aref-e Qazvini, Iran's national poet]. Ed. Seyyed Hadi Ha'eri (Kurosh). Tehran: Jāvidān, 1369/1990.

——. *Kolliyāt-e divān-e 'Āref-e Qazvini* [The complete divan of Aref-e Qazvini]. Ed. Abdorrahman Seif Azad. 6th ed. Tehran: Amir Kabir, 2536/1977.

Arvidsson, Stefan. *Aryan Idols: Indo-European Mythology as Ideology and Science.* Chicago: University of Chicago Press, 2006.

Asgharzadeh, Alireza. *Iran and the Challenge of Diversity: Islamic Fundamentalism, Aryanist Racism, and Democratic Struggles.* Basingstoke: Palgrave Macmillan, 2007.

Ashraf, Ahmad. "Iranian Identity; iii. Medieval Islamic Period." In *Encyclopædia Iranica*, vol. 13, ed. Ehsan Yarshater. New York: Bibliotheca Persica, 2006.

Atabaki, Touraj. *Azerbaijan: Ethnicity and the Struggle for Power in Iran.* Rev. ed. London: I. B. Tauris, 2000.

——. "Recasting Oneself, Rejecting the Other: Pan-Turkism and Iranian Nationalism." In *Identity Politics in Central Asia and the Muslim World*, ed. Willem van Schendel and Erik Jan Zürcher, 65–84. London: I. B. Tauris, 2001.

Atabaki, Touraj, and Erik Jan Zürcher. *Men of Order: Authoritarian Modernization under Atatürk and Reza Shah.* London: I. B. Tauris, 2004.

Ataei Fard, Omid. *Shegeftihā-ye bāstāni-e Irān* [The ancient wonders of Iran]. Tehran: Ashiyāneh Ketab, 1380/2001.

Back, Michael. "Die Sassanidischen Staatinschriften." In *Acta Iranica 18—Textes et Mémoires VIII.* Tehran: Bibliothèque Pahlavi, 1978.

Bahar, Mohammad Taqi. *Sabkshenāsi yā tārikh-e tatavor-e nasr-e Fārsi* [Stylistics or the history of change in Persian prose]. Vol. 3. Tehran: Amir Kabir, 1337/1958.

Bailey, H. W. "Arya." In *Encyclopædia Iranica*, vol. 2, ed. Ehsan Yarshater. New York: Bibliotheca Persica, 1987.

——. "Iranian Arya- and Daha-." *Transactions of the Philological Society* 58, no. 1 (1959): 71–115.

Banerjea, Surendranath. "The Study of Indian History." In *Nationalism in Asia and Africa*, ed. Elie Kedourie, 225–44. London: Frank Cass, 1974.

Banton, Michael. *The Idea of Race.* London: Tavistock Publications, 1977.

——. *Racial and Ethnic Competition.* Comparative Ethnic and Race Relations series. Cambridge: Cambridge University Press, 1983.

——. *Racial Theories.* 2nd ed. Cambridge: Cambridge University Press, 1998.

Baram, Amatzia. "A Case of Imported Identity: The Modernizing Secular Ruling Elites of Iraq and the Concept of Mesopotamian-Inspired Territorial Nationalism, 1922–1992." *Poetics Today* 15, no. 2 (1994): 279–319.

Bastani-Parizi, Mohammad Ebrahim. "Fereydun Ādamiyyat va andishehā-ye Mirzā Āqā Khān-e Kermāni" [Fereydun Adamiyat and the thoughts of Mirza Aqa Khan Kermani]. *Bokhārā: Majaleh-ye Farhangi Honari* 11, no. 65 (April–May 2008).

Bayat, Kaveh. "Āshnāyi bā pāntorkism va ta'sir-e mājarā-ye Rowshani Beyg bar ān" [Getting to know Pan-Turkism and the impact of the Ruşeni Bey episode]. In *Irān: Hoveyyat, meliyyat, qowmeyyat* [Iran: Identity, nationhood, ethnicity], ed. Hamid Ahmadi. Tehran: Mo'aseseh-ye Tahqiqāt va Towse'eh-ye 'Olum-e Ensāni, 1383/2004.

Bayat, Mangol. "Āqā Khan Kermānī." In *Encyclopædia Iranica*, vol. 2, ed. by Ehsan Yarshater. New York: Bibliotheca Persica, 1986.

——. *Iran's First Revolution: Shi'ism and the Constitutional Revolution of 1905–1909*. New York: Oxford University Press, 1991.

——. "Mirza Aqa Khan Kirmani: Nineteenth Century Persian Revolutionary Thinker." PhD diss., University of California, Los Angeles, 1971.

Bayat-Philipp, Mangol. "The Concepts of Religion and Government in the Thought of Mirza Aqa Khan Kirmani, a Nineteenth-Century Persian Revolutionary." *International Journal of Middle East Studies* 5, no. 4 (1974): 381–400.

——. "Mirza Aqa Khan Kirmani: A Nineteenth Century Persian Nationalist." *Middle Eastern Studies* 10, no. 1 (1974): 36–59.

——. "A Phoenix Too Frequent: Historical Continuity in Modern Iranian Thought." *Asian and African Studies* 12 (1978): 205–7.

Behrooz, Maziar. "Revisiting the Second Russo-Iranian War (1826–28): Causes and Perceptions." *Iranian Studies* 46, no. 3 (2013): 359–81.

Benedict, Ruth. *Race and Racism*. London: Routledge, 1942.

Benveniste, Emile. "L'Eran-vez et l'origine légendaire des Iraniens." *Bulletin of the School of Oriental Studies, University of London* 7, no. 2 (1934): 265–74.

Berger, Stefan, Mark Donovan, and Kevin Passmore. *Writing National Histories: Western Europe Since 1800*. London: Routledge, 1999.

Blanning, T. C. W. *The Culture of Power and the Power of Culture: Old Regime Europe 1660–1789*. Oxford: Oxford University Press, 2003.

Bokhārā: Majaleh-ye Farhangi Honari / *Bukhara: A Persian Review of Culture, Art and Iranology* 11, no. 65, April–May 2008.

Boroujerdi, Mehrzad. *Iranian Intellectuals and the West: The Tormented Triumph of Nativism*. Syracuse, NY: Syracuse University Press, 1996.

Boyce, Mary. "Manekji Limji Hataria in Iran." In *K. R. Cama Oriental Institute Golden Jubilee Volume*, ed. N. D. Minochehr-Homji and M. F. Kanga, 19–31. Bombay: K. R. Cama Oriental Institute, 1969.

Boyd, James W., and Donald, A. "Is Zoroastrianism Dualistic or Monotheistic." *Journal of the American Academy of Religion* 47 (1979): 557–88.

Brands, H. W. *Azerbaiganisches Volksleben und modernistische Tendenz in den Schauspielen Mirza Feth-Ali Ahundzades*. Leiden: Brill, 1975.

Breuilly, John. "Max Weber, Charisma and Nationalist Leadership." *Nations and Nationalism* 17, no. 3 (2011): 477–99.

——. *Nationalism and the State*. 2nd ed. Manchester: Manchester University Press, 1993.

——. "On the Principle of Nationality." In *The Cambridge History of Nineteenth-Century Political Thought*, ed. Gareth Stedman Jones and Gregory Claeys, 77–109. Cambridge: Cambridge University Press, 2011.

Browne, Edward Granville. *A Literary History of Persia: From the Earliest Times until Firdawsí*. London: T. Fisher Unwin, 1909.

——. *Materials for the Study of the Bábí Religion*. Cambridge: Cambridge University Press, 1918.

——. *The Persian Revolution of 1905–1909*. Cambridge: Cambridge University Press, 1910.

——. *A Year Amongst the Persians*. London: Adam and Charles Black, 1893.

Browne, Edward Granville, and Mohammad Ali Khan "Tarbiyat" of Tabriz. *The Press and Poetry of Modern Persia: Partly Based on the Manuscript Work of Mirza Muhammad Ali Khan "Tarbiyat" of Tabriz*. Cambridge: Cambridge University Press, 1914.

Brubaker, Rogers. *Ethnicity Without Groups*. Cambridge: Harvard University Press, 2004.

Cashmore, Ernest, ed. *Encyclopedia of Race and Ethnic Studies*. London: Routledge, 2004.

Chaqueri, Cosroe. "Ravesh shenāsi-e tārikhi-e Fereydun Ādamiyyat" [Fereydun Adamiyat's historical methodology]. *Bokhārā: Majaleh-ye Farhangi Honari* 11, no. 65 (April–May 2008).

Chatterjee, Partha. *The Nation and Its Fragments: Colonial and Postcolonial Histories*. Princeton Studies in Culture/Power/History. Princeton: Princeton University Press, 1993.

——. *Nationalist Thought and the Colonial World: A Derivative Discourse*. Minneapolis: University of Minnesota Press, 1993.

Chehabi, Houchang E. "The Banning of the Veil and Its Consequences." In *The Making of Modern Iran: State and Society Under Riza Shah, 1921–1941*, ed. Stephanie Cronin. New York: RoutledgeCurzon, 2003.

——. "From Revolutionary Tasnif to Patriotic Surud: Music and Nation-Building in Pre-World War II Iran." *Iran* 37 (1999): 143–54.

——. "The Paranoid Style in Iranian Historiography." In *Iran in the 20th Century: Historiography and Political Culture*, ed. Touraj Atabaki, 155–76. London: I. B. Tauris, 2009.

——. "Staging the Emperor's New Clothes: Dress Codes and Nation-Building Under Reza Shah." *Iranian Studies* 26, no. 3–4 (1993): 209–29.

Cole, Juan R. I. "Marking Boundaries, Marking Time: The Iranian Past and the Construction of the Self by Qajar Thinkers." *Iranian Studies* 29, no. 1–2 (1996): 35–56.

Corbin, Henry. *En Islam Iranien: Aspects spirituels et philosophiques*. Paris: Gallimard, 1971.

Cottam, Richard W. *Nationalism in Iran*. Pittsburgh: University of Pittsburgh Press; London: Feffer and Simons, 1979.

Crone, Patricia. "Zoroastrian Communism." *Comparative Studies in Society and History* 36, no. 3 (1994): 447–62.

Cronin, Stephanie. "Building a New Army: Military Reform in Qajar Iran." In *War and Peace in Qajar Persia: Implications Past and Present*, ed. Roxane Farmanfarmaian, 47–87. London: Routledge, 2008.

——. "Riza Shah and the Paradoxes of Military Modernization in Iran, 1921–1941." In *The Making of Modern Iran: State and Society Under Riza Shah, 1921–1941*, ed. Stephanie Cronin, 37–64. London: RoutledgeCurzon, 2003.

——. *Tribal Politics in Iran: Rural Conflict and the New State, 1921–1941*. London: Routledge, 2007.

Curzon, George N. *Persia and the Persian Question*. London: Longmans, Green & Co., 1892.

Dabashi, Hamid. *Theology of Discontent: The Ideological Foundations of the Islamic Revolution in Iran*. New York: New York University Press, 1993.

Daryaee, Touraj. *Sasanian Persia: The Rise and Fall of an Empire*. London: I. B. Tauris in association with the Iran Heritage Foundation, 2009.

Davies, Norman. *Europe: A History*. New ed. London: Pimlico, 1997.

Davis, Dick. "Iran and Aniran: The Shaping of a Legend." In *Iran Facing Others: Identity Boundaries in a Historical Perspective*, ed. Abbas Amanat and Farzin Vejdani, 39–50. New York: Palgrave Macmillan, 2012.

——. "The Problem of Ferdowsî's Sources." *Journal of the American Oriental Society* 116, no. 1 (1996): 48–57.

de Silva Jayasuriya, Shihan. "Identifying Africans in Asia: What's in a Name?" *African and Asian Studies* 5 (2006): 275–303.

Donner, Fred McGraw. *Muhammad and the Believers: At the Origins of Islam*. Cambridge: Belknap Press of Harvard University Press, 2010.

Dunlop, John B. *Russia Confronts Chechnya: Roots of a Separatist Conflict*. Cambridge: Cambridge University Press, 1998.

Durkheim, Émile, and Karen E. Fields. *The Elementary Forms of Religious Life*. New York: Free Press, 1995.

Edwards, Edward, and British Museum, Dept. of Oriental Printed Books and Manuscripts. *A Catalogue of the Persian Printed Books in the British Museum*. London: British Museum, 1922.

Elling, Rasmus Christian. *Minorities in Iran: Nationalism and Ethnicity After Khomeini*. New York: Palgrave Macmillan, 2013.

Ellison, Ralph, and John F. Callahan. *The Collected Essays of Ralph Ellison*. New York: Modern Library, 1995.

Enayat, Hamid. "The Politics of Iranology." *Iranian Studies* 6, no. 1 (1973): 2–20.

Esfandiari, Golnaz. "Historic Cyrus Cylinder Called 'A Stranger in Its Own Home.'" In *Persian Letters: Notes of an Iran Watcher*. Prague: Radio Free Europe, 2010.

Eshqi, Mirzadeh. *Kolliyāt-e mosavvar-e Mirzādeh-ye ʿEshqi* [Illustrated complete works of Mirzadeh Eshqi]. Ed. Ali Akbar Moshir-Salimi. Tehran 1322/1943.

Farahmand, Mehrdad. "Shojāʿ ed-Din Shafā: hekāyat-e din setizi az diyār-e Qom" [Shojaʿed-Din Shafa: Anti-religious accounts out of Qom]. *BBC Persian*, April 18, 2010.

Fatemi, Nasrollah S. "Anglo-Persian Agreement of 1919." In *Encyclopædia Iranica*, vol. 2, ed. Ehsan Yarshater. New York: Bibliotheca Persica, 1987.

Fattahi, Fath ed-Din. *Safarnāmeh-ye Mirzā Fattāh Khān Garmrudi beh Orupā* [Mirza Fattah Khan Garmrudi's Europe travel diary]. Tehran: Chāpkhāneh-ye Bānk-e Bāzargāni-e Irān, 1347/1968.

Ferdowsi, Abolqasem, and Dick Davis. *Shahnameh: The Persian Book of Kings*. New ed. New York: Penguin, 2007.

Feuvrier, Jean-Baptiste. *Trois ans à la cour de Perse*. Paris: F. Juven, 1899.

Figueira, Dorothy Matilda. *Aryans, Jews, Brahmins: Theorizing Authority Through Myths of Identity*. Albany: State University of New York Press, 2002.

Findley, Carter V. *Turkey, Islam, Nationalism, and Modernity: A History, 1789–2007*. New Haven: Yale University Press, 2010.

Firby, Nora Kathleen. *European Travellers and Their Perceptions of Zoroastrians in the 17th and 18th Centuries*. Vol. 14, *Archäologische Mitteilungen aus Iran*. Berlin: D. Reimer, 1988.

Foroughi, Mohammad Ali. *Payām-e man beh farhangestān* [My message to the academy]. 3rd ed. Tehran: Enteshārāt-e Payām, 1354/1975.

Foucart, Stéphane. "Rois de l'Entre-deux-Fleuves: Mésopotamie 6—Cyrus le Taiseux, Vers 550–529 avant J.-C." *Le Monde*, August 19, 2007.

Frye, Richard N. *The Golden Age of Persia: The Arabs in the East*. London: Weidenfeld and Nicolson, 1988.

——. *The Heritage of Persia*. London: Weidenfeld and Nicolson, 1962.

——. *Persia*. Rev. ed. London: Allen & Unwin, 1968.

Fussman, Gérard. "Entre fantasmes, science et politique: L'entrée des Aryas en Inde. *Annales: Histoire, Sciences Sociales* 58, no. 4 (2003): 781–813.

Fussman, Gérard, Jean Kellens, Henri-Paul Francfort, and Xavier Tremblay. *Aryas, Aryens et Iraniens en Asie centrale*. Publications de l'Institut de civilisation indienne. Paris: Collège de France, 2005.

Gellner, Ernest. *Nations and Nationalism*. Ithaca, NY: Cornell University Press, 2006.

Gershoni, Israel. "Imagining and Reimagining the Past: The Use of History by Egyptian Nationalist Writers, 1919–1952." *History and Memory* 4, no. 2 (1992): 5–37.

Gheissari, Ali. *Iranian Intellectuals in the 20th Century*. Austin: University of Texas Press, 1998.

Giara, Marzban, Ramiyar P. Karanjia, and Michael Stausberg. "Manekji on the Religious/Ritual Practices of the Iranian Zoroastrians: An English Translation of a Passage from His Travel Report in Gujarati (1865)." In *Zoroastrian Rituals in Context*, ed. Michael Stausberg. Leiden: Brill, 2004.

Gibbon, Edward, and Alexander Chalmers. *The History of the Decline and Fall of the Roman Empire*. London: T. Cadell, 1837.

Gnoli, Gherardo. "Dualism." In *Encyclopædia Iranica*, vol. 7, ed. Ehsan Yarshater. New York: Bibliotheca Persica, 1996.

Gobineau, Arthur Comte de. *Les Religions et les philosophies dans l'Asie Centrale*. 2nd ed. Paris: Didier et cie, 1866.

——. *Trois ans en Asie; de 1855 à 1858*. Paris: B. Grasset, 1923.

Gobineau, Arthur Comte de, Daniel O'Donoghue, and Geoffrey Nash. *Comte de Gobineau and Orientalism: Selected Eastern Writings*. New York: Routledge, 2009.

Goldziher, Ignaz, and S. M. Stern. *Muslim Studies*. New Brunswick, NJ: Transaction Publishers, 2006.

Golestan, Shahrokh. *The Flame of Persia*. 60 min. Iran: Edāreh-ye Koll-e Omur-e Sinamā'i-ye Keshvar [Iran National Cinema Board], 1971.

Grigor, Talinn. *Building Iran: Modernism, Architecture, and National Heritage Under the Pahlavi Monarchs*. New York: Periscope, 2009.

Gunny, Ahmad. *Images of Islam in Eighteenth-Century Writings*. London: Grey Seal, 1996.

Hairi, Abdul-Hadi. *Nakhostin ruyāruyihā-ye andishegarān-e Irān bā do ruye-ye tamad-don-e burzhuāzi-e Qarb* [The early encounters of Iranian thinkers with the two-sided civilization of western bourgeoisie]. Tehran: Amir Kabir, 1367/1988.

Haj Seyyed Javadi, Ali Asghar. "Ādamiyat, pedar-e ʿelm-e tārikh-e Irān" [Adamiyat, the father of the science of history in Iran]. *Bokhārā: Majaleh-ye Farhangi Honari* 11, no. 65 (April–May 2008): 95–201.

Hall, Stuart, and Bram Gieben. *Formations of Modernity.* Oxford: Polity Press in association with Open University, 1992.

Hall, Stuart, and Paul du Gay, eds. *Questions of Cultural Identity.* London: Sage, 1996.

Hataria, Manekji Limji. *Rishāl-e ejhār-e shiyāt-e Irān* [Essay on a description of a travel to Iran]. Bombay: Union Press, 1865.

Hedayat, Sadeq. *Kārevān-e Eslām* [The caravan of Islam]. Ed. Bahram Choubine, on-line ed. Paris: Organisation des mouvements nationalistes des universitaires, cherch-eurs et intellectuels Iraniens, 1381/2002.

——. *Parvin, dokhtar-e Sāsān* [Parvin the Sasanian girl]. Ed. Mohammad Ali Sheikh Olia Lavasani. Online ed., www.sadegh-hedayat.mihanblog.com.

Herder, Johann Gottfried. *Outlines of a Philosophy of the History of Man.* Trans. T. Churchill. 2nd ed. 2 vols. London: J. Johnson, 1803.

——. *Persepolis: Eine Muthmassung.* Gotha: Ettinger, 1787.

Hobsbawm, Eric J. *On History.* London: Weidenfeld and Nicolson, 1997.

Hodgson, Marshall G. S. *The Venture of Islam: Conscience and History in a World Civilization.* Chicago: University of Chicago Press, 1974.

Homaei, Jalal ed-Din. *Shu'ubiyeh.* Isfahan: Sā'eb, 1363/1984.

Hourani, Albert. *Islam in European Thought.* Cambridge: Cambridge University Press, 1991.

Howe, Stephen. *Afrocentrism: Mythical Pasts and Imagined Homes.* London: Verso, 1998.

Iranshahr, Hossein Kazemzadeh. *Chahār asar-e arzandeh az taʿlifāt-e Irānshahr* [Four valuable works of Irānshahr]. Tehran: Eqbāl, 1353/1974.

Jaubert, Pierre Amédée. *Voyage en Arménie et en Perse fait dans les années 1805 et 1806.* Paris: Pélicier, 1821.

Kaiwar, Vasant. "The Aryan Model of History and the Oriental Renaissance: The Politics of Identity in an Age of Revolutions, Colonialism and Nationalism." In *Antinomies of Modernity: Essays on Race, Orient, Nation*, ed. Vasant Kaiwar and Sucheta Mazumdar, 13–61. Durham, NC: Duke University Press, 2003.

Kashani-Sabet, Firoozeh. *Frontier Fictions: Shaping the Iranian Nation, 1804–1946.* Princeton: Princeton University Press, 1999.

Kasravi, Ahmad. *History of the Iranian Constitutional Revolution.* Trans. Evan Siegel. Costa Mesa, CA: Mazda Publishers, 2006.

——. *Qiyām-e Sheikh Mohammad Khiyābāni* [The revolt of Sheikh Mohammad Khiyabani]. Ed. Homa Katouzian. Tehran: Nashr-e Markaz, 1376/1998.

Katouzian, Homa. "The Campaign Against the Anglo-Iranian Agreement of 1919," *British Journal of Middle Eastern Studies* 25, no. 1 (1998): 5–46.

——. "Darbāreh-ye mellat, melli, melligerā va nāsionālism" [Regarding the terms mellat, melli, melligerā and nationalism]. In *Estebdād, demokrāsi va nehzat-e melli* [Arbitrary rule, democracy and the popular movement], 38–51. Tehran: Nashr-e Markaz, 1388/2009.

——. *Musaddiq and the Struggle for Power in Iran.* Rev. pbk. ed. London: I. B. Tauris, 1999.

——. *The Persians: Ancient, Medieval, and Modern Iran.* New Haven: Yale University Press, 2009.

——. *The Political Economy of Modern Iran: Despotism and Pseudo-Modernism, 1926–1979.* London: Macmillan, 1981.

——. "Problems of Political Development in Iran: Democracy, Dictatorship or Arbitrary Government?" *British Journal of Middle Eastern Studies* 22, no. 1–2 (1995): 5–20.

——. *Sadeq Hedayat: The Life and Legend of an Iranian Writer.* London: I. B. Tauris, 1991.

——. "Seyyed Hasan Taqizadeh: Three Lives in a Lifetime." *Comparative Studies of South Asia, North Africa and the Middle East* 32, no. 1 (2012): 195–213.

——. *State and Society in Iran: The Eclipse of the Qajars and the Emergence of the Pahlavis.* London: I. B. Tauris, 2006.

Kazemzadeh, Firuz. "Iranian Historiography." In *Historians of the Middle East*, ed. Bernard Lewis and P. M. Holt. Oxford: Oxford University Press, 1962.

Kazemzadeh, Massoud. "The Day Democracy Died." *Khaneh* 3, no. 34 (2003).

Keddie, Nikki R. *An Islamic Response to Imperialism: Political and Religious Writings of Sayyid Jamal ad-Din "al-Afghani."* Berkeley: University of California Press, 1983.

——. *Qajar Iran and the Rise of Reza Khan, 1796–1925.* Costa Mesa, CA: Mazda Publishers, 1999.

——. "Religion and Irreligion in Early Iranian Nationalism." *Comparative Studies in Society and History* 4, no. 3 (1962): 265–95.

——. *Religion and Rebellion in Iran: The Tobacco Protest of 1891–1892.* London: Cass, 1966.

Kedourie, Elie. *Nationalism in Asia and Africa.* London: Frank Cass, 1974.

Kellens, Jean. "Les Airiia ne sont plus des Aryas: Ce sont déjà des Iraniens." In *Aryas, Aryens et Iraniens en Asie Centrale*, ed. Gérard Fussman, Jean Kellens, Henri-Paul Francfort, and Xavier Tremblay, 233–52. Paris: Collège de France, 2005.

Kelly, Laurence. *Diplomacy and Murder in Tehran: Alexander Griboyedov and Imperial Russia's Mission to the Shah of Persia.* London: I. B. Tauris, 2002.

Kermani, Mirza Aqa Khan. *Āʾineh-ye sekandari* [Alexandrian mirror]. Tehran [?], 1326/1909.

——. *Sad khatābeh* [One hundred lectures]. Ed. Harun Vohouman. Los Angeles: Ketab Corp., 1386/2007.

——. *Seh maktub* [Three letters]. Ed. Bahram Choubine. Frankfurt: Alborz, 2005.

Kermani, Nazem ol-Eslam. *Tārikh-e bidāri-e Irāniyān* [History of Iranian awakening]. 5th ed. Tehran: Agāh, 1376/1997.

Khaleghi-Motlagh, Djalal. "Ferdowsi, Abu'l-Qāsem; i. Life." In *Encyclopædia Iranica*, vol. 9, ed. Ehsan Yarshater. New York: Bibliotheca Persica, 1999.

Khatibi, Abolfazl. "Beythāye 'Arab setizāneh dar Shāhnāmeh" [Anti-Arab verses in the Shāhnāmeh]. *Nashr-e Dānesh* 21, no. 3 (1384/2005).

Kia, Mehrdad. "Constitutionalism, Economic Modernization and Islam in the Writings of Mirza Yusef Khan Mostashar od-Dowle." *Middle Eastern Studies* 30, no. 4 (1994): 751–77.

——. "Mirza Fath Ali Akhundzade and the Call for Modernization of the Islamic World." *Middle Eastern Studies* 31, no. 3 (1995): 422–48.

——. "Nationalism, Modernism and Islam in the Writings of Talibov-i Tabrizi." *Middle Eastern Studies* 30, no. 2 (1994): 201–23.

——. "Persian Nationalism and the Campaign for Language Purification." *Middle Eastern Studies* 34, no. 2 (1998): 9–36.

——. "Women, Islam and Modernity in Akhundzade's Plays and Unpublished Writings." *Middle Eastern Studies* 34, no. 3 (1998): 1–33.

Kirby, Tim. "The Last Shah." Documentary series. United Kingdom: BBC, 1996.

Koerner, Konrad. "Observations on the Sources, Transmission, and Meaning of 'Indo-European' and Related Terms in the Development of Linguistics." In *Papers from the 3rd International Conference on Historical Linguistics, August 22–26, 1977*, Amsterdam Studies in the Theory and History of Linguistic Science, Series 4, ed. J. Peter Maher, Allan R. Bomhard, and E. F. K. Koerner, 153–80. Amsterdam: John Benjamins, 1982.

Kurzman, Charles. "Weaving Iran into the Tree of Nations." *International Journal of Middle East Studies* 37, no. 2 (2005): 137–66.

Lambton, A. K. S. "Major-General Sir John Malcolm (1769–1833) and 'The History of Persia.'" *Iran Journal* 33 (1995): 97–109.

Lassan, Hossein. "Shāhnāmeh khāni" [Shānāmeh reading]. *Honar va Mardom* 14, no. 159–60 (1354/1976): 2–16.

Leerssen, Joep. "Literary Historicism: Romanticism, Philologists, and the Presence of the Past." *Modern Language Quarterly*, 65, no. 2 (2004): 221–44.

Lenczowski, George. *Russia and the West in Iran, 1918–1948: A Study in Big-Power Rivalry.* New York: Cornell University Press, 1949.

Lewis, Bernard. *The Muslim Discovery of Europe.* New York: Norton, 1982.

Ligon, B. Lee. "Biography: Rhazes: His Career and His Writings." *Seminars in Pediatric Infectious Diseases* 12, no. 3 (2001): 266–72.

Lincoln, Bruce. "Rewriting the German War God: Georges Dumézil, Politics and Scholarship in the Late 1930s." *History of Religions* 37, no. 3 (1998): 187–208.

Macuch, Maria. "Barda and Barda-Dāri; i. In the Achaemenid Period." In *Encyclopædia Iranica*, vol. 3, ed. Ehsan Yarshater. New York: Bibliotheca Persica, 1989.

Mahdavi, Shireen. "Reza Shah Pahlavi and Women: A Re-evaluation." In *The Making of Modern Iran: State and Society Under Riza Shah, 1921–1941*, ed. Stephanie Cronin. London: RoutledgeCurzon, 2003.

Makki, Hossein. *Tārikh-e bist sāleh-ye Irān* [Twenty years of Iran's history]. Vol. 6. Tehran: Nāsher, 1362/1983.

——. *Tārikh-e bist sāleh-ye Irān* [Twenty years of Iran's history]. Vol. 1. Tehran: 'Elmi, 1374/1995.

Malcolm, John. *The History of Persia, from the Most Early Period to the Present Time*, 2 vols. London: J. Murray, 1829.

Malešević, Siniša. *Identity as Ideology: Understanding Ethnicity and Nationalism*. Basingstoke: Palgrave Macmillan, 2006.

Mann, Oskar. "Kāveh va derafsh-e Kāviyāni" [Kaveh and his standard]. *Kāveh*, January 24, 1916.

Marashi, Afshin. *Nationalizing Iran: Culture, Power, and the State, 1870–1940*. Seattle: University of Washington Press, 2008.

Martin, Vanessa. *Islam and Modernism: The Iranian Revolution of 1906*. London: I. B. Tauris, 1989.

Marx, Karl, and Friedrich Engels. *Selected Correspondence, 1846–1895, with Explanatory Notes*. Moscow: International Publishers, 1942.

Masroori, Cyrus. "European Thought in Nineteenth-Century Iran: David Hume and Others." *Journal of the History of Ideas* 61, no. 4 (2000): 657–74.

——. "French Romanticism and Persian Liberalism in Nineteenth-Century Iran: Mirza Aqa Khan Kirmani and Jacques-Henri Bernardin de Saint-Pierre." *History of Political Thought* 28, no. 3 (2007): 542–56.

——. "Mirza Ya'qub Khan's Call for Representative Government, Toleration and Islamic Reform in Nineteenth-Century Iran." *Middle Eastern Studies* 37, no. 1 (2001): 89–100.

Massé, Henri. *Firdousi et l'épopée nationale*. Paris: Perrin, 1935.

Matlin, Daniel. "Blues Under Siege: Ralph Ellison, Albert Murray, and the Idea of America." In *Uncertain Empire: American History and the Idea of the Cold War*, ed. by Joel Isaac and Duncan Bell, 195–222. New York: Oxford University Press, 2012.

Matthee, Rudi. "Between Aloofness and Fascination: Safavid Views of the West." *Iranian Studies* 31, no. 2 (1998): 219–46.

——. "Facing a Rude and Barbarous Neighbor: Iranian Perceptions of Russia and the Russians from the Safavids to the Qajars." In *Iran Facing Others: Identity Boundaries in a Historical Perspective*, ed. Abbas Amanat and Farzin Vejdani. New York: Palgrave Macmillan, 2012.

——. "The Imaginary Realm: Europe's Enlightenment Image of Early Modern Iran." *Comparative Studies of South Asia Africa and the Middle East* 30, no. 3 (2010): 449–62.

——. "Suspicion, Fear, and Admiration: Pre-Nineteenth-Century Iranian Views of the English and the Russians." In *Iran and the Surrounding World: Interactions in Culture and Cultural Politics*, ed. Nikki R. Keddie and Rudi Matthee, 121–45. Seattle: University of Washington Press, 2002.

Meisami, Julie Scott. "The Past in Service of the Present: Two Views of History in Medieval Persia." *Poetics Today* 14, no. 2 (1993): 247–75.

——. *Persian Historiography to the End of the Twelfth Century*. Edinburgh: Edinburgh University Press, 1999.

Melville, Charles. "Historiography; iv. Mongol Period." In *Encyclopædia Iranica*, vol. 12, ed. Ehsan Yarshater. New York: Bibliotheca Persica, 2004.

Meskoob, Shahrokh. *Iranian Nationality and the Persian Language*. Washington, DC: Mage Publishers, 1992.

——. *Sug-e Siyāvosh: Dar marg va rastākhiz* [The Sug-e Siyavosh, in death and resuscitation]. Tehran: Khārazmi, 1350/1971.

Milani, Abbas. *The Persian Sphinx: Amir Abbas Hoveyda and the Riddle of the Iranian Revolution: A Biography.* London: I. B. Tauris, 2000.

Minovi, Mojtaba, and Sadeq Hedayat. *Māziyār.* Tehran: Amir Kabir, 1342/1963.

Mirshokraei, Mohammad. "Shāhnāmeh khāni az did-e mardom shenāsi" [Shāhnāmeh reading from an anthropological perspective]. *Honar va Mardom* 14, no. 165–66 (1355/1976): 57–65.

Mohammadzadeh, Hamid, and Hamid Arasli, eds. *Mirzā Fathʿali Ākhundof: Alefbā-ye jadid va maktubāt* [Mirza Fathali Akhundov: The new alphabet and the Maktubāt]. Baku: Nizami, 1963.

Montesquieu, Anne M. Cohler, Basia Carolyn Miller, and Harold Samuel Stone. *The Spirit of the Laws.* Cambridge: Cambridge University Press, 1989.

Montesquieu, Margaret Mauldon, and Andrew Kahn. *Persian Letters.* Oxford: Oxford University Press, 2008.

Morony, Michael G. *Iraq After the Muslim Conquest.* Princeton Studies on the Near East. Princeton: Princeton University Press, 1984.

Moshar, Khanbaba. *Fehrest-e ketābhā-ye chāpi-e Fārsi* [Catalogue of printed books in Persian]. 2nd ed. Tehran: Arzhang, 1350/1971.

Motadel, David. "Iran and the Aryan Myth." In *Perceptions of Iran: History, Myths and Nationalism from Medieval Persia to the Islamic Republic*, ed. Ali M. Ansari, 119–46. London: I. B. Tauris, 2013.

——. "Qajar Shahs in Imperial Germany." *Past & Present* 213, no. 1 (2011): 191–235.

Mottahedeh, Roy P. "The Shuʿubiyah Controversy and the Social History of Early Islamic Iran." *International Journal of Middle East Studies* 7, no. 2 (1976): 161–82.

Mouritsen, Henrik. "Modern Nations and Ancient Models: Italy and Greece Compared." In *The Making of Modern Greece: Nationalism, Romanticism, and the Uses of the Past (1797–1896)*, ed. Roderick Beaton and David Ricks, 43–52. Farnham: Ashgate, 2009.

Müller, Friedrich Max. *Lectures on the Science of Language: Delivered at the Royal Institution of Great Britain in April, May and June 1861.* 5th rev. ed. London: Longmans Green, 1866.

Murray, Albert. *The Omni-Americans: New Perspectives on Black Experience and American Culture.* New York: Outerbridge & Dienstfrey, 1970.

Naderpour, Nader. "Une Contradiction: L'Âme Iranienne et l'Esprit Islamique." *Die Welt des Islams*, no. 23–24 (1984): 129–35.

Nafisi, Azar. Foreword to *Shahnameh: The Persian Book of Kings.* New York: Penguin, 2007.

Naji, Kasra. *Ahmadinejad: The Secret History of Iran's Radical Leader.* London: I. B. Tauris, 2008.

Navaʾi, Abdolhossein. *Sharh-e hāl-e Abbās Mirzā Molk Ārā* (The life of Abbas Mirza Molk Ara). 2nd ed. Tehran: Bābak, 1361/1982.

Nöldeke, Theodor. *The Iranian National Epic.* Trans. L. Bogdanov. Bombay: K. R. Cama Oriental Institute, 1930.

——. *Sketches from Eastern History.* London: Adam and Charles Black, 1892.

Omidsalar, Mahmoud. *Iran's Epic and America's Empire: A Handbook for a Generation in Limbo.* Santa Monica, CA: Afshar Publishing, 2012.

——. "Irān, Eslām va rowshanfekrān-e ʿāmi" [Iran, Islam and public intellectuals]. *Fars News Agency*, Mehr 17, 1389 / October 9, 2010.

Pahlavi, Ashraf. *Faces in a Mirror: Memoirs from Exile.* Englewood Cliffs, NJ: Prentice-Hall, 1980.

Pahlavi, Mohammad Reza. *Answer to History.* New York: Stein and Day, 1980.

Paine, Chris, and Erica Schoenberger. "Iranian Nationalism and the Great Powers: 1872–1954." *MERIP Reports*, no. 37 (1975): 3–28.

Parsinejad, Iraj. *A History of Literary Criticism in Iran, 1866–1951.* Bethesda, MD: Ibex Publishers, 2002.

Perry, John R. "Language Reform in Turkey and Iran." *International Journal of Middle East Studies* 17, no. 3 (1985): 295–311.

Pirniya, Hassan. *Tārikh-e Irān-e qadim: Az āqāz tā enqerāz-e Sāsāniyān* [History of ancient Iran: From the beginning to the fall of the Sasanians]. [Tehran?]: Khayyām, [1928?].

Poliakov, Léon. *Le mythe Aryen: Essai sur les sources du racisme et des nationalismes.* New exp. ed. Brussels: Editions Complexe, 1987.

Politis, Alexis. "From Christian Roman Emperors to the Glorious Greek Ancestors." In *Byzantium and the Modern Greek Identity*, ed. David Ricks and Paul Magdalino, 1–4. Aldershot: Ashgate, 1998.

Qajar, Jalal ed-Din Mirza. *Nāmeh-ye khosrovān* [The Book of Sovereigns]. 3 vols. Tehran: Mohammad Taqi & Ali Qoli Khan Qajar, 1868–1871.

Rafili, M. *M. F. Akhundov, Zhizn' i Tvorchestvo.* Baku: Azerbaĭdzhanskoe gos. izd-vo, 1957.

Rahnema, Ali. *An Islamic Utopian: A Political Biography of Ali Shariʿati.* London: I. B. Tauris, 2000.

Rawlinson, George. *The Five Great Monarchies of the Ancient Eastern World, or, the History, Geography and Antiquities of Chaldaea, Assyria, Babylon, Media, and Persia.* 4 vols. London: John Murray, 1862.

——. *The Origin of Nations.* New York: Charles Scribner's Sons, 1881.

Renan, Ernest. *Averroès et l'Averroïsme: Essai historique.* 4th ed. Paris: Calmann-Levy, 1882.

——. *Mélanges d'histoire et de voyages.* Paris: Calmann Lévy, 1878.

Rezazadeh Shafaq, Sadeq. *Tārikh-e adabiyyāt-e Irān barāy-e dabirestānhā* [Literary history of Iran for high school students]. Tehran: Amir Kabir, 1342/1963.

Rezun, Miron. *The Soviet Union and Iran: Soviet Policy in Iran from the Beginnings of the Pahlavi Dynasty Until the Soviet Invasion in 1941.* Alphen aan den Rijn: Sijthoff & Noordhoff; Genève: Institut Universitaire de Hautes Études Internationales, 1981.

Rieffer, Barbara-Ann J. "Religion and Nationalism." *Ethnicities* 3, no. 2 (2003): 215–42.

Ringer, Monica M. *Education, Religion, and the Discourse of Cultural Reform in Qajar Iran.* Bibliotheca Iranica: Intellectual Traditions series, no. 5. Costa Mesa, CA: Mazda Publishers, 2001.

——. "Reform Transplanted: Parsi Agents of Change Amongst Zoroastrians in Nineteenth-Century Iran." *Iranian Studies* 42, no. 4 (2009): 549–60.

Robins, Kevin. "Interrupting Identities: Turkey/Europe." In *Questions of Cultural Identity*, ed. Stuart Hall and Paul Du Gay, 61–86. London: Sage, 1996.

Rubin, Zeev. "*Res Gestae Divi Saporis*: Greek and Middle Iranian in a Document of Sasanian, Anti-Roman Propaganda." In *Bilingualism in Ancient Society: Language Contact and the Written Word*, ed. J. N. Adams, Mark Janse, and Simon Swain, 267–97. Oxford: Oxford University Press, 2002.

Ruhlen, Merritt. *On the Origin of Languages: Studies in Linguistic Taxonomy*. Stanford, CA: Stanford University Press, 1994.

Sadiq, Issa. *Tārikh-e farhang-e Irān* [Cultural history of Iran]. Tehran: Entesharāt-e Dāneshgāh-e Tehrān, 1336/1957.

Sanjabi, Maryam B. "Rereading the Enlightenment: Akhundzada and His Voltaire." *Iranian Studies* 28, no. 1–2 (1995): 39–60.

Schmitt, Rüdiger. "Aryans." In *Encyclopædia Iranica*, vol. 2, ed. Ehsan Yarshater. New York: Bibliotheca Persica, 1987.

——. "Grundriss der Iranischen Philologie." In *Encyclopædia Iranica*, vol. 11, ed. Ehsan Yarshater. New York: Bibliotheca Persica, 2003.

Schwartz, Martin. "Transformations of the Indo-Iranian Snake-Man: Myth, Language, Ethnoarcheology, and Iranian Identity." *Iranian Studies* 45, no. 2 (2012): 275–79.

Sedghi, Hamideh. *Women and Politics in Iran: Veiling, Unveiling, and Reveiling*. Cambridge: Cambridge University Press, 2007.

Seely, Robert. *Russo-Chechen Conflict, 1800–2000: A Deadly Embrace*. London: Frank Cass, 2001.

Shafa, Shojaʿ ed-Din. *Pas az 1,400 sāl* [After 1,400 years]. N.p., 2003.

Siassi, Ali Akbar. *La Perse au contact de l'Occident: Étude historique et sociale*. Paris: Ernest Leroux, 1931.

Siegert, Hans. "Zur Geschichte der Begriffe 'Arier' und 'arisch.'" *Wörter und Sachen* 4, (1941–1942): 73–99.

Skinner, Quentin. "Meaning and Understanding in the History of Ideas." *History and Theory* 8, no. 1 (1969): 3–53.

Smith, Anthony D. *Chosen Peoples: Sacred Sources of National Identity*. Oxford: Oxford University Press, 2003.

——. *Nations and Nationalism in a Global Era*. Cambridge: Polity, 1995.

Smith, Michael G. "Cinema for the 'Soviet East': National Fact and Revolutionary Fiction in Early Azerbaijani Film." *Slavic Review* 56, no. 4 (1997): 645–78.

Soroudi, Sorour. "Mirza Aqa Khan Kermani and the Jewish Question." In *Muslim–Jewish Encounters: Intellectual Traditions and Modern Politics*, ed. Ronald L. Nettler and Suha Taji-Farouki. Amsterdam: Harwood Academic, 1998.

Spivak, Gayatri Chakravorty. "Can the Subaltern Speak? Speculations on Widow-Sacrifice." *Wedge*, no. 7–8 (Winter–Spring 1985): 120–30.

Spuler, Bertold, and Ismail Marcinkowski. *Persian Historiography and Geography: Bertold Spuler on Major Works Produced in Iran, the Caucasus, Central Asia, India and Early Ottoman Turkey*. Singapore: Pustaka Nasional, 2003.

Stausberg, Michael. *Die Religion Zarathustras: Geschichte-Gegenwart-Rituale.* Band 2. Stuttgart: Kohlhammer, 2002.

Sternhell, Zeev. *The Anti-Enlightenment Tradition.* Trans. David Maisel. New Haven: Yale University Press, 2009.

Stevens, John. *The History of Persia.* London: Printed for Jonas Brown, 1715.

Stevens, Roger. "European Visitors to the Safavid Court." *Iranian Studies* 7, no. 3–4 (1974): 421–57.

Storey, C. A. *Persian Literature: A Bio-Bibliographical Survey,* vol. 1. London: Luzac, 1927.

Stuurman, Siep. "Cosmopolitan Egalitarianism in the Enlightenment: Anquetil Duperron on India and America." *Journal of the History of Ideas* 68, no. 2 (2007): 255–78.

Swietochowski, Tadeusz. *Russian Azerbaijan 1905–1920: The Shaping of National Identity in a Muslim Community.* Cambridge: Cambridge University Press, 2004.

Sykes, Percy M. *A History of Persia.* 3rd ed. London: Macmillan, 1951.

Tabari, Muhammad Ibn al-Jarir. *The Sasanids, the Byzantines, the Lakhmids, and Yemen.* Albany: State University of New York Press, 1999.

Tafazoli, Hamid. *Der Deutsche Persien-Diskurs: Zur Verwissenschaftlichung und Literarisierung des Persien-Bildes im Deutschen Schrifttum, von der Frühen Neuzeit bis in das Neunzehnte Jahrhundert.* Bielefeld: Aisthesis, 2007.

Taqizadeh [?], Hassan. *Khatābeh-ye Āqā-ye Seyyed Hasan Taqizādeh dar mozuʿe akhz-e tamaddon-e khāreji va āzādi, vatan, mellat, tasāhol* [Seyyed Hasan Taqizadeh's lectures on the subject of grasping foreign civilization, freedom, country, nation, tolerance]. Tehran: Chāpkhāneh-ye Mehregān, 1339/1960.

——. "Khiyālāt-e gunāgun" [Various beliefs]. *Kāveh,* October 3, 1921.

——. "Nowruz-e Jamshidi" [Jamshidian Nowrouz]. *Kāveh,* April 18, 1916.

——. *Zendegi-ye tufāni: Khāterāt-e Seyyed Hasan Taqizādeh* [Tempestuous life: The memoirs of Seyyed Hasan Taqizadeh]. Ed. Iraj Afshar. 2nd ed. Tehran: 'Elmi, 1372/1993.

Tavakoli-Targhi, Mohammad. "Contested Memories: Narrative Structures and Allegorical Meanings of Iran's Pre-Islamic History." *Iranian Studies* 29, no. 1–2 (1996): 149–75.

——. "From Patriotism to Matriotism: A Tropological Study of Iranian Nationalism, 1870–1909." *International Journal of Middle East Studies* 34, no. 2 (2002): 217–38.

——. "Historiography and Crafting Iranian National Identity." In *Iran in the 20th Century: Historiography and Political Culture,* ed. Touraj Atabaki. London: I. B. Tauris, 2009.

——. "Refashioning Iran: Language and Culture During the Constitutional Revolution." *Iranian Studies* 23, no. 1–4 (1990): 77–101.

——. *Refashioning Iran: Orientalism, Occidentalism, and Historiography.* St. Antony's series. New York: Palgrave, 2001.

——. "Review, Mostafa Vaziri's *Iran as Imagined Nation*: the Construction of National Identity." *International Journal of Middle East Studies* 26, no. 2 (1994): 316–18.

——. *Tajadod-e bumi va bāz andishi-ye tārikh* [Vernacular modernity and the rethinking of history]. Tehran: Nashr-e Tārikh-e Irān, 1381/2002.

Trautmann, Thomas R. *Aryans and British India.* Berkeley: University of California Press, 1997.

Vaziri, Mostafa. *Iran as Imagined Nation: The Construction of National Identity*. New York: Paragon House, 1993.

Vezārat-e Farhang [Ministry of Culture]. *Ketāb-e chahārom-e ebtedāyi* [4th grade textbook]. Tehran: Motabaʿeye Rowshanāyi, 1310/1931.

Vezārat-e Ma'āref [Ministry of Education]. *Joqrāfiyā-ye panj qatʿeh barāy-e tadris dar sāl-e sheshom* [Geography in five parts for teaching at sixth grade]. 6th ed. Tehran: Chāpkhāneh-ye Farhang, 1316/1937.

Wiesehöfer, Josef. *Ancient Persia: From 550 BC to 650 AD*. Trans. Azizeh Azodi. London: I. B. Tauris, 1996.

Yamamoto, Kumiko. *The Oral Background of Persian Epics: Storytelling and Poetry*. Leiden: Brill, 2003.

Yapp, M. E. "Two British Historians of Persia." In *Historians of the Middle East*, ed. Bernard Lewis and Peter Malcolm Holt. Oxford: Oxford University Press, 1962.

Young, Robert. *Colonial Desire: Hybridity in Theory, Culture, and Race*. London: Routledge, 1995.

Zarrinkub, Abdolhossein. "The Arab Conquest of Iran and Its Aftermath." In *The Cambridge History of Iran*. Vol. 4, *The Period from the Arab Invasion to the Saljuqs*, ed. Richard Nelson Frye. Cambridge: Cambridge University Press, 1975.

——. *Do qarn sokut* [Two centuries of silence]. 7th ed. Tehran: Jāvidān, 2536/1977 [1957].

Zia-Ebrahimi, Reza. "An Emissary of the Golden Age: Manekji Limji Hataria and the Charisma of the Archaic in Pre-Nationalist Iran." *Studies in Ethnicity and Nationalism* 10, no. 3 (2010): 377–90.

——. "Self-Orientalization and Dislocation: The Uses and Abuses of the 'Aryan' Discourse in Iran." *Iranian Studies* 44, no. 4 (2011): 445–72.

INDEX

CPSIA information can be obtained at www.ICGtesting.com
Printed in the USA
LVOW08*0836200616

493318LV00001B/1/P